ONCE JEWS

ONCE JEWS

Stories of Caribbean Sephardim

JOSETTE CAPRILES GOLDISH

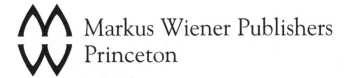

Markus Wiener Publishers
Princeton

Cover illustration: Detail of "Villa Maria" by Suzanne Perlman. A view of Curaçao's floating market and the "Villa Maria" residence built by David Ricardo in the 1880s. This house was subsequently owned by Ulises Heureaux, president of the Dominican Republic, and rented to Jeudah Senior's son, Solomon Senior, who used it as his residence.

    Oil on canvas. Photography by Johan van 't Leven. From *Motifs of Curaçao,* published by Stichting Libri Antilliani, Bloemendaal, The Netherlands. Used with permission.

For information, write to
Markus Wiener Publishers
231 Nassau Street, Princeton, NJ 08542
www.markuswiener.com

Library of Congress Cataloging-in-Publication Data
Goldish, Josette C.
  Once Jews : stories of Caribbean Sephardim / Josette Capriles Goldish.
    p. cm.
  Includes bibliographical references and index.
  ISBN 978-1-55876-493-4 (hardcover : alk. paper)
  ISBN 978-1-55876-494-1 (pbk. : alk. paper)
  1. Jews—Caribbean Area—History. 2. Sephardim—Caribbean Area—History.
  3. Jews—Caribbean Area—Identity. 4. Caribbean Area—Ethnic relations.
  I. Title.
  F2191.J4G65 2008
  972.9'004924—dc22

                    2008025006

CONTENTS

PART II: ANALYSIS AND CONCLUSIONS

APPENDIXES

ACKNOWLEDGMENTS

This book could not have been written without the help of numerous friends and relatives in many different countries.

First and foremost among my collaborators was my cousin, friend, and traveling companion Sandra de Marchena, whose painstaking work in recording the genealogy of the Sephardim of Curaçao was indispensable to the understanding of the migrants and their background. Her enthusiasm over our many discoveries together and her company in the archives of Curaçao, Santo Domingo, and Barranquilla made what could have been a fairly solitary effort something we both recall with great pleasure.

Several people were instrumental in getting this project off the ground. They were the late Dr. Harry Hoetink, Dr. Shulamit Reinharz, and my friends Diane Henriquez, Joyce de Waard, and Loretta Adams. Harry, who was an expert in Caribbean sociology and history, encouraged me early on to undertake the study and provided much needed input to the initial phases of my research. His untimely death in 2005 was a major loss to all who benefited from his brilliant academic insight. Shula's energy made me feel that this effort was possible, and her blind belief in my capabilities opened many opportunities and enhanced my self-confidence. Diane, Joyce, and Loretta funded a large portion of my trips to the locations of interest to this study and never stopped thinking of ways in which they could help me with data, connections, and ideas. In Diane's case, this included offering hands-on assistance in Coro's archives during the day and serving as a co-pilot in navigating dinner menus during our evenings in this unusual town. I feel very fortunate to have such friends.

On location, I owe much gratitude to Ena Dankmeijer, Esther van Haaren, RoseMarie de Paula, Charles Gomes Casseres, Henry van der Kwast, and Christel Monsanto in Curaçao; Arlette and Juan Hormazabal

Salas, Dr. Rafael Manuel Galán Salas, and Enrique and Aída de Marchena in Santo Domingo; Dr. Blanca de Lima, Hermán and Thelma Henriquez, and Deborah Capriles de Petit in Coro; Dr. Ricardo de Sola, Saidi Valencia, and the staff of the Museo Sefardí in Caracas; Dr. Adelaida Sourdis Nájera, Judith Segovia de Falquez, and Rodolfo Segovia Salas in Barranquilla; and Katina Coulianos and Beverly Smith in St. Thomas. I was extremely fortunate to meet Enrique de Marchena in Santo Domingo and to have access to his impressive personal archival collection before his sudden demise in 2003. And for years, I was also lucky enough to exchange many ideas with one of the best raconteurs of Sephardic life in Curaçao, Charlie Gomes Casseres, who passed away in 2006.

In Holland I received the able assistance of Ilse Chumaceiro Palm and Rene van Wijngaarden who copied and mailed me many documents that were of great help to my research. And by snail mail, e-mail, and phone, Mordechai Arbell in Israel, Sita Likuski in California, and Cheryl Pinto in Panama often shared their knowledge with me.

Dr. Sylvia Arrom of Brandeis University read through a very early version of the manuscript, providing wonderful and insightful comments, and Dr. Jonathan Sarna, Dr. Shulamit Reinharz, Rabbi Isidoro Aizenberg, Ligia Hoetink, Dr. Judah Cohen, and Rodolfo Segovia gave input at later stages of the project. Rodolfo Segovia additionally helped arrange for some of the research assistance I received in Barranquilla and taught me a great deal during our multi-hour phone conversations.

English quotations appearing in this book were often taken from publications, documents, or archival materials written in Spanish, Dutch, French, Portuguese, or Papiamentu. The accuracy of these translations is my sole responsibility, as are the opinions and conclusions expressed in this work.

A special thanks to my writing coach, Sara Levine, who refused to let me stray into incomprehensible English or to give up on the project. She encouraged me to add a personal voice to my writing and, as a consequence, I believe it now reflects some of the excitement and enjoyment of the process that led to this book. Also, kudos to my daughter, Suzanne Goldish, who was able to edit some difficult and out-of-focus photographs to obtain the images that were used.

I would never have set my sights as high throughout my professional life and all through this unusually satisfying research effort, had it not been for my husband, Lou. Although the financial aspect of research for research sake seemed somewhat alien to him, Lou's encouragement never faltered. In this way he made it possible for me to embark on a project that has been one of the most entertaining and revealing endeavors of my multifaceted career.

Thanks to all of you for your encouragement, support, and comments along the way. A special thanks to the Jewish community of Curaçao and the many descendants of the Curaçaoan Sephardic Diaspora whose lives touched mine in the past few years. Getting to know you was one of the most pleasant unexpected benefits of this research effort.

INTRODUCTION

I was born on the Dutch Caribbean island of Curaçao. My parents were Sephardic Jews* and my mother's side of the family, the De Marchenas, had been on the island since 1659. In comparison, the Capriles, my paternal ancestors, were newcomers, having arrived in the late 1750s. The Jewish community I grew up in was close-knit and supportive, and my life on the island was rooted in history. My forefathers had been well-known doctors, lawyers, and businessmen in Curaçao and had played an active part in what was once one of the most important Jewish communities in the Americas. I always thought I was lucky to have grown up in this place even though, as a teenager, it seemed somewhat small and full of nosy people. The attention given to us by these people, however, led many among my immediate friends to meet and exceed expectations. Perhaps because we knew that the pat on the back, or better yet, the communal hug, would be forthcoming.

In 1999, when I had been living in Boston for almost thirty-five years, three cousins and I organized a family reunion in Curaçao. In preparing for the reunion, we were excited to find family members in the Dominican Republic and Venezuela of whose existence we had not known. After many months of planning, we gathered together on the island where our ancestors had made their mark to reconnect and celebrate.

It was not surprising to find out that most of our Latino cousins were Catholic. Even in Curaçao, where a Jewish community has existed for over 350 years, religious assimilation had accelerated in the mid twentieth century, greatly reducing the Sephardic community. In Latin America, where structured Jewish communities were only more recently established, such absorption into the Catholic culture at a much earlier

---

* Sephardic Jews are descendants of the Spanish and Portuguese Jews who used to inhabit the Iberian peninsula.

stage appeared unavoidable. We also learned that some of our newly discovered cousins were descendants of Curaçaoan Sephardim who had
migrated from the island as long ago as the nineteenth century. I was
somewhat curious as to why these people had left when they did, but for
almost a year that curiosity remained dormant.

Once back home, the family reunion faded into the background, and,
in my spare time, I continued reading novels and memoirs about the
Caribbean, as I have done for years. Caribbean stories have always res-
onated with me. When I first read Gabriel García Marquez's descriptions
of life on the Colombian Caribbean coast or when I learned that Achy
Obejas felt that in Cuba she had always been surrounded by cousins, I
knew exactly what they were writing about. The social settings were
perfectly familiar, even though I had never been to Colombia or Cuba.
Similarly, the Dominican upper class of Julia Alvarez's political
novels and Jamaica Kincaid's sad and angry portrayal of the island of
Antigua reminded me of life in Curaçao. In a way, these authors' fic-
tional accounts kept me in touch with the Caribbean island I had left
behind.

The year following the reunion, I read Julia Alvarez's then newly published In the Name of Salomé – a novel, as it clearly states on its title page.
Part of this book takes place in the Dominican Republic in the nineteenth century. Since at the time I knew nothing about that country's
history, I began to read the book entirely as a novel, unable to distinguish
historical fact from fiction. Soon I came across the part where the pro-
tagonist of the story, the Dominican poet Salomé Ureña, meets Federico
Henriquez y Carvajal, "son of one of the Sephardic families, that had settled in the capital back when we [the Dominican people] were still occupied by the Haitians."[1] I remember thinking to myself how thorough
Alvarez always is in her research for her historical novels and how flaw-
lessly the facts are integrated into her writing. Henriquez is a very common Sephardic Jewish name found in Curaçao, Jamaica, Venezuela, St.
Thomas, and many other Caribbean locations. It was quite plausible that
one of these folks had lived in the Dominican Republic. As I continued
reading, I learned that Salomé ended up marrying Federico's brother
Francisco, and that, at some point, the couple befriended a man by the

name of Eugenio Generoso de Marchena. This caused me to pause: De Marchena, my mother's maiden name!

Had Julia Alvarez invented Eugenio Generoso de Marchena or had he really existed?* And if so, what was the connection with my mother's family? Driven by my curiosity about these immigrants from Curaçao, I began the research that led to this book.

At the time, my cousin Sandra de Marchena had begun the process of recording the genealogy of Curaçao's Sephardim and their descendants. With her help I was able to answer my first question: Who were these people? Sandra's impeccable and detailed genealogical work revealed the link between the immigrants and their Curaçaoan Sephardic ancestors. She had been most interested in connecting the names and the appropriate dates as she compiled her database. I was interested in the dash between the date of birth and the date of death – the lives of these Sephardim. There were many other questions I wanted to answer. What made them leave Curaçao? What kind of lives did they have after they left? What type of work did they do? Did they keep in touch with their relatives and friends from Curaçao? Why were their descendants Catholic? Had they converted or had they married Catholics and raised their children in that religion? Had they suffered discrimination in their new places of residence? Had their lives away from Curaçao had any Jewish content?

I decided early on to focus my research on several Caribbean locations in order to compare and contrast the lives of these migrating Sephardic Jews geographically. I also limited my data collection to the nineteenth century, since this was the period when the outmigration from Curaçao was most pronounced and its impact most keenly felt. As a result, this book examines case histories of Sephardic Jews who left Curaçao during the chosen time period to find greater economic opportunities in four other Caribbean locations. The locations I included were those that were of greatest interest to Curaçao's Sephardim during that time span: St. Thomas, Virgin Islands; Coro, Venezuela; Santo Domingo, Domini-

---

*All these personalities and names are factual. They were part of Dominican history and not merely characters invented by Julia Alvarez.

can Republic; and Barranquilla, Colombia. Archival research in these four places as well as in Curaçao enhanced and enriched my earlier library research of published materials, and was complemented by work at the libraries of the Centraal Bureau voor Genealogie in The Hague, the American Jewish Historical Society in New York City, and the American Jewish Archives in Cincinnati.

The resulting stories of these Sephardic individuals and families are presented in the first part of this book. These nineteenth century individuals are introduced to the reader in Curaçao, and their lives are followed as they make their decisions to leave and settle in diverse Caribbean ports. While these short biographies satisfied my original curiosity, a new question arose. What caused the Sephardic immigrants and their descendants to blend so quickly into their host communities?

Naturally, I was not the first person to notice this trend. In 1998, Mordechai Arbell alerted the world to the "comfortable disappearance" of Caribbean Jewry and called on Jewish leaders to find ways in which the members of still-existing Caribbean Jewish communities might survive as Jews.[2] His writing, published as a policy study by the Institute of the World Jewish Congress in Jerusalem, left unanswered the question as to why the Jews were disappearing at a different pace in each of the Caribbean communities he described. Answering this question became a focus of my analytical work. By studying the lives of Curaçao's migrating Sephardim in detail, I was able to gain an understanding of the factors that affected the rate and degree of this religious assimilation. These findings, as well as a comprehensive analysis of the importance and impact of the gender imbalance that occurred as a result of the Caribbean migration patterns, are presented in the second part of the book.

The stories of this particular group of Sephardim are of interest for reasons beyond the academic. They are part of the ancestral history of enterprising individuals and their families who, in the nineteenth and twentieth century, and in the still young twenty-first century, served and continue to serve in leadership roles in Latin American countries and other Caribbean nations. These political leaders, industrial entrepreneurs, poets, doctors, and professionals of various types are recognized as Dominicans, Venezuelans, Colombians, Panamanians, and citizens of other countries with little memory on the part of the public at large of their Jewish ancestry. Yet, these descendants of once Jewish immigrants, who are today mostly Roman Catholics, have themselves not forgotten their Curaçaoan Sephardic origins. Six and seven generations later they speak proudly of their ties to both the religion and the small Dutch island that were integral parts of their ancestors' identities. Conversations with these men and women during the course of this project revealed that they generally had a strong awareness of their migrating ancestors' place in Jewish and Caribbean history, and that they were often surprised at how little is known outside their immediate circles about the role played by these Jews in the region's social and economic development. This book aims to acknowledge and preserve this important aspect of continuity in the quest for *Tikkun Olam* – making the world a better place – by these nineteenth century Sephardim and their Jewish and non-Jewish descendants.

PART I

Stories of Caribbean Sephardim

CHAPTER 1

CURAÇAO

Nos tera ta baranca　　　　　　Our country is a barren rock
I solo ta kima;　　　　　　　　And the sun is burning hot;
Pobreza ta nos suerte　　　　　　Poverty is our fate
I bida ta pisá　　　　　　　　　And life is a heavy burden

From Cantica di Corsouw, *long-time national anthem of Curaçao
written by Fr. Maria Radulphus and published in La Cruz,
August 29, 1900.*

LIFE ON A SMALL ISLAND

As the eighteenth century drew to a close, the sun rose and set on the Caribbean every day as it had done before and would continue to do in the years to come. Its presence warmed the islands and showed off the incomparable hues of the surrounding blue sea and sandy beaches by day, while its departure at night set the stage for an unobstructed view of thousands of stars. These idyllic vistas are still evoked when the Caribbean islands are mentioned. Often they are a true reflection of happy times, but, on occasion, they also hide turmoil and distress not so visible to the naked eye.

On the Dutch Caribbean island of Curaçao, the eighteenth century ended on an ominous note. The economy was in shambles. The slave revolt of 1795 had been subdued in the cruelest of ways. The French, who had conquered the Netherlands, were on the offensive from their West Indian colonial bases. And the British were waiting on the side-

3

Partial façade of Mikvé Israel–
Emanuel Synagogue
Curaçao, Netherlands Antilles

lines to seize the island.

This chaotic situation affected all who lived in Curaçao to some degree. For the island's Sephardic Jews it marked the beginning of their dispersion across the Caribbean as, out of economic necessity, they began to look around for other locations that might offer greater opportunity. The eighteenth century, and, particularly the period between 1776 and 1790, had been a time of steady growth for these Sephardim. It had led to significant wealth for some and an overall level of comfort for most. The reversal of those favorable conditions was cause for concern. All of a sudden, members of the younger generation began to worry that they might not be able to enjoy the lifestyle they had become accustomed to in their parental homes. But how could they leave? And where would they go?

The first Sephardic Jews had arrived in Curaçao from Holland in 1651. These early Jewish colonists were descendants of the Jews of Spain who, after forced conversions, persecution, and torture, were finally expelled from that country in 1492. Many had fled from the Spanish Inquisition to Portugal, where some Sephardic families lived for almost a century. Then in 1578, King Sebastian of Portugal died without descendants. He was briefly succeeded by his uncle Henrique. After Henrique's death in 1580, Portugal was claimed by Spain, and King Phillip II was crowned king of both Spain and Portugal. Once more the Inquisition became a force to be reckoned with, and the Jews of Portugal were forced to move again and again, eventually settling in countries such as Italy, Greece, Turkey, Belgium, and Holland.

In Holland, the Sephardic Jews were dubbed Portuguese Jews, and, by 1620, they numbered approximately 1,200, with about 1,000 living in Amsterdam. Even though they enjoyed some freedoms, they were forbidden from becoming storekeepers or from practicing crafts. It was not until the emergence of colonial trade with its attendant opportunities that the Sephardic Jews achieved some prosperity in Holland.[3]

Quite early in the history of the Dutch occupation of Curaçao, the Dutch West India Company, the entity in charge of colonizing and exploiting the resources of the Americas, offered incentives to those who wished to establish themselves in the new colonies. And so it was that in the 1650s Sephardic Jews began to arrive in Curaçao from Holland, forming a community on the island which they called Mikvé Israel – Hope of Israel. In 1659 a larger group of Jewish settlers, consisting of "more than 70 souls, adults as well as children of our nation," joined the earlier pioneers.[4]

Many of these Sephardim of 1659 had been in the Americas before. At the beginning of the decade, they had been active traders in the Pernambuco region of Brazil, then under Dutch control. When Holland surrendered these Brazilian territories back to Portugal in 1654, most of the practicing Jews, fearing religious persecution, decided to leave Brazil. Some returned to Holland and others went to the Guyanas, Barbados, Jamaica, and New Amsterdam.[5] A few years later opportunity beckoned in Curaçao, and several of these Brazilian Jewish expatriates in Holland decided to give the Americas a second chance. With financial support from the Portuguese Jewish Community of Amsterdam and encouragement from their co-religionists already in the Dutch West Indies, they greatly enlarged the Jewish presence in Curaçao at a very early stage of its settlement by the Netherlands.[6]

While the Spanish who discovered Curaçao in 1499 did not truly settle the island and referred to it as "*isla inutil*" – useless island – the Dutch were more creative in their approach. Their conquest of Curaçao in 1634 had encountered little resistance. The Spanish colonists had used

Curaçao primarily as a grazing ground, and the Dutch invaders found an island with 2000 cattle, 9000 sheep and lamb, 750 horses, and 1000 goats, none of which cared if their keepers spoke Spanish or Dutch.[7] Looking after these live assets were 32 Spanish settlers and 400 to 450 indigenous Indians. There were only ten to twelve adult males among the settlers, and the Dutch conquerors evacuated most of these people to the South American mainland. In the decades that followed, Holland quickly proceeded to take advantage of the island's geographical location and natural harbor. [8]

The main enticement offered by the Dutch West India Company to potential settlers of the island was land. Those who crossed the Atlantic to come to this unknown Caribbean location were assigned plots in their new place of residence which they were expected to cultivate in order to make a living. This was the case for the early Jewish arrivals as well who were deeded a two-mile strip of land along the coast. The Sephardim had all intentions of developing the area into a productive and profitable agricultural settlement, but this turned out to be easier said than done. Infrequent rainfall and the many coral-based areas made agriculture in Curaçao a particularly difficult enterprise. Within a few decades, the Sephardim had become the island's traders, merchants, and ship owners, fully utilizing their connections in Europe to facilitate these business efforts.[9] While many continued to own plantations, the yield from these properties was usually not a sole source of income.

By the early eighteenth century, the Jewish population on the island had grown substantially, requiring the construction of a larger edifice where religious services could be conducted. In 1732 the Sephardic Jews inaugurated their magnificent Mikvé Israel synagogue, with 400 seats for men on the first floor and 200 seats for women in the balcony, a true sign of congregational growth and prosperity. Throughout the eighteenth century, the leadership of prominent rabbis, assisted by many cantors, Hebrew teachers, circumcisers, ritual slaughterers, and other synagogue officials, assured the observance of Jewish rituals by most congregants. Jewish holidays were celebrated with great reverence and joie de vivre, and Judaism blossomed in Curaçao. The degree of freedom of religious expression in this island would have amazed the persecuted Spanish ancestors of Curaçao's Sephardim. They would have been astounded by the masked and costumed Jewish boys who, without any fears for their personal safety, would parade through the streets of Willemstad for a full week around the time of the Jewish festival of Purim. And they would have marveled at the nighttime fireworks that capped off this holiday's celebration.[10]

The High Holidays were conducted with much pomp and circumstance and flowed effortlessly into the celebration of the week of Sukkot, a Jewish holiday which the Sephardim of Curaçao call *Cabana*. This name refers to the impermanent shelter constructed out of palm fronds and decorated with fruit and vegetables used during Sukkot. At Passover all members of the community received a candle from the board *"para escombrar el hames"* – to search for any remaining vestige of leavening or foods forbidden during this holiday. The synagogue also distributed *garoza (charoset)*, a fruit-and-nut delicacy used during the Passover Seder meal, to all its members. The Sabbath services brought together a large part of the community on a weekly basis, and it is clear that the synagogue and Jewish celebrations played a significant role in the lives of Curaçao's Sephardim.[11] This central importance of the synagogue, *nos snoa*, as its members still refer to it, became a key element of Jewish continuity in later years.

In many ways the eighteenth century represented a Jewish golden age in Curaçao. This did not mean that the congregants always lived together in great harmony. Disagreements arose about religious issues as well as social ones. Occasionally congregants even came to blows, requiring not only communal, but also governmental intervention to resolve disputes. Generally, however, the strong religious leadership of the eighteenth century ruled with authority on most issues that surfaced in the Mikvé Israel community.[12]

By 1789 the number of Jews on the island had grown to almost 1,500, which represented 38% of the white population.[13] They had become an integral part of Curaçaoan society, and, to them, this was the place they called home. Many Sephardic families had lived on the island for five or six generations by this time, and their relationship with the governing authorities had grown into one of mutual respect. The Sephardim were appreciative of the freedoms they enjoyed under Dutch rule, and the governing forces in turn recognized the importance of Curaçao's Jewish community to the island's overall economic growth and cultural development.[14] As such, the community wielded even more power than its relative size would suggest.

Although there had been economic recessions between the many periods of prosperity during the century and a half the Jews had been in Curaçao, the Mikvé Israel community had always managed to survive these. A *Sedaca* fund – community chest – created to help the poor, had been in existence since the early eighteenth century. Other smaller charitable organizations complemented loans and charity distributed by the *Sedaca* fund to indigent members as needed.[15]

Although it was sometimes difficult to meet the demand during economic downturns, increased charitable donations by wealthier members during those times usually allowed the community to continue without a membership fee or other type of taxation. This changed in 1810, when a *finta* – membership contribution – was introduced.[16]

Small islands with limited resources and economic structures that depend greatly on outside forces are generally more susceptible to prolonged recessions than larger more diversified countries. Curaçao's economic recession of the late eighteenth century and early nineteenth century was pervasive and exacerbated by the increased and widespread political unrest in various parts of the Caribbean. In the Jewish community, the problem expressed itself early on in the form of increased requests for charitable assistance. The community coffers had been padded during the fat years, but they began to deplete rapidly in response to the needs of an increasing number of impoverished widows, orphans, and fathers of large families.[17] Soon many loans were being given to those who wanted to leave for places of greater opportunity.

In 1802 a Mr. Pimentel acknowledged in a note written in Portuguese that he "owe[d] the *Sedaca* [the charitable fund] *of* Mikvé Israel forty-three pesos,* which have been loaned to me by the gentlemen of the

---

* The peso and the dollar are assumed to be at approximate parity through most of the nineteenth century.

Parnissim [governing board] to pay for my passage and provisions to travel from this island to New York." That same year Isaac Sarano wrote in
Dutch that he too acknowledged a debt to the *Parnassim*, which he
promised to repay upon arrival in Jamaica. And, a few years later, Judith
de Crasto Salas promised to repay a loan of 22 pesos and 4 reais to the
gabay (treasurer) of the Mikvé Israel synagogue as soon as she arrived in
St. Thomas. This letter, written in Portuguese, is signed "I.D.C." in a
hand unaccustomed to the use of a pen. A brief note, written in a firmer
handwriting by one of the witnesses, indicates that those initials repre-
sent the signature of Judith de Crasto Salas.[18]

The ancestors of these Sephardim had survived as Jews by their wit
and the historically demonstrated ability to be practical and creative in
dealing with adversity. This time too, in spite of their misgivings, a number of the younger and single Sephardim, as well as some newlywed couples, made the difficult decision to leave behind their *dushi Korsou* –
sweet Curaçao – for other shores. Although some migrated to the newly
independent United States, most chose to stay in the Caribbean. That
they chose Caribbean locations in close proximity to Curaçao is likely
indicative of the immigrants' original intent to leave only temporarily or
at the very least to have the ability to return to visit parents, siblings, and
cousins on the island on a regular basis.

Although many view the Caribbean as consisting of numerous separate
islands, the region has a character all its own to those who live there.
The Caribbean, depicted on the accompanying map, includes the core
islands usually referred to as the Antilles, starting with Cuba and running east to the Virgin Islands, and then South to Trinidad, and extending back west to include the Dutch islands of Bonaire, Curaçao, and
Aruba. The region also includes the Caribbean periphery, which consists
of the mainland countries which border on the Caribbean Sea, such as
Venezuela, Colombia, and the Central American states. While seas generally tend to separate, there is a strong element of identity and inclusion
among the islands and mainland countries of the Caribbean. This
Caribbean identity reflects the overlapping cultural, historical, economic, political, and emotional attachments that belie the large number of

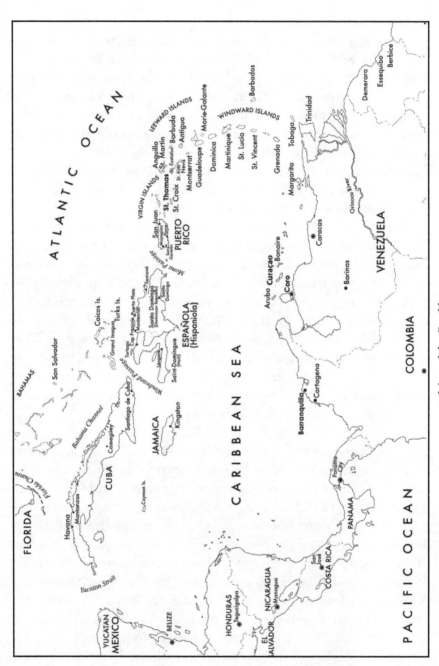

Map of the Caribbean

national identities that have existed and still exist in the region.[19]

The migration patterns of the nineteenth century Sephardim of Curaçao suggest that they viewed the region more or less in the same way as Americans moving from one place to another in the newly independent United States. While there were risks involved in migration, these risks were not perceived to be significantly greater than the move west by Americans living on the eastern seaboard. The fact that nineteenth century Caribbean migration often meant moving from one country to another, with changes in languages and political systems, added to the complexity of the adaptation process. Nevertheless, the frequency and apparent ease of migration within the region would seem to confirm that the migrants indeed thought of this area as having its own identity, albeit split among many political systems.

The greater part of the Caribbean region was still in Spanish hands as the nineteenth century began. Only a very small percentage of the total area was colonized by England, France, Holland, and Denmark. Non-Hispanic colonies included Jamaica, which was British; Saint Domingue (Haiti), which since 1791 was embroiled in its revolution to gain independence from France; and a large number of smaller islands or Lesser Antilles. Curaçao's Mikvé Israel community represented the largest congregation of Jews in the Caribbean. Yet, active Jewish congregations existed in many of the non-Hispanic locations including such islands as Barbados, Nevis, Jamaica, St. Eustatius, and the Danish Virgin Islands.

In the Spanish colonies, which included Cuba, Santo Domingo, Puerto Rico, and the Caribbean periphery, however, the Inquisition continued to be enforced. Officially these Hispanic American locations remained off limits to the Jews. The only way the Sephardim could have lived in pre-independence Latin America was as non-practicing Jews, as hidden Jews or at their peril. The memory of life in Europe before their ancestors got to Holland was still quite vivid in the minds of the descendants of Spain's expelled Sephardim. After more than a century of freedom in Curaçao, few considered that option.

To Curaçao's Jewish migrants, among the more appealing destinations open within this realm of economic and political possibilities were the Danish Virgin Islands. In the 1790s, Jews from Curaçao began to leave for St. Thomas which, under progressive Danish governance, had started to become a significant tax-free trading center.

Even though both men and women migrated to St. Thomas, it was usually the men who would make the decision to move elsewhere. They were the ones who were the breadwinners, since the Jewish women of Curaçao generally did not work outside the home. When these fathers and husbands brought their daughters and wives along with them, the women's input into the migration decision may or may not have been considered. Often, too, the Sephardim who left may have believed that their departure would be temporary, and, as will be discussed in several of the stories that follow, a number of these migrants and their descendants did indeed return to Curaçao after spending considerable time in St. Thomas and other Caribbean locations.

Understandably there was an initial reluctance to leave the Dutch island that for several generations had been a Jewish Caribbean success story. Even more difficult, perhaps, was leaving behind the close-knit Mikvé Israel society. After more than one hundred years of marriages in this place, each person was related to close to one third of the members of the Jewish community.

The size of the island and the homogeneity of Curaçao's Sephardic population had resulted in a social group with an unusually strong kinship pattern based on a bilateral, extended family. For these Jews, the Curaçaoan *Famiya* included not only the parents and their children, but all recognized relatives on the mother's and father's side along with the kinsmen of one's spouse. Social interactions in celebration of the various rites of passage were not only family affairs but, rather, total group events. In Frances Karner's concise study of the socio-cultural patterns among the Curaçaoan Sephardim she humorously highlights how "... on each birthday, whether of child or adult, the entire intricate web of relatives, near and far, was supposed to show up and pay homage. The same was the case at other events calling for celebration. Since one's extended kingroup totaled in the hundreds, it can be deduced how often these gatherings took place in the course of a year."[20]

Similarly, at the time of death, the entire group would participate in some kind of mourning. Members of the community who were not directly related to the deceased would often cancel all celebrations for a few days and even refrain from wearing bright colors for a week or so to indicate their sorrow at the recent loss. Until a few decades ago these customs were still observed. A member of the Curaçaoan Jewish community who spent much of her twentieth century adult life living in Holland would often say: "*Met de wil van God en de familie*" – with God's will and that of the family – emphasizing the important role of kinship in major and minor decisions.[21]

Despite the strength of these kinship ties, the conditions in the late eighteenth century were such that economic factors outweighed the desire of many of Curaçao's Sephardim to remain in this comfortable setting. Political instability at the beginning of the nineteenth century only served to enhance their need to leave. In 1800 the British took over Curaçao under the pretext of helping the Dutch protect the island against French invasions. They stayed for over two years and then returned in 1807 for another eight years. During British occupation, trade restrictions were implemented and the island's merchants suffered major losses when the British confiscated most of their merchandise. Many of these merchants were members of Curaçao's Sephardic community.[22]

During the same time period, other political changes were taking place on the nearby South American mainland, where the Creoles of the Spanish-occupied areas had begun their wars of independence. Refugees from the mainland were frequent visitors on the Dutch island. Here the Sephardic community was watching these revolutionary developments with a great deal of interest. Their sympathies lay with Simón Bolívar in Venezuela and Colombia and later with Juan Pablo Duarte and his cohorts in Santo Domingo. Spain – their ancestors' nightmare – had enforced many restrictive policies in the Americas pertaining to trade as well as residency. Therefore it is not surprising that, even merely from an economic perspective, Curaçao's Jews were eagerly anticipating the departure of the Spanish colonists from the area. A departure which would surely open up many untapped markets in the region.

In this atmosphere of political and economic turmoil, the religious bickering among the congregants of Mikvé Israel intensified. In March of 1815, the community's beloved Rabbi Jacob Lopez Da Fonseca died after having led the congregation for almost 52 years.[23] Since he had been ailing for a while, the *Parnassim* had already approached the Jewish leadership in Amsterdam regarding their need for someone to assist and eventually replace Rabbi Lopez Da Fonseca. Within a few months after his much-lamented death, the mother community of Amsterdam sent Jeosuah (Joshua) Piza to Curaçao to take the beloved rabbi's place.

Joshua Piza had been educated as a *hazan* – cantor – at the Ets Haim Seminary of Amsterdam and descended from a scholarly line of Sephardim who had been living in Holland since 1702. His grandfather had been a well-known author on such diverse topics as ritual slaughter and the Jewish calendar. He had also written an essay about the various names of God used in the *Torah* – the Pentateuch – that was printed as an introduction to the Five Books of Moses published in Amsterdam in 1769. Joshua's father was an instructor of *Gemara** at the seminary, the author of various works of poetry and prose, and a member of Amsterdam's *Beth Din* – Jewish Judicial Court. In short, the man chosen by the Amsterdam community to lead the Mikvé Israel congregants in Curaçao came from an impeccable Jewish background. Although he was not an ordained rabbi, the expectations were that he was sufficiently trained to lead the community.[24]

Piza arrived in Curaçao with his pregnant wife, their four-year old son, and his sister-in-law in May of 1815. His wife, Benvenida Sacutto, died within a few months after their arrival, possibly during the birth of their second son, and the cantor married his sister-in-law Esther on December 13, 1815. It had been a tumultuous year for Joshua Piza, but it only marked the beginning of his misfortunes.[25]

In January of 1816, he was reprimanded by the community leaders for some innovations he had introduced while conducting religious services. The Amsterdam community wrote to him a few months later and suggested that he adapt himself to the demands of Curaçao's *Parnassim*.[26] Unfortunately, nothing Piza did seemed to please his congregants. That same year, in the midst of his disagreements with the Mikvé Israel com-

---

* Commentary on early oral interpretations of the Scriptures as contained in the second part of the Talmud.

munity, his second wife and the twins she was carrying died in child-birth.[27] Since the community by-laws required a cantor to be married, Piza needed to find a third wife fairly quickly. Not only did he have two young sons from his first marriage who needed care, he did not want to give the congregation any additional reasons to find fault with him.

On September 15, 1816 the forty-four year old Hazan Piza married the seventeen-year-old Hannah Sasso, daughter of the assistant cantor Jacob Sasso.[28] With this single act he quickly resolved two of his problems. His sons now had someone to take care of them, and the synagogue board could not harass him for not having a wife. Lord knows he was trying to remain married! He had had three wives in a year's time, and he could only hope that this much younger Curaçaoan bride would have a healthier constitution than the short-lived and unfortunate Sacutto sisters who had come with him from Holland.

His other problems were not as easily resolved. In the years that followed, the Jewish community of Curaçao became increasingly divided about their cantor. His ways of conducting services were very different from what his congregants had been accustomed to, and some claimed that he was ignorant and tone-deaf to boot. Eventually the disagreements took on a life of their own, resulting in the secession of ninety-nine members of the Mikvé Israel synagogue. The separatists published a statement to that effect in the *Curaçaosche Courant* on the fifth of April 1819, making the internal strife a public matter on the island. [29]

The outmigration that had started in the 1790s had already caused the Jewish community of Curaçao to shrink considerably. By 1820 the number of Jews had dwindled from a high of about 1,500 to 866.[30] The resignation of so many members in 1819, representing close to half of the island's Jewish population, resulted in an additional financial burden for the Mikvé Israel community.

The separatists were undeterred. They began to conduct their own religious services. They also officiated at their own life cycle events without any guidance from Mikvé Israel's mighty *Parnassim*, purchased their own burial ground, and appeared to be well on their way to becoming an established and totally separate Jewish community. By this time the island was back in Dutch hands, and the dissenting group even wrote to the king of Holland asking him for assistance in resolving the problems surrounding Hazan Piza. Finally, through the mediation of the Dutch island governor and the Jewish community of Amsterdam, a settlement was reached in 1821, whereby Piza tendered his resignation and was promised a severance pay worth three years of his salary. The community factions reunited, and Piza was assigned a synagogue seat like any other member of Mikvé Israel.[31]

The situation in Curaçao was untenable for Hannah and Joshua Piza. Even though an agreement had been reached with the cantor, one can imagine how difficult it must have been for the ousted religious leader to sit in that synagogue as an unimportant member of the community, despised by many, listening to the various assessors (lay leaders) of the Mikvé Israel synagogue as they participated in the services and made religious decisions. He was fortunate to have some friends among the *Parnassim* who continued to care about his wellbeing. In 1824, these influential gentlemen found him a new job, and, that year, Piza departed with his young wife, his two sons of his first marriage (Moses and Judah), and two daughters (Judith and Benvenida) born to him by Hannah Sasso for St. Thomas where he had been invited to fill the post of *hazan*.[32]

CHAPTER 2

ST. THOMAS, DANISH VIRGIN ISLANDS

The absence of all restrictions on commerce and navigation in this little island, surrounded as it was by countries where a very different policy prevailed, soon attracted the notice of enterprising Europeans to it, as a point from which the manufactured goods of their respective countries could be easily introduced into the islands and continent in its vicinity.

John P. Knox, 1852

ISLAND OF OPPORTUNITY

When the Pizas arrived in St. Thomas in 1824, they found a pluralistic society of people of many races, religions, and nationalities, and a substantial Jewish community that numbered sixty-three families.[33] There had been Jewish traders on the island since the early days of Danish settlement in the seventeenth century, but, through most of the eighteenth century, their numbers had not warranted the creation of a formal Jewish community. When the nearby Dutch island of St. Eustatius was sacked by the British in 1781, however, a large number of Jews who had been merchants on that island moved to St. Thomas with their families. These Statian refugees, together with Curaçao's Sephardim who had arrived in St. Thomas in search of better economic opportunity and other Jews who had escaped the revolutionary events in French St.

Coins minted for Delvalle & Co. of St. Thomas

Domingue (Haiti), created a large enough critical mass to form a congregation in 1796, which they called Beracha VeShalom — Blessing and
Peace.[34] While they prayed in private homes in the early years and did
not have their own synagogue building, the few pioneering Jewish residents of St. Thomas had acquired land for a cemetery plot as early as
about 1750.[35] In this Savan cemetery, the Jews of St. Thomas buried their
dead for many years until the growth of the community led to the purchase of a second plot on the outskirts of the town of Charlotte Amalie
in the early nineteenth century.

The first mention of a synagogue in St. Thomas is found in the real
estate tax list of 1803.[36] In 1804 this building was destroyed by a fire that
supposedly burned down 1,200 buildings.[37] Other estimates indicate the
loss of 2,300 buildings, leaving hundreds – perhaps thousands – home-
less.[38] The island was rebuilt fairly quickly, and soon a new synagogue
arose from the ashes of the one that had been destroyed. In 1806, before
construction was completed, this structure burned down again in yet
another devastating fire. In the years that followed, religious services
were held in private homes once more, but, in 1812, another small synagogue building was erected. By 1823 this structure had become too
small to accommodate the growing community, and a decision was made
to expand the existing building.[39]

It was in this synagogue that Joshua Piza once more became the cantor of a Caribbean Jewish congregation. He had probably hoped that
Curaçao's community would be out of sight and out of mind in this new
place, but this turned out not to be the case. The community in St.
Thomas was not as homogeneous as that of Curaçao and consisted of
both Sephardim and Ashkenazim. But the number of Curaçaoan
Sephardim in St. Thomas had grown significantly during the last decade
of the eighteenth century, and they soon took over the lay leadership of
St. Thomas's Jewish community. The old by-laws of the Hebrew
Congregation of St. Thomas had been revised in 1802, and the new by-
laws showed a striking resemblance to those of the community on the
Dutch island.[40] The appointment in 1816 of Abraham Jessurun Pinto of
Curaçao to lead the congregation, added an additional Mikvé Israel
stamp on the Beracha VeShalom synagogue.[41] Over time the St. Thomas
community acquired its own flavor, but the Curaçaoan influence
remained evident for many years.

Although there were many new names among the Jewish families of
St. Thomas, there were several Maduros, de Castros, Henriquezes, and
Curiels in the island – names Piza recognized immediately, since these
Sephardim were no doubt related to those carrying the same names in
Curaçao. Many Sephardic men of the Curaçao branches of these families
had signed the petition to King William of the Netherlands in 1820,
applying for relief and dismissal of the cantor whom they described as an
"idiot, of evil mien, hoarse of voice, and incapable of performing his
duties."[42] Yet, in St. Thomas, Piza was consoled by the fact that new families such as the Benjamins, D'Azvedos, and Lopes Dubecs, and known
friends such as the Sassos and Lindos were also active in the community.
They far outnumbered the separatist names among his new congregants.
Joshua Piza could only hope that this would be the island of opportunity
he had expected eight years earlier when he first sailed from Holland to
the Caribbean. He also knew that this time around he had found himself
a formidable partner in his young wife.

A WOMAN OF VALOR: HANNAH SASSO PIZA

Hannah Sasso was born on April 27, 1799 in Curaçao to Jacob Sasso and Judith Sasso.[43] Judith was a daughter to Jacob's older brother, Moses, and as such was her husband's niece. Jacob and Moses's father, Abraham, had emigrated from London to Curaçao in the 1730s. Upon his arrival, Abraham had become the shamas – sexton – of the Mikvé Israel community, a poorly paid position that put him at the mercy of the many demands of the community's board members. His life must have rotated around the synagogue which he served for forty years. [44] He and his wife had sixteen children, and Hannah's extended family of aunts, uncles, cousins, nephews and nieces was almost a community onto itself.[45] Members of the Sasso family in Curaçao must have had varying opinions about Hannah's husband's abilities, but, in a show of solidarity, none of them sided with the separatists at the time of the Piza affair. Both Hannah's uncle (and grandfather) and Hannah's father were synagogue employees,[46] and Hannah's father's position in favor of Joshua Piza was quite clear.[47]

Based on Hannah's ancestry, it is safe to assume that she was brought up in a religious household where ritual was of considerable importance. It is also fairly certain that the family's assets were quite limited. Indeed, Hannah's sister, Ribca (Rebecca) Sasso who had married a Sasso relative, as occurred fairly frequently in that family, eventually had to borrow money from the Mikvé Israel community chest in 1822. The note acknowledging her debt of "22 Pesos and 4 reais" was signed by two witnesses, while Ribca signed her name with a circle, indicating her inability to write.[48]

Young Hannah's marriage to the much older Joshua Piza in 1816 seemed to offer some financial security since Joshua was employed as the leader of the Mikvé Israel community. The fifty year tenure of the previous rabbi must have led the Sassos to believe that in spite of the minor disagreements he had already experienced with his congregants during his first year in Curaçao, Hazan Piza's job would be a long term appointment as well. The fact that Joshua Piza ended up being the focus of the community's pent up differences of opinion within a few years after he married Hannah must have been extremely disconcerting to his wife and his in-laws.

By all accounts Hannah was not a happy young wife. In the early years it was difficult to adjust to the age difference in the marriage. Her husband was a mature and serious man, and she was barely an adult when they were wed. Her great-granddaughter Vida Lindo Guiterman writes:

Hannah Sasso Piza, 1799–1880

> Two weeks after their marriage, young Hannah became
> so exasperated with him that she vowed she would not
> be his wife any longer, and to prove it, threw her bright
> new wedding ring out of the window into the garden.
> When she got over her fit of temper, there was much
> searching for the ring, first secretly, and then with the
> aid of servants, but it was never found; so Joshua bought
> her a new one.[49]

Although this is anecdotal, the story seems quite plausible. Hannah had gone from her father's home where she had been surrounded by seven brothers and sisters to become the much younger wife of a stubborn middle-aged man, who, soon after their marriage, became an outcast in her community. Additionally, she was expected to take care of two small stepchildren who required her constant attention. Based on her actions as she matured, she must have been a very spirited woman, and her complicated life as a newlywed was most likely not what she had hoped for.

When Piza, resigned from the Mikvé Israel community in 1821, Hannah Sasso Piza was pregnant with the couple's second child. In 1820 she had given birth to their firstborn whom she had called Judith after her mother.[50] During the following three years, life in Curaçao must have been a source of irritation and grief for Hannah Sasso, as her husband became increasingly marginalized in the Jewish community which had for decades been the hub of the Sasso family's existence. The job offer from St. Thomas promised a much-needed change for the Sasso-Piza household.

Leaving the tense environment that had surrounded her in Curaçao, Hannah arrived in the Virgin Islands with the children in tow. St. Thomas was even smaller than the small island of her birth, yet it had attracted many of her Sasso relatives during the preceding decades. Her sister Rebecca and her family had moved there as well, and, although the island itself was new to Hannah, many of the Jewish faces of St. Thomas were those of relatives and friends whom she had not seen for quite a while. The *Curaçaosche Courant* had regularly printed news from this Danish island, and, even though we cannot be sure that Hannah knew how to read at that point, her husband definitely did. From these news updates, St. Thomas must have sounded appealing and far from all the ugly reminders of Joshua Piza's unsuccessful tenure as cantor of the unruly group of Mikvé Israel's Jews. Furthermore, the economy of St. Thomas had been booming since the departure of the British from that island in 1815, and, to many Curaçaoans, it was a place of opportunity. To Hannah, this new start must have seemed to be just what her family needed.

At home life seemed to settle into a happier routine. Shortly after their arrival, in November of 1824, Hannah gave birth to their first son, Jacob. In the years that followed, the Piza household kept increasing steadily with another child almost every other year: Samuel in 1827, Sarah in 1829, Esther in 1831, Rebecca in 1833, Leah in 1835, and, finally, Rachel in 1837.[51] By the time of Rachel's birth, Piza's two sons of his first marriage were already young men in their twenties and the eldest, Moses, had married Rebecca Lopez da Fonseca in Curaçao in 1835. He brought her back to St. Thomas, where he and his brother Judah were both active in the Jewish community.

Over time, disagreements between Joshua Piza and the leadership of the Beracha VeShalom community began to occur in St. Thomas as well.[52] This time, however, Hannah came to his rescue. She seemed determined that history would not repeat itself. Even though their financial condition left much to be desired, she encouraged her husband, who was by now in his fifties, to retire. In doing so she changed her life completely. She became the caretaker of this large household and the provider as well. A woman of valor, indeed!

The assumption that the family's finances were mediocre at best in their early years in St. Thomas is based on several known facts. First, both Hannah and Joshua came to the marriage with limited funds. Second, Piza's severance pay in Curaçao amounted to 500 pesos per year for three years, a sum that did not allow for many luxuries. And third, his poor relationship with so many congregants on that island had made it difficult for the maligned cantor to embark on other business ventures that might have increased his income after his resignation. In spite of this less than optimum financial condition, a small contribution was made by J. Piza & Son towards the rebuilding of the new St. Thomas synagogue when the structure of 1824 burned to the ground for a third time in 1832.[53] It is assumed that this contribution came from the cantor and one of his two adult sons of his first marriage. This donation indicates that the Pizas were charitably inclined, but not yet able to give at the same level as other Curaçaoan immigrants living in St. Thomas, such as E.A. Correa, Isaac Delvalle, and Jacob Haim Osorio. By the mid 1830s, with seven unmarried children under the age of fourteen, Piza retired.

While in Curaçao it was not common for nineteenth century Jewish women to work, the women of St. Thomas appear to have had greater freedom. Many wives worked full time in their husbands' shops and remained in charge when the men traveled away from the island on business for months at a time.[54] In the case of Hannah and Joshua Piza, however, the cantor did not run the shop; his wife did. After more than a decade in St. Thomas, Hannah had matured into a self-confident and competent woman, and lived a much more liberated and progressive life than would have been possible had she remained in Curaçao. There, the community had significantly proscribed roles for women and very strict socialization rules. But, in St. Thomas, Hannah was able to act more freely, and, when the opportunity presented itself, she took control of her life. In the mid to late 1830s, she opened a retail shop in Charlotte Amalie. Her great-granddaughter Vida Lindo Guiterman tells us that "Hannah's business throve – she seemed to have a genius for it. Her husband was not allowed inside the store: she declared she could not sell so much as a spool of thread when he was present. Though he was genial and amusing, he was most unbusinesslike."[55] Clearly there had been a significant reversal of roles in the Sasso-Piza household.

Naturally this story of Hannah's business acumen and her husband's lack thereof is based on anecdotes handed down throughout the generations and was recorded at least eighty years after the fact. Yet, it is likely that she did accumulate some wealth. Indeed, the family lore is that enough money was put aside by the Sasso-Piza family unit to allow their two eldest sons, Jacob and Samuel (or Coco and Sampi, as they were known to the family) to invest in the purchase of European goods, and sail to Panama to sell this merchandise. Somehow, during their trip across the isthmus of Central America to reach the city of Panama, all their merchandise was lost, and the two brothers had to start from scratch when they finally reached their destination.[56]

Skeptics might conclude that the two men arrived in Panama penniless, because they never had the merchandise or money to begin with, thus denying the possibility that Hannah's earnings had financed their trip and lost inventory. There is, however, an indisputable indication of some wealth in the Sasso-Piza household, which is contained in Benvenida Piza's *ketubah* – marriage contract. Joshua and Hannah's second daughter, Benvenida, married Jacob Lindo in 1844 and brought a dowry of a thousand dollars to the marriage.[57] This represented a fairly significant contribution on the part of the bride's family at a time when the cantor was no longer earning an income.* It is therefore clear that Hannah had been able to put away substantial savings from her business profits in St. Thomas to provide this dowry for her daughter. This was an impressive achievement for a woman with a household as large as hers and particularly impressive when one considers the lack of education that had been available to Hannah when she lived in Curaçao. While Hannah may have started out like her sister Ribca – unable to write – she definitely learned to count her pennies in her store in St. Thomas.

The Sasso-Piza children were of school age between the late 1820s and the early 1850s. Hannah and Joshua made sure that all their children, including the girls, were properly educated. In 1846, both Rebecca and Esther Piza, thirteen and fourteen years old, respectively, were confirmed at the Hebrew Congregation of St. Thomas.[58] Moses Nathan Nathan was the spiritual leader of St. Thomas's Jewish community during the 1840s and had instituted this ceremony as part of a more formal program of religious education which culminated in an examination of boys and girls at the end of the Shavuot** services. This curriculum and its final event on the Shavuot holiday introduced the Jews of St. Thomas to the confirmation ceremony practiced in many synagogues today. In

---

* It is likely that Joshua Piza's annual salary in the smaller Jewish community of St. Thomas was less than the 500 pesos he had earned as cantor of Curaçao's Mikvé Israel synagogue.
** The Feast of Weeks or Pentecost, which is celebrated seven weeks after Passover.

1846, when the Piza girls were confirmed, it was still considered an innovative and modern exercise.[59]

Before and after Reverend Nathan's tenure, however, many other schools and teachers came and went. In 1832 a Jewish woman by the name of Esther Jacobs announced that she was opening a school for young children of both sexes.[60] In February 1840, Isaac W. Williams, a native of Massachusetts, opened a school for "instructing in the usual branches of English Education."[61] And later that year, M.B. Simmonds announced that he had opened an evening school at his residence. Here he would teach English as well as devote some time to "the endeavor to promote a knowledge of the Hebrew tongue."[62]

In spite of these efforts, the need for a Jewish education was not always easily fulfilled in St. Thomas. In the 1850s, for example, the community did not have a rabbi, and its members not only struggled with the level of orthodoxy they wished to observe, but became increasingly concerned about the religious education of the younger generation. In 1856 a letter to the editor of the St. Thomas *Tidende* signed by "A Jewess" implored the Israelites of St. Thomas to consider the importance of such education.

> Religion must be the basis of education, or else it is
> valueless. Israel has been educated by God himself to be
> a people of religion, and how can our children know this
> fact without the aid of religious knowledge. But truly in
> nothing are we so careless and so uncertain as precisely
> in religious education ...

She ended the article by encouraging the leaders of the Jewish community to hire a "Reverend Gentleman, who will be competent to instruct our children as Jews."[63] This interest in furthering the Jewish education of the young members of the community demonstrates that the Jews of St. Thomas were well aware of the potential increase in assimilatory trends among those ignorant about their own traditions. But the community was small, and there were many years during which formal Jewish education was non-existent. Occasional periods of educational renaissance occurred, for example, during Reverend Meyer H. Myers short-lived tenure in the early 1860s and between 1871 and 1873 when Reverend Elias Nunes Martinez came from England to lead the congregation.[64] In 1877 hopes were high once more, when then lay leader David Cardoze reinstituted the congregation's Sunday school which had not operated for several years.[65] It is obvious, however that there were many educational hiatus during the second half of the nineteenth century, so that fairly substantial numbers of young people sometimes grew up without formal religious instruction.

In Hannah Sasso's household these educational voids were probably less acutely felt. Even during the years without rabbinical leadership or Hebrew School, the Sasso-Piza offspring continued to be instructed by their exposure to the Jewish elements of their home, where both Hannah and Joshua Piza observed the Jewish rituals they had grown up with.

In 1850 Reverend Joshua Piza died at the age of seventy-two. By this time the two sons of his first marriage, Moses and Judah, and three of his seven daughters born from his marriage to Hannah Sasso – Judith, Benvenida, and Sarah – were married. The sons married two Sephardic sisters from Curaçao. They were daughters of David Lopez da Fonseca, who came from a long line of Sephardic rabbis, both on the Lopez da Fonseca side as well as from David's maternal grandfather's side, who had been Curaçao's Haham Samuel de Sola.[66] Hazan Piza must have been quite pleased with these choices by his sons. Judith married her uncle, Judah Sasso. Benvenida married Jacob Lindo, a Sephardic Jew of Curaçaoan ancestry who had been born in St. Thomas. And Sarah married an Ashkenazi Jew, Herman Meyer, and spent most of the remainder of her life in Hamburg, Germany.

The stepsons both continued to live in St. Thomas and remained close to Hannah over the years. Moses Piza had been five years old when Hannah married his father. And his brother Judah had just turned one at the time of this event. Hannah had raised both boys to the best of her ability, and they thought of her as their mother. Judah, in particular, could not remember another mother, since his own mother had died when or soon after he was born, and his aunt, who had been Joshua Piza's second wife, had died less than a year later.

After Joshua Piza's death, the widowed Hannah could have decided to return to Curaçao. She did not. There were few Sassos left in Curaçao by mid century. Most of her siblings had either died or moved to St. Thomas. Her parents had passed away, and many of her cousins had migrated from the Dutch island as well. If ever she had considered the move to St. Thomas as a temporary one, it had become her permanent home by the mid nineteenth century.

Although the St. Thomas Jewish community had grown significantly from its early years, the island had only about 400 Jews in 1837.[67] In 1852 the amateur historian John P. Knox, Pastor of the Dutch Reformed Church of St. Thomas, wrote:

> The entire body of the Jews now number between four hundred and fifty and five hundred persons. They live, as they have always done in the island, under the same protection as is extended to their fellow-citizens. Many hold offices of trust and honor, and the most kindly feelings exist between them and the rest of the community. The congregation has no minister at present, the last incumbent having resigned his situation more than two years ago; services are, however, conducted by a reader.[68]

In spite of the relatively small number of Jews on the island, Hannah Sasso Piza was able to impress on all her children that they were to marry within their Jewish faith. Her offspring did not rely solely on the Jews of St. Thomas to find their mates, but branched out to many other countries to do so.

Her two sons who had set off to Panama together followed very different paths in finding their wives. Jacob, Hannah's first-born son, did not meet his wife in Panama or St. Thomas, but married Bendita Ascoli of the large Sephardic Jewish community of Hamburg, Germany in 1858, and brought her back to Panama to live. It is likely that he met her during his business trips to Hamburg where the Sephardim of the Caribbean had many connections. Although he had arrived in Panama City without any means and had later quarreled with his brother Sampi, he had built a successful business in his new place of residence which he called Piza – Piza. He was the only Piza running this enterprise, but he must have believed that the double use of the name Piza lent greater importance to the firm. It soon became apparent that Panama's climate with its many tropical diseases did not agree with Bendita Piza's constitution. As a result, the couple eventually left the Americas and moved to England where twelve of their thirteen children were born. Jacob Piza left his business to the care of his nephew, Morris Lindo, and visited only intermittently to check on its progress.[69]

Samuel's life was not quite as straightforward as that of his older brother and surely not as orthodox as one might think behooved the son of a *hazan*. Upon arrival in Panama, he fell in love with a Catholic woman by the name of Amalia Diaz and fathered two sons by her: Benjamin and Alberto. Years later, on a trip back to St. Thomas, he reacquainted himself with his niece Rachel Piza (his stepbrother Moses's daughter) and followed his mother's advice that, at almost 35 years of age, the time had come for him to marry "a nice Jewish girl." He married his niece in 1862, but, over time, remained unable to break off the relationship with Amalia, who bore him yet another son out of wedlock. He had three children with Rachel as well, but his affair with Amalia Diaz, the love of his life, only ended when she predeceased him.[70] Suffice it to say that the union between uncle and niece was not a happy one.

Samuel moved his family to Paris. After living in France for some years, Rachel moved to New York with their three children. Their firstborn daughter had been born crippled, and the family felt that she would be best cared for in New York City. It is unclear from the records if Samuel lived there with the family or remained primarily in Panama or Paris. In New York City, their son Joshua married a cousin, Florence Lindo, and their daughter Rosalie married the Reverend H. Pereira Mendes, minister of the Spanish and Portuguese Congregation of New York and a descendant of one of the oldest American Sephardic families.[71]

Like his brother, Samuel Piza had managed to accumulate considerable wealth in Panama. This is not surprising since these were the days of opportunity in that country which would eventually lead to the years of speculative investments during the building of the Panama Canal. In

1869 he was Panama's largest contributor to the Alliance Israélite Universelle, contributing 77.50 francs in order to remit the round sum of 500 franc to the Central Committee in Paris.[72]

In 1855, when she was fifty-six years old and had been widowed for several years, Hannah Sasso was living at 10 Dronningens Gade (the main street of Charlotte Amalie), accompanied by her 63-year old widowed sister, Rebecca Sasso; a 52-year old Judah Sasso, a shopkeeper by profession (conceivably their brother); her as yet unmarried daughters Rebecca, Leah and Rachel; and an unknown relative by the name of Abraham Piza. In addition to these family members, the household included a servant, a cook, the cook's twelve-year old daughter, and an eleven-year old described as a servant. Hannah herself was still running her store and is shown in this census as a shopkeeper.[73]

In her old age Hannah was fortunate to have her youngest daughter, Rachel, back in St. Thomas for extended periods. When she was a young girl, Rachel had exasperated her mother by rejecting many suitors over time. It took all of Hannah's persuasive powers to finally marry off this daughter to St. Thomas born Solomon Delvalle by which time, at age 23, Rachel was practically an old maid in her mother's eyes.[74] Delvalle set off to take his family to Barranquilla, Colombia a few years after they were wed, but ended up working for Rachel's brother Samuel Piza in Panama. Since both Rachel and Solomon had parents in St. Thomas, they returned to the island quite frequently and for fairly long stays. Hannah's other children, scattered across the globe, visited her often from these locations as well. Beyond her children and relatives, Hannah had many friends on the island. To Hannah, St. Thomas had become her home, and, unlike her children, she did not feel the need to move away.

The timing of Hannah's initial arrival in St. Thomas had been fortuitous. She was in her thirties and forties during the decades when the island was experiencing a period of steady economic growth. This environment, coupled with Hannah's fearless energy and innate business sense, broke the circle of poverty that had been her devout ancestors' fate in Curaçao. Had she arrived thirty years later, she would have faced a far different lot. Fortunately for Hannah her productive years coincided with the economic boom on St. Thomas which lasted through the

1860s. It was a time of true opportunity for those who had the wherewithal to grasp it, and the enterprising Hannah Sasso did just that.

Although the local market for goods and services in St. Thomas was
smaller than that of Curaçao and definitely could not compare to the
markets that were just opening up in Latin America, the Danish island
was extremely appealing to Curaçao's Sephardim during this period of
growth. Much of this attractiveness had to do with the free port regulations and the island's location on the trading routes between Europe and
the Americas which turned Charlotte Amalie into a trading and mar-
keting center in the first half of the nineteenth century. This was a familiar and desirable setting for Curaçao's Jewish merchants. In addition to
these economic considerations, the Danish occupiers offered a level of
political stability to the inhabitants of the Virgin Islands that did not
exist in the newly independent Spanish-speaking countries of the
Americas. Furthermore, the fact that the government of the Danish
Virgin Islands was at least as receptive to those of the Jewish faith as
Curaçao's colonial government only enhanced St. Thomas's appeal to
the migrating Sephardim.

One can speculate that it might have been the less adventurous
among Curaçao's Jews who were willing to settle in the Virgin Islands in
the nineteenth century and forego the greater, but riskier, Latin
American opportunities offered on the South American mainland. On
the surface there appeared to be no anti-Semitism on this Danish island,
and it was a comfortable place to be Jewish. Surely those who were somewhat more traditional in their personal religious observances found these
attributes attractive. It is, of course, difficult to distinguish between cause
and effect, but there is no doubt that the St. Thomas environment in the
first half of the nineteenth century allowed for a relative ease of observance of Jewish rituals. It had a synagogue building, often rebuilt, a
cemetery lot that had been filled to capacity and had been replaced by
the newer Altona burial ground, and firm community by-laws.
Furthermore, various community members had the ability to lead religious services during the years when there was no rabbi on the island,
kosher food was available, and there were local circumcisers who could
perform the required ritual circumcisions on the sons born to the Jews of

St. Thomas. These elements helped create an atmosphere conducive to Jewish continuity.

Hannah Sasso, as wife of a cantor, was of course particularly comfortable in this environment. Her family had come to the island to form part of the Jewish infrastructure of St. Thomas, and, even after Joshua Piza's retirement, they remained active in Jewish affairs. Hannah's hopes for religious continuity would have been quite common for a Jewish woman of her time. She was probably even more focused on the importance of endogamous marriage choices for her children than her contemporaries. Her husband's ancestral background and the memory of her own religiously dedicated Curaçaoan forefathers played a big role in her desire for Jewish sons-in-law and daughters-in-law. When finally her last unmarried offspring, the adventurous Sampi, married his half-brother's daughter in 1862 – albeit that the union did not turn out to be a very happy one – the widowed Hannah must have felt that her children had done well by their illustrious forefathers. They had all married Jews.

Even though not all of St. Thomas's Jews could boast the religious ancestry of the Sasso-Piza offspring, it appears that a large proportion of the descendants of the members of the St. Thomas Hebrew Congregation of the nineteenth century maintained the Jewish faith through several generations. The role of the Jewish infrastructure of St. Thomas cannot be minimized when considering this issue of continuity.

Hannah and Joshua Piza had sixty legitimate grandchildren for whom information is available. No marriage data are available for thirteen of these grandchildren. Of the remaining forty-seven, at least nine married outside the Jewish faith. The other thirty-eight married partners with Jewish last names. It is not known if all these partners with Jewish names were actually Jewish or merely of Jewish descent.[75]

The majority of the known mixed marriages among these grandchildren of Hannah Sasso Piza occurred in locations outside the Caribbean basin in countries with much larger Jewish populations than St. Thomas. Two grandchildren married non-Jews in Germany, one married a non-Jew in England, and three married outside their faith in the United States.[76] Even so, as will be discussed later, the degree of intermarriage by this group of grandchildren of the original Jewish immigrants was significantly lower than that observed among the third generation descendants of Sephardim who migrated from Curaçao to Spanish speaking Caribbean locations.

Although Hannah herself is buried in the Jewish cemetery in St. Thomas, none of her children are buried there. The places of their demise serve as a reminder that St. Thomas was a land of economic opportunity for only a very short while.

NAME	DIED IN	YEAR
Judith Piza Sasso	USA	1896
Benvenida Piza Lindo	Panama	1901
Jacob Piza	England	1886
Samuel Piza	France	1885
Sarah Piza Meyer	Germany	1907
Esther Piza Belisario Maduro	Panama	1918
Rebecca Piza Luria	Germany	1911
Leah Piza Luria	Germany	1868
Rachel Piza Delvalle	USA	1916

The fate of the Sasso-Piza children is representative of what was occurring in the St. Thomas Jewish community in the second half of the nineteenth century. Many other locations were becoming more attractive to the Jews of the Caribbean, and the growth of the Jewish population of St. Thomas decelerated and eventually reversed itself. In addition to the appeal of other places, there were several factors that affected St. Thomas specifically, making it less desirable even to those who were already there. The island's role as a refueling and transfer station was diminished by the introduction of more powerful European steamships on international trading routes which made it unnecessary for them to stop in St. Thomas for refueling. Nevertheless, a new dock was built to accommodate these larger ships that could otherwise not enter St. Thomas's shallow harbor. This dock developed many mechanical problems which remained unsolved for a considerable period. The comedy of errors surrounding the dock reached its climax in 1867 when it sank, creating an underwater hazard. The result was a less than comical situation, because now even the smaller ships that would normally dock on shore could not do so.[77]

That same year there were several outbreaks of cholera in the island, and towards the end of 1867 a number of natural disasters occurred as well. On October 29, 1867 St. Thomas was hit with a horrific hurricane which killed many and caused major damage to the buildings in Charlotte Amalie, including the synagogue. This was followed in November by an earthquake accompanied by a tidal wave, which destroyed a large number of homes and flooded the warehouses owned by the merchants. It appeared as if God Himself had unleashed His wrath on the inhabitants of this small island.[78]

The economy came to a standstill, and people began to leave in droves. As was to be expected, St. Thomas's Sephardim were once again on the move. Some returned to Curaçao, but, in the years that followed, many migrated to Panama, where, over time, they and their descendants were instrumental in establishing what could almost be called a St. Thomas Jewish colony. In this country, where soon the Panama Canal was going to be built, the children, grandchildren, and great-grandchildren of the original Sephardic immigrants who had left Curaçao for St. Thomas found new opportunities which the small islands of the Caribbean could not offer. Several of Hannah Sasso's children had left the island before 1867, but during the decade that followed, they all eventually drifted away to new places of promise.

It so happened that the only time that Hannah Sasso Piza ever left St. Thomas since arriving there from Curaçao as a young woman, was in this fateful year of 1867. Her youngest daughter Rachel, who was at that time living in Panama, had given birth earlier that year to her fifth child. She was her mother's pet, and was able to convince Hannah to come and meet her two youngest children who had been born in Panama. Hannah spent six months with Rachel and her husband Solomon Delvalle and was therefore not on the island when the hurricane and the tsunami struck. After a fairly lengthy stop in Jamaica, Hannah returned to St. Thomas with the Delvalles where the couple and their six children (another child was born to them in Jamaica) remained for four years.[79]

By the time of Hannah's return to St. Thomas, she was almost sixty-nine years old which, in those days, was considered a ripe old age. Yet it appears that she was spry enough to make the lengthy voyage to Panama and willful enough to come back to the ruins of Charlotte Amalie as it was being rebuilt. In the 1870s, safely ensconced in her St. Thomas home, she was a steadfast donor to the Alliance Israélite Universelle,[80] happy to be able to contribute to charity, instead of having to depend on it.

Age finally caught up with her in her late seventies, and she became paralyzed. Rachel, who was at this time living in London, came back to the Caribbean island of her birth with her ever-expanding family, where she vowed to stay and care for her mother.[81]

Hannah died on December 22, 1879 at the age of eighty. The inscription on her tombstone reads:

Into Thy hand I commit my spirit.
Thou hast
Redeemed me, o Lord!
God of Truth.
Ps. 31.5

In loving memory of
HANNAH
Relict of the late
JOSHUA PIZA
Died 1879
In the 80th year of her age [82]

During Hannah's long and fruitful life, she had shown herself to be a woman of unusual strength and character. In raising her children, she focused on their education and ties to the Jewish community while she herself set an example with her charitable contributions and continued devotion to the Hebrew Congregation of St. Thomas. More unusual for the times, however, she single-handedly pulled her household out of the potential cycle of poverty that might otherwise have been their lot.

St. Thomas's economy, which had allowed her to accumulate some wealth in the forties and fifties, was spiraling downwards at the time of her death. No longer was it a place of new possibilities for the generations that followed. Hannah's youngest daughter Rachel, having fulfilled her vow to care for her mother until her last breath, moved back to Panama with her twelve children to join her husband Solomon Delvalle who had been traveling back and forth between Panama and St. Thomas as his business required during the years that Rachel had spent caring for Hannah. As far as can be determined from the available records, none of Hannah's other biological children were living on the island at the time of her death. Joshua Piza's eldest son Moses had predeceased his step-mother. Although Moses's son, David, was on the island until at least the mid 1870s, when his name appeared on the rewritten by-laws of the Hebrew Congregation of St. Thomas,[83] he died in New York City in 1910, and it is not known when he moved there.[84] Hannah's other step-son, Judah Piza, still lived on the island at the time of her death and was buried there in 1892.

At its peak in the mid 1860s, the Jewish community of St. Thomas may have consisted of over six hundred Jews.[85] In 1870 the St. Thomas census counted only 375 Jews in Charlotte Amalie.[86] In 1885 the Royal Mail Steamship Line moved their headquarters from St. Thomas to Barbados, followed soon thereafter by a move of the headquarters of the French Line, Compagnie Générale Transatlantique to Martinique. Many additional Jewish families who relied on the shipping industry abandoned the island at this point. By 1890 there were 141 Jews left,[87] and a generation later, at the time of the transfer of the Virgin Islands to the United States in 1917, there were only about 65 Jews living in St. Thomas.[88]

Hannah was the matriarch of a very large family, whose descendants continue to be in leadership positions across the world even today. Her direct descendant, Paul Levy, has been the president and CEO of Boston's well-known Beth Israel Deaconess Medical Center since January of 2002. Peter Halle, a descendant of Hannah's daughter Benvenida, has had an impressive legal career as a partner in a prestigious law firm in Washington DC, while also chairing several committees of the American Bar Association. Ricardo Maduro Joest, Hannah Sasso's descendant of the same generation, was president of Honduras from 2001 through 2005.

Occasionally mixed marriages among the descendants of Hannah

Sasso Piza have taken an interesting turn, and the following case is particularly telling of the vicissitudes of intermarriage practices among descendants of other Caribbean Sephardic Jewish families as well.

Benvenida Piza (1822-1901), one of Hannah and Joshua Piza's daughters, and her husband Jacob Jesurun Lindo (1821-1885) had a daughter Clara Jesurun Lindo, who had married a Sephardic Jew by the name of Isaac Levy Maduro. They had eight children, including a son Salomon Frank Maduro, born in 1883 in Panama. In 1909, this son married a Catholic woman, Eva Lobo, of Caracas, Venezuela, after which they lived for some time in Costa Rica.

Even though Eva Lobo was a Catholic, she was the daughter of Dr. David Lobo, a Sephardic Jew and prominent doctor in Caracas. Eva's mother, however, had been a Roman Catholic by the name of Josefa Inés Pardo Monsanto, whose father, Isaac Pardo, had been Jewish, but who had been raised in her Monsanto mother's Catholic faith. Monsanto is a Sephardic name, but it would appear that the ancestors of this Monsanto had converted or intermarried in the late eighteenth or early nineteenth century.[89] Eva Lobo, like her mother before her, was brought up Catholic by her Catholic mother.

Eva Lobo and Frank Maduro (Hannah Sasso's great grandson) had six children. Again, these children of a Jewish man and a Catholic woman, for a third generation in a row, were brought up in their mother's Catholic faith. Two of these children, Richard Maduro and Olga Maduro, made a full circle geographically and ended up marrying respectively Rachel Morón and Alfred Morón in Curaçao – Sephardic Jews descending from the Henriquez Morón family who had been on the island since the seventeenth century. Olga and Alfred Morón raised their three children in their mother's Catholic faith, following the pattern established by three earlier generations of Jewish-Catholic unions on Olga Maduro's side of the family. Of the three children, the daughter married within her Catholic faith, but the eldest son married a Sephardic Jewish woman in Curaçao. Despite the fact that he did not convert, his sons were brought up in their mother's Jewish religion. After a divorce, Olga and Alfred's youngest son underwent an orthodox conversion to Judaism and chose an Ashkenazi woman as his second wife in Curaçao. Appendix A-1 illustrates this interesting generational odyssey from Curaçao to St. Thomas to Panama, Venezuela, and Costa Rica and back to Curaçao, and the accompanying shift from the Jewish religion to several generations of Roman Catholic observers and back to a new generation of Jews.[90]

A large number of Hannah Sasso Piza's descendants continue to be Jewish in the twenty-first century. Many of her Jewish and non-Jewish descendants still remember that she was the ill-fated cantor's wife. Some will also recall that when they were young, they used to be frightened of an unflattering photograph of the elderly Hannah which used to hang in their grandparents' livingroom. In the eighty years that she walked this earth, however, Hannah was much more than a wife and an aged widow. She was an independent, strong-willed businesswoman, a dedicated and loving mother, and a charitable member of the Jewish community. In many ways she was ahead of her time, showing an enterprising spirit that few Caribbean women of her era had occasion to display

DEDICATED TO HIS PEOPLE: BENJAMIN SALOM DELVALLE

During the nineteenth century most of the Sephardim who left Curaçao were single men. There were some families with children, such as Hannah and Joshua Piza, who decided to leave as well (primarily to St. Thomas), but largely the Jews who decided to migrate were the younger sons of large families, whose fathers' businesses in Curaçao could no longer accommodate the many adult sons during times of economic recession. This was the case in the household of Salomon Salom Delvalle. In the late 1820s and early 1830s, several of his sons ended up leaving Curaçao for other Caribbean locations.

Salomon Salom Delvalle was born in Amsterdam in 1767. He was twenty and his brother was nineteen when they made their decision to leave Holland. News of Curaçao's economic boom of the mid seventies to the mid eighties must have reached them in Europe and enticed them to leave the cold climates of the Netherlands for this unknown tropical place. By the time they arrived in Curaçao in 1788,[91] however, the eco-

Benjamin Salom Delvalle
1811–1876

nomic recession had just started on the island, and nobody
could have predicted its length
and depth.

In 1796 Salomon married
Deborah Motta in Curaçao's
Mikvé Israel synagogue, and in
the fifteen years that followed
they had nine children. The
youngest, Benjamin, was born
in 1811. Eight years later,
Deborah died leaving behind
five sons and four daughters.[92]
Seven of the Delvalle children
were under eighteen years of
age when their mother died,
and their father had many
mouths to feed.

It is not known what Salomon's main line of business
was, but by 1818 he owned what must have been a fairly good-sized plantation at Jan Zoutvat, valued without inventory at 10,500 pesos.[93] A few
years later in 1822, he presented a plan to the governor of the island to
start a money lending institution in Curaçao. This plan was not accepted, but it is likely that both he and his brother were involved in other
lending businesses.[94]

By 1832, sons Isaac and Abraham, born in respectively 1807 and
1809, were living in Santo Domingo.[95] It is not known when exactly the
youngest son of the family, Benjamin Delvalle, left Curaçao for St.
Thomas, but he was living there in 1832. That year had not started on a
good note on the Danish island. On January 7, 1832, the St. Thomas
Tidende's front page announced, "Destruction of half St. Thomas *By
Fire!*" The article that followed this bold-lettered headline described a
fire on New Years' Eve which had spread quickly through downtown
Charlotte Amalie and could not be contained.

> ... owing to many who would have been useful at such
> an event [the fire] being lost in the revelry of Old Year's
> Night, and the scarcity of Water from a previous drought
> the flames from their first commencement were not met
> with sufficient energy to suppress their spread. – The
> wind too which was high, carried terror and devastation
> in so many points that all opposition seemed vain ...

The newspaper estimated that 600 to 700 dwellings burnt down and that counting the "outbuildings" this number could easily reach 1,200. The damage was believed to be around three million dollars.[96]

Numerous ads by members of the Jewish community appeared in subsequent issues of the *Tidende*, thanking unnamed persons for saving their homes. But once again the synagogue, which had burned down on two other occasions, was consumed by fire. The Jews of St. Thomas did not waste any time in replacing the lost structure. By January 11, less than two weeks after the fire, a subscription list to raise funds for the reconstruction of the synagogue was started.

Benjamin Delvalle's name does not appear in this list of donors.[97] It is possible that he had not yet arrived in Charlotte Amalie in January of 1832 or that he did not have sufficient funds at that time to contribute to the rebuilding of the synagogue. But most likely, it is here in St. Thomas during 1832, that Benjamin met and befriended Judith de Castro Curiel and her husband Salomon Haim Curiel. Both Judith and Salomon had been born in Curaçao and, like Benjamin, had moved to the Danish Virgin Islands. On August 7, 1832, Salomon Curiel died suddenly at the age of 29. The widowed Judith fell in love with Benjamin Delvalle, and although she was twenty-six and he was only twenty-one years old and just starting a new life on the island of St. Thomas, they decided to get married.

It did not take them long to find out that their marriage was not going to be a straightforward event. According to the laws of the levirate* – *Halitza* in Hebrew – the childless Judith could only remarry if she mar-

---

* *Levir* is a husband's brother in Latin.

ried one of her husband's surviving brothers. In Dr. J.H. Hertz's written commentary on the relevant biblical portion of Deuteronomy, he indicates that a levirate marriage was intended to "avert the calamity of the family line becoming extinct, of a man's name perishing and his property going to others. [Therefore] the surviving brother of such a childless man was required to marry the widow, so as to raise up an heir to that man's name."[98]

Why the matter was dealt with by the Mikvé Israel community of Curaçao and not by the St. Thomas Jewish community is not clear. Conceivably it was because both Benjamin and Judith originally came from that Dutch island, and because their respective fathers still lived there. It is also likely that at some point after she was widowed, Judith had returned to Curaçao. Be it as it may, in the Sephardic Curaçaoan community of the 1830s, laws dealing with *Halitza* were upheld and given very serious consideration. Judith's brother-in-law, Elias Curiel, a prominent member of the Mikvé Israel synagogue board, was married and therefore did not qualify as an available brother-in-law. A second brother-in-law, Jacob, refused although he was not yet married. And for some reason the youngest brother Moses, who was in Aruba, could not comply either. The matter was therefore brought to Curaçao's *Beth Din* – Jewish judicial court.[99]

The Mikvé Israel community had no rabbi during this time, leaving the lay leaders to resolve this issue with little guidance. In the end, the *Beth Din*, pressured by the synagogue board, came to a compromise which the historian Rabbi Isaac Emmanuel, writing in the 1970s, criticized as "too daring for the period." They allowed the widow to remarry on the condition that it would be her duty " *ainda despois de casada de observar a todo tiempo o preceito de Halisa quando hum dos cunhados for disposto a efectuallo ...*" – even after she was married, to observe the precepts of Halitza at all times, whenever the two brothers-in-law might be willing to comply. In other words Judith had to promise that even after she was married, she would obey the law of *Halitza* and marry one of her brothers-in-law if he were to be so inclined. This ruling meant that she would have to obtain a divorce from Benjamin Delvalle if one of her first husband's brothers would decide at a later date that he wanted to marry her.[100] Not only was the ruling too daring for the period, it was extremely odd for any period.

Throughout these deliberations of August and September 1833, Judith was pregnant with her first child. Finally on September 25, 1833 the couple was allowed to marry according to Jewish law.[101] Daughter Deborah Delia Delvalle was born on December 6, 1833 in St. Thomas.[102]

Analysis of birth dates of individuals versus the marriage dates of their parents indicates that premarital pregnancies were not that unusual among the Caribbean Sephardim.[103] That is not to say that these situations were not at the time the focus of gossip among the members of the community. In spite of these complicated beginnings, Judith and Benjamin Delvalle settled down once more in Charlotte Amalie after these legal issues had been resolved where they proceeded to have seven additional children after Deborah Delia.

Although the problems with Hazan Piza had culminated during Benjamin Delvalle's pre bar mitzvah years, he must have had a solid Jewish education in Curaçao. Such teachers as David Rodrigues, Moses Lindo, Jacob Rodriguez Pereira, and Mikvé Israel's assistant cantor, Jacob Sasso[104] must have taught Benjamin quite a bit about Jewish ritual, and it appears that he often assisted the latter during services at the Mikvé Israel synagogue. In St. Thomas, too, he served as reader and occasional *hazan* when needed, and he became a well-respected member of the Jewish community on the Danish island.[105]

Benjamin Delvalle's commercial progress over time is reflected in the Virgin Islands' census data. The information collected in such surveys of St. Thomas would indicate by name all persons living at a particular address, showing each person's place of birth, age, marital status, profession, his or her relationship to the head of household, and sometimes additional information considered of importance by the census taker. Like most young men first starting out in business in nineteenth century St. Thomas, Benjamin Delvalle was a clerk when he first settled in the island. In 1835 he received his *Burgher Brief*. This was a license granted by the Danish government to upstanding businessmen who had been sponsored by at least two other St. Thomas burghers to be a business agent.[106] By 1846, he lived at 15 Dronningens Gade, the main street of

Charlotte Amalie where several other Jewish families lived, including the Pissarro family of artistic fame who were Delvalle's neighbors at #14.[107] The house Delvalle lived in was at the time owned by Elizabeth Vetter.[108] As was common in those days, he probably lived over his store, and he is shown in the 1846 census records as a shopkeeper.

In the 1855 census, Benjamin Delvalle is registered as living at 16 & 17 Dronningens Gade, a property owned by Mr. A. R. Ligett. This new address may indicate a renumbering of the street or an expansion of his residence to accommodate his large family. He lived there with his wife Judith and his children Solomon, Rachel, Rebecca, Jacob, Isaac, and David, as well as a servant who had been born in St. John.[109] His daughter, Deborah Delia, had by this time already married Joseph Gomes Casseres, and had her own household on the island.[110]

The 1873 tax records show that Benjamin Delvalle owned three properties in town that year: 5B Commandants Gade, which he rented out to David Sasso, 6A Wimmelskaft Gade, and 9 Crystal Gade, across the street from the synaggogue. The latter, on a hill with a wonderful view of the harbor of Charlotte Amalie, was Benjamin Delvalle's own residence in 1870 when he was 60 and Judith was 64. At that time he referred to himself as proprietor and not merchant or shopkeeper, indicating his semi-retirement.[111]

Jewish life was of great importance to Delvalle. He served on the board of the St. Thomas synagogue for many years and was considered a pillar of the community. He was a board member in 1867, when a schism in the St. Thomas Jewish community resulted in the creation of the Reformed Congregation Beth Elohim. As such he was a co-signer to a letter dated April 1, 1867 directed to the Vice Governor of St. Thomas, whereby the board of the St. Thomas's Hebrew Congregation reminded the Danish official of the illegitimacy of the act of secession of some of its erstwhile members from the only legitimate synagogue in the Virgin Islands.[112]

Even in retirement he remained very much a part of synagogue politics, sometimes strongly disagreeing with the actions taken by his co-religionists. In 1872 he wrote an indignant letter to the Governor, informing him that:

Section 41 of the present Code of Laws actually governing the [Israelite] Congregation states "that no alteration
of or addition to these laws can be made without the
consent of 3/5 of the voting members of the Congregation. After the same has been proposed by the Representatives & to which the approval of His Majesty must
afterwards be obtained." -------- further in the confirmation of the said laws by His Majesty in conclusion it
reads as follows -------- "We order also all and every one
to abstain from impeding what has been enacted."

Delvalle's letter then explained that members of the Jewish congregation
had decided to go ahead with alterations to the community by-laws without consideration of this legal code and without heeding the Danish
king's directive "to abstain from impeding what has been enacted." As a
member of the "Israelite Congregation of this island" the writer stated
that in his humble opinion he considered the steps taken to frame new
by-laws without due process illegal and begged to be excluded from having any responsibility for said actions.[113] The writing in both letters is
somewhat pompous and legalistic, giving the impression that Benjamin
Delvalle was both someone who adhered to every letter of the law as well
as a person very confident of his interpretation of the intent of such laws.

Nevertheless, efforts must have been made to pacify and satisfy Delvalle, who, after all, was an elder of the Jewish community and a wealthy
one at that. When the revised by-laws were published in 1875, a year
before his death, the names of two of his sons, Solomon B. and Jacob B.
Delvalle, featured prominently on the title page of the revised Code of
Laws, indicating their participation in the process.[114] It seems inconceiv-
able given the close-knit nature of this family that Benjamin Delvalle's
children would have served on the committee to revise the synagogue
constitution if they had not had their father's blessing to do so.

At home Delvalle's involvement in community life and adherence to
Jewish traditions set an example for his children. One of Benjamin and
Judith's children, Esther, had died before her first birthday, but the other
seven offspring all married Sephardic Jews. Benjamin and Judith also

adopted a niece, Esther Henriquez Delvalle, who married a Sephardic Jew as well. Unlike the Piza offspring, who traveled far and wide to find their spouses, six of these Delvalle weddings took place in St. Thomas while two took place in Curaçao. Among the St. Thomas weddings, every single one was either to a Sephardic Jew who had been born in Curaçao or to someone who had at least one parent born there.[115] This further reinforced the connection with that island among the offspring of Judith and Benjamin Delvalle. The St. Thomas weddings included that of son Solomon who married Rachel Piza, daughter of Hannah and Joshua Piza.

While his commercial activities and his life as a Jew were quite important to Benjamin Delvalle, he and Judith must also have participated in the many cultural activities available to them in St. Thomas. Considering the size of the island, cultural life in the nineteenth century was quite varied. Men and women who could afford the price of admittance had frequent access to traveling theatre groups and concerts. The upper layers of St. Thomas society, and particularly the merchants, tended to be multilingual. As such, they attended plays in French, were entertained at the Commercial Hotel with English comedies in 1841, and marveled at the magic tricks performed on stage by the "celebrated Obaldino Milton, only 14 years of age" at this same locale in 1857. They were active members of the International Club in the 1870s and were able to see a performance of Shakespeare's Othello and other plays in English at the Apollo Theatre in 1875, where they also attended concerts given by Latin American musicians. All in all, many recreational activities were available to those who were interested and had the wherewithal to avail themselves of them.[116]

Like many other nineteenth-century Jews, Benjamin Delvalle was also a Freemason. He was initiated on April 6, 1842, passed on May 4, and raised on June 1 of that same year at the Harmonic Lodge in Charlotte Amalie.[117] Freemasonry is a secular society of men concerned with moral and spiritual values. Although Freemasonry is not a religion or a substitute for religion, the essential qualification for admission as a Mason is the belief in a Supreme Being. The organization is often referred to as a secret fraternity because of its secret rites and is frowned upon by the Roman Catholic Church and some other religious institutions. However, most Jews have considered its tenets of brotherly love, charity, and truth to be an appealing complement to their own religious beliefs.

Benjamin Delvalle's Masonic lodge in St. Thomas, the Harmonic Lodge, had been founded in 1818 in response to the fact that the Danish lodges would not allow either "Jews or free-coloreds" to join.[118] This exclusion seems inconsistent with the idea of Universal Brotherhood on which Freemasonry is based. It is also surprising in view of the much-touted acceptance of the Jews by the Danes in St. Thomas. Worshipful Brother John D. Woods of St. Thomas's Harmonic Lodge, writing at the time of the 175th Anniversary of that institution in 1993, excuses these restrictions by the Danes by suggesting that "[e]ven if they [meaning the Jews and free-coloreds] had been able to visit or join, they would have found it difficult to follow the ceremonies which were in either Danish, German or French."[119] Language, however, was not the issue, since the ostracized group in St. Thomas who wanted to join the Freemasons could have formed a lodge under the Danish charter which could have conducted its ceremonies in English – the lingua franca on the island. However, this solution was not an option entertained by the Danish Freemasonry movement.

In the end, the excluded group bypassed the Danish system and applied for a charter from the Grand Lodge of England in 1818, which was granted at the end of that year. A few months there-after, in April 1819, the Government of St. Thomas informed the leaders of the Harmonic Lodge that it had "no objection whatsoever to the establishing of a Freemason's Lodge as stated in your petition."[120] Among the fifteen founding Masonic Brothers of 1818 were six Sephardic Jews. For the year 1827-1828 all nine leaders of the lodge were Jews, with David Pardo serving as Worshipful Master.[121] Between 1818 and 1870 there were twenty-three different Worshipful Masters of the Harmonic Lodge, of which seventeen were Jewish.[122]

Unlike the situation in many other locations, Freemasonry was not a conduit for the Jews of St. Thomas to mingle with the non-Jewish Caucasian elite, since upper-class Danes did not belong to the Harmonic

Lodge. As the century advanced, two other lodges were established on the island under the jurisdiction of the Supreme Council of France. Jews joined these lodges as well, but it is not known if discriminatory practices against non-Caucasians existed in these lodges operating under the French charter. While Delvalle was a Freemason, the brotherhood took second place to his activities on behalf of the Jewish community. He was never among the leaders of Freemasonry on the island and instead, dedicated his leadership talents to his beloved synagogue.

With all the merchandise coming through the Virgin Islands, Benjamin Delvalle and others who belonged to St. Thomas's higher strata of society in the nineteenth century did not lack the niceties of life. Based on advertisements in the *Tidende* they owned silk jackets and parasols, perfumed themselves with French eau de cologne, wore gold chains and diamonds, bought dressed dolls for their children and concertinas, pianos, music books, and novels in several languages for their own entertainment. They ate imported fresh salmon from England, spread their bread with strawberry and gooseberry jams, drank Martell and Hennessy cognac after dinner, and smoked Havana cigars to round off a pleasant evening.

An inventory taken of the contents of Benjamin Delvalle's residence shortly after his death reveals that he could have entertained many guests at his home at 9 Crystal Gade. Delvalle's hall (living room) contained, among other items, a sofa, a couch, four rocking chairs, ten chairs and a China spittoon. Also listed among the contents of his house were 17 large foot glasses, 6 small foot glasses, 23 liqueur glasses, 18 champagne glasses, 12 wine glasses, and a "China Dinner Sett Complete."[123] It is true that Benjamin Delvalle had a large immediate family, but the numerous glasses for alcoholic beverages point to festive tropical evenings spent with family, friends, and business associates.

The Jews of St. Thomas were a worldly group. The *Tidende*, and later the *St. Thomas Times*, kept its readers apprised of happenings around the world, ensuring that they were well read and well informed. These newspapers and the fact that the Jews traveled with some regularity allowed them to feel connected with others across the planet. In 1840 they expressed their "feelings of disgust and abhorrence" about the murders of

Jews in Damascus. In 1856 they rejoiced when the government of Santo Domingo offered amnesty to President Baez, in exile on their island, collected funds for France's flooding victims, and worried about Roman Catholic persecutions of Freemasons in England. In the late 1860s the possibility of annexation of the Virgin Islands by the United States was high on the agenda, but it took almost another fifty years before these Danish colonies were sold for $25 million to the USA in 1917.

As had occurred to a lesser extent in Curaçao at the end of the eighteenth century, poor economic conditions and the calamities of the 1860s slowly but surely brought an end to this life of Jewish and secular pleasures for the Jews of St.Thomas. The places where Benjamin Delvalle's children died illustrate once more how short the sojourn in St. Thomas ended up being for the descendants of the original Curaçaoan immigrants.[124]

NAME	DIED IN	YEAR
Deborah Delia Delvalle Gomes Casseres	Curaçao	1872
Solomon Delvalle	U.S.	1882
Rachel Delvalle Fidanque	St. Thomas	1882
Rebecca Delvalle Penso	Curaçao	1897
Jacob Delvalle	Curaçao	1920
Isaac Delvalle	Panama	1900
David Delvalle	St. Thomas	1909
Esther Henriquez Delvalle Osorio	Curaçao	1876

Yet, the places of death do not give the whole story, because Delvalle's sons Solomon, Jacob, David, and Isaac lived in St. Thomas on and off for many years, where all four of them were in the dry goods business. Even after the Jewish outmigration of the late 1860s, they were still making money in St. Thomas. At the time of their father's death in 1876, all four men were residents of the Danish island.

Benjamin and Judith Delvalle's sons continued to invest in St. Thomas more than a decade after the Jews had started leaving the island. In 1875, Delvalle & Co. had an advertisement in the *Saint Thomas Times* indicating that the brothers had opened another establishment at No. 87

Kronprindsens Gade under the management of Isaac B. Delvalle.[125] Isaac, one of Judith and Benjamin's younger sons, had been a bachelor for a long time, but in 1870 at age 37, he had married Esther Jesurun Lindo in St. Thomas. They only lived there as a married couple for about six years. Shortly after his father passed away in 1876, Isaac put an ad in the *Tidende* announcing that he was selling his "well kept household furniture – all of elegant and superior quality, equal to none" and moved to Panama.[126]

Of the four brothers, Solomon was the eldest. He was married to Rachel Piza and their peripatetic lifestyle, which took them to many other countries with several long interludes in St. Thomas, was detailed in the previous discussion of the Piza family. Their children were born in St. Thomas, Panama, Jamaica, London, and San Francisco, indicative of their wanderings in the second half of the nineteenth century. When he lived in St. Thomas, Solomon was active in synagogue affairs, and he was the driving force behind Delvalle & Co. His brother Jacob was his partner in this enterprise.

Jacob Delvalle stayed on in St. Thomas after Solomon's departure in the early 1880s, running the business essentially by himself. Delvalle & Co. minted its own currency in the 1880s, struck for Jacob B. Delvalle by the Birmingham Mint in England.[127] It was fairly common in the nineteenth century for large commercial enterprises to mint their own coins and print their own paper money. In the 1890s, the Maduros of Curaçao and several other companies on that island issued paper money that was commonly accepted for payment of all kinds.[128] Clearly, Delvalle & Co. was a similar major player in the St. Thomas economy at the end of the nineteenth century.

Jacob Delvalle remained involved in Jewish life and Jewish charities. In 1895, he wrote a letter to the Alliance Israélite Universelle to accompany the annual remittance to that organization by St. Thomas's Jews. The size of their contribution that year was indicative of the diminished condition of the island's Jewish community as the century drew to a close. While in 1864 the members of the Hebrew Congregation of St. Thomas had contributed a total of 700 francs to the Alliance,[129] Delvalle's letter, written a little over thirty years later, explains:

> We subjoin a list of the members and their individual con-
> tributions for the present year amounting to One Hundred
> Francs, which sum we have the pleasure of handing you
> enclosed in a Bank of St. Thomas draft.... We regret that
> the contribution is not larger which is owing to the num-
> ber of Israelites residing at present in St. Thomas being
> much less than what it was in former years.[130]

Eventually Jacob Delvalle left the Virgin Islands as well. At least three
of his children had found Curaçaoan marriage partners in the Mikvé Israel
community, and, in their middle age, he and his wife Hannah chose to be
nearer to their Curaçao-based children. By the late 1890s, they were back
on the island where Jacob's father, Benjamin, had been born.[131] In
Curaçao, when he was already in his late fifties, Jacob founded the firm El
Globo, which was the last Jewish retail establishment to close its doors on
the Sabbath on that island.[132] It appears that Jacob had continued to
adhere to his father's religious traditions. Elderly members of the Jewish
community of Curaçao who spoke of him at the end of the twentieth century, remembered this aspect of his life quite clearly.[133] His wife Hannah
died in Curaçao in 1901, but Jacob survived her by nineteen years. He died
at the age of eighty-one and was buried in Curaçao's Jewish cemetery.[134]

Jacob Delvalle's great-grandson, René Maduro, served as president of
Curaçao's Mikvé Israel – Emanuel congregation for many years in the late
twentieth century and presided over that community's celebration of its
350th anniversary in 2001. His great-granddaughter Ena Maduro Dankmeijer and her mother, Rachel Louise Brandao Maduro, founded the
S.A.L. (Mongui) Maduro Library in Curaçao in 1974, a depository of
Antilliana and Judaica collected by Ena's father Mongui Maduro. This collection continues to be enhanced daily by the dedication and energy of
this female descendant of Jacob B. Delvalle and her savvy staff.

The youngest of Benjamin Delvalle's children, David B. Delvalle, born
in St. Thomas in 1845, was married on that island on July 9, 1873 to Grace
Cardoze.[135] On March 14, 1875, a child was born out of wedlock to an
Episcopalian woman named Henrietta Lucas, and baptized in St. Thomas's
Catholic Church on April 28 of that same year. The church records named

David Delvalle as the father of this child. It was by no means an uncommon occurrence in the Jewish community of St. Thomas for men to have children out of wedlock. During the eighteenth and nineteenth centuries, such liaisons occurred fairly frequently on the island. David Delvalle, of course, was already married when Henrietta Lucas conceived this child, but it appears that this fling during his first year of marriage to Grace was forgiven. He and Grace had nine children between 1876 and 1890, three of whom died as infants.[136] David was not in business with his brothers and ran his own dry goods business in Charlotte Amalie.[137] In the late 1880s or early 1890s, he left for Panama, hoping to make more money there than he had been making in the declining economy of St. Thomas. He left Grace and his children in the care of Grace's father, Reverend David Cardoze, only to return to the Danish island penniless. Shortly thereafter, he was paralyzed, most likely from a stroke, and his wife was left to care for her invalid husband and her surviving six children.[138] Later several of the Cardoze-Delvalle children migrated to Panama, where some of their descendants still live.[139] David Delvalle is the only son of Benjamin and Judith Delvalle who is buried in St. Thomas.

Judith and Benjamin Delvalle had 52 known legitimate grandchildren born from the endogamous marriages of their eight surviving children and their spouses. Of the 28 marriages known to have been contracted by these grandchildren, 25 were to persons with Jewish surnames.[140] In other words, a very large percentage of the second-generation descendants of the original Curaçaoan Sephardic immigrant to St. Thomas, Benjamin Delvalle, married within the Jewish faith. They did so in such diverse places as St. Thomas, Curaçao, Coro, Panama, New York, Chicago, and Nicaragua.

Judith de Castro Delvalle predeceased her husband on June 23, 1871. Her obituary in the *Tidende* stated:

> Today we record with deep regret the death of Judith, wife of Mr. B. Delvalle, who departed this life on the evening of the 22nd instant at the age of 65 years.
>
> The deceased was universally respected and beloved

by all who knew her, and her death has cast a gloom on
all who held her dear. She has left an affectionate husband, eight dutiful children, and numerous relatives and
friends to mourn her loss, for she was a good wife, a dear
mother, and a true friend. Her mortal remains were con-
veyed to their last resting place yesterday afternoon followed by a very large concourse of friends.

May her soul enjoy the peace which is reserved for
those who have led a pious life here below, and may He
who is the soother of all grief grant strength, fortitude,
and consolation to those who mourn the loss of one who
was so good and kind.[141]

This was a comparatively long obituary and reflects the respect held
for Benjamin Delvalle and his family in the community at large, as well
as the appreciation expressed for the deceased. The epitaph on her tombstone was equally elaborate and was mostly likely drafted by her husband.
It reads:

Sacred
To the memory of
JUDITH
The beloved wife of
BENJAMIN DELVALLE
Born in the island of Curaçao
On the 5th of October 1806
Died in the island of St. Thomas
22nd June 1871
Her children rise up and call her blessed
Her husband also, and he praiseth her.
Many daughters have done virtuously;
But thou excellest them all
Give her of the fruits of her hands and
Let her own works praise her in the gates.
Prov. C. 31. V. 28-29-31[142]

This *Eshet chayil* prayer from Proverbs is recited every Shabbat eve by observant Jewish men for their wives. Its use on Judith's grave is indicative not only of Benjamin's love for his wife, but also of his knowledge of the appropriate prayer.

A year later, Benjamin and Judith's firstborn, Deborah Delia Delvalle Gomes Casseres passed away in Curaçao a day after giving birth to her tenth child.[143] And in 1876, Benjamin Delvalle was put to rest as well. Benjamin's tombstone in the Altona cemetery of St. Thomas is fully covered with Hebrew and English inscriptions and is the gravestone with the greatest amount of text in this cemetery. His lengthy epitaph reflects a life dedicated to his God and his family and reads:

Sacred

to the memory of

BENJAMIN SHALOM DELVALLE

Born in the island of

Curaçao 8th August 1811

Died in St. Thomas on the

holy day of atonement

28th September 1876

Piously inclined from his youth, he steadfastly adhered through life to his ancestral religion, rearing in unity with his dear wife a numerous family in the fear of God, and in the firm belief that those who trust in the Lord shall not want any good, the reward of which in this world he lived to enjoy, seeing around him his progeny following in his footsteps. Truly it may be said of the departed "May my end be like his, for his death was that of the righteous."

His favorite quotations were:

"The fear of the Lord is the beginning of wisdom;

And good success attendeth all who keep

His commandments." "I rejoiced when

they said unto me: let us go unto the house of the Lord."[144]

He left behind a very impressive estate and showed his charitable leanings even in his will, where he carefully earmarked donations to be made
out of this estate to the St. Thomas Hebrew Congregation, the Mikvé
Israel synagogue in Curaçao, and the Lutheran Church of St. Thomas.[145]
This last will and testament ends with Article 14th, which reads:

> This will & testament made this day in the island of
> St. Thomas, Danish West Indies, we desire to be consid-
> ered legal, valid, & to take effect wherever we may here-
> after reside.
> In the name of God Amen
> Signed in presence of witnesses in the island of St.
> Thomas this third day of May 1864.

The addition of the sentence "In the name of God" in this otherwise
legal document was exactly what might have been expected from
Benjamin Delvalle. He was a true believer whose communal activities
were a logical extension of a life dedicated to doing God's work. In exe-
cuting this will with which he confronted his own and Judith's mortali-
ty, he once again put himself in the hands of his Maker who had guided
him through all his years.

MEMORIES OF ST. THOMAS

Going down the ninety-nine steps that lead to the main business area of
Charlotte Amalie, the sea sparkles at a distance, and the sun is already
hot at seven o'clock in the morning. On the left of this steep incline is
the nineteenth century home that used to belong to the Sephardic
Morón family. With its wide second story wood balcony, it is a perfect
spot to cool off in the late afternoon after a day of hard work. In the
twentieth century it served as the Virgin Islands Government Finance
Office, and it appears unoccupied at this time.[146] At the bottom of the
steps on the right is the 1829 Hotel, the building still standing more or
less as it did in the year it was built. And then, because it is still early, it

St. Thomas Hebrew Congregation
St. Thomas, U.S. Virgin Islands

is possible to walk down Wimmelkafts Gade (Back Street) and Dronningens Gade (Main street) without the assault of shopkeepers and taxi drivers who will soon be encouraging tourists to buy their wares and use their services.

In these early morning hours the buildings are a spruced-up version of what they must have looked like in the nineteenth century. The store-keepers are arriving, coffee in hand, and have started to open their shops. On Dronningens Gade, Benjamin Delvalle's store is now partitioned and includes an ice cream parlor. His property on Wimmelkafts Gade houses a restaurant. A little further, at 10 Wimmelkafts Gade, is a building orig-inally constructed in 1833 as a residence for a French Jewish merchant named Aaron Robles. The Freemasons of the Harmonic Lodge now meet here as they have since they first occupied this tall building in 1874.[147] And finally, climbing up a steep hill from Wimmelkafts Gade, the syna-gogue appears, brilliantly framed by flowering bougainvillea and palm

trees. Across the street, its community hall and archives at 9 Crystal
Gade are located in the home where Judith and Benjamin Delvalle spent
the last years of their lives. Benjamin's spirit must be smiling down at the
members of the Hebrew Congregation every Shabbat as they say *Kiddush*
– the prayer over wine – in what used to be his former home.

In spite of many fires, hurricanes, and other natural disasters that have
hit St. Thomas over the years, the places where the Sephardim worked
and lived in the nineteenth century can still be seen. The Sephardim
themselves, however, are gone.

St. Thomas's Hebrew Congregation, Blessing and Peace and Loving
Deeds, as it is formally known today, continues to operate as a Jewish
congregation with weekly services and special events, but its members no
longer include the Delvalles, Sassos, Pizas, Maduros, Cardozes, de
Castros, and Fidanques. Instead the synagogue's Board of Representatives for 2006 included such names as Coulianos, Goldman, Ebenholtz,
Feuerzeig, Blackhall, Miller, and Werbel. With their American born
rabbi, Arthur Starr, these dedicated people are determined to sustain
Jewish life in this small island. Their task is not an easy one. On many
Saturday mornings, as is also the case in Curaçao, Jewish tourists out-
number the local membership at Shabbat services in the historic building. Yet the Jewish presence remains.

It is actually amazing that this Jewish community has continued to
exist. In 1940 there were only about fifty Jews left in St. Thomas, and,
while outmigration had leveled off, intermarriage had begun to take its
toll.[148] It did not seem that the community would last much longer. In
1946, however, the first direct flights from New York to San Juan, Puerto
Rico were instrumental in bringing new life to the Hebrew Congregation. From Puerto Rico it was only a very short trip for the New Yorkers
to visit St. Thomas, and this they did. Reform American Jews who came
to the synagogue in Charlotte Amalie in the late forties and early fifties
were at first surprised at the Sephardic rituals. As short term visitors, it
was all a part of the exotic that had lured them to St. Thomas in the first
place, and no doubt they returned home with many stories about this little synagogue in the Caribbean with its sand on the floor. Over time, a
number of the more regular visitors decided to settle on the island per-

manently. As their numbers increased, their energy and needs trans-formed the religious ritual into a Reform service with only a hint of its Sephardic past. In later years the ritual was further adjusted in response to the new membership of the Hebrew Congregation.[149]

Until the 1960s, there were still a handful of Sephardim living in St. Thomas. Among these last Jewish descendants of Curaçao's Sephardic immigrants was Morris Fidanque de Castro. His grandmother Rachel had been a daughter of Benjamin and Judith Delvalle, who had married Mordechay (Morris) Fidanque in 1856.[150] Mordechay had moved to Panama in 1890,[151] and his daughter Adah had married Daniel de Castro in Panama City in 1899. Adah and Daniel's two children, Esther and Morris, were born in Panama, but when Adah died unexpectedly in 1906, Daniel de Castro moved back to St. Thomas where he had been born, and where his mother still resided. His son Morris spent most of his childhood on the island and, as an adult, filled a number of functions in island government before becoming governor of the U.S. Virgin Islands from 1949 to 1954.[152,153] He was an active member of the Hebrew Congre-gation through much of his adult life. In 1966, when he was serving as synagogue president, he suffered a heart attack and died at the relative young age of 63.[154] Deeply mourned by Jews and non-Jews on the island, he was buried in St. Thomas' Jewish cemetery.

Another Sephardic Jew who made his home in St. Thomas through the 1960s was Moses (Molito) Sasso. He was born in St. Thomas on February 2, 1894 and was the fourth generation of his family to be born in this island. His great-great-grandfather, Abraham Sasso, had been among the early Curaçaoan immigrants who had come to Charlotte Amalie in the late eighteenth century. This Abraham had married Hannah Sasso's aunt Leah Sasso around 1795, and the couple had arrived in St. Thomas shortly after they were wed.[155]

More than a century later, when Molito Sasso was still quite young, his parents moved from St. Thomas to Panama. But in 1912, Molito returned to the island of his birth. For two years he served as assistant reader to the Hebrew Congregation, helping out the elderly Rabbi David Cardoze who was then leading the community. In 1914 Rabbi Cardoze died at the age of 90, and Sasso remained in charge. He led the St.

Thomas Jewish community for 52 years until his retirement in 1966.[156]

Jews from all over, including members of Curaçao's Jewish community were invited to the celebration of his Golden Jubilee anniversary,
which consisted of a "Solemn Thanksgiving Service" held in his honor
at the St. Thomas synagogue on July 1, 1964.[157] In his book on the history of the Jewish community of St. Thomas, Judah Cohen indicates that
this was "[p]erhaps the last celebration of the congregation's active
Sephardic tradition."[158] On that day, as Molito Sasso entered the synagogue, former Governor Morris de Castro welcomed him with the hymn
"Baruch Aba"[159] – blessed be he who comes – a Sephardic tune still used
in Curaçao's Mikvé Israel to welcome a bride and newly elected members
of the synagogue board. The ceremony was indeed "a fleeting glimpse of
the Sephardic Jewish world"[160] that had touched St. Thomas for less than
two centuries.

Today the St. Thomas phone book still lists some of the Sephardic
names of the nineteenth century, such as Maduro, Sasso, Morón, de
Castro, Marchena, and de Jongh, but none of these Virgin Islanders is
Jewish. However, some of these Christian descendants of St. Thomas's
Sephardic Jews are quick to identify themselves as having had Sephardic
ancestry. It appears that Curaçao's Sephardic Diaspora left behind a lega-
cy in St. Thomas that has remained part of the self-identity of these non-
Jewish descendants.

The majority of the Jewish descendants of St. Thomas's Sephardim
now live in Panama, Costa Rica, and the United States. Here, four or
five generations after their ancestors left the Danish island, they too
have experienced religious assimilation. And even when these
Sephardim marry within their Jewish faith, they tend to marry into the
much larger Ashkenazi communities of the countries which are now
their homes. Yet the lure of the Caribbean often brings them back to
Charlotte Amalie to climb the hill to the Hebrew Congregation of St.
Thomas. Among the "Chai Members" of the congregation who make a
small annual contribution to belong to this group are several descendants
of the Sephardic men and women who, for a brief period in history, worshipped in this building on Synagogue Hill. These visitors embrace their
ancestors' short interlude in St. Thomas as part of their own history.

CHAPTER 3

CORO, VENEZUELA

GLORIA AL BRAVO PUEBLO
QUE EL YUGO LANZÓ

(GLORY TO THE BRAVE PEOPLE WHO THREW
OFF THE YOKE)

First sentence of the Venezuelan national anthem.
Words by: Vicente Salias; music by: Juan José Landaeta; adopted: 1881.

Curaçao's early Sephardim were well aware of the commercial potential that existed in the vast, unexplored regions beyond the Caribbean ports of the South American mainland. The coastal towns of these territories lay invitingly close to the Dutch island. Close, but yet so far! Trading with these countries and living there at the beginning of the century were risky endeavors. Spain's stronghold on the greater part of South America had been guided by monopolistic regulations that prohibited foreign vessels from importing goods to the Spanish colonies while, at the same time, requiring all exports to be transported on Spanish vessels. These limitations, coupled with the fact that the Tribunal of the Inquisition was headquartered in Cartagena de las Indias on the Caribbean coast of Colombia (or Nueva Granada, as it was then called), had been somewhat of a deterrent for the Sephardim of Curaçao. The Tribunal would bring in for questioning all individuals "accused of judaizing, Mohammedanism, Lutheransim, bigamy, heretic propositions and

Blanca de Lima on the dunes of Coro, Venezuela

blasphemy. They were all included under the generic name *brujos* – sor-
cerers."[161] One would think that most Jews would want to avoid being
included among these *brujos*. Most Jews, but not all! Some of Curaçao's
Sephardim appeared unfazed by these threats.

In the late seventeenth century, a Sephardic Jew named Jacob Senior,
also known as Captain Philippe Henriques, regularly ferried merchandise
and slaves between Curaçao and Cartagena. One of his trips took him
back to this Colombian port in 1699. As usual, his goods and merchandise were transferred off the ship and delivered to his local agent. When
Senior tried to come ashore himself, however, he was denied permission
to land. After several days, soldiers boarded his ship and arrested him. He
was incarcerated for seventy-three days, and, for a period of two months,
he was not told why he was in custody. Eventually he was informed of
the charges against him, which included trafficking in the West Indies in
a trade prohibited to the Jews by order of the King of Spain and doing so
with full knowledge of this prohibition. He was furthermore accused of
having tried to convert his crew to Judaism.[162] With the aid of many letters back and forth between officials of the Inquisition in Cartagena and
the Dutch governor of Curaçao, Bastiaan Bernagie, Senior was finally
released. He arrived back in Curaçao on December 8, 1699.[163] In spite of
this harrowing experience, he continued sailing back and forth to the
Spanish colonies on the mainland until 1711.

Over the years, other Jews also developed relationships with the Creole* population of the Caribbean periphery. Yet to the Sephardim, a personal, more permanent presence on the mainland would have been much more desirable. Their early attempts made them realize, however, that such sojourns would not last very long. For a very short period, a group of Sephardic traders managed to settle in Tucacas, Venezuela, where they purchased cacao beans from local farmers, which were then sent to Curaçao for processing. At some point during the second decade of the eighteenth century, they even erected a synagogue in Tucacas, but it was soon destroyed (either by the Spanish or by the departing Jews themselves) in November of 1720.[164]

During Spain's war of succession in the early eighteenth century, the governing forces in the Iberian peninsula turned their focus to internal affairs and away from their widespread empire in the Americas. Through sheer neglect on the part of the mother country, its colonies entered a severe economic depression. European shipments were slow to arrive and consumer goods, from basic necessities to luxury items, were simply not to be had.[165] At the same time, however, the Spanish colonies were producing enough agricultural products that could be used as barter payment for the much-needed imports. Since European goods were generally more readily available in some of the non-Spanish colonies, the unfilled demand in Hispanic occupied America could fairly easily be met without reliance on Spain. Growers and traders in the Spanish-occupied territories began to establish new commercial ties with merchants and traders in the British, French, and Dutch colonies of the Caribbean, alleviating some of the shortages they had been experiencing. These early contacts set the stage for the very lucrative, but illegal, trading activities which, from then on, became a routine aspect of the economies of the Caribbean periphery. The greatest beneficiaries of this illicit trade were the Sephardic Jews of the Caribbean and in particular, the Sephardic Jews of the island of Curaçao, which lay at a distance of less than fifty miles from the Venezuelan coast.[166]

In an attempt to truly monopolize Venezuelan commerce, and with

* Residents who were born in the colonies were referred to as Creoles – *Criollos*.

the hope of preventing this lucrative trade with other countries from dominating the Venezuelan import/export scene, Spain created the Royal Guipúzcoa Company in 1728.[167] The Company would send armed Spanish ships to Venezuela on an annual basis in an effort to clear the coast of smugglers and control all shipments to and from Venezuela. In the process it took away the rights of the local farmers to use a third of the capacity of any ship to export on their own account. This and many other restrictions resulted in great resentment towards the Royal Guipúzcoa Company among Venezuelan landowners, leading to a number of protests and uprisings and adding to the bad feelings that were steadily increasing towards the Spanish government. While many Curaçaoan vessels carrying smuggled goods to and from Venezuela were captured during the years that the Company exercised its privileges, the illicit trade continued pretty much unabated.[168] In 1781 the King rescinded the Company's contract, and, in 1785, the operation came to a halt, allowing the highly profitable trade between Curaçao and the Spanish colonies to flourish.

In spite of considerable discontent among the Creoles towards Spain, it took a while for these feelings to solidify into action. It was not until the invasion of Spain by Napoleon's forces in 1808 and the subsequent civil uprising in that country that independence became of greater interest to the inhabitants of Venezuela and Nueva Granada. The mistrust between the Spanish governors and Nueva Granada's Creole leadership in Bogotá finally reached a climax on July 20, 1810, when the Creole elite expelled the Spanish viceroy from that city,[169] setting the stage for Cartagena's declaration of absolute independence from Spain on November 11, 1810.[170]

In Venezuela, the first phase of independence was spearheaded and controlled by the Caraqueños. As was to be expected, leaders in other localities thought themselves equally well qualified to lead this effort and did not automatically follow the footsteps of the revolutionaries in Caracas. Thus, despite the Venezuelan declaration of independence on July 5, 1811, it took several years of infighting and the development of leaders in areas beyond Caracas to arrive at an independence ideology behind which most of the population could unite.[171]

In Nueva Granada the uprising following Cartagena's declaration of independence of 1810 was accompanied by similar internal disagreements among its revolutionary leaders, while Spain desperately tried to reestablish control. The Spanish reconquest from 1816 to 1819 was particularly brutal, but in August of 1819, Simón Bolívar's forces defeated the royalists at the Battle of Boyacá, changing the course of the revolution.[172]

At the Congress of Angostura of 1819, the Republic of Gran Colombia was created, encompassing Venezuela, Nueva Granada (which included Panama), and Ecuador.* Simón Bolívar became its first president with General Francisco de Paula Santander serving as vice president.[173] True independence in Venezuela was not achieved until 1821 with a victory over Spain at the battle of Carabobo. Yet, even after this event, there continued to be many pockets of resistance across the new nation. Various cities and towns, including the coastal town of Coro, Venezuela, remained loyal to the Spanish or anti-Bolivarian Creole leaders for several years after the defeat of Spain at Carabobo.

In the midst of Venezuela's struggle for independence, the Constitution of 1811 had declared the Catholic religion to be the state religion, adding that it would be the only religion to be observed in the country.[174] The charismatic Simón Bolívar who was spearheading the uprising against Spain was a liberal thinker, however. Supposedly a Freemason and a man who had many Jewish friends, he was in favor of encouraging foreigners to settle in the newly formed Republic. In 1826 his more liberal views prevailed, and it was decreed that foreigners were now officially allowed to enter the country. Bilateral treaties were signed with the United States as well as with Great Britain, and, in 1829, the Treaty of Peace, Friendship, Navigation, and Commerce was ratified between Gran Colombia and the Netherlands. This treaty provided reciprocal rights to the citizens of both political entities to trade freely, to anchor in each other's ports, and to rent and use homes and shops for commercial purposes. Furthermore, article 15 stated that "Subjects of H.M. the

---

* After Bolívar's death in 1830, the rivalries between Venezuela and New Granada caused the Republic of Colombia to collapse, resulting in three separate national entities.

King of the Netherlands who are residents of the Republic of Colombia, even when they do not profess the Catholic religion, will enjoy [assurances] that they shall not be hampered [... because of] their religious beliefs in the proper exercise of their faith, as long as they do so in private homes and with the required decorum."[175]

Although this statement was by no means an unconditional invitation to the Sephardim of Curaçao, the stage had now been set for many new ventures and adventures.

AN EARLY SUCCESS IN CORO, VENEZUELA: JEUDAH SENIOR

Jeudah Senior was born in Curaçao in 1817 to Jacob Senior and Hannah Cohen Henriquez. He was the youngest of five sons in a family of eight children[176] and was the fourth generation of his family to be born on the island.* At the top of a hill, not too far north of the area where his parents lived, Jeudah could look south over the Caribbean Sea that separated Curaçao from Venezuela. On a clear day, he could see the outline of a strip of land on the horizon. This was the Paraguaná peninsula, Venezuela's closest point to Curaçao. Slightly east on the neck of this peninsula lay the town of Coro with its seaport called La Vela.

At the time of Jeudah's birth, the British had left Curaçao, the Dutch were trying to re-establish some order, and the revolutionary war in South America was in full swing. Venezuela and Nueva Granada achieved their independence when Jeudah was in his teens. Lured by the promise of adventures and opportunities, some of his older cousins left Curaçao for these newly emerging nations. It is believed that Jeudah's brother David was also among these immigrants to South America and that he migrated to nearby Coro, Venezuela in the early 1830s.[177] It is not surprising that this unknown land across the glimmering sea captured young Jeudah's imagination as well.

---

* Notably, he was a descendant of David Senior, a brother of the daring slave trader who was incarcerated in Cartagena in 1699.

Due to its proximity to Curaçao, Coro had often been the destination of Dutch ships, carrying contraband to Venezuela in the times before independence. Those who sailed back and forth to La Vela included many Curaçaoan Jews who were eager to tap the markets and resources that lay beyond the port. Yet, in spite of the proximity and the considerable trade between Curaçao and Coro, the first permanent Jewish resident, a man by the name of David Hoheb, did not settle there until 1824, a year after the liberation of the town by Bolivarian forces.[178] At that time, the town of Coro had fewer than 3,000 inhabitants and the province had a population of slightly over 23,000.[179]

Jeudah Senior
1817–1896

Jeudah Senior, who was then about seven years old, was safely esconced in his parents' home in Curaçao, and knew little about Coro.

By 1831, however, a census taken by Governor José María Tellería showed that "21 Dutch citizens" lived in Coro, all Jewish, all merchants, and, one can presume, mostly single, since no mention is made of other members of their household. The gentlemen listed in this census were: David Maduro, José (Joseph) Curiel, Isaac Abenatar, Gabriel Abenatar, Elias Curiel, Isaac Maduro, Samuel Maduro, Josua Lopez, Salomón Brandao, Guillermo Alvarez, David Valencia, Isaac Curiel, M. Cohen Henriquez, Jacobo Pereira, Elías Lopez, Jacobo Salcedo, Antonio Salcedo, Abraham Curiel, Isaac de Lima, Jacob Morón, and Honorato Fonseca. The last names of these men were all names found among the membership of the Mikvé Israel synagogue of Curaçao.[180]

These early immigrants had come to a place that was not quite what it had seemed from across the sea or even what they remembered from their brief stays in Coro prior to their more permanent settlement. The reality of Coro in the first few decades of the nineteenth century was harsh. A few years before the Sephardim settled there, Simón Bolívar had written in a letter of 1821, "Coro is like Lybia, where there is not even water to nourish human beings."[181] This comment must have reflected the revolutionary leader's first impressions of the town. He must have approached Coro on a hot day, riding over the beautiful, but desolate dunes that lie north of the village. Such an introduction would have reminded even the greatest optimist of the Sahara and could not have resulted in flattering comments. Ten years later, Governor Tellería's short narrative about the socio-economic conditions of the town does not sound much more encouraging. He writes that the area's resources had been exhausted and that many essential consumer goods were simply unavailable. He furthermore mentions the existence of schools, none of which were operational at the time. Only one benevolent hospital, able to treat a total of five patients, represented the health care facilities of the town, which boasted the services of three doctors.[182]

These descriptions evoke the image of an economic wasteland. Yet, despite this fact, the Curaçaoan Jews came. They came because, bad as the conditions may have been in Coro immediately after Venezuela's independence, the new republic promised a greater diversity of possibilities than the stagnant economy of Curaçao.

When Jeudah's brother and cousins decided to join their friends in Coro in the early 1830s, their elders must have impressed on these young men that life in Venezuela was going to be very different from the life they knew in Curaçao. Although the new Venezuelan constitution of 1830 had assured all foreign residents that they would enjoy the same personal security and guarantees for the safety of their property as Venezuelan nationals,[183] Coro was known as a very conservative town. It had been one of the last towns to be liberated by Bolivarian forces, and a large portion of its inhabitants did not agree with Bolivar's liberal leanings which had become part of the country's constitution. Orthodox Catholic views and latent pro-Spanish loyalties were the two key ingredients that fostered the conservative and xenophobic beliefs of many Corianos.[184]

When Jeudah was fourteen years old, Curaçao's Mikvé Israel community received disturbing news about anti-Semitic actions in Coro. It all began on the evening of September 25th, 1831, during the Jewish holiday of Sukkot. That night the Sephardim of Coro were gathered at the home of David Valencia to celebrate the holiday. Some time during the evening, a group of uninvited and disguised Corianos showed up at Valencia's home. When Samuel Maduro, one of the Jewish celebrants, came to the door and asked what was going on, he was summarily beaten up. The group of thugs then moved on and vandalized several other Jewish homes in the area.

Early the following morning, Coro's Curaçaoan Jewish population awoke to find posters attached to the streetlights calling for "the Dutch" to leave the country within eight days or risk beheading. To make it quite clear which Dutch the posters were referring to, another notice, crudely assembled by cutting letters out of newspapers and regluing them, stated: "JEWS!!! The People informs you: Die or Leave Coro."[185] Disturbances of this type continued off and on for several months, until finally, with significant assistance from the local and state government, the incidents came to a stop at the end of the year.[186]

A few Jews returned to Curaçao during these disturbances, but most of these men went back to Coro once they felt that it was safe to do so. It was at this point in time that Jeudah Senior's cousins, older brother, and other Curaçaoan Jews decided to try their luck in Coro as well. New stores began to open up in the small town, and the reports sent home by the new immigrants must have been positive enough to make many more decide to sail to La Vela and join their Curaçaoan friends in the small Venezuelan town, where they appeared to be doing so well.

Mail between Coro and Curaçao flowed back and forth daily, and, as the years went by and the disturbances of 1831 receded to the subconscious, the enthusiastic letters from Jeudah Senior's brother and cousins must have encouraged Jeudah to emigrate to Coro as well. By 1838 he had joined the growing Curaçaoan Jewish community in Coro,[187] and by 1841 he owned a store in that town, a fact known to us today because of a court case indicating that some textiles had been stolen from his shop that year.[188] Most of these shops sold a large variety of items, ranging from dry goods to groceries, in an attempt to cater to the comprehensive needs of their clientele in this small town. It is likely that this store was Jeudah's first attempt at making money in Coro.

A few years after his arrival, Jeudah had earned enough to start a family. He asked his cousin Jael to marry him, and they were wed on November 30, 1842. The marriage was recorded in Curaçao's Mikvé Israel marriage register without a dowry[189] – often an indication that it did not take place in Curaçao. It is also possible that Jael was not provided with a dowry. Since her father had passed away in Curaçao twenty years earlier, her family may not have had the wherewithal to make this customary contribution to the union.[190] The couple's first son, Salomon, was born in Coro in 1844, where he was circumcised according to the Jewish rites by Joseph Jacob Curiel.[191]

By the time of Jeudah and Jael's first son's birth, the Jewish community in Coro had grown significantly, yet there were still only about one hundred and fifty Jews in town.[192] In spite of this small number, several of the Curaçaoan immigrants had enough learning to lead religious services, perform circumcisions, marriages, and burials, and to handle the kosher slaughtering required for the observance of Jewish dietary laws.[193] Even though they never had a rabbi to lead them, the Sephardim of Coro had organized into a fairly effective community early on. In 1832 they bought a cemetery plot, which served to bury eight-year-old Hannah Curiel who had passed away that year. She was the daughter of two of the earliest Jewish residents of Coro, Joseph Curiel (the aforementioned circumciser) and his wife Deborah Levy Maduro.

From the early 1830s on, the Jews of Coro conducted weekly Shabbat services and holiday celebrations at the home of David Valencia. By 1847 the location for these services had been switched to the home of Abraham M. Senior, one of Jeudah's first cousins (see Appendix A-2 and A-3). Most likely Jeudah Senior attended these religious services, since later developments reveal that he was a leader of the Jewish community of Coro as well as of the Mikvé Israel synagogue in Curaçao. In Abraham Senior's home, the ladies must have shown up with their handheld fans to survive the stifling heat that would have prevailed during the day. In Curaçao, the Mikvé Israel synagogue had large windows on both long sides of the building, which were kept wide open, producing a cross-window ventilation that allowed the congregants to be comfortable during most of the religious services. In Coro, however, the Jewish worshippers did not have such luxury. Here they made sure not to offend their neighbors and kept all the windows of the room assigned for prayers shut, in spite of Coro's suffocating heat. It was not until 1853 that the Sephardim requested and received permission from Mr. Senior's neighbor to open two windows that looked out on this Mr. García's property. They carefully explained that this request was being made so that they could "facilitate fresh air and ventilation for the room assigned for their prayers."[194] Yet, Jeudah and his co-religionists appeared at services regularly, even before the new arrangements finally made the physical environment more agreeable. The Jewish Chronicle of London reported in 1847 that Coro's Jews met "for prayers every Friday evening, Sabbath morning and evening, and all the holy days; and [that] there [was] always a congregation of above twenty present."[195]

Beyond their religious lives, Jeudah and Jael Senior lived like people in most frontier communities. Jeudah traveled often and Jael must have tried to replicate as best she could the niceties of the more established Curaçaoan society in the new territory that had become her home. Crime was fairly prevalent in Coro, and archival documents pertaining to civil and criminal cases show numerous robberies, street fights, anti-Semitic cases, and cases of illicit trade.

In addition to the robbery at Jeudah Senior's store mentioned earlier, the following are examples of some other thefts that occurred in town. In January of 1845, several pieces of gold and merchandise were stolen from Isaac Namías de Crasto, who lived in the same house as Benjamin Penso.[196] In 1852 Elias H. Lopez reported the theft of twelve pieces of colored chintz, eight pieces of blue and red striped material, eight pieces of French striped material, one piece of white drill (strong cloth), and various other pieces of textile.[197] On December 26, 1853 a robbery occurred at the home of Cecilia de León Henríquez. Taken were a golden thimble with her initials, two pairs of golden earrings, a pair of scissors made of ivory and inlaid with gold, and several other items.[198] These archival documents shed light on the consumer goods sold and owned by Coro's

Sephardim at the time. In spite of Coro's rough and tumble environment, the Jewish women who lived there still expected to use French textiles for their party dresses and show off their gold earrings when they went out.

Fistfights between the men often occurred in drunken rages, even between Jewish acquaintances. In 1832, there was a case against Samuel Maduro who bludgeoned Elías H. Lopez at the home of Joseph Curiel, at which time both men were taken into custody. Curiel, who was Maduro's brother-in-law, testified that the latter was inebriated, and after a brief stay in jail, both men were released.[199]

Individual anti-Semitic incidents were also plentiful. An example was a court case against Nicolasa Catoche and other women pertaining to offending statements made by them to David Hoheb and Jacob Henriquez in 1825. The ladies declared in court: "We have not said that the Dutch and Hebrew gentlemen are thieves nor that they are bands of thieves who have come to rob this province of Coro … and if in the heat of the argument … of that same night we expressed those thoughts … we desist from them …"[200] In another court case, charges were brought against Pedro Leal who had caused injuries to the Jew Isaac Abenatar. A witness, who happened to be a Curaçaoan who worked for Abenatar, testified that Mr. Leal had offered an acquaintance of his twenty-five pesos to stab Mr. Abenatar. The witness said that Mr Leal had told his aquaintance that such action was justified, since "killing a Jew was the same as killing an animal."[201] Occasionally the Jews responded in kind. In an argument witnessed by many in 1834, Mr. David Cohen Henriquez purportedly expressed himself in a derogatory manner about the Christian faith, referring to it as a "filthy fiction."[202]

Numerous cases involving illicit trade are recorded in the archival documents of Coro. A court case of 1841 describes the importation of merchandise in excess of the amounts indicated on customs declarations in order to evade import duties. The two importers accused of this misrepresentation were a gentleman of La Vela by the name of José Perón and Jeudah Senior of Coro.[203] It is clear that Jeudah participated in these illicit trade practices which most importers on the Venezuelan coast considered to be the normal way of doing business in those days. In other cases, merchandise was allegedly delivered to the homes of Curaçaoan Jews living in Coro without ever having passed through customs. Several court documents also reveal that a great deal of smuggling occurred by means of rowboats which would come ashore on the beaches in the vicinity of Coro carrying merchandise for Coriano businesses.

These civil and criminal cases occurred primarily in the male social realm of society, while the females of Coro's social elite remained at a great distance from most of these chaotic events. Jeudah and Jael Senior soon became accustomed to this new environment, and Jeudah branched out beyond retailing. In 1851 he joined José Henriquez and Samuel Levy Maduro, both Curaçaoan Sephardic Jews living in Coro, in the business entity "Henriquez, Maduro y Senior." The partners began to trade directly with the United States from Coro, bypassing the shipping and agency assistance of the Curaçaoan Sephardim, through whom most of the Coriano Jews had been trading in earlier years. Company documents show shipments in the tens of thousands of pesos, mostly to New York, utilizing American ships which often had Biblical names, such as *Abram* and *Sarah*, presumably owned by Jews.[204] Although Henriquez, Maduro y Senior seemed to flourish, the partnership was short-lived and was dissolved in 1854.

Jeudah was an aggressive businessman. In a relatively short time, he managed to accumulate significant wealth. By 1854 he owned a house and a pond in La Vela, the seaport of Coro. In addition to his house in Coro, he had a coffee plantation with one thousand trees, a farm with eight hundred goats, a sugar plantation, eighty donkeys, a mule, and a horse. In nearby Barquisimeto, he had a house with a tiled roof and three coffee plantations. In the same parish he owned additional sugar plantations, two thousand goats, two hundred cows, ten mares, twelve horses, and seven mules. In short, he was a man of means and was the highest taxpayer in town.[205]

It is no wonder that Jeudah Senior's name appears in many municipal archival documents, where he is shown to have served as a witness in numerous court cases and to have been a party to many contracts. Court case records show that his stores were robbed on several occasions, and they also indicate that there were times when he was accused of illegal imports. In other words, all the evils of Coro's environment were part of Jeudah Senior's life there as well.

If Coro's Catholics had to find someone to hate, Jeudah surely represented all that they envied and resented. He was financially successful, and he was a practicing Jew and a leader among Curaçao's Sephardic Diaspora of Coro. Following the custom of providing "voluntary" loans and contributions to the state government, Jeudah Senior had loaned the governor 500 pesos on December 31, 1854. He did so in spite of the fact that similar loans made by the Jewish community were still outstanding.[206]

In January 1855, an additional loan was requested from the Jews to pay for the garrison's payroll. When the community declined this request, the people of Coro remembered once more how much they hated these Jews. Anti-Semitic letters and posters made their unwelcome appearance again, and, during the night of February 4, 1855, a serious riot broke out. A group of about thirty armed men ran through the streets of Coro, shooting at Jewish homes, breaking down doors, and sacking businesses. Looting was widespread while the men shouted: "*Mueran los judíos y viva su dinero!*" – Death to the Jews and long live their money! Many more posters with anti-Semitic and libellous messages continued to appear during the next few days. And this time the Jews of Coro were really frightened! They did not perceive much support on the part of the local government as had occurred during the disturbances of 1831 and their businesses had incurred major losses.[207]

The first Sephardic families left Coro for La Vela on the afternoon of February 5, 1855. There they boarded a Curaçaoan schooner that left for the island on that same day. When they arrived, they immediately asked for a meeting with Governor Gravenhorst to bring him up to date on what had been going on in Coro. Within a day and a half, the latter sent two Dutch warships to La Vela de Coro to protect the Dutch citizens and their possessions. Upon arrival in Coro, the two ship captains proceeded to the home of Jeudah Senior where they met with the town's Jewish leaders. Here they drafted a letter to the governor of the province, which they presented to him on behalf of Coro's Jewish community. In spite of the fact that Governor Carlos Navarro received these emissaries quite politely, he refused to put in writing that he would guarantee the safety of the Jews and their assets. Using what was perceived as a delaying tactic, he indicated verbally that he would do so the next day. While he followed through with his promise the following morning, the governor also let it be known that, in his opinion, the fault for all the rioting lay with the Jews themselves since they had refused to loan the government the additional funds needed to pay the salaries of the local garrison.[208]

It became increasingly clear to Jeudah Senior and the few Jews who remained in Coro that whatever protection they could expect to receive would be provided reluctantly. The time had come for everyone to leave. On February 10 and 11, Jeudah and some of his relatives joined the families who had stayed behind and sailed on two of their own ships, accompanied by the two Dutch warships, back to their island of origin. Two hundred and fifty-six persons, consisting of one hundred and sixty-eight Jews and eighty-eight slaves, landed in Curaçao during that week. Here, the refugees immediately started working with the Dutch government in their attempt to be reimbursed for the damages incurred.[209] In the years that followed, the governor of Curaçao and the Dutch government, through its representatives in Venezuela, pressed the Venezuelan government repeatedly for a resolution to this issue. The Dutch requested the assistance of the American and British ambassadors to Venezuela as well, and, after much diplomatic maneuvering and implicit and explicit threats, a deal was finally struck in August of 1857. It took a little longer before the Jews of Coro were indemnified, but, by the end of 1858, most of the monies that were supposed to change hands had been paid out, although some families had to wait much longer to receive their reimbursement.[210]

Jeudah Senior traveled to Caracas immediately after his arrival in Curaçao in an effort to recover his own very considerable losses from the Venezuelan government. He was unsuccessful in that endeavor. Between 1855 and his demise in 1896, he continued to own many assets in Coro and its environs, but he never returned to live there. Instead, he relied on his relatives and friends to recover some of his Venezuelan wealth. Even in his old age he remained in close contact with his cousins Isaac A. Senior & Son in Coro, occasionally using their services to collect outstanding receivables in this place that must have held so many bittersweet memories for him.[211]

After 1855, most of his daily business interests in Venezuela were handled by Felipe Lopez of Coro, who had power of attorney to act for Senior. In this capacity, Lopez bought and sold cattle for him in 1859,[212] and sold a schooner owned by Jeudah Senior in La Vela to Juan Ricardo.[213] In spite of the fact that Senior no longer resided in town, his property there continued to be the target of attacks by various parties. The municipal archives of Coro reflect a protest filed by Felipe Lopez in 1861, acting for Jeudah Senior, against the Federal forces that invaded Coro that year. While this invasion was not an anti-Semitic event, the effect of the ensuing political chaos was the confiscation of private property belonging to various businessmen. Part of the protest reads:

> ... since the [local] authorities did not have sufficient forces to defend the population [of Coro] and [chose] to confine themselves in San Francisco, they left the foreigners and their properties over to their own fate, without advising them ahead of time of these decisions in order to [enable them to] ensure their own safety as well as saving their properties. That Mr. Senior's commercial enterprise was located two blocks from the temple [church] of San Francisco, and was being managed by me and which on the day of the invasion, the sixteenth of this month, was occupied by the invading forces, who took all the merchandise, goods, and interests there-in, as well as the property of Mr. Jeudah Senior and that of Messrs. Raimundo Correa, Rafael Cohen Henriquez, Luis Razetti, and A. Lemoine & Co.[214]

This protest intimated that a great deal of ill will still existed among the local authorities towards the foreigners who continued to do business in Coro. It should be noted that three of the five gentlemen who were prejudiced by the invasion of the Federal forces into Coro – Senior, Correa, and Cohen Henriquez – were Curaçaoan Sephardim. The protest concluded by formally filing a claim for the losses incurred.

Throughout the remainder of his life, Jeudah Senior continued to seek reimbursement for the losses he had sustained in 1855. In 1876, the Venezuelan government acknowledged that it owed him 3,538,726 Bolívars. At the time, the country's Treasury indicated, however, that it did not have the funds to pay out that amount. It was not until 1903 that the estate of Jeudah Senior & Son received 1,000,000 Bolivars (worth between $150,000 and $200,000) to settle the claim.[215] Neither Jeudah, who had died in 1896, or his wife Jael, who died in 1902, were around to receive this compensation for losses incurred almost half a century earlier.[216]

When he resettled in Curaçao, however, Jeudah Senior did not sit around waiting for his money to arrive from Venezuela. He was 38 years old and full of energy. Based on his past achievements, it was not surprising that he became involved in all the key issues of the day in the small island community.

One of the most important projects that caught his attention was the need to expand the business area of Willemstad. In the 1850s it had become clear that the city walls surrounding the downtown area of Punda, where most of the Curaçaoan Jews worked and lived, were beginning to hamper commercial and residential growth. Jeudah Senior's brother, Abraham J. Senior, had requested in 1859 that the government permit him to demolish part of the walls. His house was built right up against the ramparts and he wanted to make some residential improvements and also thought that it would be important to open up the town in order to accommodate additional commercial growth. This request was denied. But Abraham then combined his request with a more explicit letter to Governor Crol, dated December 15, 1859. This time the proposal was co-signed by Jeudah Senior, Abraham Capriles and Joshua and Elias Jesurun Henriquez, all up and coming Curaçaoan Jewish businessmen. The governor responded by requesting a more detailed proposal from these gentlemen, who quickly wrote back on January 24, 1860. In this letter they described how their proposed project would positively impact commerce on the island, and how they were convinced that it would contribute tremendously to the beautification of the town. The letter was signed by the same individuals who had signed the December 15 letter, plus their new partner, the energetic and savvy businessman Salomon Elias Levy Maduro. The permit was granted, and work began in May of 1861. It took four years to demolish the walls and fill in part of the inner harbor. It was yet another two years before all the debris was removed.[217]

This demolition and land-making project created a large new area available for future development. It was a real business coup for the five men who first envisioned and executed these plans that allowed the city to expand. They subsequently received land concessions from the government to build new streets, houses, and shops, and, most importantly, to add new wharves for their vessels along the shore of the newly filled in area. As a result, their businesses grew and prospered, and majestic homes were built in the beautiful new residential area of Scharloo.

Up to this time, the most important shipping company in Curaçao had been the firm of J.A. Jesurun & Sons. To the Jesuruns, the new wharves presented an unfavorable change in the status quo on the island. Prior to the demolition of the city walls, the limited number of available wharves had made it almost impossible for other shipping companies to expand. Now this was no longer the case, and the Jesuruns were suddenly confronted with a level of competition that had not existed in the walled city prior to the 1860s.

Between 1843 and 1875, the Jesuruns owned a mercantile fleet of more than one hundred vessels. They were truly the shipping magnates of the island.[218] When the city walls were demolished, however, several other members of the Sephardic community, in particular S.E.L. Maduro, were able to expand their shipping businesses, benefiting greatly from the newly created wharves. In 1874, Maduro established the firm S.E.L. Maduro & Sons, which in later years became the most important shipping and trading company on the island.

Jeudah Senior too saw his shipping business grow. Upon arrival in Curaçao he had continued the shipping and trading activities that had been part of his undertakings in Coro, Venezuela. His biggest ship of 87 tons was called *El Coriano*** and was valued at 10,000 florins in 1856.[219] Over the years he owned many other smaller vessels[220] and branched out in other areas as well. In 1865, he established a partnership with his son Salomon, founding the firm Jeudah Senior e hijo. Father and son were in the dry goods business, and, in addition, they were the agents for the Compagnie Générale Transatlantique which sailed five times a month

---

* Jeudah's continued attachment to Coro is apparent from the name of this ship.

from Curaçao to Colombia and to Europe.[221]

Jeudah's land speculations also paid off well. He had bought several plots of land in the reclaimed area, and, only a few years after he purchased one of these parcels for 1,000 florins, he sold it for 17,100 florins. A tidy profit in a very short time.[222] He was also the first member of the Senior family to own a house in the new Scharloo neighborhood – a residential address that soon became a true sign of wealth and stature among Curaçao's elite.[223]

Jeudah's son, the Coro-born Salomon Senior, had returned to Curaçao with his parents after the pogroms of 1855. Here he married Esther Jesurun in the Mikvé Israel synagogue in 1868. Her dowry of thirteen thousand florins (approximately ten thousand dollars) represented a true fortune in the nineteenth century.[224] Clearly the couple enjoyed great wealth on both sides of the family, even before their assets were further enriched by the compensations received from the Venezuelan government in 1903.

The Senior-Jesurun couple lived and entertained in style. In November 1892, they sent out gold-lettered invitations to all their family and friends, requesting their presence at the celebration of the fiftieth wedding anniversary of Jeudah and Jael Senior at their home.[225] Jeudah's contemporary, Leah Monsanto, carefully pasted this souvenir of the evening in her scrapbook, no doubt remembering this gala event for many years afterwards.

Salomon and Esther Senior had six children, one son and five daughters.[226] None of the five daughters married. They lived their entire lives in Curaçao. In the mid twentieth century, they were known as sweet old ladies who gave the most lavish birthday parties.[227] The son, Julio, emigrated to Santo Domingo in the 1890s. Here he met and married Margarita León in 1902. She was the daughter of a Sephardic Jew and a woman whose father had been an English Jew called Delvalle, but whose mother had not been Jewish. The five spinster sisters in Curaçao were purportedly unhappy about this aspect of the marriage, but it did not bother Julio Senior in the least.[228] Yet, his sisters' disapproval of Julio's marriage decision shows that the families of Curaçao's Sephardic community tried to exert some pressure on the marriage choices of their male relations, albeit often to no avail. None of the surviving descendants of the Senior-León couple are Jewish.

In addition to Salomon, Jeudah and Jael Senior had one daughter who survived to adulthood. The daughter, Hannah, married Salomon Rodriguez Pereira in 1881 and the couple had three children. Marriage information is available only for their eldest son, Jacob. He married a Sephardic woman from Panama, Lily Esther Cardoze, who was the granddaughter of Reverend David Cardoze of St. Thomas. Jacob and Lily Esther Pereira both lived and died in Panama City.[229]

In Curaçao Jeudah continued to be active in community matters. He served on the board of the Mikvé Israel synagogue from 1857 to 1859 and again in 1863 as the Jewish community entered yet another phase of its existence. Between the death of Rabbi Lopez da Fonseca in 1815 and the arrival of Rabbi Aron Mendes Chumaceiro in 1856, Curaçao's Jewish community did not have a rabbi to lead them. During that time, family feuds and other personal as well as religious issues remained unsolved and festered. The new rabbi was a scholar, but he soon found himself at the center of long-brewing conflicts between the more liberal and the conservative-leaning factions of the Jewish community. These frictions exacerbated in the 1860s and as the rift widened between the parties, it became inevitable that the liberal element would secede from Mikvé Israel. On May 28, 1864, twenty-five members of the opposition formed the Dutch Jewish Reform Community. The following year the new community, Temple Emanuel, was recognized by the Dutch government. Although some members of the Senior family joined the new reform congregation, Jeudah Senior and his son remained steadfast members of Mikvé Israel.

In 1858 Venezuela elected a new president, Cipriano Castro. Soon after this election some of the Jewish refugees who had finally been reimbursed for their losses let it be known to Castro that they wished to return to Coro. In response, President Castro ordered the governor of Coro in no uncertain terms to protect and respect the Jews. And so, unbelievable as it may seem after what they had gone through, a fairly large group of Curaçoan Jews went back to Coro in 1858. They were accompanied by a special envoy from Holland, Mr. P. van Rees, and by

Curaçao's Rabbi Chumaceiro. The presence of these two officials was most likely intended to make the return of the Sephardim seem like an official act, which was undertaken in response to the Venezuelan president's appeal to the local authorities.[230]

Even though Jeudah Senior was not among those who chose to return to Coro, he had left his stamp on the town. In the 1840s and early 1850s, his enterprising spirit had permitted him to benefit from the diverse opportunities offered by the then newly independent Venezuela, and his resulting wealth was an example of the possibilities awaiting those who dared follow in his footsteps. Younger men who came after him hoped to achieve such heights and were willing to overlook the constant political and anti-Semitic upheavals the early migrants had encountered in Venezuela. The opportunities in Coro had been exciting enough to counterbalance such disturbances when Jeudah Senior was younger, but, as he approached middle-age, Curaçao offered a much more predictable and comfortable environment for a man of means.

Home of Josias Senior
Coro, Venezuela

CORO, THE SECOND TIME AROUND:
ABRAHAM, ISAAC, AND JOSIAS SENIOR

¿Qué nuevas esperanzas	What new hopes
al mar te llevan? Torna,	take you to the sea? Return,
torna, atrevida nave,	return, fearless vessel,
a la nativa costa.	to the native coast.
Aún ves de la pasada	Still you see from tempests
tormenta mil memorias,	past, a thousand memories,
¿y ya a correr fortuna	and already for a second time
segunda vez te arrojas?	you fling yourself to brave the
	storm?

From: A la Nave, poem written by Andres Bello
(Caracas, Venezuela 1781 – Santiago, Chile 1865)

Jeudah's cousin, Abraham Mordechay Senior, who had hosted religious services for Coro's Jews at his home from 1847 until their hasty departure of 1855, was among the Curaçaoan Sephardim who returned to Venezuela in 1858.[231] He had been one of the early immigrants to Coro and had originally settled there at the beginning of the 1830s.[232] Unlike so many who were single when they immigrated, Abraham had been married and had brought along his wife (and cousin) Leah Senior and their four underage children, David, Isaac, Jacob, and Clara, who had all been born in Curaçao.[233] Coro had become home to this family unit. Although both Abraham and Leah were up in age at the time of their return in 1858, their commitment to their Sephardic friends who were trickling back into town must have been strong. Prior to their unplanned escape to Curaçao, the Senior home in Coro had been almost like a community center for the Jews of that town, and old or not, Abraham must have wanted to participate in the re-establishment of Jewish life in this place that, despite all the troubles, had been his residence for almost twenty-five years. The fact that all three sons decided to come back to

Coro during this second period of Jewish settlement was, of course, an additional incentive.

At the time of the pogrom of 1855, David, Isaac, and Jacob Senior had been adult members of the Jewish community of Coro, but they had all still been single. It is not clear if they were in business together when they were in their twenties, but it is likely that they owned at least one retail establishment. An accounts receivable journal belonging to the eldest son, David A. Senior, and covering the 1850s, begins with a heading on the first page that reads "Coro, 1° Enero 1851," and continues with entries through February 10, 1855, all recorded in Coro. Immediately following this February 1855 entry is a page with the heading "Curaçao 2 Marzo 1855," indicating David Senior's renewed business efforts in Curaçao soon after he had fled the Coro uprising in early February of that year. Business appears to have been much slower during the years that David Senior spent in Curaçao as compared to the four years recorded in Coro prior to the violence of 1855. Entries for the four years and one month in Coro covered 174 pages, whereas entries for the three years and four months in Curaçao take up only 25 pages. The last entry recorded in Curaçao in this book is dated March 8, 1858, with the first entry made by David Senior upon his return to Coro dated May 9, 1858.[234] At this time David was no longer single, having married Sarah Cohen Henriquez in Curaçao two years earlier.[235]

Within a few years after their second settlement in Coro, Isaac Senior followed his brother's example, choosing himself a wife as well. On January 9, 1861, he married Raquel Lopez Henriquez, daughter of one of Coro's early Sephardim. The wedding was performed in Coro by Isaac Namias de Crasto, a member of Coro's Jewish community. Witnesses were Josias Dovale Jr., J.A. Senior,* Joseph Curiel, and Elias Penso Suares – all part of the Curaçaoan Sephardic Diaspora of Coro.[236] Isaac and Raquel's first child, called Abraham after his grandfather, was born on June 17, 1861 in Coro. It is possible that this child was sickly, and

---

* This J.A. Senior was probably Isaac's brother Jacob. According to Jewish law, two witnesses who are not directly related to the bride or groom need to sign the *ketubah*. Since the other three witnesses were not relatives, the *ketubah* was perfectly legal and Jacob Senior's signature merely reflected his brother's desire to honor him.

that he was taken to Curaçao for health reasons. It is not clear if he died there or if he was only buried there. [237] His death took place about three weeks before the birth of the couple's second son, Josias Senior, born on November 30, 1862. One can only imagine that Josias's birth in this house of mourning was doubly cherished by his grieving family.

In the following years, Isaac and Raquel Senior had four additional sons and one daughter. In 1865 when their third son was born, they named him Abraham Haim, the addition of *Haim*, meaning life, distinguishing this child from his deceased brother. The other sons were called Morris, Jacob, and Seigismundo, and the daughter's name was Auristela.

Isaac Senior was a man of great insight. The business he and his brother David had left behind in Coro when they fled to Curaçao picked up quickly upon their return, but Isaac had bigger things in mind. David Senior's accounts receivable journal shows receivables from Jews and Gentiles for a very wide variety of goods, which presumably he imported and sold in his store. They included handkerchiefs, buttons, ivory combs, forks and knives, cologne, colored thread, playing cards, mousetraps, umbrellas for ladies, cooking oil, powder, wine, tobacco, white flour, Dutch butter, shoemaker's thread, needles, various textiles, and candlesticks. In short, mostly items for personal consumption. [238] Isaac was intent on importing and exporting both consumer products and intermediate products used in manufacturing. In 1884, when he was in his late fifties, his dreams began to come to fruition. He founded a new firm called *Isaac A. Senior e Hijo* – Isaac A. Senior & Son – and with young Josias by his side, the Seniors began to put together a network of hubs within Venezuela and abroad. [239]

In spite of the accepted adage that there was only a limited internal market in Venezuela, these enterprising men soon managed to develop and cater to an internal demand for consumer products as well as a demand for key industrial materials. They continued to import products for mass consumption, such as rice, starch, spices, beer, wheat, butter, cheeses, sweet and dry wines, inexpensive textiles, china, matches, agricultural tools, and colognes. Luxury items for the conspicuous consumers of the elite class, such as "canned hams as well as fresh ones, pickled fish, fresh grapes and apples, black tea, mushrooms, corn, pears, canned peas, crystallized sweets and cookies" were also among the shipments they received.[240] And for the growing manufacturing sector, they supplied Venezuela with shoe glue, machines, spare parts, stearin (which was used for the manufacture of soap and candles and in textile sizing), and various other intermediate manufacturing products. On several occasions, building materials, luxury office furniture, and jewelry were also shipped to the Seniors of Coro for their personal use.

The principal products exported by Isaac Senior & Son were coffee grown in the Andes region, animal hides, and products of the dividivi tree, a tropical American tree (*Caesalpina coriara*) used both for its wood and for its pods, which, when dried, produced an extract used in tanning leathers. Clearly, father and son were no longer merely storekeepers who imported goods to be sold in their shops to the local Corianos. They were now serious participants in Venezuela's import and export business.

A complex network of connections was maintained by the Seniors to facilitate this ever-growing enterprise. In foreign countries they relied heavily on their Jewish and familial connections. In New York they dealt with D.A. de Lima & Co. and De Sola, Bros & Pardo, both companies founded by Sephardic Curaçaoan Jews, as well as other firms such as Kunhardt & Co. and Neuss Hesslein & Co. In England their contacts were Jaffe & Sons, Jaffe & Brothers, Simon & Co., B. A. Dehn & Heine, and many other firms. In Hamburg their chief counterparts were Sigismundo Weil and Isidoro Weil. The Seniors and De Limas had had common ancestry in Curaçao and in later years one of Isaac Senior's sons, Morry, married Esther A. de Lima, related to the De Limas of New York. The Weils of Hamburg were even more closely related. Sigismundo Weil was married to Isaac Senior's sister, Clara, and their son, Isidoro Weil, was Isaac's nephew.[241]

In Venezuela the Seniors had intermediaries in a large number of towns south of Coro as well as on the Paraguaná peninsula who would buy the animals or hides from the farmers, coffee from the small and large plantations, and dividivi from various ranches. Certain Venezuelan villages became the hubs of smaller network systems. Here intermediate processing would take place, before shipping hides, coffee, and dividivi to the Seniors in Coro and La Vela, which in turn served as the shipment center to and from Curaçao for exports and imports.[242]

Supply of the exported agricultural products depended greatly on weather and political climate, and I.A. Senior and Son did not always have an easy time obtaining the required products of the quality requested for their export market. The prices for these products also fluctuated significantly, and often sales were held back until such time as a favorable price could be obtained. Nevertheless, the company's product diversification provided some flexibility during times of climate-related shortages and quality problems, and their business prospered.

At all times, Curaçao remained a part of the equation. The shipment routes were back and forth between La Vela and Curaçao, and then from Curaçao to New York or Europe and vice versa. Even though the Seniors of Coro were agents for a shipping company, they established relationships with many fleet owners from Curaçao, including the Jewish firms of Moses L. Maduro, Maduro Jr. & Co., Chumaceiro, Edwards Henriquez & Co., and Próspero Baiz & Co.[243] In the archives of S.E.L. Maduro & Sons of Curaçao, numerous remittances to and from Coro are recorded in the company's ledgers. This business continued in spite of the inordinately high import duties that Venezuela had begun to charge in 1881 on all foreign merchandise arriving from the Antilles.

It took time for this intricate network system to become operational. The many contacts and relationships formed over a lifetime by Isaac Senior had been instrumental to the company's early import/export activities, but the elder Senior died at age 59 in 1885, less than two years after he founded the firm. Therefore, all subsequent growth and I.A. Senior & Son's success and name recognition throughout the Caribbean have to be attributed to the business acumen of the generation that followed.

It must have been a tremendous burden on the young Josias Senior to take over this business at a mere 23 years of age, but he managed to do so with great determination and energy. At home were his widowed mother and his younger siblings Abraham Haim age 20, Morris age 12, Seigismundo (age unknown) and Jacob and Auristela, both under ten years old.[244] Throughout his life he continued to feel responsible for the wellbeing of his family. During a trip to Curaçao in 1895 he wrote frequently to his *"queridos hermanos"* – dear brothers – admonishing them to take good care of "*la querida mamá*" during his absence.[245] And in another letter on that same trip he writes again from Curaçao to his brothers and sister and ends the letter with "…you must know that I miss you all and that my greatest pleasure is to always live together. Auristela, my pigeon, love. Mama, hugs. From your Chia."[246]

On March 30, 1887, a little over a year after his father's death, Josias had married Carmen Alvares Correa, daughter of long-time Coro residents Raymundo and Julia Alvares Correa.[247] This marriage was short-lived. Carmen died later that year, most probably during childbirth, and was buried in the Jewish cemetery of Coro.[248] In 1891 Josias remarried, choosing Carmen's sister Sarah as his second wife.[249] Three children were born from this union, representing the fourth Jewish generation of this Senior branch in Venezuela.

Although the Seniors had been among the more observant Sephardim of Coro, Josias's brother Abraham Haim married a Catholic woman by the name of Rosario Molina on March 15, 1894. On that occasion the press in Coro reported:

> … as far as we know: this is the first time that we see in Coro the case of a young man of Jewish blood, fully breaking with the old traditions of his race and without foreswearing his rooted religious beliefs, uniting his life and his fate with a deserving daughter of Coro's native soil. [250]

Not too long thereafter, Seigismundo Senior also entered into a mixed marriage and married Rosario's sister Eugenia Molina. It would appear that during the last decades of the nineteenth century, some of the religious cohesion among the Sephardim of Coro had begun to disappear. The social relationships in the Jewish community still remained strong, but it was no longer centered on the weekly religious services, which by this time were not taking place as regularly as they used to prior to the pogroms of 1855.

Several months after the first exogamous marriage in the family, on August 3rd, 1894, Josias's sister Auristela married the Sephardic Jew

Alberto Henriquez in Coro.[251] Alberto was a bright twenty-three year old, and Josias was excited to have him join the growing enterprise of Isaac A. Senior & Son. During his first years in the business, Henriquez traveled frequently through the hinterlands of Venezuela to check on the company's many contacts and supply sources. On one of these trips, in the fall of 1896, he drank contaminated water and died at the premature age of twenty-five, leaving Auristela with a small daughter and pregnant with their second child.[252] The outpouring of condolences contained in the Senior archives is indicative of how terrible a blow Alberto's demise was to the family and all who knew him. Auristela never remarried.

Josias's brothers Morris and Jacob also married within their faith. In 1897, Morris, nicknamed Morry, married Emma Alvares Correa, yet another of Raymundo Correa's daughters, at a ceremony conducted in Coro by Josias Senior.[253] It is the only wedding ceremony in this town at which Josias officiated, and it must have been quite a thrill for him to be marrying his younger sibling to his sister-in-law. Again, however, tragedy struck. Emma died in 1902 at age 22,[254] leaving behind three young children.[255] Morry subsequently remarried in 1905, choosing another Sephardic woman by the name of Esther A. de Lima as his wife. An additional four children were born from this second marriage. Jacob Senior, nicknamed Coco, was married to Amelia Jesurun in 1898 in Curaçao's Mikvé Israel synagogue and they had no descendants.[256] In 1900 Morry and Coco became partners in the business run by their brother, Josias, and so the family remained united in all their endeavors.[257]

The generation of Isaac Senior's children was the generation of transition in Coro. During the second settlement of the Sephardim in Coro, the ability and drive of the Jewish community to maintain the rituals that had been observed during the first period of settlement began to suffer some setbacks. Some of these changes had to do with the decline in the number of Jews in Coro. Among the group that lived in this town in the second half of the nineteenth century there were not as many individuals familiar with ritual and tradition who could offer the sort of leadership the community had enjoyed when the Sephardim first settled in Coro. After 1860, more and more non-biblical names were found among the Coriano Jews, while, during the same period, biblical names were still being used among Curaçao's Sephardim. Furthermore, instead of having access to a local *mohel*, the Jews of Coro now had to rely on Curaçaoan circumcisers who were willing to travel. And, towards the end of the nineteenth century and the beginning of the twentieth century, they needed such services less often, as the lure of other Venezuelan cities caused some to leave Coro. The diminished adherence to tradition can be noted in the Jewish cemetery as well. Although, even in the earlier years, no Hebrew lettering was used to mark the cemetery graves of Coro, the tombstones in Coro had been similar to the ones in the Sephardic cemetery of Curaçao. Over time, however, sculptures of human figures began to appear on the Jewish tombstones of Coro, ignoring the Jewish commandment against graven images.[258]

Slowly but surely the Sephardim of Coro became less and less observant. After four generations of Jewish life in Coro without rabbinical guidance or teachings, knowledge about religious tenets and traditions became almost non-existent. The historian Blanca de Lima interviewed one of the last Jews of Coro, Thelma Henriquez, who elaborated on her childhood memories of the 1920s:

> I remember that my father commemorated – I think that is the word – [Yom] Kipur, but he commemorated it this way: he would close his business and he would take us for a ride. To La Vela. To Cumarebo. I began to believe that [Yom] Kipur was a festive day, not a day of forgiveness. We did not prepare any special food or anything like that.[259]

While Jewish religious observance did not flourish in Coro, the Coriano Sephardim continued to be among the top echelon of the commercial and cultural scene. Isaac A. Senior & Son's business kept growing and gained recognition all across the Caribbean. Correspondence with important businessmen in the region is evidence of this fact. Julius L. Penha, writing in 1899 from Curaçao, asks Josias to find him some freight for the return trip from Coro to Curaçao of the ship *Colibri* belonging to A. Henriquez in Curaçao. "With the great relationships [connections] that you have I don't doubt that it will be easy [for you] to do so."[260] In a letter dated October 26, 1896, Moses S.L. Maduro asks Josias to exert his influence on his brother Abraham Senior so that he (Maduro) may be named the agent for the Seniors in Curaçao.[261] From Maracaibo, Venezuela, C.G. Pinedo commends Josias's ability to find him the requested cattle hides in Puerto Cabello.[262] And from Havana, Cuba, the agent for Stoller Commission Co. of Kansas City Stock Yards, Missouri, asks Josias if he could sell him cattle.[263]

Curaçaoan relatives and friends maintained regular correspondence with Josias Senior as he continued to make a name for himself. Some of the correspondence in the Senior archives is of a purely personal nature, written by family members who cared for each other and kept in touch quite frequently. Thus the archives contain chatty letters from Josias's maternal uncle Jacob Henriquez and his paternal uncle David Senior, who had returned to Curaçao after many years in Coro. Both these men offer advice, ask for favors, and send gifts to their relatives in Coro. Edwin Senior, an important businessman in Curaçao, was a distant relative with whom the Seniors of Coro had a personal relationship as well as a business relationship. To give an example, he had been asked by Josias to buy and ship sweets from Curaçao for a party to be given in Coro on July 15, 1899 on the occasion of Josias's son Isaac's fifth birthday and wrote to confirm that he was taking care of this request.[264] Later that year, Edwin Senior wrote an extensive letter detailing his efforts to negotiate a fee for a commercial shipment to Josias in Coro. He added a personal note to this business letter, indicating that his wife Rosaura would be happy to take care of anything Sarita (Josias's wife) might want to order from Curaçao.[265]

Josias too appears to have done many favors for friends and relatives in Curaçao. In 1898 he was asked to pay the rent and one other debt incurred by Alfonso Capriles in Coro. "[T]he father is only paying for maintenance: room rent, nothing else," Moses Maduro wrote to Josias on his company's letterhead – Palais Royal – from Curaçao. In a later letter written from Curaçao in June of the same year, it appears that the father, Moisés Capriles, had been ailing, and on paper with the letterhead El Siglo XX – The Twentieth Century – J.D. Capriles of Curaçao asks Josias to inform Alfonso of his father's death.[266] Alfonso's father, Moisés Capriles, and Manasés Capriles Ricardo of Coro had been first cousins, and one might have thought that the parties in Curaçao would have asked Manasés's sons to watch over their cousin Alfonso in Coro and communicate his father's death to him. This was, however, not the case. These Curaçaoan friends must have considered Josias more reliable and mature than Manasés's sons to handle these issues.

The Seniors contributed greatly to Coro's economy and were certainly among the most important businessmen in town. In addition, they were also involved in almost all the cultural activities available to the citizens of Coro. As early as 1843, Isaac Senior had been a member of the Sociedad Estudiosa, an association whose members' aim was to familiarize themselves with republican practices, which were, at the time, still quite novel in Venezuela.[267] During the second settlement period, they focused on literary publications and theatre productions. In 1893 Josias Senior was president of the Sociedad Armonía, while Abraham Haim Senior served as editor of the periodical published by this literary group.[268] All these organizations had many Catholic and Jewish members, and Coro's Sephardim mingled with great ease in these settings, often taking leadership roles.

One of the early places where liberal Coro Catholics met with their Jewish counterparts on an equal footing was at the Masonic lodge of Coro. The town's first Masonic lodge, La Unión Fraternal No. 44, was founded in 1856. A Sephardic Jew by the name of David Curiel* was one of the co-founders.[269] Other lodges were formed in later years, but some of these merged with the original lodge to form the Unión Fraternal No. 17. This Masonic center was a very important gathering point for Coro's importers and exporters in the last quarter of the nineteenth century, and most of the Sephardic Jews of that town, including Isaac Senior and his sons, were members of this fraternal order.[270] The Masonic meetings introduced liberal thought to Coriano society and also represented a place where the merchants, importers, and exporters could socialize and discuss their business endeavors as well as their political views. As the

* Most likely a son of Joseph Curiel and Deborah Levy Maduro of Coro.

century advanced and the weekly Sabbath observances were discontin-
ued in Coro, the Jewish men of Coro derived spiritual guidance primarily from the moral elements of the Freemasonry movement. In 1899 Josias
Senior was the orator of this Masonic lodge and his brother Morry was
also listed as a member.[271]

By the twentieth century the Seniors' level of integration into
Venezuelan society had become so complete that during a short stay in
Hamburg in 1911, Josias Senior donated a religious statue to a church in
Puerto Cumarebo – a town close to Coro. Even in far away Germany, this
Coriano Jew still remembered his Catholic friends in Venezuela by means
of this generous, although somewhat unusual gift.[272]

Despite such close relationships with Catholic Corianos, religious and
political persecutions were never far from the consciousness of the Jews
of Coro and their descendants. In her book about the lives and business
endeavors of Isaac Senior and his descendants, Blanca de Lima states
that "[t]he oral memory of the Sephardic descendants evoke[d] a hidden
fear and the necessity to be ready at any time to leave for Curaçao, as well
as the expression of a need to become integrated because they lived in
this community."[273] Over time, this fear was reinforced repeatedly by representatives of the Catholic Church who made it clear that no matter
how long the Jews remained in Coro, they would always be unwanted.

The degree of the dislike for the Jews of Coro by some of the more rad-
ical members of the Church became apparent to the Seniors once more
in 1900. That year Abraham Haim Senior, one of Isaac Senior's sons who
had married outside the faith, left Coro for political reasons. This
prompted the priest José Dávila González to write in the periodical *La
Revista Católica*: "It is said that all the Jewish men and women who live
in Coro will follow the same path [i.e., will leave Coro]. This measure
will be applauded by all Catholics, because it will signify the spiritual and
material salvation of Coro." This article received strong reactions from
members of the Jewish community,[274] as well as from Catholic friends of
the Coriano Jews who printed a response that ended with: "...we protest
solemnly against Father José Dávila, Curate of the State, who, as a representative of our religion, shames the Christian faith and the Christian
society of Coro, to which we proudly belong."[275]

Dávila, who was the editor of the aforementioned Catholic periodical, was not the least bit chastised by these protests. He responded with an even stronger affirmation of his anti-Semitic views, scolding in passing those Catholics of Coro who had criticized his views and had written in defense of their Jewish friends.

> The Jew, who has not managed to be pardoned by any nation, as if he were the wandering and selfish rabble, whose tents [have been] without ideal[s] or the warmth of the principles of generosity and love;
> The Jew, who is despised in republics, persecuted in kingdoms, eternal stranger in all eras and among all peoples; *Caifás* [high priest of the Sanhedrin during the time of Jesus], nomad, who is burdened with the dust of Salomon's destroyed temple, without the land on which to rebuild it, and with the hate of his beliefs and without the conscience on which to base it...
> ... against that Jew, miserly and egoistic ... against him I [express] my convictions, my ministry, my energy, and my word.

And as if this were not sufficient he adds:

> It hurts and saddens [me] that honorable persons sign leaflets in defense of the eternal enemies of our religion.

And concludes:

> I am a Catholic priest, and therefore an enemy of the Jew, and I cannot conceive of a Christian, who with the same lips mixes up religious prayer and the kiss of Judas.[276]

Although the violent anti-Semitism experienced by the first generation of Jewish settlers in Coro did not repeat itself, this exchange with Father Dávila clearly shows that almost half a century later, strong anti-

Semitic sentiments continued to exist among some of the more conservative leaders of the Catholic Church in this Venezuelan town. It is no
wonder that the Jewish community failed to grow and flourish under
these circumstances. With this under-current of anti-Semitism, a lack of
influx from surrounding Jewish communities, and an increasing number
of mixed marriages, the size of the community decreased precipitously in
the early twentieth century.

The fact that mixed marriages were occurring at an ever-increasing
rate demonstrates that the opinions about the Jews held by Coro's
Catholic upper class and those of the Church did not necessarily coincide. This changing and more relaxed attitude among some of Coro's
non-Jewish residents made the possibility of intermarriage more palatable, in spite of the official condemnation of the Jewish faith by Church
leaders such as Father Dávila. With the local marriage market for the
Jews of Coro shrinking drastically due to the decrease in the size of the
Jewish community, exogamous unions became of greater interest to the
Sephardim as well. After all, as a Curaçaoan visitor to Coro had noted a
few decades earlier, the Corianitas were indeed pretty and cute and outgoing and coquettish,[277] and these were the women who Coro's Jewish
men saw on a daily basis.

At first, intermarriages occurred primarily between Jewish men and
Catholic women, while many of the Jewish women remained single
rather than marrying outside the faith. As time wore on, however, the
Jewish women of Coro also married Catholics, and, by the end of the first
decades of the twentieth century, the Jewish community had practically
disappeared.[278]

The decline in numbers of the Curaçaoan Sephardic Diaspora of Coro
and the degree of its dispersion among Venezuela's coastal towns is also
apparent from the records of the Alliance Israélite Universelle. In 1874,
Elias de Sola of La Guaira, Venezuela listed thirteen Jewish members of
the Alliance Committee in that region, who contributed a total of close
to 200 francs. Among the donors, four lived in Caracas, two in La
Guaira, four in Puerto Cabello, one in Coro, and two in Cumaná. Mr. de
Sola's letter accompanying this remittance to the Central Committee of
the Alliance and his letters to that organization in subsequent years indi-

cate great difficulty in collecting these donations.

> If I have delayed so long in remitting to you this year's
> contributions it has been entirely owing to the habitual
> apathy of some of the contributors, but I am today, at
> length, enabled to hand you herewith an order for the
> amount collected as per note hereunder.[279]

Filed with this letter by De Sola, but written in a different handwriting, the Alliance officials in Paris noted fourteen members of the Venezuelan committee who had not honored previous pledges. On this list, under the heading of *"n'ont pas payé"* – have not paid – are listed eleven Jews of Coro: Manassé [Manasés] Capriles, Raymond A. Correa, Isaac de Castro Jr., Moses A. de Lima, David L. Fonseca, Isaac L. Fonseca, Manuel P.D. Henriquez, Elias Haim Lopes, Mordecay L. Navarro, Moses H. Penso, and Isaac A. Senior. Marriage data for nine of these eleven indicate that they were all married to Jewish women,[280] so that their degree of apathy cannot be blamed on religious assimilation which might have caused them to distance themselves from the less fortunate Jews who were the beneficiaries of the funds collected by the Alliance Israélite Universelle. Possibly this list was an indication that these men had pledged a contribution which had not yet been received.

In 1881 De Sola wrote from Caracas that the results of his fundraising efforts for the Alliance were not very satisfactory that year and explained that he had distributed the circulars mailed to him by the Central Committee in Paris to "the few of our people residing here" receiving only six contributions.[281] By 1886, there was an improvement in the number of donors. That year the names of the contributors from Caracas indicate the arrival in Venezuela of Sephardic Jews from North Africa with names like Bentata, Bendelac, and Abehatar. Members of the Curaçaoan Jewish Diaspora, who had by then begun to settle in Caracas, were even less responsive to requests for donations to the Alliance in 1886 than they had been in the 1870s.[282]

When the weekly Shabbat services in Coro came to an end, the Senior family donated their Torah scroll, which had been used by the community in Coro, to the Mikvé Israel synagogue in Curaçao.[283] The small community that remained in Coro continued to meet on Yom Kippur for several years, but, in the early twentieth century, there were times when the Sephardim who still lived in Coro were not even sure what the dates for Passover were unless someone had been to Caracas or Curaçao on business and had returned with *matzo* from those locations to remind the few Jews who were still in town that the holiday was about to begin or had just begun.[284]

The contacts between Coriano Jews and Curaçao were much more frequent than those which existed, for example, between the Jews of Santo Domingo and Barranquilla and their relatives and friends on the Dutch island. The reasons for these intense relationships are multiple: first, of course, the proximity of the island to the Venezuelan coastal region; second, the history of Coro's persecution of the Jews; and thirdly, the extremely important business connections that the Coriano Jews had established with family and friends in Curaçao. While Curaçaoan Jews had business relations with Curaçao's Diaspora communities in other places, the magnitude of nineteenth century commerce between Curaçao and Coro was much greater than that between Curaçao and any of the other locations discussed in this work. Mixed marriages did not hamper these commercial relationships nor did they affect the existing social relations to any great extent. A scrapbook that used to belong to the Jewess Leah Monsanto of Curaçao (1814 – 1902) shows dozens of engagement, wedding, and birth announcements, thank-yous for expressions of condolence and other such cards from Jewish as well as non-Jewish friends of Sephardic descent in Coro and other cities and towns in Venezuela.[285]

It would appear that many Jewish families who were in Coro for extended periods or even for several generations in the nineteenth century moved back to Curaçao or to other parts of Latin America after their stay in that town. Indeed, in the twentieth century, the relatives in Coro, no matter how successful, were considered big fish in a little pond by Curaçaoan Sephardic Jews who had migrated to other parts of the Caribbean. A Cuban great granddaughter of Isaac Senior of Coro explained that the saying "*El conde que va a Coro no es conde*" – the count who goes to Coro is not [really] a count – was commonly used in Cuba among her relatives to indicate that there was nothing impressive about Coro.[286]

In summary, Jeudah Senior and his first cousin Abraham M. Senior made diverging decisions with regard to their migration to Coro. For Jeudah Senior and his descendants, Coro ended up being only a temporary residence, although it would appear that they might have remained in that town had it not been for the degree of persecution and property destruction that they experienced. For Abraham Senior, his son Isaac, and Isaac's children, Coro became their permanent new home, although Abraham, Isaac, and Josias were all buried in Curaçao. Isaac's children and grandchildren continued to live in Coro for many years and several members of these later generations are buried in Coro. A few of Isaac Senior's descendants still live there, but many now live in Caracas or have moved away from Venezuela. A small number of these descendants are still Jewish, and most of these Jewish men and women have married non-Jews.

Retired judge Edna Molina Senior de Suarez of Coro, Isaac Senior's great-granddaughter and granddaughter of his son Seigismundo Senior, who had married outside the faith, recalled the following story about her grandfather. Seigismundo, nicknamed Don Chimú and called Papá Mun by his grandchildren, had remained Jewish in spite of his marriage to Eugenia Molina Franco. He had four daughters and one son who were all raised in their mother's Catholic religion. The son, Pedro Isaac Senior, married a woman by the name of María Luisa Carías in Coro. At some point in the early twentieth century, Pedro Isaac was diagnosed with cancer, and his wife made a promise to the Almighty that if her husband were to survive, she would try to convince her father-in-law to convert to Catholicism. Pedro Isaac Senior had surgery and recovered. True to her word, María Luisa asked the bishop of Coro, Francisco José Iturriza, to speak to Seigismundo. The latter listened to the bishop and replied that he would be damned forever were he to forsake his God for the love of his son. According to Seigismundo's granddaughter, the bishop respected this decision and remained her grandfather's life-long friend. As a consequence, when Don Chimú died, the bishop was one of the first to arrive at the home of the deceased to offer his condolences. This led many in Coro to believe that Don Chimú had finally converted to Catholicism on his deathbed. But the family knew that this was not the case, and with the assistance of his sister's nephew, Alberto Henriquez, Seigismundo Senior received a Jewish burial in Coro, albeit next to his wife in the Catholic cemetery.[287]

VENEZUELA, HERE WE COME!
THE CAPRILES-RICARDO FAMILY

The Corianitas are all bonitas and graciositas and comadritas and coqueticas.[288]
(The girls from Coro are all pretty and cute and outgoing and coquettish.)
David Ricardo Capriles, July 1858

After the original Sephardim of Coro returned to Venezuela in the late 1850s, visitors from Curaçao once more began to go back and forth to the Paraguaná peninsula for business and special events. Vessels carrying merchandise sailed between La Vela and Curaçao on a daily basis, and news from Coro was reported regularly in the *Curaçaosche Courant*. The Curaçaoan Sephardim no longer perceived any major deterrent in emulating some of their friends and relatives who were once again acquiring great wealth in Coro.

Manasés Capriles Ricardo was one of the young Curaçaoans who had been waiting for an opportunity to settle in Venezuela. He had been born in Curaçao on August 17, 1837 to Joseph Capriles and Bathsheba Ricardo and was their ninth child. His parents had many mouths to feed and with the birth of their last child at the end of 1855, Manasés, who was then eighteen years old, needed more than two hands to count his five sisters and ten brothers.

It is likely that he had heard many stories about Coro from the refugees who had returned to Curaçao in 1855 after the anti-Semitic unrests. And in 1858, when it became safe to go back, exciting first-hand reports from Sephardic Jews visiting the Paraguaná peninsula for the first

Tombstone of Manasés Capriles (1837–1894)
in Curaçao's Jewish cemetery at Berg Altena

time must have reached him as well. On June 17, 1858 two of Manasés's contemporaries, his first cousins Dr. David R. Capriles and Joseph Capriles, left Curaçao for a pleasure trip to Venezuela. They sailed to La Vela, arriving in Coro at 8 o'clock of the following evening. These two young men, born in respectively 1837 and 1836, were both still single at the time of this trip. David Capriles's diary only provides a summary of his experiences in Coro, but it may be assumed that upon his return he recounted his adventures in Venezuela with great flourish to his friend and cousin, Manasés, fueling the latter's desire to experience Coro's hospitality himself. In his diary David wrote:

> Friday, June 18. Yesterday I left Curaçao in company with my brother, Joe and after quite a pleasant little trip by sea and by land we finally arrived this evening at 8 o'clock in the village, or rather city of Coro (Venezuela).
> Sunday, June 20. Everything goes on quite smoothly so far; the people are most amiable towards me, a fact which generally makes one like a place wherever it may be.
> Tuesday, June 22. This evening we made an extremely pleasant visit to the family of F. L...z, where I had the fortune of meeting one of the sweetest birds in this romantic place. Yes, I must confess that the effects of Niña L...a's piercing eyes came quite near my heart....
> Monday, July 26. Last night I was quite happy amongst a party of Coro beauties. We went to see some fireworks which were displayed in the 'public place,' and as I was not in a public place but under a very romantic 'balcony' I had a romantic approach to the temple of Cypres. Oh! Sweet recollections! Oh! Dreams of voluptuousness! Few mortals can live for a long time in your ecstacy, or I should crave you to last forever.[289]

Because he does not provide complete names of the people with whom he interacted, it is not known if Capriles had been socializing with members of the Jewish community of Coro. It is likely, however, that F. L...z was Felipe Lopez, the gentleman who took care of Jeudah Senior's affairs in Coro after Senior chose to remain in Curaçao. It also appears that the young bachelor had himself a wonderful time in this town that had frightened away so many of his friends a few years earlier, and that he felt most welcome indeed. Nevertheless, he returned to Curaçao, where he married Hannah Senior on September 7, 1859, and where he practiced medicine and continued to live for the remainder of his life.

It is not known if Manasés, like his cousins David and Joseph, visited Coro before he decided to settle there permanently, but by the beginning of the 1860s, he and his brothers Madison (born 1834), David (born 1836), and Julio (born 1839) had all migrated to the South American mainland. In the decade that followed, most of the other members of this Capriles-Ricardo family unit also followed suit.[290] The parents, Joseph and Bathsheba, joined their children in Venezuela as well and are both buried in Puerto Cabello.

Manasés, Julio, and Elias Capriles Ricardo settled in Coro, while their other siblings scattered among various other Venezuelan towns, including nearby Puerto Cabello, Caracas, and the lesser known Barcelona and Piritu located further away from Coro in the eastern state of Anzoátegui.[291] Migration away from Curaçao was not that unusual in the nineteenth century, but to have almost an entire family unit of eighteen leave over a period of ten years or so was not very common. To fully understand the attraction that Venezuela had for these Capriles-Ricardo siblings, it is important to step back in time and briefly describe the connection between their maternal grandfather, Mordechay Ricardo, and the South American Liberator, Simón Bolívar.

Mordechay Ricardo was born in Amsterdam in 1771 and studied law in Holland. In the late eighteenth or early nineteenth century he left Europe and migrated to the Americas. After a short stay in New York, he arrived in Curaçao in 1802, during the first English occupation of the island. That same year he married Esther Frois de Sola.[292] Many of the Ricardos of Mordechay's generation had by then left Holland. His uncle, Abraham Ricardo, for example, had moved to England with his offspring, where his son David later became the well-known British economist. Mordechay had at least one brother and one sister who had also migrated to Curaçao.[293]

Although Mordechay Ricardo arrived in Curaçao at a time of economic downturn and political upheaval, he became gainfully employed almost right away, and soon made a name for himself as an able attorney. Professionally he held many important posts on the island, both during the English occupation and later when the Dutch returned to Curaçao. As a lawyer he frequently represented his co-religionists in their business transactions and court cases, and, at the time of his death in 1842, he was auditor of the island's National Guard.[294]

The Mikvé Israel community played a large role in Ricardo's life. He served on the synagogue board for many years, and was its president in 1822, and again from 1826 through 1829, a period requiring much leadership after the turbulent times with Hazan Piza.[295]

It is mostly through his other activities, however, that Mordechay Ricardo has remained well known in Curaçaoan and Venezuelan history. At the beginning of the nineteenth century, Curaçao's Jews had kept abreast of the revolutionary developments on the South American mainland. Refugees from the revolution and leaders of the movement frequently passed through Curaçao and on occasion lived there in exile for prolonged periods of time. In 1812, the most important individual of that war of liberation, Simón Bolívar, arrived on the island as a refugee. The first part of that year had been difficult for Bolívar. The revolutionary forces had been defeated in Puerto Cabello, and Bolívar was forced to leave Venezuela. Through the good graces of his friend Francisco Iturbe, who obtained a safe conduct passage for him out of his beleaguered country, he managed to get to Curaçao.

Although he arrived in the island without funds and feeling depressed and discouraged, he befriended two important individuals during his stay in Curaçao. The first was the Curaçaoan Pedro Luis Brion, who later joined the Venezuelan cause as admiral of its fleet. The second was Mordechay Ricardo, who was, by this time, well established and had accumulated some wealth. Ricardo offered the exiled Bolívar financial assistance for the revolutionary war efforts, and Bolívar, who was twelve years younger than Ricardo looked upon the older man as a mentor.[296]

These friendships were quite important to Bolívar. In a September 10, 1812 letter to his friend Iturbe, Bolívar informs him of the new friendships he has made, and his melancholic mood seems much improved. He writes, "Never do we lack a compassionate friend to help us and one should not be ashamed to receive the help of [such] a friend." His stay in Curaçao reenergized him, and the month after he wrote this letter, Bolívar left Curaçao for Cartagena, Colombia, where he presented his Manifest of Cartagena, a document he had worked on during his stay in Curaçao, and which he had apparently discussed with his new Jewish friend.[297]

He completed this important manuscript in Cartagena and presented it there in December of 1812. This manifest of Cartagena showed Bolívar to be a man of vision and ensured his role as the true leader of the revolution. In it he described a strategic plan to liberate both Nueva Granada and Venezuela by means of a professional army instead of the random militias that had been battling the Spanish up to that point. He also encouraged the leaders of Nueva Granada to form a united front with Venezuela in throwing off the Spanish yoke. Although 1813 did not mark the end of the hostilities, it was a successful year for Bolívar, and his victories that year gained him the title of Libertador – Liberator.

In 1815, Bolívar called on Mordechay Ricardo to host his sisters who were eager to abandon the terrors of war in Venezuela. María Antonia and Juana Bolívar stayed in Curaçao at Ricardo's country estate El Octagón for a significant period, during which the ladies befriended many members of the Sephardic community. Ricardo's descendants are proud to possess a letter, written by the Libertador from exile in Jamaica to Mordechay Ricardo in Curaçao, thanking him for "the kindness with which you have treated my unfortunate sisters."[298]

Although Manasés Capriles had not yet been born at the time of these visits, these were days when history was being made on the South American continent. Simón Bolívar was a charismatic leader and the courage of those who fought the revolution against Spanish dominion was much admired by the Sephardim in Curaçao. From these early years of the fight for Venezuelan independence and throughout the remainder of his life, Mordechay Ricardo's world began to include Venezuela. He traveled there on several occasions, but never made a permanent move. In 1842 he was buried in the old Jewish cemetery in Curaçao.[299]

Not surprisingly, Mordechay and Esther Ricardo's children grew up with a special feeling towards Venezuela. The couple had five children, three sons and two daughters. Of the three sons, one died as an infant and the other in his teens. The surviving son, Moisés Ricardo, married Henriette Tavares in Kingston, Jamaica, and, although he lived most of his life in Curaçao, he became the itinerant *mohel* of the Caribbean and traveled to Venezuela very frequently.[300] In the large households of the two daughters, Bathseheba and Rachel, who married the brothers Joseph and Abraham Capriles, respectively, the name Bolívar evoked those exciting times when Mordechay Ricardo had, in his own way, contributed to the revolutionary war on the South American mainland. His grandchildren in both Capriles-Ricardo households (all twenty-eight of them) grew up with these magical stories. To them Venezuela was the site of heroic deeds and future promise. Even four and five generations later, at the end of the twentieth century, Mordechay Ricardo's descendants continued to be well aware of their forefather's role in Venezuela's fight for independence. One can only imagine how much more vivid the stories were a century and a half earlier when Manasés Capriles Ricardo and his brothers and sisters were growing up in Curaçao among people who had witnessed history being made.

Between the children and grandchildren of Batsheba Ricardo and Joseph Capriles, almost all of whom ended up living in Venezuela, and some of the grandchildren of Rachel Ricardo and Abraham Capriles, who later joined their many cousins in that country, they eventually flooded Venezuela with Caprileses. It is often said that in Venezuelan towns one can always find *"un jefe civil, un cura, un boticario y un Capriles"* – a town official, a priest, a pharmacist, and a Capriles.[301] This saying reflects the effect that the migration of so many Caprileses had on Venezuela's demography. Although it was the perceived economic opportunities in Venezuela that drew these Sephardim to the country in the second half of the nineteenth century, the romantic stories told in the Capriles-Ricardo households about the friendship between Simón Bolívar and Mordechay Ricardo must have provided an extra draw for the members of these large households.

In 1859, Manasés Capriles Ricardo married Sarah Cecilia Senior in Puerto Cabello, Venezuela, a town located at about 130 miles from Coro. Although Sarah Cecilia was Jewish (a distant relative of the Seniors of Coro), Rabbi Chumaceiro of Curaçao refused to record the marriage in the Mikvé Israel marriage register, since the couple had married on Hoshanah Rabah, a Jewish holiday falling during the week of Sukkot.[302] Manasés and Cecilia (or Sally, as she was often called) must not have cared or known about such prohibitions, and Rabbi Chumaceiro's lack of recognition did not affect their marriage in any discernable way. Within three years the union had produced a daughter and two sons – all three born in Coro. The first-born son, José Manasés, was circumcised by his great-uncle, Moises Frois Ricardo, who traveled from Curaçao to Coro for this occasion in April of 1862. The *mohel* was there again in 1865 for the circumcision of another son, Abraham.[303] In total, the couple had thirteen children who survived to adulthood. In the 1870s some of these children were born in Curaçao. It is therefore not clear when Manasés Capriles became a permanent resident of Coro or if he moved back and forth between Curaçao and Coro every few years.[304] Indeed, very little information is available about his business activities of the sixties and early seventies in Venezuela.

By the late seventies, however, he owned a soap factory in Coro, which in 1878 was capable of producing 250 cases of soap a day. According to Venezuelan historian and Coro expert Blanca de Lima, the soap factory was the first manufacturing concern in the state of Falcón,[305] a state that, despite much growth in other areas of Venezuela, had remained under-populated and relatively poor as the nineteenth century drew to an end. Its economy consisted of small farmers and cattle breeders who would send their products to the large import/export companies in Coro, such as I.A. Senior & Son, which was where the real money was being made.[306] By 1872, Coro's population had grown to 8,172, which meant that it had almost tripled in forty years. In the twenty years that followed, the economy of the state of Falcón was stagnant, and, as was mentioned earlier, many left Coro for other more promising cities of Venezuela. In 1891 the population of the town of Coro stood at 8,752.[307]

It is estimated that the number of Jews hovered slightly below one hundred at the time.*

In such a declining economic environment, it had to be guts or madness that guided the businessmen of Coro to continue to invest in that town in the 1880s. But this is exactly what people like Isaac Senior and Manasés Capriles and their sons did. Manasés expanded his manufacturing concerns to include the production of candles, hides, and castor oil and, with this diversified base, he was Coro's first industrial mogul.[308]

In the late 1880s and early 1890s, Capriles switched his business focus to the construction of a railroad between Coro and its port of La Vela.[309] Since the early 1870s individuals involved in the import/export trade had been interested in improving the connection between Coro and its Caribbean port. The idea was to build a railroad that would start in Coro and end at a pier in La Vela, streamlining the region's import and export procedures. Steamships importing and exporting goods to and from Coro could not, at the time, dock in La Vela. Instead they would anchor away from the shore and a burdensome transfer of imported goods from those ships to smaller vessels would take place in order to unload cargo in La Vela. To export the agricultural products arriving in La Vela from Coro and the Venezuelan hinterlands, the same inefficient operation had to be repeated in reverse. Small vessels in La Vela had to be loaded with the products that arrived by land, and these boats would then transfer the export items to the steamships anchored a bit further offshore.[310] It was obvious that this multi-step process had to be improved.

In 1874, a gentleman by the name of Pedro Mártir Consuegra received a contract from the state to build a railroad and new pier that would eliminate these transportation inefficiencies between Coro and La Vela – a distance of 12.5 kilometers (7.8 miles). His efforts were not successful and the project remained idle for another ten years. In 1884 a Coro businessman, Alejandro Cesáreo Salcedo, spearheaded a second attempt at this railroad. He formed a corporation and included several elite busi-

---

* Estimate calculated by counting the number of household members in eight family units who lived in Coro at the time and adding several other Jews living in Coro for whom no genealogical details were available.

nessmen from Coro in his efforts. Among them were Jaime and Juan Blanch, Manuel Leyba, Manasés Capriles, Eduardo Iturbe, José Lopez Fonseca, and José María Gil. Salcedo, Leyba, Capriles, and Fonseca were all of Curaçaoan Sephardic descent. This second effort was equally unsuccessful, and Salcedo withdrew from the project. A new contract was awarded to Manuel Leyba and Nicolás Schotborgh in 1888. This duo also failed to make much progress.[311] To most Corianos, the project seemed doomed to failure. When it became apparent that Leyba, like those who came before him, was not going to be able to accomplish what he had set out to do in a timely fashion, the Coro press wrote with poetic insight:

A *Salcedo no convino*	It did not suit Salcedo
El contrato a realizar	To fulfill the contract
Ya Leyba va en camino	And Leyba is well on his way
Dejarlo caducar	To let it expire [312]

Leyba's contract was indeed not renewed. It would appear that the project had died an agonizing death and could not be revived. To Manasés Capriles Ricardo, however, the idea of the railroad appeared to be within the realm of the possible, and he refused to give up. In December of 1892, he sold all his manufacturing concerns, the building in which they were housed, and all the accompanying fixed assets to Isaac A. Senior & Son, in order to have enough capital to invest in the Coro-La Vela railroad. He was fifty-five years old and his sons José Manasés and Abraham, who had both been in the manufacturing business with their father, joined him in this new effort.[313]

Manasés did not live to see this railway realized. He died at age 56 on January 6, 1894,[314] leaving the railroad endeavors in the hands of his sons, whose financial condition was, at that point, highly leveraged and in need of additional capital to execute the project of their father's dreams.

Manasés's body was transferred to Curaçao for burial. He was buried in the part of the Jewish cemetery on Berg Altena reserved for the Reform community – the only Capriles buried in that portion of the cemetery, since all other family members had remained loyal to the Mikvé Israel synagogue at the time of the formation of Temple Emanuel in 1864. His tombstone is quite elaborate, even for Curaçaoan Sephardic standards, and is adorned, somewhat controversially, with a very large bust of the handsome Manasés.

Back in Coro, his offspring and widow now had to deal with the realities of the day. They transferred the contract to build the railway to a group of North American investors, but remained involved in the ensuing developments. José Manasés Capriles was given power of attorney by the company's new president, Jacob Baiz, authorizing him to arrange for a larger subsidy from the Venezuelan government, and he and his brother Abraham became the agents in charge of issuing bonds to refinance the project. Although the new company, The Coro and La Vela Railroad and Improvement Company, was incorporated in New York, the principal investors, Jacob Baiz and the De Lima brothers of that city, were all of Curaçaoan Sephardic origin. Manasés Capriles's sons were somewhat casual about their business dealings, and soon major disagreements developed between the two brothers and Jacob Baiz. The problems facing José and Abraham Capriles did not end with Baiz's demise in 1899.[315]

By the end of the century and the beginning of the twentieth century, the two Capriles brothers in Coro were desperately trying to stay afloat, while, finally, in December of 1897, the train connection between Coro and La Vela became a reality. Construction costs ended up being over a million Bolivars, and, although the railroad had a few profitable years in 1899, 1900, and 1904, it never became a truly viable enterprise.[316] The company was declared bankrupt on December 14, 1907,[317] and was eventually taken over by the State.

From Curaçao, S.E.L. Maduro & Sons were persistently trying to collect payments for outstanding debts owed to them by the brothers J. & A. Capriles. In a letter written on January 14, 1901 the Maduros reminded the two men that they had been promising to pay back their loans for more than two years and suggested various solutions to amortize the debt. A few months later, the management of S.E.L. Maduro & Sons appears to have become more concerned about the ability of the two brothers to repay their debt. They now wrote to the young men's uncle, Elias

Capriles Ricardo, who had agreed to be the guarantor for the loans that had been extended to his two nephews.

> 15 March, 1901
> Dear Friend,
> Since we had the pleasure on the 28th of January inst. to announce to you the delivery that we made of your 20 tins, we have not been favored with your news.
> Today we have taken the liberty to include a copy of a letter that since the 14th of January we addressed to Messrs. J. & A. Capriles and which has not merited an answer from them.
> From this letter you will see that we proposed to those friends that they accept our demand for $100 each month, to see if this way we can manage to amortize to some extent the large sum that they owe us.
> We appeal to you that you help us in this matter, [and] we hope you will be able to succeed, so that we shall not have to call upon you as lender and principal debtor, since it is a very large share of the [total] amount that is owed to us by those friends.
> It does not please us to have to call on you for the loan made to them, but once [it has been established] that there is no way for them to settle with us, we have no other recourse but to insist that you meet this obligation.
> Awaiting your answer we are,
> Your affectionate friends and servants
> [signed]
>
> We have taken the liberty to add a bill that you have outstanding to our firm for [the sale of] wood, so that you may include the amount whenever you have [the opportunity] to remit to us. [318]

The letter is business-like and does not contain any of the familial chitchat that was often seen when the Maduros corresponded with other

Sephardic friends and relatives who had moved away from Curaçao.

Finally, by March 26th, the Maduros heard back from the Caprileses in Coro, who appear to have rejected the suggestion that they pay $100 each month towards the monies owed to S.E.L. Maduro & Sons. The Maduros did not seem too surprised or disturbed and responded to this development by indicating that they were "sorry to see from your letter of the 22nd that you cannot comply with the proposition made by us on January 14, when we thought that the monthly surrender of a relatively insignificant sum would be a reasonable way to amortize your account." Most of the rest of this correspondence then discusses a promissory note in favor of Cecilia S. de Capriles, Manasés's widow, and finally, the letter ends with a request that the Caprileses provide the Maduros in Curaçao with some information about the estate of a recently deceased Jew of Coro, who owed the Maduros a great deal of money. "Has the [business] been liquidated? Is somebody in charge of this enterprise? Any information that you may be able to provide us will be treated confidentially ..."[319] It is interesting to note that, despite the problem of non-payment by the Capriles brothers, the Maduros still considered them an important source of information with regard to monies owed to the Curaçaoan firm by yet another Sephardic enterprise in Coro.

Of all of Manasés Capriles's sons, these two, José and Abraham, remained closest to the Jewish community of Curaçao. José had married Ana Capriles Senior, daughter of Mordechay Capriles Ricardo (Manasés's first cousin), in Curaçao in 1891, and Abraham had married Enriqueta Ricardo a few months earlier in Curaçao as well.[320] The couples visited Curaçao often from nearby Coro, and one can only hope, for the sake of all the participants, that the difficulties with the Maduros, who were good friends of the Curaçaoan Capriles branches, were resolved subsequent to the letter exchanges described above.

The marriage choices of Sally and Manasés Capriles's children reflect how difficult it was to enter into endogamous marriages in Coro at the end of the nineteenth century. Marriage information is available for ten of the thirteen children. Five married Jews and five did not. Many of these marriages occurred in a very small circle of acquaintances, as the market for acceptable spouses for the Jews of Coro continued to shrink.

José, Abraham, and David all married women who were their cousins,* while Rosalina, Belén and Julio César married three Ashkenazi siblings by the name of Mayerston. Another of the Mayerston sisters was married to Elias Capriles Ricardo, uncle of these young men and women. Several of these couples had to apply to the State of Falcón to receive permission to marry in view of their close family relationship. In 1905, Julio César Capriles and his first cousin Alicia Capriles Mayerston had to apply for a state waiver of their "cosanguinity in the fourth degree" before they could marry. And in 1879, Belén Capriles and Jacob Mayerston also had to receive a state dispensation in order to marry. As far as can be determined, Belén and Jacob were not at all related by blood. But presumably the many Capriles-Mayerston marriages in Coro were just too confusing for the authorities of the time, and the couple must have decided to be on the safe side and applied for the special permit nevertheless.

In the generation that followed, Manasés Capriles's forty-one known grandchildren became almost fully assimilated religiously. Only two granddaughters married males with the Jewish last names of Delvalle and Maduro – which would indicate that their husbands may have been Sephardim or descendants of Sephardim.[321]

It is not clear if Manasés and Sally Capriles participated in any aspect of Jewish life in Coro's rapidly diminishing Jewish community of the last decades of the nineteenth century. There is evidence, however, that Manasés was vocal about the anti-Semitic slights that continued to occur in this religiously conservative Venezuelan town. Most of these sentiments expressed in Coro subsequent to the problems of 1855 tended to be provoked by Church officials, and the Jews generally kept a low profile during Holy Week, when many priests used the pulpit to incite their congregants against the killers of Christ. In response to such a sermon given in 1884, Capriles wrote to the offending priest:

> Reverend Father: You delivered a sermon at the 'Matriz Church' [the cathedral] last night, which

---

* Notably, David's wife Luisa Ricardo, a granddaughter of the *mohel* Moisés Ricardo, was Catholic, since she was brought up in her mother's faith.

undoubtedly would have brought honor to some obscure
clergyman of the 14th, 15th, and 16th centuries – those
centuries of the Inquisition and persecutions – but for
which today you are not envied by even the most fanat-
ic clergy of Christianity in this century of brotherhood
and love.

What sentiments guided you to pronounce such
senile words against a race which far from antagonizing
your Church, tries to fraternize with it? What sentiment
induced you to insult an inoffensive people with the
most injurious epithets?

In the present age, when all races try to forget mutual injuries and look to unite in an embrace of charity and
tolerance, your sermon was inopportune, Reverend
Father. With that sermon, lacking any deep thought
whatsoever, you maybe had two goals in mind. First, to
predispose the honest and tolerant inhabitants of Coro
against the Jews who reside in this city and whom they
value because they know their charitable feelings and
their conduct which is according to the strictest [rules]
of irreproachable integrity. Secondly, you [must] have
wanted to show yourself as an erudite expert of the most
tragic drama of the Calvary and of the history of the
Jewish people. But permit me to say to you that you have
not achieved your goals.[322]

Capriles continued for several paragraphs assuring the priest that
Corianos would not listen to his propaganda and that, in fact, the content of his sermon was against the latest teachings of his own Church.
The letter ends with Capriles informing the priest that he does not
expect to hear him expressing his views again, since little is to be gained
from such an experience. Isidoro Aizenberg, who wrote a seminal book
about the Jews of Coro, recounts that, unfortunately, anti-Semitic comments were not merely isolated sentiments attributable to the Church,
but continued to occur among the population at large as well. Jews in

Venezuela were quite often accused of usury and false conversions to Catholicism for the purpose of accumulating wealth.[323]

Although this letter represents a strong protest on the part of Manasés Capriles, it is of interest to note the Masonic overtones inherent in his statement regarding "brotherhood and love," as well as his assertion that Coro's Jews, "far from antagonizing [the] Church [try] to fraternize with it." This shows a marked change in the cross-cultural practices of the Jews in Coro in the last part of the nineteenth century as compared to the concerns with Jewish ritual and the focus on Jewish community events that the early migrants to Coro had embraced in the first half of that century. It is not surprising that Capriles's statement shows Masonic influences. He was a 33rd degree Freemason and Grand Master of his lodge in Coro.[324]

As mentioned earlier, Freemasonry became an extremely important aspect of the life of Coriano Jews in the second half of the nineteenth century. Its importance increased, while simultaneously Jewish religious practices declined among the mostly second and third generation members of the Curaçaoan Jewish Diaspora as well as among the more recent immigrants. Without the ritual of their own weekly religious services, which had ceased as the community shrank, Jewish men began to attend mass with their Catholic wives and children. By the end of the century, Jews were frequently buried in Catholic cemeteries, in spite of the fact that the Jewish cemetery in Coro remained available to them.

Julio Capriles Ricardo, who had migrated to Coro around the same time as his brother Manasés, married a French Catholic in Aruba. Other than the fact that all his children were born in Coro, little is known about him.[325]

Elias Capriles Ricardo, Manasés's younger brother, who had guaranteed the loan for his nephews J. & A. Capriles, had also settled in Coro, although it is not known when he arrived there. He was thirteen years younger than Manasés, and it is likely that he arrived in the late 1860s or early 1870s. In 1875 he married Sara María Mayerston in Coro, and most of their eleven children were born in that town.[326] His fondness for his older brother and sister-in-law is reflected in the fact that he named one of his sons Manasés and also had a daughter called

Cecilia.* Five of the eleven children in this Capriles-Mayerston household entered into endogamous marriages.[327] As mentioned earlier, Alicia
married her cousin Julio César Capriles Senior. Rosalta and Cecilia married two Salas Baiz brothers who were Curaçaoan Sephardic immigrants.
Isbelia married Jacob Mendes Chumaceiro, grandson of Curaçao's rabbi
Aron M. Chumaceiro in Curaçao, and the couple lived in the island for
a few years before moving back to Coro. Manasés Capriles Mayerston
married Deborah Lopez Fonseca, whose grandparents had been among
the early Curaçaoan Sephardic immigrants in Coro.

Deborah Capriles, who today owns a pharmacy in Coro, does not
remember her grandfather, Manasés Capriles Mayerston, since he died
when she was still a baby. Her father, Elias, born of two Jewish parents,
did not practice any aspect of Judaism and was somewhat of a rebel. Her
mother was Catholic and Deborah was brought up in the Catholic
Church. In conversation she was able to discuss various Jewish holidays,
although occasionally she seemed to be confused about the customs associated with each holiday. For example she mentioned among Passover
customs matzo, bitter herbs, four candles, and salt. When asked what she
knew about Jewish dietary laws, she indicated that Jews were not to eat
pork and could only eat white fish with scales. She is very proud to be of
Jewish descent, and although she and her family are all Catholic, she
claims not to be a regular churchgoer.[328] She maintains a close friendship
with Coro's last Jewish survivors, her cousins Thelma and Hermán
Henriquez.

All the descendants of Curaçao's Sephardim who still live in Coro
today are related to one another. The Caprileses married the Ricardos,
Mayerstons, and Lopez Fonsecas; the Lopez Fonsecas married the
Maduros and the Henriquez; the Henriquez married the Seniors and the
Baiz; the Seniors married the Alvares Correas and the De Limas; and all
of them married relatives with the same last names and continue to call
each other *primos* – cousins – no matter how far removed the relationship may be. Although it may seem unusual to outsiders, it is perfectly
normal for most of these descendants to know exactly whose great-

---

* Unlike the Ashkenazim, Sephardic Jews often name their children after living relatives.

grandmother was a sister to whose great-grandfather, more than a century after the original players were born.

CORIANOS AND THEIR JEWISH NEIGHBORS

On the day that I arrived in Coro with my friend Diane, we had paid in cash to fly in a frighteningly small aircraft from Curaçao over the sandy dunes on the northern edge of Coro into the airport that sat right across from our hotel. Even though I had never met or spoken to Thelma and Hermán Henriquez before that day, there they were, waiting for us at customs together with Professor Blanca de Lima who had offered to facilitate our access to the private and municipal archival resources in town. And so it was to be throughout our trip. We would be in a museum, and Hermán would pop up, asking us if we were being shown everything in a satisfactory manner. We would be going to the cemetery with Blanca,

Jewish cemetery of Coro, Venezuela

and there were Thelma and Manche, as Hermán is called, to give us their personal insights about the many relatives buried in this sacred spot. We would be photographing manuscripts at the Senior Archives, and there was Thelma, reminding the caretaker to put toilet paper and soap in the restrooms.

Everybody knew them. And everybody showed them great respect. They were the last of the once despised Sephardim of Coro, but they were no longer a source of hate for the population of Coro. "*Hola, Don Manche. Buenas tardes, Doña Thelma* ..." Everybody was very courteous.

"Don't you believe it is all gone," says Thelma, sharp as a tack, in spite of her eighty years. She is referring to the anti-Semitism that sent some of her Lopez Fonseca and Curiel forefathers running from Coro in 1855. Oh, sure, she has many good friends and acquaintances in town, but she remembers some unpleasant episodes that happened not too long ago. In the 1960s, when at most ten to twenty Jews still lived in Coro, Thelma and Hermán's mother, Eliana Lopez Fonseca de Henriquez who was already up in age at the time, used to sit on her porch in the afternoons, hoping for a cool breeze to end the sticky heat of the day. Every afternoon a well-known and respected gentleman who lived in the neighborhood would walk by and tip his hat to Mrs. Henriquez. She, of course, would return the greeting and would look forward to the gentleman's old-fashioned salute each day. One day Mrs. Henriquez mentioned to one of her Catholic acquaintances how politely her neighbor always acknowledged her on his afternoon walks, to which her friend replied: "That is because he does not know that you are Jewish." Thelma winces when she tells the story, annoyed after all these years to think that her mother had to put up with such insolence.

She herself is made of tougher material. Not too long ago she too experienced a similarly obnoxious comment. She had been in church at the christening of a friend's grandchild, when someone came up to her and asked what business she had being in a Catholic church. Irritated at having to actually respond, she pointed at the crucifix hanging over the altar and said, "If Jesus Christ who was a Jew can be here, I can be here too."

And yet, Coro is charming. People seem friendly and the Catholic descendants of the Sephardim are fully integrated into this small society.

In retrospect, the people of Coro may even remember the Sephardim of the nineteenth century somewhat fondly with the passage of time. Some believe that they had already begun to like their Sephardic neighbors better when the Jewish focus of Coro's Sephardim began to fade in the second half of the nineteenth century. Sephardic and Catholic Corianos increasingly mingled in business and social settings, and, in addition to their participation in Coro's cultural life, the Sephardim and their descendants, quite importantly, became involved in Venezuelan politics as well.

The cultural contributions of the Sephardim in Coro are hard to ignore. The Corianos fell in love with the poems of Elias David Curiel, one of which became the text for the regional hymn of the state of Falcón. They eagerly read the literary contributions of Elias's brother José David Curiel, and the three Lopez Fonseca brothers, Salomón, David, and Isaac. And they were thrilled with the creation of two literary societies, Sociedad Alegría and Sociedad Armonía in 1890, whose founding members included such prominent Jews as Jacob Mayerston, Julio Capriles, R. A. Correa, David Ricardo, and, of course, several of the aforementioned Coriano writers of the Jewish faith. In 1891, when the Sociedad Armonía inaugurated its new theatre, one of the major donors towards the construction of this venue was Julio Capriles.[329] How could one not interact with such benefactors who brought the finer things of life to Coro? And how could the people of Coro not appreciate the attentive services of the Curiels who owned the pharmacies in town, and José David Curiel and Pola de Lima who were Coro's beloved teachers? And where would they be without the excellent care they received from such dentists as Dr. Ricardo, Dr. Lopez Henriquez, and Dr. Maduro, and Coro's general practitioner, Dr. José Curiel Abenatar? All these individuals had become integral parts of the Coriano tapestry of the late nineteenth and early twentieth century.[330]

Many Sephardim were active in Coro's municipal council as well as in state government. And then there were those Sephardim who were good friends and supporters of Guzman Blanco and later of Cipriano Castro and Vicente Gómez, who all became presidents of Venezuela.

Isaac Capriles, son of Manasés Capriles Ricardo, was more than a good friend to President Joaquín Crespo. He was his son in law. Although Isaac had been trained as a medical doctor, he too became involved in the political scene. Aside from being Director of the Military Hospital of Caracas, he was General Director of the Venezuelan Postal Services, Inspector of the Community Hospitals of Caracas, and a member of the Venezuelan delegation in Washington in 1892 and 1893.[331] Three other sons of Cecilia and Manasés Capriles were also politically active. Raul Capriles served as a member of a Venezuelan delegation in Paris and held several other political posts. Mario Capriles was a deputy in the Venezuelan National Congress, and Abraham Capriles too was active in the Legislature. Several of these men moved away from Coro, gravitating towards Caracas, which, in addition to being the nation's capital, was quickly becoming a magnet for many members of the Curaçaoan Sephardic Diaspora and their descendants.[332]

As the twentieth century began, the small remnant of Coro's Sephardim was no longer looked upon only as astute and successful businessmen. They were now members of the state's elite society with important connections in high places. Their names were increasingly found in Venezuelan politics, where, for better or for worse, they demonstrated that their citizenship was first and foremost Venezuelan. The Jewish religion in Coro at the end of the nineteenth and in the early twentieth century had become an issue of ancestry more so than beliefs and practices, even to those who were still of the Jewish faith. Superficially it appeared that that the integration of the descendants of the nineteenth century Sephardic immigrants had been complete and successful. Yet, in spite of this blending of the cultures, the descendants of the once practicing Jews of Coro never forgot who their ancestors were, and neither did their Catholic neighbors.

CHAPTER 4

SANTO DOMINGO, DOMINICAN REPUBLIC

SETTLING IN UNSETTLED SANTO DOMINGO

The island of Hispaniola, discovered by Columbus in 1492, was Spain's first foothold in the Americas. The western third of the island was ceded to France in 1697, but the eastern part, Santo Domingo, continued to be controlled by Spain through most of the eighteenth century. As the Spanish empire expanded to include vast areas of the Central and South American mainland, Spain's ability to keep up with the needs of the colonizers in Santo Domingo was severely tested. The resulting scarcity of everyday consumer goods opened up many opportunities to enterprising traders and shipping agents in the region.[333] In spite of Spain's monopolistic trade practices that prohibited direct trade with foreign colonies, ships from these colonies arrived in Santo Domingo on a fairly regular basis. Between 1754 and 1775 almost twenty percent of these ships anchoring in Santo Domingo were from the islands of St. Eustatius and Curaçao.[334] This clear violation of Spain's trade prohibitions reflected the lax attitude by the governing officials in Santo Domingo in enforcing the trade restrictions imposed by the mother country.

Trading and shipping in the Caribbean was a Sephardic specialty in the eighteenth and nineteenth century, and the rulers of Santo Domingo realized that they had to accommodate this fact in order to obtain such necessities as flour, oil, wine, salted cod, cheese and even shoes on a reg-

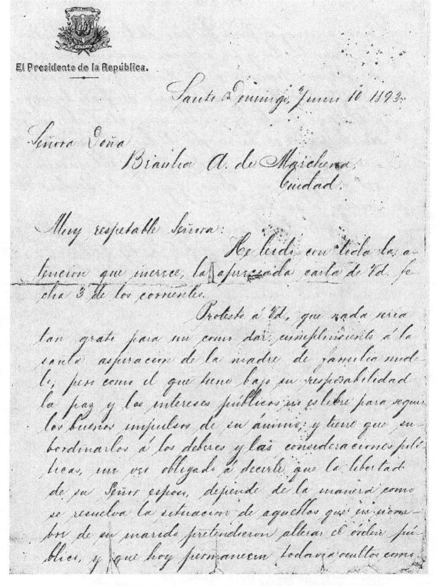

Letter from Ulises Heureaux, president of the Dominican Republic,
to Braula de Marchena, wife of Eugenio Generoso de Marchena
Santo Domingo, June 10, 1893

ular basis. As a consequence, the island's governors were fairly lax about Spain's prohibitions, and Jews were allowed to do business in the colonial city of Santo Domingo in the eighteenth century. However, other contact was absolutely not tolerated. The Roman Catholic Church was adamant about preventing any and all socialization between visiting Jews and the Catholic population. Therefore, when Jewish merchants were in town, they had to reside in convents or other religious institutions, watched by guards who had the job of preventing the entry of non-merchant visitors into the convent cells. The guards also had to accompany the visiting merchants each time they left the convents to walk around town. These very unpleasant and harsh limitations on their freedom of movement did not seem to be as discouraging as one might think, and the Jews would often spend months in the city.[335]

Occasionally the Church let its power be felt in no uncertain terms. In April of 1785, a young David Gómez Cáceres, a Sephardic Jew from Curaçao, had the audacity to arrive in Santo Domingo to see a young lady with whom he had "*relaciones amorosas.*" He was captured and thrown in jail. The affair was even more scandalous in view of the fact that the object of David's affection belonged to one of the most distinguished families of the city. The lovelorn Curaçaoan Jew spent three months imprisoned in the convent of San Francisco and all his worldly goods were confiscated. David was a minor, which accounts for his relatively mild punishment. His incarceration was meant to serve as an example and warning to other Jews who might have the inclination to visit Santo Domingo for any reason other than business. Social contact with that "*pérfida nación*" was definitely not allowed by the Catholic Church, no matter what benefits the Dominicans derived from their commercial contacts with the Jewish merchants.[336]

As the eighteenth century drew to an end, rebellions in French Saint Domingue became a source of major concern to the French and Spanish colonizers on Hispaniola. In 1789, the revolutionary idea of *liberté, égalité et fraternité* had been quite popular in France, but this slogan clearly did not extend to France's colonies. Haiti was clamoring for its *liberté* on the western side the island, and the French were intent on stopping the rebels from achieving this goal. As part of their efforts to position themselves strategically and prevent the loss of Saint Domingue, France attacked the eastern part of the island, and in 1795, Spain was forced to cede the colony of Santo Domingo to the French.

Within a few years after the French occupied the Spanish part of the island, the Real Audiencia and a large number of Roman Catholic clergy left Santo Domingo for Cuba. While the threat of religious persecution in Santo Domingo diminished during this French occupation,[337] the subsequent political and economic instability became a significant deterrent to immigrants of any race or creed. Indeed, by 1809, the population of what was once the Spanish part of the island had dwindled to less than half of what it was in 1789.[338] For more than twenty-five years, France, Spain, and Haiti fought to gain control over Santo Domingo, ruining the country in the process. Spain's last settlement, from 1809 to 1821 is generally referred to as the *España Boba* period – Foolish Spain period – reflecting the ineffective way the colony was ruled during those twelve years. By the 1820s the Dominican economy was in shambles.[339]

It was during these oppressive times that revolutionary thoughts and liberal ideas took hold in this country that was to become the Dominican Republic. On November 30, 1821, a lawyer by the name of José Nuñez de Cáceres (possibly of Jewish descent) led an uprising, declaring the independent state of Spanish Haiti. The Spanish, of course, resisted as best they could, and at some point during the struggle, Nuñez de Cáceres sent a request to President Jean Pierre Boyer of Haiti for assistance in their mutual defense against the colonial powers. The Haitian army appeared in the city of Santo Domingo in February of 1822, and Haiti remained in control of the eastern part of the island for almost twenty-two years.[340]

The first Jews from Curaçao are known to have arrived during this relatively long period of Haitian governance, although it is possible that some came to Santo Domingo even earlier. It is believed that a Sephardic Jew from Curaçao, Mordechai de Marchena, was an active participant in Nuñez de Cáceres's independence movement of 1821.[341] Mordechai de Marchena was a young man during the 1821 uprising in Santo Domingo, and he returned to Curaçao within the next decade and a half, where he married Jael Curiel in 1836 and remained for the rest of his life. He is the forefather of the Jewish De Marchenas still living in Curaçao in the twenty-first century.[342]

As these early Sephardim of the 1820s and 1830s were getting settled, the political situation in Santo Domingo heated up once more. Revolution was in the air. In 1838 the secret society La Trinitaria was formed with the objective to create an independent Santo Domingo on the eastern part of the island. On the South American mainland and in neighboring Haiti, which at this point represented the occupying force of the eastern part of Hispaniola, the people had freed themselves from colonial powers. The members of La Trinitaria were intent on achieving such freedom for all Dominicans as well. The Jews and their descendants embraced the cause of liberty, both through direct participation as well as financially. As a result they were held in high regard by the early leaders of the new nation.[343]

When independence was declared on February 27 of 1844, Juan Pablo Duarte, who had been a key player in the independence movement, happened to be in exile in Curaçao, where he had many Jewish and non-Jewish friends. He quickly returned to Santo Domingo on a ship owned by one of the leaders of Santo Domingo's Jewish community. In spite of Duarte's much-admired leadership in La Trinitaria and his participation in the rebellions against the Haitians in 1843, he was eventually exiled to Venezuela, where he died in poverty. In the late 1840s and 1850s, a struggle for the presidency ensued between two other leaders of the independence movement, General Pedro Santana and Buenaventura Báez.[344]

From these early days and continuing through the twentieth century, the Dominican Jews and their descendants played important roles in the country's politics.

THE DE MARCHENAS OF SANTO DOMINGO

In 1835 three brothers arrived in Santo Domingo from Curaçao. They were Rafael, Benjamin, and Isaac de Marchena. Rafael and Benjamin were in their twenties and single, while Isaac was 41 years old and married.[345] It is most likely that Isaac had merely accompanied his

Rafael de Marchena
1813–1890

younger brothers to assist them in setting up their business in this new land, and that his stay was intended to be of a temporary nature.[346] Indeed, once Rafael and Benjamin were more or less settled, Isaac returned to his wife and children in Curaçao.

The two brothers could just as easily have chosen to migrate to Coro, but, possibly because of their older brother Mordechai's participation in the Dominican uprising of 1821, they may have had a romantic notion about Santo Domingo and chose to try their luck there instead. They arrived with sufficient funds to purchase haciendas and open retail establishments in their new place of residence. Their stores, like those of Sephardic immigrants in other Caribbean locations, offered a wide variety of imported merchandise for sale, and it would appear that their retail business was a success. Soon they were also exporting some products from their haciendas.[347]

Rafael and Benjamin came from a large family. Their parents were Abraham and Esther de Marchena whose ten children represented the seventh generation of the De Marchena family in Curaçao. The first De Marchena had arrived on the island in 1659 with the first large influx of Sephardic Jews from Holland.[348] Throughout the years that had elapsed since those early beginnings, members of this family had been actively involved in Curaçao's Jewish affairs. They had been elected to the Mikvé Israel board and had donated many religious artifacts to the synagogue, including two Torah scrolls, offered to the community between 1764 and 1815. When the synagogue building which is currently in use was built in the early 1730s, various De Marchenas paid for the purchase of the

rabbi's bench and the bench on which the board members sat in the synagogue – the banca. Four silver lamps that to this day adorn the banca
were donated by a member of the De Marchena family as well, as was
one of the imposing chandeliers that still hang in the Mikvé Israel
sanctuary.[349]

Rafael and Benjamin's father, Abraham de Marchena, was a wealthy
and powerful member of the Jewish community.[350] But he was also a man
of strong opinions. In 1819, when the Curaçaoan Jewish community
became divided about the Hazan Piza's leadership, Abraham de
Marchena sided squarely with the separatists. Later that year, when he
was billed for penalties he owed to the Mikvé Israel synagogue, he
responded indignantly:

> Curaçao November 11, 1819
> Sir!
> In answer to your letter of the 5th instant requesting
> payment or a guarantee to the holy synagogue to which
> I owe penalties associated with [prior] [non]payments, as
> you imply several times, my circumstances unfortunate-
> ly do not permit me to do so for now. And second, I con-
> sequently consider it an affront [on your part] to demand
> this and [ask you] not to humiliate me by soliciting it;
> I am
> One of the Separatists,
> Abm. De Marchena [351]

Notably, the circumstances that prevented De Marchena from paying
up his debts to the synagogue were possibly not financial in nature. In
1814 he had given his daughter Esther a dowry of 2,500 pesos when she
married Abraham Haim Naar a few weeks after her mother passed
away,[352] and the dowry provided to his youngest daughter Leah at the
time of her marriage to Benjamin Jesurun amounted to an even greater
sum of 6,000 pesos in 1836.[353] Conceivably 1819 could have been a bad
year financially for De Marchena, but the tone of the letter and the way
he identified himself as "one of the separatists" almost suggests that he

was refusing to pay because he no longer considered himself a member of Mikvé Israel.

Abraham and Esther de Marchena had married on October 14, 1795, and their ten children were born at intervals of a year or two between 1796 and 1814. About a week after giving birth to her tenth child, Gabriel, in 1814, Esther died, leaving behind six children under the age of ten. At the time, Rafael was one and Benjamin was three years old.[354] Their father Abraham de Marchena was left with the full responsibility to care and educate these younger children.

It is possible that their father's temporary separation and alienation from the Mikvé Israel community caused some interruption in the religious education of De Marchena's younger sons. In addition, because of their mother's premature death and the resulting void in their home, the sons who migrated to Santo Domingo may have been less immersed in Jewish life and observances than their older siblings, parents, and grandparents had been. Therefore, even though they came from an actively Jewish background, they may have been less rooted in Jewish tradition than their ancestry might imply, facilitating their subsequent integration into Dominican society. There is no way to truly prove this, however, since multiple factors affect the decision to marry outside the faith. Also, as is discussed later, offspring of other separatists who left Curaçao around the same time did not necessarily intermarry when they arrived in the host countries that eventually became their homes, even though their descendants eventually may have done so. It is therefore difficult to point the finger at the religious and familial opheavals in the lives of Abraham de Marchena's children to explain the subsequent integration of some of his children into Santo Domingo's Catholic environment.

For Rafael, religion was not a hindrance in his social relations. Within some years after his arrival in Santo Domingo, he met and fell in love with Justa Sanchez Carrera.* Justa was the daughter of a Spaniard from the Canary Islands, who had most likely arrived in Santo Domingo during the Spanish efforts to attract more white colonists to the island dur-

---

* Sanchez is spelled Sanches in some of the archival documents, but the current usage by the Dominican De Marchenas was maintained.

ing the last decades of the eighteenth century.[355] Justa's father, Alejo Sanchez, was originally from Santa Cruz de Tenerife and had migrated to Santo Domingo with his widowed brother and this brother's only son. Notably, this cousin of Justa's became a priest in Santo Domingo, and it may be fair to assume that the family's Catholicism was an important aspect of the Sanchez's lives.[356]

Rafael and Justa proceeded to have four children in rapid succession. Emilia and Abraham Rafael were both born in 1843, Eugenio followed in 1845, and Julia in 1846.[357] It was not until November 9, 1848, however, that Justa and Rafael were officially married.[358] As was customary in the Dominican Republic, they first posted a *promesa de matrimonio* – a marriage promise – in February of 1848 and were wed later that year at a private home in Santo Domingo. The fact that the marriage did not take place in a church is indicative that Rafael de Marchena did not convert in order to marry Justa. At the time of their marriage, Rafael formally recognized the four children as being his legitimate children, and this official declaration was appended to the marriage registration in the government documents.[359] It is not clear if Rafael and Justa's delay in marrying was due to their hesitancy about their religious differences, but once they made the decision to do so, they were together for forty-two years, until Rafael predeceased his wife. The union produced a total of eight children who survived to adulthood. (see Appendix A-4)

Cándida Amelia Cohen de Marchena, Rafael's granddaughter, writes that her great-grandfather "was of the Hebrew faith, but my grandfather Rafael married my grandmother according to civil law, and did not oppose the Catholic baptism of all his daughters."[360] This confirms the information provided by today's descendants of this couple that the sons of this nineteenth century union were raised as Jews, while the daughters abided by their mother's faith.[361]

Apparently this type of compromise was sometimes agreed upon in mixed marriages of the time. Why the family would choose to bring up the sons and daughters in different religions is not very clear. One can speculate that the parents wanted their sons to be more like their father and their daughters more like their mother. Or conceivably they may have thought that a continued affiliation with the Jewish religion for the sons would enhance their business opportunities later in life, an advantage the daughters would not have any use for, since, generally, they were not expected to work for a living. This differentiation has been seen in other families where the sons of Catholic fathers were raised Catholic, while the daughters were raised in the mothers' Protestant faith. Nevertheless, such differential treatment of the religious upbringing of sons and daughters of mixed marriages was not found elsewhere in this study among offspring of Sephardic exogamous unions. In that respect Rafael and Justa de Marchena were somewhat unique.

According to orthodox interpretation of Jewish law, a person is only considered Jewish if his or her mother is Jewish or if he or she converts to Judaism. Therefore Rafael and Justa's sons were not technically Jewish, even though their father may have considered them as such. In essence, therefore, all the children of this family unit were lost to Judaism. A factor which made it even less likely that the sons were raised as Jews was that Santo Domingo never had an organized Jewish community in the nineteenth century. Religious services, if any, were held irregularly at private homes, and Jewish education for the children of the Sephardic immigrants born in Santo Domingo must be assumed to have been negligible. Therefore these sons of mixed marriages would have had little or no exposure to Jewish rites when they were growing up, with the exception perhaps of an occasional prayer service at a private home on the High Holidays.

As was to be expected, Rafael and Justa de Marchena's sons who married all chose Catholic women to be their spouses.[362] Yet some of them continued to identify themselves as Jews through most of their lives. Eugenio de Marchena, Rafael's second born son, had married Adelaida Damirón Burgos in Santo Domingo. When he died at the relatively young age of fifty, his Catholic wife and children did not consider it appropriate to adorn his grave with any Christian markings. And so his tombstone in Santo Domingo stands devoid of such decorations in a cemetery full of graves with crosses, an indication that this son of a Jewish father and a Catholic mother did not consider himself a Roman Catholic.

The life of Eugenio's brother, Rafael's eldest son, Abraham Rafael de

Marchena, took a very different turn. As a young adult Abraham moved to Haiti, where he married the daughter of a French diplomat. Her name was Isaure Brun.* This union produced two sons, Albert and Ernest, both born in Jacmel, Haiti. When the children were quite young, Abraham and Isaure de Marchena moved with their family to France. In contrast to the open acknowledgement of their Jewish roots by the De Marchenas of Santo Domingo, Abraham's Jewish ancestry was not an issue that was discussed among the family members of the De Marchenas who moved to France. His great-granddaughter, Ernest de Marchena's granddaughter, wrote the following from Paris:

> I never heard that we had Jewish people in our ancestry (mind you, I have nothing against the Jews and have many excellent friends among them …). We usually refer to a Franciscan father who was Queen Isabelle's confessor – a certain Father Juan Peres de Marchena at the monastery la Rabida, Spain and being a great friend of Christopher Columbus, he obtained from her the three "caravelles" boats, thanks to which he discovered America. His brother is supposed to be our direct ancestor and to have taken part in the 2nd expedition to America. We have a family tree which goes back to the 14th century.[363]

The story of Queen Isabelle's confessor, De Marchena, is known to the De Marchenas of Curaçao, but this letter from Mme. Roux de Bézieux showed that she had no idea that subsequent branches of De Marchenas, including her own ancestors, had felt free to practice the Jewish religion for many centuries after their expulsion from Spain, returning to their roots when they lived in Holland and later in Curaçao.

---

* Cándida Amelia de Marchena writes that Isaure Brun's father was the French consul in Port au Prince, while the French descendants of Abraham and Isaure de Marchena believed that Isaure Brun's father was the Dutch consul in Haiti and that the couple got married in Jacmel and not in Port au Prince.

Further correspondence with Michel Hadengue, a grandson of Abraham's son Albert, revealed the interesting fact that Abraham arrived in France calling himself Abraham Raphael de Marchena, subsequently shortened to A.R. de Marchena, and eventually dropping the Abraham altogether in favor of a newly-spelled Raphaël. Not only did he find it prudent to drop his very Jewish name, but he also adopted the noble title of Marquis. His great-grandson speculates that he very much wanted to ensure that his family would be included in the best society possible in France. As a result, he did everything in his power to facilitate the transition from his Caribbean Sephardic roots to a more prestigious French Catholic circle that would benefit his family's prospects in his new place of residence. Indeed, he did such a great job, that the knowledge of their Jewish heritage was totally obliterated among the French De Marchenas who came after Ernest and Albert.[364]

Abraham R. de Marchena's granddaughter, Ernest's daughter, Mrs. Marguérite Hoppenot, née de Marchena, fully assimilated into French society. She became quite active in the French Catholic movement and was the founder of Mouvement d'Action Catholique Sève in France and author of several books on spiritual topics.

It must have been relatively easy for the De Marchenas to follow through with their new identities in France. First, even though Rafael's sons, including Abraham, were supposedly brought up as Jews in the Catholic environment of Santo Domingo, there is no way to know what this encompassed, and it is likely that Abraham knew little about the Jewish religion. And secondly, Abraham's fluency in many languages facilitated the invention of a socially more desirable past.

Because of Abraham's lack of a solid Jewish background and his marriage to the Catholic Isaure, it may be assumed that Ernest and Albert de Marchena had little or no exposure to Judaism prior to their arrival in France. If they even knew about their father's Jewish ancestry, it would not have been from any religious practices that they might have observed at home.

While Abraham's descendants attribute his multilingual skills to his purportedly having studied at Oxford, England, these talents were not uncommon for someone of his background in the Caribbean region of the nineteenth century. His acquired nobility, which the "de" in the name De Marchena made even more plausible, coupled with his language skills, secured his access to French society.

Abraham's need to fabricate a background that would fit the life he desired in Paris may be better understood if one remembers that this was, after all, the France of Alfred Dreyfus that these De Marchenas had moved to. Being of Jewish stock was not such a favorable attribute in the anti-Semitic atmosphere that existed in that country in the late nineteenth century. Although his parents considered him Jewish, Abraham must have felt that since he was not Jewish according to Jewish law, it was totally unnecessary to disclose his religious ancestry. The acquisition of a noble title might have been a stretch of the imagination, but it did achieve its purpose. The family mingled among the elite and his sons were both quite successful in their new country of residence.

The discussion of this French interlude presents a marked contrast between the ties to Judaism maintained by Rafael's descendants who remained in the Dominican Republic versus the lack of such ties among his descendants who emigrated to France. It would appear that the warm welcome extended to the arriving Sephardim by the people and leaders of the Dominican Republic was key to the subsequent strong self-identity observed among the Catholic descendants of the Jews in Santo Domingo. On the other hand, the anti-Semitism that existed in France made it more prudent for the French branch to ignore their religious and cultural roots. Surviving in the best possible way was the key concern of the De Marchenas. While their individual approaches and the sociopolitical environments of the host countries in which they chose to live might have differed, they adapted to their new realities with creativity, albeit with little emphasis on the continuity of their religious pasts.

The positive attitude towards the nineteenth century Jewish settlers in Santo Domingo was reflected early on in a letter written in 1846 by President Santana in response to a complaint against some Jewish merchants in La Vega. He wrote unequivocally:

> It is stated in the petition that four or five Jews are doing considerable harm to the people because they purchase

ounces of gold and the country's produce at exorbitant prices, etc. These words alone indicate clearly that it is not the populace who is complaining, for there is no farmer to whom it would occur to complain that a Jew gives him a hundred pesos for a *quintal* of tobacco for which a Dominican would pay him only fifty, therefore, far from [resulting] in harm to the people, it is instead a manifest benefit that will continue to increase [...].

The president's lengthy letter then proceeded to admonish the anonymous complaining gentlemen by pointing out that:

Those four Jews whom they persecute there, and others who reside here, have been the first to hand over their funds without delay to defray the war expenses, at the same time when some Dominicans were not only doing nothing, not even making loans, but were through their bad example discouraging the good patriots who showed themselves determined to defend the freedom of the Republic.[365]

This forthright official appreciation of the Jews living on Dominican soil continued throughout the ensuing century and a half and was a very important variable in the integration of the immigrant Sephardic Jew in Dominican culture.

Even before independence, the Dominicans in colonial Santo Domingo had a fairly relaxed attitude towards the Jews with whom they traded, largely ignoring the sanctions imposed by Spain and the Catholic Church. The influence of the Church diminished yet further when members of the clergy left Santo Domingo at the end of the eighteenth century after the French conquest and again during the subsequent Haitian take-over in 1822. Hence the positive feelings extended towards the Jews apparent in the new republic were not a sudden phenomenon but something that had slowly developed over the decades leading to the country's independence in 1844.

In this atmosphere of acceptance, it is likely that Rafael and Benjamin de Marchena attended Jewish prayer services at the home of Jamaica-born Abraham Cohen, who was the most prominent Jew in the city of Santo Domingo when the brothers arrived in 1835. Here, to the best of their ability, members of the Jewish community conducted religious services on the Jewish holidays.[366] Archival sources consulted do not mention that weekly Shabbat services were held in the nineteenth century. Neither is there any mention of *kashrut* – observance of dietary laws. It appears that there were no ritual slaughterers among the Jews who made their homes in Santo Domingo, nor did the nineteenth century Dominican Jews have access to a local ritual circumciser. Instead they relied on traveling circumcisers from the surrounding islands whenever a male child was born. As a consequence, circumcisions rarely took place on the specified eighth day after birth, and sometimes not at all.[367]

While the Jews were unable to find or form a religious center to serve their spiritual needs in Santo Domingo, they became quite active in the Masonic movement. In April 1847, Benjamin de Marchena cosigned a letter from the Freemasons of Santo Domingo to the Grand Commandeur of the French lodges, thanking him for having appealed to the Prussian monarch to compel Prussian lodges to accept German-Jewish applicants as members.[368] Rafael too was a dedicated Freemason and was a member of the same lodge to which his brother Benjamin belonged.

Although Rafael de Marchena considered Santo Domingo to be his new home, the political realities of the country caused him to seek refuge in other parts of the Caribbean more than once. The fact that he returned to the Dominican capital after each of these absences makes it quite clear that this was where his heart was. In the 1850s he lived in Puerto Rico during yet another war between the Dominican Republic and Haiti which had broken out in 1849. His descendants are not sure why he went there, but they speculate that the war and the unfavorable economic conditions that existed in the Dominican Republic during this upheaval were enough of an incentive for him to make this move with his wife and children. Several of Rafael's younger children were born during this stay in Puerto Rico, and it appears that he was well established on that island with a store and three slaves to his name.[369]

In Puerto Rico the De Marchena family met the widower Juan
Agustín Cohen* who later married Rafael's daughter Emilia. Like Rafael
de Marchena, Juan Agustín was also a Freemason, and the two men soon
became very friendly. At this time, Emilia de Marchena was still quite
young, but when she was almost eighteen, her father took the family
back to Santo Domingo, and Juan Agustín Cohen joined them. Rafael
de Marchena's descendants believe that they left Puerto Rico for the
Dominican Republic in 1860 primarily because Freemasonry was not
permitted in Puerto Rico, which was then still a Spanish colony.[370]
Whether this is true or not, Rafael de Marchena's grandchildren and
great-grandchildren in the Dominican Republic considered Freemasonry
to be a very important aspect of this ancestor's life.

Soon after the family came back to Santo Domingo, Emilia married
her father's widowed friend, Mr. Cohen. At the same time, Rafael
became more actively involved in Dominican politics. President Pedro
Santana was at that time trying to solve the young nation's problems by
seeking Spain's help in his endeavors. Rafael de Marchena disagreed
with this approach to such an extent that it became politically unsafe for
him to remain in Santo Domingo. Shortly after the re-annexation of the
Dominican Republic by Spain became a reality, he and his family took
refuge in Curaçao.[371]

The return of the Spanish to Santo Domingo was a disastrous event.
In 1863 the opposing parties in the Dominican Republic rose up against
Santana in an attempt to extricate the country yet again from Spain's
clutches. This War of Restoration concluded with Spain's permanent
withdrawal from Dominican shores in 1865.[372] Rafael de Marchena and
his family spent some of this period of political upheaval waiting in
Curaçao for the situation in Santo Domingo to turn around. At some
point during the War of Restoration, Rafael was back on Dominican soil,
however, and government records in Santo Domingo indicate that in
1864 he provided the Dominican government with "war materials and
gun powder."[373] Presumably this merchandise was smuggled into the

* Cohen's father had been Jewish, but his mother was not.

Dominican Republic from Curaçao to be used in the fight against Pedro Santana and Spain.

Rafael's great-great-grandson, Enrique de Marchena y de Marchena, was in the midst of writing a complete history of the De Marchena family in Santo Domingo at the time of his untimely demise in 2003. In his unpublished work in progress, he explains that it is likely that Rafael de Marchena smuggled the war materials into the country through what the family referred to as *"el tunel de los Marchena"* – the tunnel of the Marchenas. He recalled that during his youth he used to hear stories about the existence of such a tunnel from his elders and that he always found them amusing, but never gave them much credence. As an adult, he was very surprised to learn that when the Plaza de España was restored (no date is given), a large and spacious tunnel was found, which was believed to have been constructed during colonial times and which reached from this centrally located plaza to the river Ozama. With this discovery, the stories seemed to be more securely based on fact, although it was not positively determined that the contraband brought in by Rafael de Marchena actually traveled this route.[374]

Contact with the Jewish relatives in Curaçao was maintained for several generations. Not only did the island serve as political refuge for many of the Sephardic migrants in various parts of the Caribbean, but the Dominican Sephardim and their descendants continued to visit family and friends in Curaçao and vice versa for several generations.

Eugenio de Marchena, who was the eldest of Rafael's sons living in Santo Domingo, sent all his daughters to board at the "Welgelegen" school in Curaçao in the 1880s. This was a fashionable thing to do in the second half of the nineteenth century. Daughters of many wealthy or politically connected Latin Americans would often spend a few years in boarding schools on the Dutch island. Eugenio de Marchena had been a teenager in Curaçao during the years that his father Rafael sought refuge in his place of birth in the 1860s. Not only had he lived there for a while in his youth, but, by the 1880s, he was a Dominican who was both wealthy and politically well connected. A successful businessman in Santo Domingo, he was listed fourth among the top corporate taxpayers in that city in 1881. Other Jewish names included on this list of the eight most highly taxed firms were those of José María Leyba, Namías y Compañía, and Jacobo de Marchena (Eugenio's first cousin and son of Benjamin and Clara de Marchena). Based on his very Christian given name, Leyba was most likely of Jewish descent, but no longer Jewish.[375]

Like his father, Eugenio de Marchena was a dedicated Freemason. He achieved the rank of 33rd degree Mason and was Sovereign Grand Commander of his lodge. He was the co-founder of a lodge called "Logia La Fé," and was active in many philanthropic organizations. In addition to these fraternal activities, Eugenio de Marchena was the honorary consul of Portugal in the Dominican Republic.[376] In the last decades of the nineteenth century, he was a man of considerable importance in Santo Domingo. He died at the relatively young age of fifty in 1895 and was buried in the old Catholic cemetery on the Avenida de la Independencia in Santo Domingo. In later years his descendants moved his remains to a newer cemetery that was believed to provide better care and maintenance of its grounds.

It is interesting to note the early involvement of Rafael de Marchena and his descendants in the politics of their host country. It appeared to be a family trait. Rafael's nephew, Eugenio Generoso de Marchena, whose middle name distinguished him from Rafael's son Eugenio, was even more dedicated to Dominican politics than his uncle and cousin. He was the son of Gerardo de Marchena, Rafael's half brother, who had been born out of wedlock in Curaçao to Abraham de Marchena in 1818 after his wife's demise. Rafael's younger brother, Gabriel, and this even younger Gerardo both migrated to Santo Domingo some years after Rafael and Benjamin did. In spite of his illegitimacy, Gerardo was openly recognized by his father – a fairly common practice among Curaçao's Sephardim of the time.[377] He was raised in his mother's Catholic religion, and, upon arrival in Santo Domingo, he married Ana Joaquina Peláez in 1841. They had numerous children, including Eugenio Generoso de Marchena, who was born in 1842.[378] (see Appendix A-5)

In the 1880s, this grandson of Curaçao's Abraham de Marchena was instrumental in obtaining a major European loan for the Dominican Republic. The initial 770,000-pound sterling loan was issued by the Westendorp banking firm of Amsterdam in 1888, "undoubtedly supported by [Eugenio Generoso de Marchena's] Curaçao and Dutch connections."[379] This financial institution lent the Dominican Republic an additional 900,000 pounds sterling in 1890 for the construction of the Puerto Plata-Santiago railroad line. The loans were the cause of much finger pointing concerning their misappropriation. When shortly after the second loan the Westendorp banking firm collapsed, the loan contracts were transferred to another firm. At that point the president of the Dominican Republic was the dictator General Ulises Heureaux, also known as Lilís by the population at large. Upon his urging, the Dominican government decided not to recognize the transfer of the loan contracts and a major financial debacle ensued. Finally, in 1893, new contracts were signed with a new firm, the San Domingo Improvement Company. Leading up to the execution of these contracts, Eugenio Generoso de Marchena had opposed the increased power of the Improvement Company, and his disagreements with Heureaux on this matter and other issues reached a climax when he ran against him as a presidential candidate of the Dominican Republic in 1892. From then on his political involvement took a more dangerous turn.

Heureaux won the election. He was a man known to achieve his goals through bribes and coercion and did not take dissent lightly. De Marchena felt that Heureaux's electoral triumph had been achieved though fraud and was not shy about publicizing this. His continued opposing opinions and actions were a constant thorn in the president's side. The final blow occurred when De Marchena, being an executive of the National Bank of Santo Domingo, ordered the bank to refuse all credit to Heureaux and to freeze all his accounts. Heureaux struck back immediately, and De Marchena was taken prisoner.[380]

He remained in prison for more than a year. Eugenio Generoso's wife must have written to President Heureaux requesting leniency on behalf of her husband, because in a handwritten letter, adorned with many official stamps and seals, the President responded to her on June 10, 1893:

> Most Respected Madam:
> I have read your appreciated letter, dated the 3rd of the
> current month, with all the attention it deserves.

> I declare to you that nothing would be more pleasing to
> me than to comply with the holy aspiration of the moth-
> er of a model family, but as the person who has the
> responsibility for peace and the public interest, who is
> not free to follow the good impulses of his soul, and who
> has to subordinate them to duties and political consider-
> ations, I am obliged to tell you that the freedom of your
> husband, depends on the manner in which the situation
> of those who in your husband's name pretended to alter
> the public order and who today remain hidden is
> resolved ... [381]

Unfortunately, the situation Heureaux refers to was not resolved. De
Marchena's cousin, Cándida Amelia, describes in her memoirs that fires
were stoked in enclosed areas of the fortress where Eugenio Generoso
was being held to make the prisoners choke in the smoky environment.
By means of such torture the jailkeepers were hoping to obtain confes-
sions about others who had participated in actions against Heureaux.
Finally, in December of 1893, Eugenio Generoso de Marchena was
ordered shot and killed.[382]

In the twentieth century, Rafael's great-grandson Enrique de
Marchena Dujarric continued the family's involvement in national politics. He became an active member of Rafael Trujillo's government and
served for several years as Minister of Education. He was also a representative of the Dominican Republic at the United Nations and was thrilled
to be there on the day when yet another Catholic descendant of Curaçao's Sephardim, Dr. Max Henriquez Ureña, in his role as U.N. ambassador of the Dominican Republic, welcomed Israel into the United
Nations in 1948.[383]

Curaçaoan Jews and their descendants did not adopt passive attitudes
in their new places of residence. Their strong involvement usually resulted in their complete integration into these new societies. Because of
their leadership positions, the Sephardic Jewish names of Curaçao
became recognizable and identifiable in many cities and towns of the
Dominican Republic. In Santo Domingo several streets and thorough-

fares are named for Curaçaoan Sephardim and their descendants, reflecting their contributions to multiple aspects of life in that capital city.

Not only in politics, but also in the Catholic Church did the name De Marchena appear in the Dominican Republic. One of Eugenio Generoso de Marchena's sisters, Enriqueta, had married General Lowenski Lamarche. Their son Florentino Armando Lamarche Marchena was born in 1866 and was ordained a priest in 1888.[384] He rose through the ecclesiastical hierarchy to obtain the title of Monseñor[385] and was also a member of the National Congress of the Dominican Republic. Monseñor Lamarche Marchena was known to lament that he always came in second. He said that he often almost won the first prize [in the lottery], and that he lost the vote to become the provisional president of the Republic in 1922 by one vote. Similarly, even though he headed the archdiocese of Santo Domingo, he was never named an archbishop.[386] Abraham de Marchena of Curaçao would have been surprised to know that one of his descendants had become a high-ranking official in the Catholic Church of the Dominican Republic less than a century after he had been worrying about Hazan Piza's performance in the Mikvé Israel synagogue.

Yet, for his children, grandchildren, and great-grandchildren in Santo Domingo, the fact that some of them were Jewish and others were Catholic was much less important than the pleasure and security of their family ties. With his brothers Benjamin, Gabriel, and Gerardo living close by with their families, Rafael and Justa and their children were surrounded by De Marchena relatives. Benjamin, who had married within the faith, had six children; Gabriel, who had married a Dominican woman of Jewish descent, had two children who survived to adulthood, and Gerardo had thirteen. The families were close and visited each other often. The numerous mixed marriages and multiple religions in these families did not appear to be a problem for any of the individuals involved.

When Rafael de Marchena passed away in 1890, his Catholic wife and children arranged for an authentic and traditional Sephardic funeral. His granddaughter, Cándida Amelia Cohen de Marchena recorded the ceremony in her memoirs as something extraordinary that she had not seen before and that she presumed others would find unusual as well.

> I remember that when my grandfather died the coffin
> was made of wood, without any lining or paint, and the
> priest, praying with a book in his hand walked around
> the coffin. This was the priest of the Jews, who they
> called the Rabbi – there were a lot of Jews here then, all
> decent folks.[387]

Whether or not a rabbi had been brought in to perform the rituals at this funeral, the circling of the coffin described by Cándida Amelia is a Sephardic orthodox custom, occasionally still practiced at Curaçaoan funerals. It is customary that prior to the actual burial, seven circuits be completed around the coffin of an adult male in the Casa de Rodeos, or House of Circuits, a structure built for that purpose on the cemetery grounds.[388] Of course, no such structure existed in the Catholic cemetery of Santo Domingo where Rafael de Marchena was buried. Nevertheless, it is quite interesting to note that fifty-five years after his arrival in that city and after a total religious assimilation of his family into the Catholic culture, his nearest and dearest respected his Jewish faith sufficiently to give him these final honors.

A century later, Rafael's great-great-grandson, Enrique de Marchena y de Marchena wrote: "All I can tell you is that the descendants of all the old Sephardic families [of Santo Domingo] are very proud of their heritage though they (we) are all catholics."[389]

LATER SEPHARDIC IMMIGRANTS:
SAMUEL CURIEL AND MOISÉS SALAS BAIZ

The De Marchenas were among the early Sephardic immigrants to Santo Domingo, but throughout the nineteenth century, other Curaçaoan Sephardim continued to immigrate to this rapidly growing capital of the Dominican Republic. During the last decades of the nineteenth century, some of the newcomers had already searched for better economic and

Tombstones of Hannah and Samuel Curiel, Santo Domingo, Dominican Republic

social conditions in other Caribbean locations, where, apparently, they had not found what they had been looking for. For these men and women who had lived in other Latin American countries before their arrival in the Dominican Republic, the friendliness of the population and the live-and-let-live attitude of the native Dominicans vis-à-vis newcomers seemed very appealing. And for the Sephardim who arrived in the sixties and seventies, the integration of the Jewish immigrants of the thirties and forties into Dominican society was proof that this easy-going approach extended to those who were not of the Catholic religion as well. With political and economic conditions seemingly improving after the War of Restoration, many decided to make Santo Domingo their final destination in their Caribbean search for economic advancement.

Samuel Curiel was born in Curaçao in 1837.[390] Like most young men of the nineteenth century who lived in the Dutch colony surrounded by the growing economies of the newly independent countries of the

Caribbean and the Caribbean periphery, he too wondered if he should
try his luck elsewhere. His father, Abraham Curiel, and uncle, Joseph
Curiel, had both been attracted to Coro during the early years of
Sephardic migration to the South American mainland and were both
living there in 1831.[391] Joseph Curiel and his descendants remained in
Coro, but Abraham Curiel moved back to Curaçao. Here he married
Ribca Hoheb in 1833,[392] and it is believed that he continued to live in
the island. The early anti-Semitic tone set by the less tolerant inhabitants of Coro may have played a part in Abraham Curiel's decision to
abandon Coro. Nevertheless, later correspondence with those who settled in Venezuela in the the late thirties and the forties made the country seem quite palatable, and it is understandable that Samuel would
reconsider his father's decision.

The Curiel family had been in Curaçao since the second half of the
seventeenth century. Throughout the ensuing century and a half, they
remained active in the Mikvé Israel community and appear to have been
religiously inclined.[393] In 1815, three weeks after Rabbi Da Fonseca's
death, Samuel Curiel's grandfather, Jacob de Abraham Curiel, was
appointed *Moré Din* – judge and lawgiver – for Curaçao's Jewish community, an indication that he was considered well versed in Jewish law.[394]
A few years later, however, he was one of Hazan Piza's chief detractors
and eventually had a falling out with the synagogue board about the
much-maligned cantor. Curiel considered Piza to be "hoarse and deaf,"[395]
and joined the separatists in 1819.[396] After these dissidents made peace
with the synagogue board in 1821, Jacob Curiel resumed his membership
of the Mikvé Israel community. His descendants continued to be steadfast supporters of Mikvé Israel, even after the Reform Temple Emanuel
was formed in 1864.[397]

In spite of the fact that Samuel Curiel's father's stay in Coro had been
temporary, Venezuela seemed attractive to Samuel. Like his friend and
contemporary Manasés Capriles Ricardo, he ventured to Puerto Cabello
and lived there for some length of time in the 1850s. It is possible that
he was there with his parents, as he was in his late teens during that period. Nevertheless, there is no mention of his father being present at any
of the events in Puerto Cabello at which Samuel appeared, and it is more

likely that Samuel was working in Venezuela on his own between ages sixteen and eighteen, and possibly for some years thereafter. In early 1853 he attended a Jewish wedding in Puerto Cabello between Rachel Lobo, daughter of the Sephardic Jew David Lobo, and Mr. Raphael Polly of Hamburg, Germany.[398] That same year he was among the Sephardim who gathered at Mr. Lobo's home for Yom Kippur services.[399] As late as April 1855 Samuel was still in Puerto Cabello and was present at the circumcision ceremony of Joseph Daniel Lobo.[400]

By the late 1850s and early 1860s, Curiel was back in Curaçao. In 1863 he had a seat assignment in the Mikvé Israel synagogue,[401] and later that year he was left in charge of Manuel Alvares Correa's business in Curaçao during the latter's absence from the island.[402] The following year, he was named to a committee to study the possibility of ritual reform in the synagogue.[403] Led by Rabbi Aron Mendes Chumaceiro and with the approval of the Consejo de Ancianos –the Board of Elders – this group recommended some significant changes in the orthodox ritual observed by the Mikvé Israel community. At age 27 Samuel Curiel was the youngest member of this committee – a clear indication that his opinion was valued by the Council of Elders which had nominated the members who constituted the advisory committee.

One of the unorthodox recommendations that came out of this process was a plan for "[t]he formation of a mixed choir provided that there was a special enclosure for each of the sexes. This choir was to be accompanied at all services, excepting those of Yom Kippur, by an organ to be played by a non-Jewish organist."[404] Samuel Curiel and Mordechay Capriles were in charge of organizing the choir and proceeded to get together a group of sixty persons, which made its debut during Hanukkah of 1864. Curiel was obviously an important participant in the affairs of Curaçao's Mikvé Israel community, and Rabbi Chumaceiro must have hoped that some of the innovative ideas offered by such young men as Samuel Curiel and Mordechay Capriles would stem the defections of Mikvé Israel members to the newly formed Temple Emanuel.

Samuel Curiel's marriage to Hannah Rodriguez Pereira in 1870 was recorded in the Mikvé Israel annals without a dowry, which suggests that, most likely, the wedding ceremony did not take place in Curaçao.[405]

In a search through the Mikvé Israel birth registers, Hannah Rodriguez Pereira's name was not found. However, this omission is not conclusive evidence that she was not born in Curaçao, where the Sephardic Pereiras had been living since the seventeenth century. While the birth and circumcision of the sons of Curaçao's Sephardim was faithfully recorded by the Jewish community, the birth of baby girls was only sporadically noted. It is quite possible that Hannah was born in Santo Domingo. It is known that members of the Pereira family were among the early migrants to the Danish Virgin Islands and the Dominican Republic. Furthermore, Hannah's mother was a Lopez Penha and many of this family migrated away from Curaçao as well (to St. Thomas, the Dominican Republic, Venezuela, and Colombia). In any case it is not known where Hannah Pereira and Samuel Curiel met or where they were wed. What is known is that by the early 1870s the couple had established themselves in the Dominican capital.

Samuel Curiel had two brothers and one sister. His eldest brother Jacob and his sister Rachel both remained in Curaçao, while his youngest brother, Isaac, migrated to Coro, Venezuela.[406] For Samuel and Hannah, Santo Domingo became their permanent home. The political situation in the Dominican Republic was still in flux in the 1870s, but it did not prevent Samuel Curiel from opening a hardware store in downtown Santo Domingo. The location of that store in a central part of the city is still referred to as "la esquina de Samuel Curiel" – Samuel Curiel's corner.[407] In addition to his retail activities, Curiel also ran a lottery that was widely played throughout the Caribbean. His relatives and friends in Curaçao were among those who participated in this lottery, and Samuel would receive regular instructions from the island regarding the disposition of the winnings of Curaçaoan gamblers who requested that their funds be deposited on a particular account, be used to cancel a debt or be sent to them.[408]

Curiel was a known entity to the Sephardic community of Curaçao. Not only had his family been on that island for four generations, but his activities on behalf of the Mikvé Israel community upon his return from Venezuela had not gone unnoticed. By the time he left for Santo Domingo he had the respect of his co-religionists and was considered an

enterprising and trustworthy young man. It is likely that many of the
items sold in his store were imported into the Dominican Republic via
his friends from Curaçao. And as is clear from his correspondence with
these Curaçaoans, Samuel Curiel often served as a go-between for his
Sephardic acquaintances back home.

Among those who held him in high regard were the Maduros who
lived on the Dutch island. In later years, Curiel and his sons brokered
wood and timber for S.E.L. Maduro & Sons. Correspondence between
Samuel Curiel & Co. and this Curaçaoan firm reveal that a strong personal relationship permeated their business relationship throughout the
years, extending to the following generation as well. In a letter to Samuel
Curiel & Co. dated March 15, 1901, the Maduros write to Curiel's sons:

> Dear Friends,
> A million thanks for the information pertaining to
> wood that we received by means of your kind letter of
> the 8th, which we have before us.
> We are doubly sorry that due to a recurrence of Doña
> Henny's illness, Don Samuel's trip had to be postponed;
> [a trip] which we believe to be highly necessary because
> of the bad eyesight of the latter. We sincerely hope that
> that lady's afflictions will subside soon, so that he may
> undertake the trip. ... [409]

Many business letters between Curaçaoan businessmen and their ex-
countrymen in the Caribbean have this dual aspect to them. In between
the business issues, the writers express interest and concern for the
goings-on of the family. These expressions of empathy were very important in maintaining the emotional bond between the Jews who migrated
from Curaçao in the nineteenth century and their friends and relatives
who remained on the island.

In the last few decades of the nineteenth century, between ten and fif-
teen Curaçaoan Sephardic families made their homes in Santo
Domingo. There was, however, no structured Jewish community for
Samuel Curiel to involve himself in as he had done in Curaçao in the

1860s. Yet he remained active in whatever might affect the few Jews in town.

In 1880 he was part of a group of men who formed the Sociedad Cosmopólita in the capital city. The officers of this new society were Jacobo de Lemos, president; Eugenio de Marchena, secretary; and Namias de Crasto, treasurer – all Jewish or of Jewish descent. The purpose of this group was to try to resolve the problem of cleaning up the non-Catholic part of the cemetery on the Avenida de la Independencia. This area had been used and was still sporadically used for Jewish and Protestant burials, and no entity was willing to take on the responsibility for its maintenance. It was unclear who owned this part of the cemetery, leading to the lack of upkeep that the new society was trying to address. At some point the British consulate had been in charge of the terrain, but, by the end of the nineteenth century, both Jewish and Protestant burials occurred so infrequently in this Catholic city's old cemetery that the tombstones and the area around them had started to fall into disrepair. Sometime between 1914 and 1918 this part of the cemetery, also called the Cosmopolitan Cemetery, was finally transferred to the municipality of Santo Domingo and the division between the two burial grounds – meaning Catholic and non-Catholic – was removed. With this act, the responsibility for the upkeep of the entire burial ground came to rest on the city of Santo Domingo. This formal transfer did not, however, prevent the deterioration of many of the Jewish graves.[410] Clearly Curiel belonged to the small group of Sephardim and descendants of Sephardim who were concerned about these issues. Several decades after the formation of the Sociedad Cosmopólita both he and his wife were buried in this cemetery. The tombstones continued to deteriorate throughout the twentieth century, and Samuel Curiel would not have been happy with their current state, had he been around to view them.

Like many other Jews in the Dominican Republic, Curiel was considered a member of Dominican elite society. In the second half of the nineteenth century, Santo Domingo had several social clubs which accepted members according their social standing. It was difficult for recent immigrants to be admitted to these clubs, and, as a consequence, some groups ended up creating their own community centers, such as for example the Syrian-Lebanese Center, and societies for those of Chinese and Italian descent. Many Sephardic Jewish immigrants, including Samuel Curiel and his son Samuel, were, however, accepted with open arms into the famous Club Unión, which was started in 1892. Indeed, one fifth of the founding members of this organization were of Jewish descent.[411]

Hannah Pereira and Samuel Curiel had at least six children.[412] Despite Curiel's involvement in the Jewish community while he lived in Curaçao, only one of his children, his daughter Rebeca, married within the faith. The Jewish community in Santo Domingo, was, of course, very small, and the market for Jewish marriage partners in the republic was therefore quite limited. Yet, the Curiels traveled to Curaçao frequently, where, at the time, there were a disproportionate number of single Jewish girls.[413] In November 1889, for example, Samuel's son, Abraham Curiel, who was then eighteen years old, arrived for a visit in Curaçao, where the Home Journal of the Young Men's Hebrew Association of Curaçao bade him a hearty welcome.[414] He returned to Santo Domingo a single man, and, after many years as a bachelor, he married a Dominican Catholic when he was thirty-eight.[415] Conceivably Abraham and his two brothers might have found themselves partners among Curaçao's Sephardic beauties during these visits, but they did not.

Daughter Sarah Curiel married into the Dominican De La Rocha family, and Rosalia Curiel married Miguel Ángel de Marchena, Eugenio Generoso's son.[416] Although Miguel Ángel was of Curaçaoan Sephardic descent, that branch of the De Marchenas had been Catholic for three generations. This marriage once again suggests that the descendants of Curaçao's Sephardim continued to interact socially for many generations in the countries their forefathers migrated to. Similar to the pattern observed in Coro, these descendants of the orginal Sephardic immigrants formed an informal Curaçaoan Diaspora in Santo Domingo, maintaining social attachments long after the Jewish religion ceased to be a common factor.

Only Rebeca Curiel, serendipitously, ended up marrying a Sephardic Jew. His name was Moisés Salas Baiz, and he appeared on the scene in Santo Domingo in the early 1890s, detemined to meet Rebeca because he had heard that she was quite beautiful.[417] His friend, Julio Senior, who was also a bachelor, traveled with him from Curaçao, and the two settled in Santo Domingo, where they soon became acquainted with the Curaçaoan Sephardim living in town. Julio was a grandson of Curaçao's wealthy Jeudah Senior, and Moisés Salas Baiz was also a Jew of Curaçaoan Sephardic descent, whose grandfather and namesake had for many years been the Reader for Temple Emanuel in Curaçao during those periods when that Reform congregation had no rabbi to lead the services. Samuel Curiel, of course, knew both young men's parents and grandparents quite well and must have welcomed them in his house. Here Moisés met and fell in love with Rebeca Curiel.

On September 8, 1894, the two were wed in a solemn Jewish ceremony. Rafael Namias Curiel officiated at the event attended by the entire Curaçaoan Diaspora of Santo Domingo. The *ketubah* – wedding certificate – designed for the occasion shows a triangular gable held up by two pillars on either side of the document with the initials of bride and groom in the bases of the pillars. The Spanish text of the document reads:

> In the city of Santo Domingo, capital of the Dominican Republic, on the eighth day of the month of Elul of the five thousand six hundred and fifty-fourth year of Creation, which corresponds with the eighth day of September of one thousand eight hundred and ninety four of the Common Era at nine post meridian, there appeared before me, Rafael Namías Curiel, acting as officiant, and before the majority of the Israelites who reside in this city [acting] as witnesses, *Moisés Salas Baiz*, legitimate son of Isaac Salas and Leah Julia Baiz, and *Rebeca Curiel Pereira*, legitimate daughter of Samuel Curiel and Hannah Pereira, and they declared that they wish to unite in holy matrimony, according to and in compliance with the precepts of the laws of Moses and Israel, promising to sustain, honor, respect, and protect each other according to the practices and customs of the Israelites.
>
> In view of this declaration, I proceeded to consecrate

this marriage according to the Hebrew rites prior to the signing of this document in the presence of the parents of the bride, Mr. Levy Baiz and his wife Naneta Baiz de Baiz, representing the widow Leah Julia Baiz de Salas, and the undersigned witnesses.

In addition to the signatures of those whose names are mentioned in the text, nine additional individuals signed as witnesses. Their last names were all common Curaçaoan Sephardic last names including Namias de Crasto, Curiel, Cohen Henriquez, Osorio, and Senior – the latter being the autograph of the groom's friend Julio Senior who would continue to be single for another eight years.

The story about Moisés Salas coming to Santo Domingo with his friend merely to check out Rebeca's good looks during a short vacation cannot be totally discounted. He was twenty-eight years old when he married Rebeca Curiel, and their subsequent travels would tend to confirm that Moisés Salas's original intent had not been to settle permanently in Santo Domingo.

Although the Salases had been living in Curaçao since the first half of the eighteenth century, the numerous periods of economic malaise in the nineteenth century had caused many of them to temporarily as well as permanently leave the island for other destinations. Moisés's grandfather Moisés had lived for many years in Ríohacha, Colombia (from the late 1830s until 1864) where he was a partner in the firm "Mendez Salas & Co." His partners were his brothers-in-law Jacob and Isaac Rois Mendez, a connection which was made even closer by the fact that Jacob Rois Mendez was married to Moisés Salas's sister, Esther.[418] Theirs was a sophisticated concern that participated in imports and exports to and from South America, utilizing letters of credit, and conducting business with agents and brokers in various parts of Europe.[419] In 1864, the elder Moisés was named Consul of Colombia in Curaçao,[420] and he returned to the place of his birth and lived there until his death in 1893 at the age of eighty-two.

Moisés Salas Baiz's father, Isaac, was the first son born to Abigail Rois Mendez and Moisés Salas. He was born in Curaçao in 1836, before his

parents moved to Ríohacha, but he too moved around during his lifetime. While he grew up in Colombia during his parents' long stay in that
country, he lived for some time in Venezuela, where, in 1863, he married
Leah Baiz in Barcelona. Several of the couple's thirteen children, including Moisés Salas Baiz, were born in the small Venezuelan coastal town of
Barcelona. When Moisés was five years old, his parents moved back to
Curaçao.[421]

Moisés spent his school years in Curaçao. As a teenager he attended
the Penha School in the Pietermaai area of Willemstad, a prestigious
school started in 1875 by a Sephardic Jew named Jacob Lopez Penha.[422]
When Moisés graduated, his father, Isaac, presented him with a bible
containing both the Old and New Testament in Spanish. It would
appear that Isaac did not give much thought to the fact that he was pre-
senting his son with a part of Scripture that was not an element of
Judaism. Isaac Salas was not ignorant about his religion, but it is proba-
ble that he had not received as rigorous a Jewish education as his own
father, after whom Moisés was named. Living in Riohacha, Colombia
and in Venezuela, without the structured religious educational resources
that were available in Curaçao to the members of the Mikvé Israel community, he had learned most of what he knew about Judaism at home.

The young Moisés, as was to be expected, treasured his beautiful bible.
Over time, he pasted newspaper clippings inside it with articles pertaining to his family. Included among these clippings is a thank-you column
written by Isaac Salas in 1885, shortly after Moises's brother and sister
died within a six-month span. At the time, Isaac Salas was living in
Trinidad where he was the editor of *The Trinidad Chronicle*. The thank-
you column was addressed to his friends who had offered their condolences on his heavy loss. The article reflects the writer's Jewish roots as
he ends it with "*Bendito y alabado sea el Santo nombre de Dios*" – Praised
and exalted is God's holy name – echoing the words of the *Kaddish* –
mourners' prayer – he must have recited for his children after they died.
At the time of these tragedies in his father's life, the first-born son,
Moisés, was nineteen years old and most likely no longer living in his
parents' home.[423] But Moisés's ties to his family were strong, and he kept
these mementos taken out of foreign newspapers printed in Venezuela

and Trinidad in his most important family possession, the bible his father had given him. When he moved to Santo Domingo, he brought the two leather-bound volumes with him and today they belong to one of his Dominican grandsons. Almost one hundred and fifty years after they were printed, the two tomes are still as handsome as they were when Moisés received them in 1877.

After their wedding in 1894, Moisés and Rebeca Salas spent some time in Santo Domingo, but they appear to have moved shortly thereafter. Their first-born daughter, Octavia, was born in New York City in 1895, and in 1898 the couple was back in Curaçao, where Rebeca gave birth to their second daughter, Ángela. Also their daughter Olga was born in Curaçao in 1906, while the youngest of the family, Victoria Luisa, was a native of Santo Domingo, born there in 1910.[424] In 1910, however, Moisés Salas Baiz left for Colombia, presumably leaving his wife and young children under the watchful eyes of her Curiel and Pereira relatives in Santo Domingo. In Barranquilla, Colombia, he became the administrator of a new concern called Fábrica Nacional de Fósforos – National Match Factory – which was incorporated that year. The three principal shareholders in this enterprise were Jacob Cortissoz, Enrique Alvares Correa, and Moisés Salas Baiz, all of Curaçaoan Sephardic descent. The business was dissolved the following year and at that point, Moisés moved back to Santo Domingo.[425]

Moisés Salas Baiz had gained considerable experience while running the short-lived match manufacturing firm in Barranquilla, and in 1914, when he was already in his late thirties, he started a similar match company in Puerto Plata, Dominican Republic. From then on the family stopped moving around and settled permanently in the Dominican Republic. In later years, Salas Baiz also invested in the manufacture of cardboard boxes. This firm, Industria Cartonera Dominicana, is no longer in family hands but continues to be operational.

The travels of Moisés Salas Baiz and his family were not that unusual for the times. Although many of the Sephardim who left Curaçao for other Caribbean locations migrated to a particular place and just stayed there, there were quite a few who did not do so and who continued looking for a place where they could live without fear of persecution while at the same time making a good living. When either of those two factors appeared to be lacking in their chosen places of residence, they just picked up their families and moved elsewhere. This pattern was noted among the Coriano Jews who returned to Curaçao when anti-Semitism became too violent, among the Dominican De Marchenas who waited out political unrest in Puerto Rico and Curaçao before returning to Santo Domingo, and among the many Sephardim of St. Thomas, who left for Panama and Curaçao when the economy of the Danish island had ceased to grow. Similarly, it was not until Moisés was older and had achieved some commercial success in the Dominican Republic that this country became his permanent residence.

Once Moisés Salas Baiz settled down in Puerto Plata, he became the consul of the Netherlands in that town. In this capacity, he was knighted by the Dutch queen in 1938. At age 71 this decoration was a real feather in his cap, and he celebrated the event with much fanfare. There had been enough Curaçaoans and descendants of Curaçaoans in the Dominican Republic to warrant the celebration of Queen Wilhelmina's birthday in August of each year. In 1938, a gala evening at the Club de Comercio, one of the social clubs of the elite founded in 1874, celebrated not only the Dutch monarch, but also the newly knighted don Moisés and his "distinguished wife doña Rebeca Curiel." Officers of a Dutch ship that happened to be in the harbor that day participated in this festive event, and a large picture of the queen was hung in the ballroom at the club.

Throughout the years, the family continued to feel a strong connection to Curaçao and the ruling Dutch monarchs of the House of Orange, whose religious tolerance over the centuries had allowed the Sephardim in the overseas colonies to live in a fairly non-discriminatory environment. When Princess Beatrix of the Netherlands was born, the Salas-Curiel family in the Dominican Republic carefully clipped the picture of her father, Prince Bernhard, carrying the newborn princess from a local newspaper. More than sixty years later, when Beatrix was already queen of Holland, I visited the descendants of this family, and they proudly displayed this clipping, as well as the actual decoration Moisés had received from Beatrix's grandmother when he was knighted.

Moisés Salas Baiz's grandson, Juan Hormazabal Salas, recalls that although his grandparents, Moisés and Rebeca Salas, remained Jewish until they died, they had no qualms about their daughters marrying outside the faith. By this time, both sides of the family had seen many non-Jewish unions, since all of Rebeca Curiel's siblings had married outside the faith and at least two of Moisés's brothers had intermarried as well. The marriages of the Salas-Curiel girls included quick conversions to Catholicism prior to the wedding. Hormazabal explained that none of the four girls had had the opportunity to participate in a Jewish community while they were growing up. In Puerto Plata, where they were raised, they only knew of one other Jewish family, the Paiewonsky family. Hormazabal writes that the Paiewonskys were *"polacos"* – Polish – and that they originally came to the Dominican Republic from St. Thomas.[426] The Paiewonskys are a well-known Jewish family in St. Thomas, and, in the 1960s, Ralph Paiewonsky was the governor of the U.S. Virgin Islands. Mr. Paiewonsky of Puerto Plata was Moisés Salas's business partner and was a relation to the St. Thomas Paiewonskys. Even if he he had been a practicing Jew, his Ashkenazi observances would most likely have differed significantly from those of the highly secular Curaçaoan Sephardic Jews living in the Dominican Republic at the end of the nineteenth century.

According to Hormazabal Salas, the four daughters of Rebeca Curiel and Moisés Salas never practiced the Catholic religion to any great extent after their conversions. Nevertheless, daughter Olga appears to have entertained serious spiritual thoughts, leaving behind a multi-page essay directed to her immediate family, detailing her religious views. In this exercise, she contrasts Old and New Testament views and presents her ideas of what she would hope the readers of her essay would come away with: "This is the religion that I would want for you: one which provides an eternal balm, illuminating the dark moments of our path, augmenting the oases of our desert, and representing the secret chamber we can turn to in our search for rest when weariness disheartens us." There is no doubt that in spite of her non-religious upbringing, the writer had found strength and solace in the New Testament, liberally sprinkling her writing with references to Jesus.[427]

The travels of Samuel Curiel and Moisés Salas Baiz provide a true
sense of the search for economic betterment by the Caribbean
Sephardim in the nineteenth century. They were not really adventurers
who went from one place to the next just for the pleasure of doing so.
They worked and invested in the countries to which they migrated, but
sometimes their first choice of residence was not the most satisfactory
one. When these immigrants eventually settled in Santo Domingo, however, they were fairly quickly fully absorbed in the local Roman Catholic
culture, no matter how actively they and their ancestors had participated in Jewish affairs in Curaçao in years gone by. One generation after
Samuel Curiel's migration, all but one of his descendants had intermarried. His four Jewish granddaughters, born to his daughter and his only
Jewish son-in-law, not only intermarried, but also converted to
Catholicism prior to their weddings.

HAIM LOPEZ PENHA
AND HIS DOMINICAN SONS

A Sephardic family name still found in the Dominican Republic today is
that of the Lopez Penhas. Many of these twenty-first century Dominicans descend from Haim Daniel Lopez Penha, a Curaçaoan Jew, whose
migration to Santo Domingo in the mid nineteenth century ended up
being of a temporary nature.

Haim Daniel Lopez Penha was born in Curaçao on May 17, 1820, to
Moseh Lopez Penha and Clara Cohen Henriquez. He was their seventh
child, and they gave him the name Haim, meaning life in Hebrew, to distinguish him from their first-born son, Daniel, who had died as an infant.
Five sisters had been born before him as well, and five more siblings were
to follow his birth. Haim – for that is how he was known - was the couple's eldest son to survive to adulthood.[428]

Shortly after he was born, the unfortunate Hazan Piza was fired. After
Piza's departure, the Mikvé Israel congregation entered a prolonged period without any rabbinical guidance, relying on knowledgeable lay leaders to conduct religious services. Haim's father, Moseh Lopez Penha, ful-

Street in Santo Domingo, Dominican Republic

filled this function for many years, rendering his services pro bono until his death in 1854.[429] With his learned father to guide the family, Haim grew up in a household where Jewish observance and involvement in the community were considered important aspects of life.

On November 19, 1842, Haim married Rachel Levy Maduro, a descendant of a Sephardic family which had been in Curaçao since the late seventeenth century.[430] The decade of the 1840s was one of active outmigration for the Curaçaoan Sephardim, and some time between 1842 and 1845 the young Penha-Maduro couple moved to the Dominican Republic.

In Santo Domingo Rachel bore Haim three daughters, Clara, Sara, and Esther, and three sons, David, Moses, and Elias.[431] The birthplace of their first-born son, Abram Oriel, is not known. In spite of the fact that there were close to one hundred Sephardim in Santo Domingo when the Penhas arrived,[432] the Jewish observance they encountered in that city was a far cry from the bustling Jewish community they had left behind. Although the ability to live an active Jewish life was limited in their new place of residence, Haim and Rachel were intent on observing their religion to the best of their ability. In 1849, they took their son Moses back to Curaçao to be circumcised by the resident cirumciser, Moises Frois Ricardo, and in 1854, Ricardo traveled by boat to Santo Domingo to perform the circumcision of son Elias at home. [433]

Haim Lopez Penha was most likely a merchant or import/export broker when he lived in the Dominican Republic, but no concrete information is available on his business dealings in his new place of residence. Like many of the more religious Sephardim who attempted the move to Santo Domingo in those days, he must have worried about the secular and religious education of his children. He must also have missed the tight-knit community he had left behind. In spite of the Jewish vacuum they encountered in their new place of residence, Haim and Rachel and their ever-growing family lived in the Dominican Republic for at least ten years.

All the while, however, this Lopez Penha household continued to think of Curaçao as its true home, and a few years after his father's death in 1854, Haim moved the family back to the Dutch island. Haim's son David always referred to the ancestral mother island as *"la patria que la casualidad me robó"* –the country that was stolen from me by chance,[434] and the family settled back among their old friends and relatives in Curaçao with great ease after the interlude in Santo Domingo. Soon the couple had yet another son, Joseph, who was born in Curaçao in 1858.[435]

Unfortunately, their happiness was meant to be short-lived. An epidemic of smallpox struck the island in 1862[436] and in September of that year, both their first-born son, Abram Oriel, and their younger son Aaron succumbed to this disease. The sixties were to be a nightmarish time in Haim and Rachel's lives. In March of 1865, a still-grieving Rachel gave birth to another son, Abraham Zacarías, only to lose Joseph at age six to another epidemic a few weeks after she had given birth. Three of their ten children had now died before reaching adulthood.[437]

It is hard to imagine how the family unit recovered from these tragedies, but Haim was greatly consoled by his strong religious beliefs, and life went on for him at a fast pace. He threw himself into community work in the 1860s, particularly after the schism that took place in the Jewish community in 1863, resulting in the creation of the liberal congregation, Temple Emanu-el. He and his family remained devoted to the Mikvé Israel synagogue, and he was a member of Mikvé Israel's executive board from 1867 through 1869.[438] In 1867, Rabbi Mendes Chumaceiro named him associate judge of the *beth din* – judicial court.[439]

Rachel Lopez Penha died in July of 1875. Born in St. Thomas to Curaçaoan Sephardim, her family had returned to Curaçao, where she had met and married Haim. Then she moved to Santo Domingo with her husband, and after a decade or so, she settled back in Curaçao. The last decade of Rachel's life was filled with anguish over the death of her three children. Unlike her three sisters who died at the ages of sixty-nine, eighty, and eighty-nine, Rachel was only fifty-six when she passed away.

A little over a year later, Haim remarried. This time he married a sister of Samuel Curiel, also named Rachel. She bore him a son and a daughter and helped him raise his youngest son Abraham Zacarías, who had been ten years old when his mother died.

Although Haim Daniel Lopez Penha's migration to the Dominican Republic had been only of a temporary nature, two sons of his first marriage, Elias and Moses, decided to return to their place of birth when they were young adults. They settled in Santo Domingo, determined to succeed. Their commitment to Jewish continuity was, however, not as firm as that of their father. In 1877, a year after Haim had married for a second time, Elias Lopez Penha announced that he intended to marry a Catholic Dominican by the name of Natalia Quesada. Haim was very unhappy with his son's choice. But the far away demands coming from Curaçao were no match for the less restrictive Dominican environment, where intermarriages between the Curaçaoan Sephardim and the local Catholic population had been occurring quite regularly, even a generation earlier. On July 23, 1877, Natalia and Elias were wed, and in the years that followed, Haim and his son, Elias, became estranged.

While today's descendants of the De Marchena, Curiel, and Salas families who migrated to the Dominican Republic believe that the eventual abandonment of Judaism for the Catholic religion in their families was a fairly casual issue, this was clearly not the case for Elias Lopez Penha. His father was a very important member of the Sephardic community of Curaçao, and his ancestors had been members of Curaçao's *Beth Din* – Jewish judicial court. It was to be expected that the elders of such a family who descended from learned and devoted Jews would hope that their children would follow in their footsteps. It was therefore not surprising that Elias's break with Jewish tradition was poorly received by his father.

Although he must have been very much in love with his new bride, the severed relationship with his beloved father was extremely painful. In 1883 Elias decided that it was time to make up with Haim, who was, by this time, in his sixties. He arranged to travel to Curaçao "*con el único objeto de reconciliarme con mi padre, a quien respeto y venero ...*"— with the only objective to be reconciled with my father, whom I respect and worship.[440]

It would appear that the visit with his friends and relatives in Curaçao did not turn out to be what he he had hoped for. Upon his return to Santo Domingo, he reacted to events that had occurred on the Dutch island by publishing a seven-page pamphlet entitled *Reivindicación* – literally meaning recovery and referring to his attempt to reclaim his good name. His written explanations were directed to "*la mayoría sensata del Gremio Hebreo de Curazao*" – the sensible majority of Curaçao's Jewish Society – and the pamphlet seems to have circulated widely among the island's Sephardim.

Elias begins his essay by stating that during his visit to Curaçao, he had been insulted in the synagogue on Saturday the 27th of January of 1883, and that he was therefore providing the appropriate documents to prove that he was not "a deserter of the Jewish ranks" as was suggested during the confrontation on that Sabbath day.[441] He then provides a description of his wedding ceremony of July 23, 1877 to Miss Natalia Quesada in the Dominican Republic and has this description certified by the bride's uncle, a priest by the name of Miguel Quesada, who had been a witness at the time. In this polemic he explains that the ceremony took place in a private home in Santiago where there was no altar and where he was not required to confess or genuflect. There were also no Catholic sacraments involved in the event. According to Elias, the entire wedding ceremony consisted of bride and groom affirming their intent to be wed in the presence of the required witnesses. After describing this part of the ceremony, Lopez Penha goes through great pains to point out that subsequent to this assent by both bride and groom, he stepped aside so that his bride could receive the religious benediction. The sole purpose of the benediction was to guarantee that the children of this marriage, who were to be brought up in their mother's religion, would be considered legitimate in the eyes of the Church. He then reiterates that he was never baptized or confirmed, nor was he required to sacrifice his religious beliefs in any way, shape or form. Never, says Lopez Penha, did he participate in any act that could affect his "quality and dignity as a Jew."[442] It was obviously very important to Elias Lopez Penha that Curaçao's Sephardic community accept him back as one of their own, in spite of his marriage outside the Jewish faith six years earlier.

The writing does not indicate whether father and son were eventually reconciled. It does appear, however, that the trip to Curaçao had created additional problems for Elias Lopez Penha, and it is not known if he returned to the island at a later time.

By the time this pamphlet was published in 1883, Elias's brother Moses who was also living in Santo Domingo had married outside the Jewish faith as well. In 1879, Moses Lopez Penha had married Adelaida de Marchena, whose father, Gerardo, had been born out of wedlock to Abraham de Marchena of Curaçao.* There is no indication that Moses and Adelaida's marriage was cause for the kind of recriminations that the union of Elias and Natalia had endured. Maybe Adelaida's Curaçaoan Sephardic antecedents mitigated the fact that she was Catholic. Or maybe Moses was less dramatic than Elias. Whatever the case, Moses was never inclined to publish any essay to justify his behavior to Curaçao's Sephardim.

Adelaida bore Moses Lopez Penha one son and four daughters. The son, whom they called Haim Horacio in honor of his grandfather, was born on December 13, 1878, a month before his parents were married.[443] He was a bright little boy and his uncle, David Lopez Penha, Jr., who was single and wealthy, ensured that he received an education befitting his intellect. From Barranquilla, Colombia, Uncle David provided the funds that enabled his nephew to be educated in Germany from a very early age. When Haim returned to Santo Domingo at age eighteen, he became active in government circles.[444] Among the many public positions held by this Dominican Penha was that of Senator of the Republic in the

* Adelaida de Marchena was a sister of Eugenio Generoso de Marchena.

1940s. He was also President of the Dominican Committee for Jewish Immigration in 1946, formed when President Rafael Trujillo invited Jewish victims of Nazi persecution to settle in the Dominican Republic, making 100,000 visas available to these refugees. During this post-war year, the United States was admitting only 2000 European refugees a month. But Trujillo believed that the European Jews would bring their entrepreneurial skills to the Dominican Republic to the benefit of both parties, just as the Sephardim had done a century earlier, and his immigration policy reflected this conviction. The Catholic Haim Lopez Penha travelled frequently to the United States in the 1940s and spoke on behalf of the surviving European Jews on many occasions.[445] In Santo Domingo his memory lives on, and a street has been named after him.

CATHOLIC JEWS

It is a sunny afternoon in Santo Domingo. Rush hour is rapidly approaching, and the traffic on Avenida George Washington, more commonly referred to as "El Malecón," is intense. In the very early morning, joggers and strollers use the wide sidewalk on the southern side of this long stretch of roadway along the Caribbean Sea before the sun makes it too hot for any outdoor exercise. Sea grapes grow in the small parks that jut out into the walkway, and restaurant workers are cleaning up debris from the night before to start yet another day. Here and there a wave splashes over the seawall of the Malecón. At that early hour of the day, the air smells fresh, and Santo Domingo looks beautiful and serene, framed by the sea. On this afternoon, however, my cousin Sandy and I are standing at the back entrance of our hotel, inhaling the fumes of the cars that zip by, while we wait to be picked up by Rafael Manuel Galán Salas, grandson of Moisés Salas Baiz, who will be taking us to a tea party given in our honor.

We are *las primas de Curazao* – the cousins from Curaçao – and have found many new relatives in this friendly capital of the Dominican Republic. A great-great-grandson of Rafael de Marchena, Enrique Eduardo de Marchena, and his wife Aida Kaluche have had us over for

Descendants of Curaçaoan Sephardim in Santo Domingo

drinks a few days earlier and have invited us for dinner at their home before we leave. Moisés Salas's grandsons have picked us up at the airport, toured us around town, taken us to nearby resorts, marched us through cemeteries, looking for the graves of their descendants, and entertained us with their stories about their grandparents and great grandparents. Now, Juan Hormazabal Salas and his wife Arlette Casals have invited a large number of descendants of Santo Domingo's Sephardic Jews to meet us at their home. When Nonín* finally pulls up into the hotel lot, he is late and has choice words for the poor drivers and traffic jams. By the time we get to Juancho's home, many of the guests are there,

---

* Nicknames are de rigeur among this group. Rafael Manuel is Nonín, Juan José is Juancho, Olga is Cuqui.

and we are introduced to each and every one. They do not shake hands and say: "pleased to meet you." Instead, everybody hugs and kisses us, because, after all, we are cousins.

We walk around talking to our newly found friends, nibbling on the delicious food that Arlette has prepared. It occurs to me that right here in this living room I am looking at what the historian Enrique Ucko called "the fusion of the Sephardic Jews and the Dominicans." This warm and outgoing group of people is the result of two coinciding factors encountered by their migrating forefathers: first, the lack of a religious center and Jewish leadership in Santo Domingo, and second, the relatively uncomplicated acceptance of the Sephardim by the local elite. Although, within a generation, the descendants of these immigrants became totally integrated into Dominican society, four and five generations later, these folks with Sephardic ancestry have remained socially close. At this affair organized by the Hormazabals, it is clear that all the guests know each other well. They ask about children, traveling husbands, ailing mothers, and, most of all, they want to know exactly how we are related. They are thrilled that Sandy is able to tell them that their great-grandfather and ours were brothers, or, among the older guests, that their grandfather and our great-great grandmothers were siblings. And Sandy, of course, is excited to fill in the blanks in her family data base for the current Dominican generations. There is a comfortable awareness of the common religious and Curaçaoan background of more than a century ago, but first and foremost, these new cousins are Dominicanos, and, of course, they are all Catholic.

This level of integration combined with an easy-going dual self-identity can probably best be summarized by a conversation we had that afternoon with one of Juancho's guests, Marianela Lopez Penha. She tells Sandy that her father was Haim Lopez Penha y de Marchena – a man with a very Jewish first name and two very Curaçaoan Sephardic last names. Then she mentions that she is *judía* – Jewish. This is an exciting discovery! Even in the Jewish cemetery, inaugurated in Santo Domingo in the twentieth century, we had found only one tombstone with a Sephardic name among the Ashkenazim buried there. I sit down with her, eager to hear more. Where in Santo Domingo does she attend synagogue services, I ask. Her answer sums it all up. Quite amazed at such a silly question she says, "*No, no, mija! Soy católica, ... pero soy judía!*" – No, no, my child! I am Catholic, ... but I am Jewish!

Today, this is what remains of the Sephardic migration to the Dominican Republic: the fully integrated Catholic Jews whose forefathers came from Curaçao and who wear their Jewish ancestry as a badge of honor.

CHAPTER 5

BARRANQUILLA, COLOMBIA

TRADE EMPORIUM OF THE CARIBBEAN

There is ... one spot which peculiarly claims attention; this is the port of Savanilla, at the mouth of the Magdalena. The lands here are finely timbered, and the temperature refreshed by strong breezes; but the principal advantage consists in its being the natural port of the Magdalena, in which capacity, there is little doubt, it will one day become the emporium of the whole trade of the interior ...

From Colonel F. Hall's Pamphlet on Colombia, *as quoted in* Journal of a Residence and Travel in Colombia during the Years 1823 and 1824 *by Capt. Charles Stuart Cochrane*[446]

In the first few decades of the nineteenth century, Barranquilla, Colombia was a small village of a few thousand inhabitants located near the confluence of the river Magdalena and the Caribbean Sea. It was a place of little significance, existing in the shadow of Cartagena, which was then Colombia's principal Caribbean port. In the 1820s, the town of Sabanilla, only about ten miles from Barranquilla, was an even smaller fishing village on the Caribbean. It was hard to imagine then that by

Home of Ernesto Cortissoz
Barranquilla, Colombia

1836 the exports through Sabanilla would be triple those passing through Cartagena,[447] transforming Barranquilla into the emporium of trade visualized by a handful of people a decade or two earlier.

Charles Stuart Cochrane, an Englishman who traveled through Colombia during those early years immediately after independence, met one of these visionary men in Barranquilla in March of 1823. John Glenn was a Canadian merchant who had been in Colombia for eight years. He was, according to Cochrane, "making a fair fortune." Glenn told Cochrane that he had no doubt that "after three years' peace the trade of the country would nearly triple."[448] Such a prospect would have been very exciting for many an entrepreneur and reflects the expectations of the new immigrants who settled on the Colombian coast in the nineteenth century.

Sabanilla's improved status in the 1830s was largely the result of the clogging of the Canal del Dique which linked Cartagena to the Magadalena River. This obstruction shifted a large portion of that port's import/export traffic to Santa Marta, a coastal town east of Barranquilla. Even tiny Sabanilla benefited from the decreased trade through Cartagena. Soon the merchants of Santa Marta began to feel threatened by the growing commercial activities in Sabanilla and Barranquilla. With their encouragement, a declaration was issued in 1838, requiring all Colombian exports to go through Santa Marta. It was not until 1842 that imports and exports were able to enter and leave Colombia legally via Sabanilla, marking the beginning of a new era for Barranquilla.[449]

The export of Colombian goods through Barranquilla was not a simple endeavor. Goods would be brought on the Magdalena River from interior parts of Colombia to the city and transported by land or sometimes taken by means of very primitive rafts through the barely passable Canal de la Piña to Sabanilla. Here the export products would be loaded unto larger ocean-going vessels and shipped to various parts of the world. Similarly, ships carrying products from foreign lands to Colombia would anchor in Sabanilla and the same difficult route via Barranquilla would be undertaken in reverse.[450] It was obvious that at some point this burdensome transportation process had to be improved for Barranquilla to achieve its full potential as a major trading center.

In the 1820s, a German immigrant by the name of Juan Bernardo Elbers owned the exclusive rights for steamboat navigation on the Magdalena River. This monopoly may not have seemed so valuable in those early years of the nineteenth century, but as Barranquilla's prospects for trade grew, so too did the importance of transportation. Some Colombian historians have indicated that Elbers was one of the first Jews to establish himself in Coastal Colombia,[451] but others believe that he was born to Protestant parents. It is possible that his close association with the early Jews who came to Barranquilla led people to believe that he was Jewish.[452]

Be it as it may, by the 1830s there were quite a few foreigners living in Barranquilla. Among them were individuals called Cohen and Pardo who were most likely Jewish or of Jewish extraction.[453] Their numbers increased significantly in the 1840s, when the restrictions on Colombian exports through Barranquilla were lifted. At this point in time, Cura-çaoan Sephardic names such as Alvares Correa, de Sola, Rois Mendez, and Pinedo began to appear in town. The foreigners' interest in the import/export business stimulated the once dormant little village and, by the mid 1840s, the economy of Barranquilla was poised for take-off.

ENTREPRENEURS PAR EXCELLENCE: THE ALVARES CORREA–CORTISSOZ FAMILIES OF BARRANQUILLA

Jacob Alvares Correa was one of the early Curaçaoan Sephardim to set-tle in Barranquilla. He arrived there in 1841 and would later become a very wealthy man and a leader of the Sephardic community in this rapid-ly growing town.[454] Jacob was born in Curaçao in 1809 to Mordechay Alvares Correa and Clara Pinedo. He represented the fifth generation of Alvares Correas to be born in Curaçao.

Jacob's ancestor, Manuel Alvares Correa, was the first member of the family to emigrate from Europe to Curaçao in the 1670s. He was among the small number of Curaçaoan Jews active in the slave trade. In spite of his reprehensible source of income, he was a religious and chari-table man and served the Mikvé Israel community in many different capacities, including as Treasurer and President of the Board.[455] The gen-erations of Alvares Correas that came after him remained religiously involved and participated actively in the affairs of Curaçao's Jewish com-munity in the eighteenth century.

Jacob's father, Mordechay, had been one of the separatists during the problems with Cantor Piza in Curaçao. He was so outraged about the decisions made by the leaders of the Mikvé Israel congregation, that he revised his will in 1821, setting forth that he wished not to be buried in the Jewish cemetery, providing several alternatives as to what was to be done with his remains.* He ended this list of options by indicating that

---

* Either he changed his mind later in life or his children did not honor his will, because when he died on July 4, 1841, he was buried in the Jewish cemetery at Blenheim in Division I, Row G, #175. Emmanuel, *Precious Stones of the Jews of Curaçao*, p. 498.

if they were all disallowed, his corpse was to be cast into the sea "to be preyed upon by the fishes rather than be [interred] in a cemetery under the management of [a] community whose principles do not coincide with mine." He forbade the members of Mikvé Israel to lave his corpse, and his brother Manuel Haim Alvares Correa who had sided with the synagogue board during the Piza affair was not allowed to be present at his funeral.[456]

It is not known for certain if Mordechay Alvares Correa's son, Jacob, lived in other locations before he decided to move to Barranquilla. But he must have spent some time in St. Thomas, where he married Rachel Jesurun Pinto,[457] daughter of Abraham Jesurun Pinto and Sarah Lopez Fonseca.[458] Rachel's father had been hired by the St. Thomas Jewish community to lead the congregation in 1816 and had migrated to the Danish colonies from Curaçao.[459] It is most likely that his daughter Rachel was born in St. Thomas during the period that her parents lived on that island. Religion played an important role in the Jesurun Pinto household, and Rachel and her siblings were very familiar with Jewish traditions and observances.

Since both Rachel and Jacob's ancestors had been active members of the Jewish communities in which they lived, the young couple must have tried to maintain some level of Jewish observance once they got to Barranquilla. This was not an easy task. The number of Jews in Barranquilla was quite small in the forties and fifties, and it is unclear if the Sabbath or the Jewish holidays were observed in a formal way by the ten to fifteen Jewish families who lived there during those years. It took more than three decades after Jacob Alvares Correa's arrival in Barranquilla for the Jews of this town to finally create an officially recognized organization which they named the Colombian Jewish Community. This institution came into being on March 6, 1874 and had a governing body which could deal with Jewish community matters. Jacob Alvares Correa, who had been instrumental in the formation of this entity, became the organization's first treasurer. Agustín I. Senior was president; David de Sola, secretary; and David Haim Dovale and D. H. Senior were board members without portfolio. All these gentlemen were part of the Curaçaoan

Sephardic Diaspora living in Barranquilla in the seventies.[460]

A census taken in 1875 shows sixty-seven foreigners from Curaçao living in that Colombian town that year.[461] It is likely that most of these Curaçaoans were Sephardim, since, according to the historian Isaac Emmanuel, the Jewish presence in Barranquilla "numbered 64 souls" in 1874.[462] Aside from these Sephardic Jews, there were quite a few German Jews in Barranquilla as well, such as the Wessels, Hoenigsberg, Wolf, Helm and Heilbron families. The Colombian historian Adelaida Sourdis Nájera speculates that women and children were not included in the aforementioned census figures and estimates that the number of Jews in Barranquilla must have been three or four times greater than is indicated in these census tabulations. In other words, she believes that a few hundred Jews resided in Barranquilla in 1875.[463] If this is true, it is likely that the Jewish community of Barranquilla in the mid 1870s was at least as large as, if not larger, than that of Coro, Venezuela at the end of the first phase of that town's Jewish settlement in 1855. A community of this size should have had a large enough critical mass to meet regularly for religious services. Nevertheless, it appears that, even in the 1870s, such gatherings did not occur with the same regularity of place and time in Barranquilla as they did in Coro in the early 1850s.

Whenever the Jews of Barranquilla got together for prayers, however, it was fairly certain that Jacob Alvares Correa and his sons were included among the worshipers. Before the creation of the Colombian Jewish Community, religious services were held at the homes of miscellaneous Jewish Barranquilleros. Rodolfo Cortissoz (Jacob Alvares Correa's grandson), explained to the historian Itic Croitoru Rothbaum that his ancestors in Barranquilla "used to timidly get together on the holy days of Rosh Hashanah (the Jewish New Year) and Yom Kippur (the Day of Atonement) to recite the traditional prayers."[464] The word "timidly" leads one to believe that in spite of the number of foreigners in town, the environment in Barranquilla was not always favorably inclined toward Jews arriving from Curaçao and other locations. The many years that nearby Cartagena had been the headquarters for the Inquisition in Spanish-occupied Nueva Granada had clearly left their mark. Nevertheless, Barranquilla was considered a place that was welcoming to immigrants and considerably more liberal and open-minded vis-à-vis those who were not Catholic than many other Latin American locations. It is possible that the timidity of the Jewish Barranquilleros of the time, with regard to their observance of the Jewish High Holy Days, merely reflected their desire to keep a low religious profile in order not to provoke the always feared and often latent anti-Semitism. After the creation of the official Colombian Jewish Community, services were held in the home of Abraham (also known as Agustín) Senior, the Community's first president.*

Jacob and Rachel Alvares Correa had nine children. At least one son entered into an exogamous marriage, but one son and two daughters married within the faith. Serafina Alvares Correa married into the German Jewish Helm family of Barranquilla,** and another daughter and a son married into the Sephardic Cortissoz family. Alejandro Alvares Correa married Rebecca Cortissoz, and Julia Alvares Correa married Jacob Cortissoz, Rebecca's brother. These Cortissoz siblings were children of Joseph Cortissoz and Esther Jesurun Pinto. The latter was a first cousin to Jacob Alvares Correa's wife Rachel.[465] Therefore the Cortissoz-Alvares Correa couples were second cousins (see also Appendix A-6 and A-7). As was seen in other small Jewish communities, cross and parallel cousin marriages[466] occurred with some regularity among the endogamous marriages in Barranquilla, where ancestry was often more important than wealth. Rachel and Jacob Alvares Correa must have approved of their children's unions with the Cortissoz siblings, even though it is likely that Jacob Cortissoz and his sister arrived in Colombia with few assets.

---

* Notably, the well-to-do Agustín Senior of Barranquilla was a first cousin of the wealthy Jeudah Senior of Coro, who was by this time living in Curaçao.

** An interesting aspect of the Jewish community in Barranquilla, which was not seen to the same extent in Curaçao, Santo Domingo, or Coro, was the easy mixing of Ashkenazim and Sephardim in this coastal town. Although the first board of the Colombian Jewish Community in Barranquilla consisted entirely of Jews of the Curaçaoan Sephardic Diaspora, the Ashkenazim and Sephardim of Barranquilla were business partners and marriage partners at a very early stage of their settlement on the Caribbean coast of Colombia. Adelaida Sourdis Nájera, "Sefardíes y Ashkenazis en Barranquilla en la Segunda Mitad del Siglo XIX – Negocios y Compañías Comerciales," in *Paper presented at XII Congreso Colombiano de Historia* (Popayán, Colombia: 2003), p. 4

Jacob Cortissoz
1848–1936

Rachel and Jacob Alvares Correa were not taken aback by their new son-in-law's limited wealth. Although her husband had acquired a great deal of wealth in Colombia, Rachel Alvares Correa was quite familiar with less favorable financial circumstances. Her father, Reverend Abraham Jesurun Pinto, had not earned a very good living when he lived in the Virgin Islands, and his brother Jacob, who was Rebecca and Jacob Cortissoz's maternal grandfather, was downright poor. He was the sexton of Curaçao's Mikvé Israel, where his dire financial condition caused him to write a letter to the synagogue board in 1837 in which he begged these "Most Dignified Gentlemen" to excuse his humble request for some financial relief. He explained in this letter that due to his *"primitivo salario"* as *shamas* (sexton) and even supplementing this salary with his income as *shohet* (ritual slaughterer), he was unable to have a new suit made. He begged the board to help him out since his only black suit which he had to wear on Shabbat and holidays was in a deplorable state. Because he believed that it was his sacred duty to offer his services as *shamas* and *shohet*, his inability to dress properly for his profession presented a true dilemma. He ended the letter by reminding the board that he was a *"pai di familla"* (head of household) of an ever growing family and signed off as *"humilde servidor de vose Q.S.M.B."* – your humble servant who kisses your hands.[467]

When Jacob Jesurun Pinto's daughter Esther married Joseph Cortissoz, there was no dowry. A generation later, the marriage of their son Jacob

Cortissoz into the well-established Alvares Correa family of Barranquilla was considered a real step up.[468] In lieu of wealth, Jacob Cortissoz had his energy and entrepreneurial spirit going for him. It is likely that the Alvares Correas were favorably impressed by the charismatic and dynamic young man. Their confidence in their son-in-law was soon rewarded by Jacob Cortissoz's many successes in Barranquilla in the years that followed.

Jacob Cortissoz was born in Curaçao in 1848. When he was quite young, his parents, Joseph and Esther, moved with their five children to Puerto Cabello, Venezuela. In Venezuela Esther gave birth to two more sons, and the Curaçao-based *mohel* (circumciser) Moises Ricardo travelled to Puerto Cabello to circumcize these children in 1855 and 1857. At some point thereafter Esther Cortissoz passed away, and, eventually, Jacob's father married for a second time, choosing a non-Jewish woman named Eudacia as his wife.[469]

This second marriage of Joseph Cortissoz produced two daughters, Sara and Esther, and a son, called Abraham Haim, born in Puerto Cabello in 1864. In spite of the fact that Joseph's second wife was not Jewish, Eudacia agreed to bring up Abraham Haim as a Jew. In a letter to Moises Frois Ricardo, dated July 19, 1867, Eudacia Cortissoz formally requested that the *mohel* circumcise her son, indicating her wish "to educate the boy in the Jewish religion into which I too wish to be initiated." This letter was witnessed by Isaac Pinheiro and A.E. Levison, both members of the Jewish community of Puerto Cabello, with all signatures officially certified. Ricardo travelled to Puerto Cabello later that month and performed the religious circumcision of Abraham Haim Cortissoz on the 30th of July 1867.[470]

Jacob was in his teens when his father remarried. He did not get along too well with his stepmother, however, and at some point, when he was still young, he moved back to Curaçao.[471] Many relatives of Jacob's deceased mother still lived on the island at that time, and it is likely that upon his return he had significant interaction with these pious relations. Therefore, even though his formal religious upbringing may have been interrupted by his move to Venezuela as a child, he probably had considerable exposure to Jewish ritual and observances.

When he came to Barranquilla with his brother Manuel and his sister Rebecca, he was young and single. An enterprising man, he very quickly became involved in dozens of businesses and became one of the movers and shakers of Barranquilla's rapidly growing economy. His marriage into the Alvares Correa family proved to be fortuitous, and his in-laws became his favorite business partners. With his brother-in-law, Joseph Helm, he formed a company called J. Helm & Cia. Many of Cortissoz's investments were made in the name of this entity. Thus Helm & Cia. was one of the original shareholders of the Banco de Barranquilla, the nation's second financial institution, which was founded in 1873. Seventeen Jewish shareholders, most of Curaçaoan Sephardic descent, controlled 31% of the original shares of this bank.[472]

In 1871, Barranquilla and the seaport of Sabanilla had been linked by the Ferrocaril de Bolívar railway, greatly improving the cumbersome transportation of imported and exported goods that existed earlier between these two sites. By 1873 Sabanilla's total imports and exports exceeded those of rival Santa Marta by a factor of five.[473] In the 1870s, Barranquilla was the nation's most important trade center, used primarily for the forwarding and distribution of merchandise. With their network of relatives and friends throughout the Caribbean, the United States, and Europe, it is no wonder that the Jewish Barranquilleros, who at that point had already been residing in the city for thirty-some years, were able to derive great benefit from the commercial growth of this Colombian city. Indeed, in many ways, their presence and efforts and that of other immigrants were instrumental in Barranquilla's development.

In this city that had become a hub for trade between the interior of Colombia and Europe and the Americas, members of the Jewish community made their living importing and exporting. It was therefore quite logical that they would become involved in all aspects pertaining to transportation. Two years after the inauguration of the railway, a group of businessmen, including many from the Jewish community, published an open letter to the president of Colombia, with the hope that he would assist them in rectifying what they considered to be excessive freight charges levied by the railroad company on certain agricultural export products, including corn, cotton, berries, and dividivi. Again Helm &

Cia. and also Jacob Alvarez Correa appear as signatories to this letter.[474] A couple of weeks later, the local newspaper, *El Promotor*, published a response from the executive branch of the government, which instructed the Ferrocaril de Bolívar to lower its freight charges and admonished the company for not operating on a punctual schedule. The train company executives were reminded that the latter was an important aspect of their contract with the Colombian government, and the president's representative encouraged them to implement the suggested operational improvements at their earliest convenience.[475]

In March 1873, Helm & Cia. were among the initial shareholders of a modest new company, Compañía de Omnibus, which operated mule-trams in Barranquilla. As was the case with the formation of the bank a month earlier, about one quarter of the founding shares of this company belonged to Jewish Barranquilleros.[476]

It is evident that Jacob Cortissoz, like his father-in-law, belonged to the group of proactive businessmen of Barranquilla who left no stone unturned to ensure the smooth operations of their many and varied enterprises. The efficient transfer of goods between locations was a key element of the city's economy, and efforts to improve the means of transportation in and around Barranquilla therefore became a logical focus for Barranquilla's Jewish businessmen. Jacob Cortissoz was quite aware of this all-important connection between the region's transportation services and economic advancement. In later years, he was also a director of the board of the Compañía Colombiana de Transporte, which was formed in 1886 from the merger of three firms: a transportation company owned by a Cuban engineer, a German Jewish navigation company, and a navigation company owned by two Curaçaoan inhabitants of Barranquilla, David Lopez Penha, a Sephardic Jew, and Cristobal Hoyer, a non-Jew.[477]

Through the firm Cortissoz & Cia. which Jacob founded with his eldest son Rodolfo and his son-in-law Benjamin Senior, he invested in a beer brewery with Alberto Osorio and Ricardo Alvares Correa, both of Curaçaoan Jewish descent. With his brother-in-law, Enrique Alvares Correa, he co-founded another financial institution called Cortissoz Correa Crédito Mercantil, and, towards the end of his life in

Barranquilla, he and Enrique joined Moisés Salas Baiz in the manufacture of matches in Barranquilla.[478]

Jacob Cortissoz was an active participant in the construction and management of a much needed water purification system for Barranquilla. This Acueducto de Barranquilla, which held its first shareholders meeting on July 14, 1879, aimed to supply the city with potable drinking water. During the early months of construction, the project ran into numerous difficulties, including major flooding of the river Magdalena in the area where the aqueduct was being built.[479] In spite of these problems, the first test of the water works in February of 1880 was highly successful, and the local newspaper reported that all interested parties could view three samples of water exhibited at the offices of Sres. Jimeno Hermanos. One sample came from the swamps of Barranquilla – pure mud, according to the reporter – and represented the water the public was at that time drinking. A second sample contained unfiltered water of the river Magadalena. And a third sample was water from the same river, which had been filtered by the machinery of the Acueducto de Barranquilla. The latter, according to the reporter, was *"una agua enteramente cristalina"* – crystal clear water.[480] The aqueduct officially began its operations on April 1, 1880. That same day Rafael Nuñez, former governor of the state of Bolívar, was sworn into office for his first term as president of Colombia.[481] Barranquilla, which is located in Bolívar, benefited from both events.

In 1892 Jacob Cortissoz was secretary of the board and co-signer to an announcement that appeared in the weekly newspaper discussing the purchase and installation of a new pump and a new boiler for the Acueducto de Barranquilla. From time to time, the waterworks project experienced difficulties in collecting its receivables and, over the years, several notices were posted in *El Promotor* advising consumers to pay up their bills or risk having their water supply shut off. One such notice, signed by Cortissoz, ended with the somewhat humorous statement:

> ...To the Company's debtors we must express the wish that they pay their bills without delay: the moral support which we generally receive [just] is not enough for us; it

is also necessary, when the opportunity arises, for compensation to be received for the services which the company is rendering ...[482]

As was the case with so many of the infrastructure projects that were initiated in Barranquilla during the last three decades of the nineteenth century, the aqueduct too was largely owned by Jews, many of whom were of Curaçaoan Sephardic stock. Of the 406 voting shares, at least 255 were in Jewish hands.[483] For many years the company's president was a Sephardic Jew of Curaçaoan ancestry by the name of David de Sola.

While the businessmen of Barranquilla were focused on implementing the many structural changes necessary to keep up with and facilitate the economic growth of the 1870s, they also tried to enhance other aspects of their lives in this commercial city. Jacob Cortissoz was on the forefront of these efforts. In 1882 he was one of the key organizers of the second social club in the city, the Club Barranquilla. Cortissoz became the first president of this prestigious organization, where Barranquilla society met, played, and celebrated for almost a century.[484] In 1888 Jacob Cortissoz was once again one of the founding members of the Compañía Teatro de Barranquilla, an organization which set out to raise the necessary funds for the construction and operation of a new theater in Barranquilla. He became treasurer of the original executive board of this organization, which greatly enhanced the cultural lives of the Barranquilleros in the late nineteenth century.[485]

As was the case among the Sephardim in other Caribbean locations, Freemasonry was an important aspect in the lives of the Alvares Correa and Cortissoz men of Barranquilla. This organization served as an important unifying element among the foreigners – meaning the immigrants – who lived in town. Among the early Freemasons were individuals with German names (Jewish and non-Jewish), such as Heilbron and Berne; English names like Fairbanks, Price, and Ladd; and Curaçaoan names (Jewish and non- Jewish) such as Senior, de Sola, Dovale, Hoyer, and Quast. On November 21, 1864, some of these gentlemen joined with liberal thinkers among Colombian Catholics to form the honorable lodge El Siglo XIX – No. 24.[486] Although the Jewish men of Barranquilla were not part of the original executive board of El Siglo XIX, they were almost all members of this lodge.

Conservative forces and the Catholic Church in Colombia were Freemasonry's natural enemies. On many occasions, the Church used its considerable influence to inform the Freemasons and the public at large of its displeasure regarding the membership of Catholic citizens in this secret organization. A particularly poignant case was that of the first secretary of the Barranquilla lodge, Manuel Román y Picón. Román was the owner of Barranquilla's most important weekly newspaper, *El Promotor*. His daughter, Soledad Román, was married to Dr. Rafael Nuñez, a man who later became President of Colombia. In short, Román was an important and well-connected figure in Barranquilla. Because of his liberal views and his involvement in the Masonic movement, and, upon specific instructions from Bishop Medina of Cartagena, Román was excommunicated and denied last rites by his priest in Barranquilla. A letter by Domingo González Rubio, cofounder of *El Promotor*, to the bishop questioning this decision was answered by the latter in an insolent tone. In his letter the bishop of Cartagena asked González Rubio to inform him if he was "… Jewish, Protestant, Muslim, gentile, Catholic, Quaker, etc. …" A question made even less relevant and more insulting by the fact that the bishop knew Cartagena-born González Rubio and his Roman Catholic family quite well.[487]

Later in the nineteenth century the Jews of Barranquilla became more prominent leaders of the lodge. In 1894, for example, the executive committee of the lodge included the Venerable Master Rafael Ma. Palacio, First Celebrant Jacob[o] Cortissoz, Second Celebrant Alejandro A. Correa (Jacob Cortissoz's brother-in-law), Orator Jacobo R. Mendez Jr., and Secretary Miguel E. Diago.[488] That year, three of the five leaders of the lodge, Cortissoz, Alvares Correa, and Rois Mendez, were Sephardic Jews.

Jacob Cortissoz, like most of the Caribbean Sephardic immigrants of the nineteenth century who left Curaçao in search of better financial opportunities, gave liberally to charity and other fundraising efforts once his purse permitted them to do so. Over the years, he contributed generously to both public and private causes. Through José Helm & Cia., he gave money for the establishment of a non-denominational cemetery, the Cementerio Universal.[489] This cemetery was a joint effort between the Jews, Protestants, and Freemasons of Barranquilla who needed a burial place that was not under Catholic jurisdiction. The issue of June 14, 1873 of the weekly newspaper El Promotor listed the contributors to this effort. Of the 400 pesos raised up to that point in time, eighty-nine pesos were contributed by Jewish Barranquilleros, who arranged for a separate walled section to be set aside for Jewish burials.[490] Prior to the creation of this cemetery, Jews were buried in a burial ground that had been purchased by David A. Senior near the San Mateo Park of Barranquilla. The remains of some of the Jews buried in this original cemetery were transferred to the new location once it was put into use.[491]

Today this section of the Cementerio Universal is referred to as the Cementerio Viejo Sefardita – the Old Sephardic Cemetery. Its oldest graves with legible inscriptions are those of David Goldsmit who died in 1858 at the age of 18,[492] and Isaac Wolf who died in 1862 at the age of 17.[493] These names are testimony that both Ashkenazi and Sephardic Jews had found their way to Barranquilla by the 1850s and 1860s and that in spite of the name Cementerio Vieja Sefardita several Ashkenazim are buried here as well.

On a personal basis, Jacob Cortissoz never forgot his humble beginnings. He tried to help his relatives as best he could. He brought his father to Barranquilla, where Joseph Cortissoz lived out his last years, and where he is buried in the Cementerio Viejo Sefardita.[494] At some point, Jacob also arranged for his half sisters, Sara and Esther, and his half-brother, Abraham, to leave Venezuela and join him in Barranquilla. By this time Cortissoz had already amassed a fortune and was able to finance Abraham's dental studies in the United States. Upon Abraham's return to Colombia, his wealthy half-brother once again helped him with the necessary financial assistance to set up his dental practice in Barranquilla.[495]

Jacob Cortissoz also contributed to Jewish charities. In 1874 he pledged to donate 6 francs for each of the following five years to the Alliance Israélite Universelle.[496] And in 1884, when the treasurer of the Barranquilla committee of the Alliance apologized about the decreased

amount of the community's total remittance to this international charitable organization, Jacob was still contributing to the Alliance with a
five year pledge of 36 francs.*[497] In this aspect he was very much like his
father-in-law, Jacob Alvares Correa, who had been president of the
Alliance committee in Barranquilla in 1870 and had that year collected
76 francs from his Jewish friends and relatives in town for the benefit of
his "coreligionists, who in diverse regions suffer the rigors [imposed by]
despotic and uncivilized governments."[498]

Julia and Jacob Cortissoz had taken to heart the biblical commandment to go forth and multiply. They had fourteen children of which
twelve survived to adulthood. By the time the children were growing up,
Barranquilla's Jews had established a modest religious infrastructure with
the 1874 formation of the Colombian Jewish Community, the purchase
of a burial place, and somewhat more regularly occurring religious services, conducted by Moisés and Samuel de Sola.[499] Jacob and Julia tried
as best they could to provide their children with some Jewish background. Jacob and his sons often attended religious services at the home
of Agustín Senior. Even without an actual synagogue structure or a formally trained rabbinical leader, both his sons, Rodolfo and Ernesto,
became Bar Mitzvah. In a letter to Ernesto just before his thirteenth
birthday, Jacob wrote: "The thirtieth of this month you will turn thirteen, which is the age when, according to our religion, you will count in
our community. At this event, which is so pleasing to our hearts, receive,
with the blessings of your parents, the expression of their most fervent
wishes that they may soon see you become a useful man."[500] It is of interest to note that Ernesto was at that time studying in Germany, and it is
not clear whether he had a bar mitzvah ceremony there or returned to
Barranquilla to receive his first *Aliyah.*** Sourdis Nájera does tell us that
his brother Rodolfo's bar mitzvah was celebrated "*con alborozo en el hogar*"
– with merriment in the home.[501]

---

* This was probably a six-year pledge.
** A religious ceremony whereby a Jew is called to join the reader of the *Torah* during reli-
gious services. The person given this honor must be at least thirteen years old to receive an
Alyah.

Jacob and Julia's fourteen children included ten girls and four boys. Rodolfo and Ernesto married two Catholic sisters in Barranquilla, and Alfredo and Augusto married American women – presumably not Jewish. Of the ten daughters of the Cortissoz-Alvares Correa family, one died at birth and another died young. Five married Jews, two married non-Jews, and one of the daughters remained single. Interestingly, two daughters, Raquel and Renata, were both married to Arquímedes Salas Baiz (Renata married him after Raquel's demise), and a third sister, Rebeca Cortissoz, married Arquímedes's brother, Clodomiro Salas Baiz. These men were brothers of Moisés Salas Baiz, whose migration to Santo Domingo was discussed earlier.[502]

Of all these children, Ernesto Cortissoz probably remains the best known. Ernesto was born in Barranquilla on December 30, 1884. Here he and his brother Rodolfo attended the Colegio Ribón, a school run by Carlos Meisel. Meisel was a German who had been invited by the Colombian government to modernize education in Barranquilla. For those who could afford the expense, the logical extension of this schooling was further study in Germany. When Ernesto graduated Colegio Ribón, he left for Europe where he completed his formal education at the *Realschule* of Bremen. Once back in Colombia, he joined his father's many business activities and worked in the offices of Cortissoz y Cia., which were managed by his older brother Rodolfo.[503]

In many ways, he followed in his father's footsteps, both in business as well as in his civic activities. Among the latter it is noted that from 1910 to 1912 Ernesto was the Venerable Master of his Masonic lodge[504] as well as an active participant in the affairs of the Club Barranquilla, the social club his father had helped organize in 1882. He also served as president of the Carnival in 1913, a major citywide event which is still one of the annual highlights of today's Barranquilla.[505]

Soon after his permanent return from Germany, he fell in love with the beautiful Esther Rodriguez of Barranquilla. In his diary Ernesto Cortissoz wrote about their religious differences:

> We talk about religion and it pleases me immensely to
> see that she has nothing fanatic about her.... It turns out

that we understand each other well, particularly regarding a delicate point which some day we shall be forced
to broach: religion.... I think that I will never doubt her
true love. She only breathes sincerity. In every one of
her gestures and her words, one can discern the purity
and greatness of her soul, incapable of a lie.[506]

Ernesto's marriage to Esther had his parents' blessings. Both he and
Esther were bright, goodlooking, and much admired by members of the
elite society in which they circulated. It would appear that a wonderful
future lay ahead for the young couple. They were married in 1908 and
agreed to raise their children as Catholics.[507] Although Ernesto Cortissoz
never converted to Catholicism, he did not observe even the most
important Jewish holidays. His daughter Clarita indicates that in spite of
the fact that he would attend the break fast after Yom Kippur at the
home of Rabbi Samuel de Sola, he never fasted on that day. Others in
his family, such as his aunt Memé (his mother's sister) and his cousin
Jacobo Alvares Correa did, however, observe Yom Kippur by not eating.[508]

    As Ernesto's father, Jacob Cortissoz, began to spend more time in the
United States, withdrawing from his Colombian business affairs in his
later years, Ernesto took over some of these activities. While managing
his father's many enterprises in the first two decades of the twentieth
century, Ernesto was introduced to a German by the name of Werner
Kaemmerer, who had been trying to sell First World War airplanes to
Latin American countries without too much success. He found a willing
investor in Ernesto, who convinced some of his many contacts in
Barranquilla to help finance his novel plans for a commercial airline.
Thus SCADTA (Sociedad Colombo Alemana de Transporte Aéreo) was
founded on December 5, 1919, reflecting the joint effort of Colombians
and Germans and representing one of the first few commercial airlines in
the world.[509]

    Air travel captured Ernesto imagination. The company was started
with two hydroplanes, and six more were added in 1923. In the early
1920s SCADTA handled mail service, provided aerial reconaissance services, and soon began to transport passengers. Ernesto had great plans for

the enterprise including the expansion of its air services to more Colombian towns as well as Venezuela and the nearby Caribbean islands.

In June 1924 Barranquilla was celebrating the widening and deepening of the mouth of the Magadalena River, the Bocas de Cenizas, which would allow larger vessels to moor. As part of the celebrations, there was to be a fly-over by one of the hydroplanes with SCADTA's president, Ernesto Cortissoz, on board. The plane crashed, killing all aboard. Ernesto's premature death at age thirty-nine was greatly lamented, and most businesses in Barranquilla shut down on the day of his funeral so that Barranquilleros of all walks of life could offer their last respect to this enterprising young man. He left behind his pregnant wife and five children and was also survived by his father. Although Ernesto did not live to see his vision for SCADTA realized, by 1930, the Barranquilla-based airline was flying to Bogotá, Medellín, Cali and several other Colombian towns. It also included Maracaibo, Venezuela, and Curaçao in its scheduled flights, and advertised its services in English to the American market, boasting of "12 years of flying experience in the tropics" by "South America's OLDEST air service."[510] In its founder's memory the Barranquilla airport is called Aeropuerto Internacional Ernesto Cortissoz.[511]

Even though by the 1930s the name Cortissoz in Barranquilla was associated only with the Catholic descendants of the Jewish Cortissoz, some of Jacob Cortissoz's daughters had married within the faith. The story of a descendant of one of these daughters enhances our understanding of the difficulty in maintaining a sense of Jewish continuity among the later generations. The Jewish household of Clodomiro Salas Baiz and Rebeca Cortissoz – Ernesto's sister – had five children. Shortly after the birth of their fifth child, Rebeca Cortissoz de Salas died, leaving Clodomiro to raise his young family by himself. In most Latin American countries, private Catholic schools tend to provide a better education than public schools. Therefore it was to be expected that the Salas-Cortissoz children would all attend Catholic schools in Barranquilla. Rebeca's granddaughter, Judith Segovia de Falquez, says that her grandfather, Clodomiro Salas, used to go to the schools and tell the nuns not to teach his children too many [Catholic] prayers. With

essentially no Jewish educational resources to assist him, this was all
Clodomiro Salas could do to indicate that he wished his children to
remain Jewish. It was obviously not a very effective way to offer an alternate, non-Catholic lifestyle.

Nevertheless, his daughter Raquel, who was Judith Segovia's mother,
remained nominally Jewish in spite of her Catholic schooling and did
not convert when she married Ignacio Segovia in a mixed marriage ceremony. It was agreed, however, that Raquel Salas and Ignacio Segovia's
offspring would be raised Catholic. Clearly, Raquel was surrounded by
Catholic relations: her husband, her children, and many of her aunts,
uncles, and cousins were all Roman Catholic. And, she, of course, had
not been given any Jewish education whatsoever. Over time, the exposure to this Catholic culture made that religion increasingly attractive to
Raquel. She finally converted to Catholicism, with her own eighteen-
year old daughter Judith serving as her *madrina* – godmother – at the ceremony.[512]

Intermarriage in Barranquilla at the turn of the nineteenth century
into the twentieth was considered a matter of personal choice with very
little pressure on the part of the dwindling Jewish community to marry
within the fold. And the Church made sure that all children of such marriages were brought up Catholic, whether or not the mother happened to
be the Jewish partner. While members of the De Sola family of
Barranquilla led the Jewish community in prayers on the High Holy Days
and possibly on other occasions, they were lay leaders who had not
received rabbinical training. Educating the Jewish offspring of the small
number of endogamous marriages was not a focus for the services they
offered to the vanishing Sephardim of Barranquilla. More and more, this
segment of the population became Jewish in name only, in a society
where the Catholic Church provided spiritual comfort and a structured
religious and moral education to its parishioners. It was only natural that
some of the nominally Jewish Barranquilleros in search of spiritual guidance would turn to the only source of such support: the Church.

Interestingly one of Judith Segovia Falquez's daughters married an
American Jew and has converted to Judaism in the twenty-first century.
As a consequence, and also due to her many friendships with members

of Barranquilla's Ashkenazi community, the Catholic Judith Segovia is probably more knowledgeable about Jewish ritual and holidays than her Jewish-born mother Raquel ever was.

Not all of Jacob and Julia Cortissoz's offspring remained in Colombia. Jacob and Julia Cortissoz were truly dedicated to offering their children the best education possible. As mentioned earlier, Ernesto and Rodolfo completed their studies in Germany, and, in order to afford their younger children and grandchildren an American education Jacob and Julia lived in New York in the late nineteenth and early twentieth century. Many of these American-educated children and their descendants remained in the United States and the current generation of Colombian Cortissoz appears to have lost track of these relatives.[513] Jacob and Julia traveled back and forth to Colombia quite frequently, but they did not return to live in Barranquilla, ending their lives in the United States.[514] Yet, it was in Colombia that Jacob's entrepreneurial skills flourished and where he made his fortune.

In the case of the original Sephardic immigrant to Barranquilla, Jacob Alvares Correa, about half his children entered into endogamous marriages, and fewer than half of the Jewish second generation (primarily the women) born in Barranquilla married within the Jewish faith. If this occurred among the descendants of one of the more religiously active Sephardic families of Barranquilla, one can imagine that among the more secular Jews of the time, intermarriage was even more prevalent. By the mid twentieth century, only a handful of these Jewish descendants still lived in the city that had offered such great opportunities to their ancestors in those heady years of the nineteenth century.

CONTRASTING LIVES: THE LOPEZ PENHAS OF BARRANQUILLA

De la luna al fulgor de suave armiño,   In the moon's soft, ermine
   Las ondas descogían   resplendence, The waves unfolded
Sus encajes de perlas y de espumas;   Their mosaic of pearls and foam;
En nuestra sed de amor, jamás pensamos   In our thirst for love, we never thought

Que ocultaban la muerte en sus abismos.	That in their abyss, they were hiding death.
Hoy que al fin he sondeado en tu conciencia,	Today, when at last I have explored your conscience
Tú, mi santa adorada de otros tiempos!...	You, my beloved saint of times gone by! ...
Hoy sé que puede el alma	Today I know that
Tras el poema de luz de una sonrisa	Behind the poem's smiling light
Ocultar los abismos de la muerte.	The soul may hide the abyss of death.

Abismos, *a poem written by Abraham Zacarías Lopez Penha, 1893*

Three siblings arrived in Barranquilla from Curaçao in the latter half of the nineteenth century. They were all children of Haim Daniel Lopez Penha who, after residing in Santo Domingo for more than a decade, was living in Curaçao once more at the time of his children's migration. The experiences of these three were colored by the timing of their arrival in Colombia, as well as by their particular talents and reasons for migration. David Lopez Penha Jr., settled in Barranquilla around 1868,[515] just during the city's growth spurt of the 1860s and 1870s. He was followed almost a decade later by his sister Sarah, and, in the early 1880s, their youngest brother Abraham Zacarías followed suit. David and Abraham Zacarías lived widely different lives in Barranquilla, reflecting their own abilities within the city's strongly commercial focus. Sarah's stay in Colombia may not have been an active choice. She ended up in Barranquilla as a result of her marriage. Each of these individuals had a unique role in Barranquilla's society during the last three decades of the nineteenth century.

David Lopez Penha Jr.

David Lopez Penha Jr. was born on June 20, 1846, in Santo Domingo, Dominican Republic. By the time he was ten, his parents, Haim and Rachel, returned to Curaçao where they had both been born. Although David was sent to school when he arrived in Curaçao, it is believed that he did not complete the formal education available on the island at that time. He hated school and considered the material taught there "narrow,

David Lopez Penha Jr.
1846–1893

Abraham Zacarías Lopez Penha
1865–1927

dry, and deadly." Instead he was fully self-taught and devoured books in many languages, the contents of which he was able to recall verbatim even years later.[516] The Curaçaoan lawyer, Abraham Mendes Chumaceiro who was five years David's senior recalled how the young David used to spend hours "reading works in a language that was not his, and of which, at the beginning, he could not understand a thing, so that each word had to be explained to him; and how, after a short while, he would have mastered that language [and] learned to love it."[517] Chumaceiro acknowledged that "soon he passed me by to take flight [to heights] where I could not follow him." This was no trivial compliment from a man of Chumaceiro's intelligence and training.[518]

In 1862 David's eldest brother, Abraham Oriel, died, and, at age sixteen, David became the oldest son in the household of Rachel and Haim Lopez Penha.[519] David was by then already considered a young genius, but he was also considered a kind person and a good son. He treated his parents and siblings with love and affection, and, to his friends and acquaintances, he was equally generous and pleasant.[520] When he decided to move to Barranquilla, Colombia, his admirers in Curaçao followed his progress proudly, read and saved the speeches he gave, enjoyed his many visits to the island, and marveled at the way in which, over time, he became one of the business leaders of Barranquilla.[521]

David was twenty-two years old when he left Curaçao. He left behind behind his parents, his brothers Moses (age 18), Elias (age 13), and Abraham Zacarías (age 2), and his two single sisters, Sara and Esther, ages 20 and 16, respectively. His older sister, Clara, was living in Santo Domingo with her husband, Isaac de Marchena, at the time. Their daughter, Julita, was David's first of many nieces and nephews.[522]

Soon after his arrival in Barranquilla, David Lopez Penha had occasion to reveal his forthright nature to his new countrymen. A conservative Colombian intellectual by the name of José María Vergara y Vergara had written disparagingly about Curaçaoans in a letter dated April 21, 1871. This letter was published in *La Ilustración*, a popular national Colombian publication. David knew Vergara y Vergara quite well and had considered him a friend. The article in *La Ilustración* really bothered him. As David Lopez Penha's biographer Dr. David R. Capriles rightfully wrote, *"plus l'offenseur est cher, plus grande est l'offense"* – the more beloved the offender, the greater the offense.[523] On the 13th of May 1871, David wrote a rebuttal, which according to his friends softened, calmed, appeased, disarmed, convinced, and conquered his adversary.[524] On the 29th of May of the same year, Vergara publicly apologized in writing. This written debate was widely read by Colombian intellectuals of the time and marked the beginning of David's popularity in literary circles.

By 1874, David Lopez Penha Jr. had already become known as a good writer and an excellent orator in Barranquilla. On the occasion of the sixty-third anniversary of Cartagena's declaration of independence from Spain, the 11th of November 1874, he was invited to speak at a gathering on the Plaza de San Nicolás in Barranquilla. He brilliantly weaved the recent history of Spanish oppression in South America and the subsequent revolutionary wars that led to Colombia's independence with the history of the eighty-year war fought by the Netherlands against Spain in the sixteenth and seventeenth centuries. He ended with an important charge to the citizens of the still young republic.

> Adelante Colombianos! – Onward Colombians! March on towards that noble and holy end [of universal brotherhood]! Crown the splendid achievement of your political emancipation with the sublime achievement of your moral growth. Let discord escape this land terrified as did its barbarian conquerors! May your motto be Unity and Peace! Onward! Your path is widened and your journey is shortened by the liberal dogmas and democratic teachings that give flesh to the gospel truths of your model constitution. Onward! Be for the regenerative cause of Brotherhood what your eminent progenitors were for the cause of Liberty – soldiers of integrity; fervent patriots; selfless apostles.[525]

Not only is his Spanish in this speech sophisticated and impeccable, but he sounds like a patriot, in love with his new country – almost like a politician running for office. If his presentation was as persuasive as his writing, he must have been an inspiration to his audience. At the time he gave this speech, he was twenty-eight years old and had only been living in Colombia for six years.

David Lopez Penha wrote other rebuttals to articles he disagreed with as well. In 1875, Dr. José María Samper, chief editor of the national publication *La Unión Colombiana* and a prominent Colombian politician, had referred to the government of the Colombian province of Antioquia as being served by "*Israelitas políticos*" and had indicated that he believed the title *Israelita* to be synonymous with "disloyalty, avarice, and immorality." He furthermore referred to the synagogue as a refuge for merchants and traders. This time, David Lopez Penha, Jr., descendant of some of Curaçao's most devoted Sephardim, was truly livid. He responded to these anti-Semitic comments with a nineteen-page letter which was printed in Barranquilla and widely distributed.

In his letter, he countered Samper's comments point by point in his eloquent style.

> The Synagogue, Mr. Samper, is not what you through ignorance or bad faith represent it to be. The Synagogue is not a Stock-Exchange, nor much less a public market. It is a house of prayer, like many others, which is built by human frailty as a Sanctuary where [worshippers] can offer to the Supreme Being the faith of their devotion, the repentant tributes of their belief. The synagogue is the sacred site where the faithful sons of Abraham congregate with veneration to worship the Universal Father, in spirit and truth, recognizing with ever-growing fervor his Oneness![526]

On the matter of avarice and usury, Lopez Penha explained that it is quite common for those who accuse the Jews of these habits to blame them for the evils and character defects that they themselves compelled people of the Jewish faith to be inspired by. He then proceeded to provide the history of the persecution and marginalization of the Jews in Europe, which, Penha argued, made them realize the importance of money as a way to get things done. Or in his words: "their wealth assisted them most powerfully [in dealing] with those who, [though] deaf to the voice of Charity and Reason, did not show themselves to be equally indifferent before the altars of the Golden Calf."[527]

He ended his letter to Samper as follows:

> What are your concepts based on? I encourage you to give me the reasoning behind your affirmations. If you manage to prove them to me, I offer to foresake [my religion] and to find in the regenerating waters of Baptism the ablution that will *purify* me of my *Jewishness*. But if you do not justify your premises; if you [can]not lessen the strength of the [assertions] that I present to you in this letter, then, Dr. José M. Samper, I shall consider it my right to consider you an UNJUST MAN![528]

It is obvious from these writings that David was a man who stood up for his beliefs, even to well-respected, established authors and politicians like Vergara and Samper who were respectively fifteen and eighteen years older than Penha. It was impossible for him to let a slight directed to any group of which he considered himself a part go unanswered. He could easily have ignored the writings of these men and continued with his business affairs and other occupations. But it was not in his character to do so, and, as such, he was the pride of the Jewish community in Barranquilla and in Curaçao.

David was not only a speech and letter writer. He translated many works from French into Spanish and wrote original poetry and prose as well. Being a practical man, however, he was first and foremost a businessman. In the early 1870s, two of his most important investments in Barranquilla were in the Banco de Barranquilla of which he was a founding member, shareholder, and, in 1873, its managing partner[529] and the Compañía Colombiana de Transporte of which he was the managing director. The latter handled transportation of cargo and passengers on the Magdalena River, facilitating their transfer to seafaring vessels that would sail to the United States, Europe, and many Latin American countries, including Mexico, Argentina, Brazil, Chile, Venezuela, Peru, Ecuador, and Cuba.[530]

From these positions he branched out into many other business dealings. David Lopez Penha's accounting books provide an interesting picture of his investments in the 1890s. In addition to his financial positions in the aforementioned two companies, he owned stocks and bonds of the Tranvía Eléctrico de Panamá – the Electric Tramway Company of Panama – and had investments in an insurance company as well as the Santander Hydraulic Company, a rum business, a salt mining company, and various other small manufacturing concerns. He also owned residential and commercial real estate, some of which provided rental income. In March of 1893, the Tranvía Eléctrico de Panamá was sold to United Electric Tramways, Limited of London. As a result, all shareholders equity was liquidated. At the time, David's share in this enterprise was 28,516 pesos. A year later, financial statements pertaining to his estate show his total assets to be about 124,400 pesos, a hefty sum in the 1890s.[531] Arriving in Barranquilla at a moment of great opportunities, he had taken full advantage of this fortuitous timing.

Penha was a charitable man. He provided funds for the Cementerio Universal,[532] contributed to a bazaar to benefit a new hospital building,[533] made contributions to purchase bricks for the church Iglesia de Nuestra Señora del Rosario,[534] gave freely of his time to address the students of the Colegio de Niñas at their musical and theatrical performances,[535] contributed annually to the Alliance Israélite Universelle,[536] and, in short, was involved in all aspects of business, religious, and social life in Barranquilla.

In 1879, David Lopez Penha, Jr. was appointed vice consul of the Netherlands in Colombia, and in 1884, he was promoted to consul general. A few years later, his diplomatic efforts on behalf of the Dutch colonies made him a hero in the eyes of Curaçao's commercial establishment. In 1887, a law had been proposed by the Colombian legislature entitling the government to levy import duties of an additional thirty percent on all merchandise imported from other countries (i.e. Europe and the U.S.A.) if they were transferred to Colombia through the Antilles. Since most imports were arriving in Colombia via Curaçao and Cuba, this new law would have meant a true *coup de grâce* to the lucrative trade between the Sephardim of Curaçao and those of Barranquilla and other Colombian ports of importance in those days. David Lopez Penha, Jr., in his capacity as consul of the Netherlands* and by means of his many political connections and his usual eloquence and persuasive power, managed to dissuade key Colombian government officials from proceeding with these plans. As a result of his efforts, the law was not ratified, and a large part of the Curaçaoan trade with the South American continent was thus preserved. In Venezuela, the champions of Curaçao-Venezuela trade relations had not been equally successful, and in 1881, Venezuela had introduced the excessive thirty percent duties, putting a dent in Curaçao's trade with that country. It was therefore doubly important to ensure that trade between Curaçao and Colombia would not be similarly affected.[537]

---

* Notably, David Lopez Penha Jr. was also the consul of Chile and Spain in Barranquilla.

Following the defeat of the proposed law, the Dutch warship, Queen Emma, arrived in Sabanilla on a good will visit in January of 1888. David Lopez Penha accompanied the ship's captain to meet with Barranquilla's government officials and reported that they had amicable discussions about the new tax agreements of the previous year which, thanks to Penha's intervention, were favorable to the trade relations between Curaçao and Colombia. Penha then departed on board the Queen Emma for an official visit to Cartagena as well. Apparently, the visit of this Dutch warship was meant as a follow-up to the important accomplishments of 1887, with the Dutch officially expressing their appreciation for the outcome of the negotiations to the officials in the important ports of Colombia.[538]

David Lopez Penha Jr. had excellent political contacts. He was a personal friend of Dr. Rafael Nuñez and his wife Soledad Román, and, during Nuñez's presidency of Colombia (1880-1882 and 1884-1894), Penha was a frequent visitor at the Presidential Palace in Bogotá[539] and at Nuñez's residence in Cartagena.[540] He was also a close friend of the publisher of the weekly paper *El Promotor* and had been a co-editor of the paper. As such, his comings and goings, speeches, and business activities were always duly noted in this publication. After a stay in Curaçao in 1888, the editor of *El Promotor* affectionately and profusely welcomed him back to Barranquilla, concluding: "[Penha's] pen is brilliant when he writes and his clear talents throw off diamonds that glimmer as apparitions in rough terrain. Welcome to him who is so much esteemed in this city."[541]

David Lopez Penha's importance in Colombia's political dealings beyond issues that were directly related to the countries which he represented as consul is evident from his presence and involvement at many official events that affected Colombia's economic future. An example was his early relationship with Count Ferdinand de Lesseps. When De Lesseps arrived in Barranquilla in late December 1879, David Lopez Penha Jr. was among the individuals chosen to toast him during his visit.[542] De Lesseps was at that time finalizing the necessary groundwork for the construction of the Panama Canal, running between the city of Colón and the city of Panama, a project which was officially started on

January 1, 1880. Panama was then a province of Colombia, and it was important for the promoters of this project to receive the support of the many businessmen of Barranquilla and other Colombian ports who had most to gain from expanding the routes of transportation for the region. Colombian leaders and men of commerce had great hopes for this project. But in spite of the initial enthusiasm, it turned out to be quite difficult to complete the canal. The endeavor resulted in various bankruptcies of the entitites involved and the declaration of independence from Colombia by Panama in 1903. In the end, the United States essentially took over the final construction efforts and operations of the Panama Canal, which officially opened to traffic in 1914.

During the early years of the construction of the Canal, Penha continued to be in touch with Count de Lesseps about the project. An announcement in *El Promotor* of February 13, 1886 indicated that he was leaving for Panama to meet with De Lesseps and that he had promised to send the newspaper his impressions of the Canal project. Subsequent to his trip to Panama, he was scheduled to go to Bogotá, most likely to report his findings to the Colombian President, his friend Dr. Rafael Nuñez. During his absence, the consulate of the Netherlands was left in the care of Mr. Oswald Berne, while the consular affairs of Spain and Chile remained in the hands of Penha's friend Benjamin T. Senior.[543] Both these men were David Lopez Penha's Masonic Brothers and personal friends.

David's consular appointments required him to participate in many ceremonial activities in the city, and he acquitted himself of these tasks with significant élan. As consul general of the Netherlands, he organized celebrations to honor the birthdays of members of the Dutch royal family. He hosted one such party on the occasion of Princess Wilhelmina's eleventh birthday in 1891, and Barranquilla's newspaper gave a full report of the festivities, including descriptions of the reception room at the consulate, the food served, presents offered to the attendees, and speeches given by some of the party-goers. David de Sola addressed the gathering as the representative of "la Colonia Curazoleña" in Barranquilla, and David Lopez Penha Jr., the host of this elegant event, also spoke on this celebratory occasion.[544] Although he was single and did not have a wife to co-host and plan the reception with him, it appears that every decorative and gastronomic detail had been carefully taken into account.

At official events and anniversaries, David's consular position also ensured his participation. For example, in 1892, when the town commemorated the 400th year of the discovery of America by Columbus with many citywide festivities, all foreign diplomats in Barranquilla attended a celebratory mass. These dignitaries, of course, included David Lopez Penha Jr.[545] Probably the only reason he did not give a speech at this event was that as a Jew he was, most likely, not allowed to do so in a Catholic church.

As consul of Spain in Barranquilla, he was decorated with the order of Carlos III and, very ironically, with the order of Isabela la Católica. The latter decoration is, of course, named for the Spanish queen who finalized the expulsion of the Jews from Spain in 1492. In spite of his pride in receiving this honor from Spain, it is clear from the aforementioned exchange with Dr. Samper that David was keenly aware of Spain's unfortunate history vis-à-vis its Jewish citizens. The Lopez Penha family in Spain and later in Portugal had suffered greatly under the vigilant eye of the Inquisition, and David's grandfather, Moseh Lopez Penha, had recorded the family's oral history in a widely circulated manuscript written in Portuguese. In this document, he recounted the torture and imprisonment his forefathers had endured in Lobón, Spain during the times of the Spanish Inquisition. He also elaborated on their subsequent migration from Spain to Portugal where the Inquisition eventually caught up again with the Sephardim and the flight of the Lopez Penhas from Portugal to Smyrna, Turkey. It is likely that most members of the Penha family, and particularly David who loved to read, had read this narrative and the accompanying genealogical chart. Copies of the document in the original Portuguese as well as in a Spanish translation were found among the belongings of many descendants of the Lopez Penha family in the twentieth century.[546]

David's attention to business and official affairs did not diminish his compassionate concern and love for his family. Having the wherewithal to be of financial assistance to relatives who needed a helping hand, he never hesitated to reach out to them. As mentioned previously, he provided the funds for his nephew, Haim Lopez Penha of Santo Domingo, to study in Germany from a very early age, when presumably Haim's father could not afford to pay for such an expense. Had David been around to witness Haim's many accomplishments in Santo Domingo in the twentieth century, he would have considered the yield on his investment in his nephew's education even more satisfying than that on many of his other financial investments.

David Lopez Penha, Jr. also looked after his sister Sarah's legal and financial affairs in Barranquilla. Sarah and Clara were the two siblings closest in age to David, and he had a particularly strong bond with Sarah. After Sarah was widowed, he had power of attorney to act for her with regard to her husband's estate, and he also appears to have taken care of her personal accounting.

On May 12, 1893, the 47-year old David Lopez Penha Jr. filed a sealed copy of his last will and testament with Barranquilla's primary notary public, Juvenal Francisco Herrera. Whether the timing of this act had to do with the fact that Penha was embarking on a longer than usual trip or whether he had not been feeling well and decided to put his affairs in order is not known. In his will, Penha set out exactly how his very significant estate was to be distributed. He designated his father as his universal heir and executor of the estate, were he to survive him, and named alternate executors in case this was not to be. These executors were all Barranquilleros of Curaçaoan Sephardic descent and included Benjamin Tavares Senior, Abraham Zacarías Lopez Penha (David's brother), Jacob Cortissoz, and Jacob Senior.[547] In addition to distributions intended for his immediate family, the document indicated that the four children of Abraham (Agustín) Senior and Rebeca Tavares, Sephardim residing in Barranquilla, were to be given five percent each of the total value of his estate. This statement was followed by the following sentence in which he addressed these four individuals directly: "I beg of them to accept this limited token of the brotherly affection I feel towards them and of the unending gratitude I owe them for more than twenty-five years of uninterrupted signs of graciousness and kindness [bestowed on me] by their dear parents and themselves."[548] These individuals were among his nearest and dearest in Barranquilla.

To the great dismay and heartbreak of his many friends and relatives, David Lopez Penha died on the 24th of October 1893 of an undisclosed disease at the age of forty-seven. He was in Holland at the time, possibly on consular business, and was buried in a very simple grave in the Jewish cemetery of Ouderkerk aan de Amstel, outside Amsterdam.

From his obituaries and his last will and testament, it is known that he was single when his life was so unexpectedly cut short. Did David not marry because he did not find himself a Jewish wife? Surely a man of his capabilities, wealth, good looks, and social standing could have found a wife in Barranquilla's society of the nineteenth century. But unlike their brothers Elias and Moses Benjamin in Santo Domingo, who married outside the Jewish faith, David and his brother Abraham Zacarías, living in Barranquilla, both remained single.

David's Colombian friend Francisco Parias Vargas wrote a four-column obituary at the time of his passing in which he hints at lost loves and secrets taken to the grave, ending with:

> Love! At the first ray of light that brightens the sky of the deserted pole a surprising flower is born. How much more so in tropical regions, where the shadows are phosphorescent, aromatic, and passionate!
>
> Nevertheless Penha dies, and in the resplendence of the loving moon that reverently illuminates his tomb, the white feather of a deserted nest does not shine in the shadow of the cypress that shades it.[549]

There is a puzzling reference to his "orphans" in an obituary written by D.H.S. of Curaçao (only initials are provided by the author of this obituary). This may refer to David's charitable activities at an orphanage, since Penha's testament makes it very clear that he never had children of his own: "*No soy ni he sido casado; ni tengo ni he tenido hijos naturales o adoptivos*" – I am not nor have I been married; nor do I have or have I had children of my own or adopted children.[550]

His death left a void in Barranquilla's business community. For more than twenty-five years, David Lopez Penha Jr. had been among the most important entrepreneurs in this growing city. Throughout those years he had remained loyal to the religion of his fathers, and in all his actions he had reflected the unusually broad cultural perspectives he brought with him from Curaçao. He was a Renaissance man par excellence and Barranquilla's gain was, to some extent, Curaçao's loss.

Sarah Lopez Penha

Sarah Lopez Penha was only a little over a year younger than her brother David. During their early years in Santo Domingo and later, in Curaçao, the two were quite close. In the 1870s, when David was already making a name for himself in Barranquilla, Sarah remained in Curaçao under her parents' care and appeared headed for spinsterhood.

In the mid 1870s, however, her life changed dramatically. Her mother died in July of 1875, and Sarah, at age twenty-seven, was now in charge of her father's household. Her sister Esther was several years younger and already an adult, but their youngest brother, Abraham Zacarías was only ten. Based on his personality as an adult, it is likely that he was not an easy child. Sarah's seniority and increased responsibilities did not last very long. A little over a year after her mother's demise, her father remarried, and the two single daughters now shared the management of Haim Lopez Penha's home with their stepmother Rachel Curiel.[551]

Some time after this wedding, when Sarah was almost thirty, she met her future husband, Jacob Senior. It is not clear if she got to know Senior on a trip to visit her brother David in Colombia or if Jacob Senior, who lived in Barranquilla, was in Curaçao visiting his relatives when the two met.

Jacob was a widower. He had married Leah de Castro* in 1849 at a wedding ceremony that did not take place in Curaçao. When the couple's daughter, Esther, was born, they were living in Barranquilla, and, in 1875, when Leah died, they were still in that town. Leah was buried

---

* She was a younger sister to Judith de Castro, who married Benjamin Delvalle after the complicated resolution of her status as a *halitza*.

there in the old Sephardic cemetery. Her tombstone shows her birth and death dates and an inscription that reads, "Her husband and daughters always lovingly preserve the memory of her tenderness," implying that she was survived by more than one daughter. Nevertheless, when subsequent to his death, the exact disbursements from Jacob Senior's estate were agreed upon in March of 1884, the documents listed only one legitimate child of his first marriage to Leah de Castro – Esther Senior Wolff.

Jacob Senior was 55 years old when he asked the 29-year old Sarah Lopez Penha to marry him. It is hard to know if Sarah's father's remarriage, her stepmother's subsequent pregnancy, or the rambunctious Abraham Zacarías influenced her decision to marry this much older man. She may have been eager to leave Curaçao and her father's household or she may really have been in love with Jacob. In any case, the wedding date was set for June 20, 1877, and the family began to prepare for the event.

It is interesting to note that although Sarah's father had provided a dowry of five thousand guilders at the time of his daughter Clara's marriage to Isaac de Marchena in 1865, he did not provide such a dowry for Sarah in 1877.[552] It is possible that his financial condition was not what it had been twelve years earlier. But it is even more likely that Jacob Senior, who was a very wealthy man, refused Haim Lopez Penha's offer of a dowry. Instead, the groom gifted his bride a very large sum of 25,000 guilders, specifically indicating that Sarah was to consider this sum hers at all times under the customary laws of marrying without common property – *buiten gemeenschap van goederen*.[553]

There were many legal issues that had to be resolved for the ceremony to take place in Curaçao as planned. Birth certificates and Jacob's first wife's death certificate were needed for the civil ceremony. Obtaining these proved to be impossible. In the marriage document the groom indicated that he was unable to produce a birth certificate for himself, since no birth registers existed on the island of Curaçao when he was born; nor was he able to produce a death certificate for his deceased wife Leah, since death registers were not kept in Barranquilla, Colombia at the time of her death. This argument was accepted by the bride as well as by the Dutch island's civil servant J.F.K. van Eps who performed the civil ceremony. Notably, Sarah Lopez Penha could not produce her birth certificate either, stating that she was born in Santo Domingo where no such records were kept.[554] In Latin American countries, birth and death records were kept by the Church parishes, where, of course, Jewish life-cycle events would not have been recorded.

Once these statements by the bride and groom had been notarized, the bride also obtained a certificate from Doctor David R. Capriles of Curaçao, in which he declared that "as a consequence of her nervous condition [she] could not appear at the City Hall" for the ceremony. Instead the couple was wed at the bride's father's home in the residential area of Pietermaai in Curaçao.[555] It is not known if this "nervous condition" was truthful or used to bypass the government agency's requirement that couples be married in an official location. Getting married in Haim Lopez Penha's Pietermaai home was, no doubt, a great deal more comfortable and elegant than the usual setting for civil wedding ceremonies. In Curaçao today, these ceremonies continue to be separate from the religious ceremonies and are usually enacted prior to the religious event. It is possible, of course, that Sarah was truly concerned and nervous about marrying a much older man who already had a married daughter and grandchildren of his own. Nothing in her subsequent life, however, would seem to indicate that she had a delicate psychological disposition, and, nervous or not, Sarah was swept off to Barranquilla soon after the ceremony.

The wedding festivities were attended by many members of the island's Jewish community and, most likely, also by out of town guests. The men who signed the *ketubah* were representative of the migratory background of the bride and groom. Both had lived away from Curaçao for periods of their lives. Sarah Lopez Penha had been born in Santo Domingo and was living in Curaçao at the time of her wedding, and Jacob Senior was born in Curaçao and had lived most of his adult life in Barranquilla, Colombia. The witnesses at this Curaçaoan wedding were also Sephardic Jews who had traveled and lived in many different places.[556]

The first witness was Samuel Curiel (age 41) a merchant who, as was discussed earlier, was at that time living in the Dominican Republic but who had remained close to his relatives and business associates in

Curaçao. Curiel's wife, Hannah Pereira, and the bride were first cousins, and Curiel was a brother to Sarah's stepmother. The second witness was Isaac de Marchena (age 28), Curaçaoan merchant and brother-in-law of the bride. Sarah's sister, Clara, and her husband Isaac de Marchena had also lived in Santo Domingo where several of their twelve children were born. Although the couple had moved back to Curaçao by late 1875, their presence added to the Curaçaoan-Dominican flavor of the wedding ceremony. The third witness was Abraham Senior (age 53), the groom's brother. Strange as it may seem, Jacob Senior had two brothers named Abraham. Abraham I. Senior was a half brother, born to Isaac and Leah Senior in 1815 in Curaçao.[557] He was better known as Agustín and lived in Barranquilla at the time of Jacob and Sarah's wedding.[558] Jacob Senior's younger brother, Abraham, lived in Curaçao and was the son of Isaac Senior and Esther Belmonte. Based on the ages of the witnesses, which are indicated in the Senior-Penha marriage document, it was the Curaçaoan Abraham who served as witness at this wedding.[559] Mordechay Capriles (age 40), an acquaintance of the couple, was the fourth witness. While Mordechay lived in Curaçao at the time of the wedding, he was as intrigued by Venezuela as his cousin Manasés Capriles Ricardo had been, and his descendants eventually moved to Venezuela where they joined the many Capriles cousins already established in that country.[560]

Dr. David Ricardo Capriles who had graciously supplied the medical opinion which allowed the wedding to take place at Sarah's parental home in Pietermaai had also spent considerable time away from the island. He had studied medicine at Columbia University in New York City, receiving his degree in 1857. Before settling down in Curaçao, where he had been born, he spent several months traveling in Venezuela, visiting family and friends who had migrated to that country.[561]

Whereas, at first glance, the marriage and legal documents pertaining to Sarah's marriage to Jacob Senior may seem filled with small-town details, the people involved were very worldly and well-traveled. Yet, even as they moved from one part of the Caribbean region to another and frequently traveled to the United States and Europe for business, plea-sure, education, and health reasons, they kept in touch and often used Curaçao as their hub.

Once settled in Barranquilla, it did not take long for Sarah to become pregnant. On June 28, 1878 she had a son, whom she called Isaac. When Isaac was four, his sixty-year-old father died, leaving behind a will and testament that made no mention of Sarah and bequeathing his considerable estate to his two legitimate children, Esther Senior Wolff and Isaac Senior.

Sarah's response to this slight or oversight, which only became known to her after Jacob Senior's demise at the end of 1882, was not at all that of a woman with a nervous condition. She was fortunate that throughout the ensuing legal dilemma, she was able to count on the support of her brother-in-law, Abraham (Agustín) I. Senior, and of her brother, the much-esteemed Dutch Consul in Barranquilla, David Lopez Penha, Jr. She contested the disposition of the estate. Her legal case consisted of several multi-paged documents and took quite a while to resolve. These legal ramifications serve as a reminder that, although there was great fluidity in the places of residence of these Curaçaoan Jews, the laws and customs of the different Caribbean islands and countries were quite diverse. Jacob Senior's will also disclosed once more the degree to which the Curaçao-connected Sephardim of Barranquilla's Diaspora continued to trust and rely on each other in various capacities. The executor of the estate was none other than the enterprising Jacob Cortissoz.

Sarah's initial presentation to the Provincial Judge in Barranquilla is written in a very formal style and was obviously prepared by someone with a legal background. She begins by providing proof that she was indeed the wife of the deceased and that she had dutifully fulfilled all her wifely obligations during the five and a half years that they were wed. The partial translation provided below clearly reflects the subservient position of upperclass women in Colombia of the late nineteenth century.

> I, Sarah Lopez Penha de Senior, native of Santo Domingo and a resident of this city [Barranquilla], disclose [the following] to you with due respect: 1st On the 20th of June of the year eighteen hundred and seventy-seven Mr. Jacob Isaac Senior and I were married in Curaçao according to the conditions in force there; 2nd

From the moment we celebrated our wedding until the
death of my husband, he and I always lived together and
in perfect harmony; and even though he was absent
once from the place where we had established our shared
home to move for a short period to this city for purposes related to his mercantile business established here,
this took place in agreement and by our mutual consent.
During his other absences I accompanied him, except on
one occasion when we were in New York for reasons of
his health. He continued on to Europe to better climates, leaving me in the care of his legitimate brother
Mr. A.I. Senior and his family, who were also staying in
said New York City. In this as in all other cases during
our married life, I have always and constantly submitted
myself to [his] marital authority; 3rd On the fifth of
August of eighteen hundred and seventy-nine, my aforementioned husband executed a testament in this city,
which has already been recognized and acknowledged as
his last will, and registered in due form; ... [562]

It does not appear that this 1884 appeal by Sarah was contested by her
stepdaughter, Esther, whose family stood to lose most from the requested
review of Jacob Senior's last will and testament. Notably, Abraham Wolff
represented his wife Esther Senior in all the legal affairs that ensued.
Both the tone of the paragraph quoted above and the fact that Esther
and Sarah were not to involve themselves directly in these legal and
business affairs emphasize the submissive and secondary roles played by
the Latin American Jewish women of the era. Their passive participation
contrasts sharply with the aggressive entrepreneurial character of most of
the migrating Sephardic men and their male offspring. A woman's role
in Barranquilla in the 1880s was also much more restrictive than that of
women in St. Thomas where, three decades earlier, Hannah Sasso Piza
had been running her own retail establishment quite successfully.

Although Sarah and Jacob had been married in Curaçao under Dutch
law without common property, the laws of Colombia prevailed in the

end. After subtraction of various expenses and specific gifts indicated in the will (including provision for the dowry her husband had given her at the time of her marriage), the remainder of the estate was divided among Sarah, her son Isaac and her stepdaughter Esther, with Sarah receiving one fourth of the estate and the children three eighths each.[563]

Once she was widowed, Sarah had to decide what she wanted to do. Should she stay in Barranquilla or would it be better to raise her son in Curaçao? Barranquilla of the late nineteenth century had grown significantly from the little village described by Captain Cochrane in 1823. Its level of comfort, however, had lagged behind this growth to a great extent, as is apparent from a travel report provided by Charles H. Emerson, an American journalist, who arrived in Barranquilla by train in 1898. He writes that he was taken by carriage on a winding route from the station to his hotel, riding through dusty and often smelly streets and alleys. Upon his arrival at the hotel, he and his companions were dying for a hot bath, but such refinements were not available at Barranquilla's best lodging place. He describes the city as one big market place of about 40,000 souls with inconsistent architecture and irregular public roads often littered with garbage.[564] Yet, descriptions of such events as Princess Wilhelmina's birthday party celebrated at the Dutch consulate of Barranquilla in 1891 do give the impression that a degree of elegance and conspicuous consumption had become discernable among the well-to-do of Barranquilla. Her marriage to the wealthy Jacob Senior had put Sarah Lopez Penha smack in the middle of this elite circle. Still, it is likely that the comforts of Curaçao must have seemed appealing to the recent widow, and, some time after her husband's demise, she moved back to the island.

Colombia was not without its attractions and happy memories for Sarah, and in 1888 she travelled for a visit from Curaçao to Barranquilla, accompanied by her brother David.[565] At that point, the distribution of her deceased husband's estate had not yet been finalized. On April 20, 1889, *El Promotor* published a notice signed by Sarah Lopez Penha indicating that the liquidation of the assets of the estate of J.I. Senior would be managed by Jacob Cortissoz and that, in his absence, these affairs would be taken care of by David Lopez Penha Jr. (Sarah's brother) or

Abraham Wolff (Jacob Senior's son-in-law).[566] While Jacob Senior had left behind a very large estate of over 270,000 pesos (one could live amply on 2000 pesos a year in those days), much of the estate was tied up in fixed assets and investments which had to be liquidated in order to be distributed.

Sarah had made many friends in Barranquilla during the time she lived there, and it is not clear whether she was in Colombia temporarily in 1888 and 1889 visiting these acquaintances and taking care of her financial affairs or if she still considered the city her primary place of residence at that time. What is known is that towards the end of her life, she lived in Curaçao. She died there in 1921 and was buried in the old Jewish cemetery at Blenheim near her brothers Aaron and Joseph Lopez Penha who had succumbed to various epidemics in the 1860s before reaching adulthood.[567]

Sarah and Jacob's only son, Isaac Senior, was schooled both in Curaçao and in Barranquilla. When he was twenty-two, he married his first cousin, Celina, daughter of Clara Lopez Penha and Isaac de Marchena, in the Mikvé Israel synagogue. Celina and Isaac Senior had four children, all born in Curaçao. The youngest son, Alex, died at age four and was buried on the island. The eldest daughter, called Sarah after her grandmother, also died young. She was twenty-two when she passed away in 1937 in Barranquilla. The fact that she was buried in Barranquilla suggests that Celina and Isaac Senior had returned to live in that town in the 1930s, even though their two surviving children were both living in Curaçao at the time. Soon after Sarah's death, they moved back to Curaçao.

Isaac, however, continued to be drawn to Barranquilla. Toward the end of his life, he left Celina behind on the Dutch island and returned to his Colombian place of birth by himself. He died and was buried there in 1942. His wife and surviving children continued to make their home in Curaçao.[568] His daughter, Noemi, was a beloved, but strict, teacher of Spanish in Curaçao's public schools, and his son, Otto, was an entrepreneur who established the first ice cream and dairy factory on the island. Otto Senior was also very dedicated to Curaçao's Mikvé Israel community and served as president of that congregation for many years. His presidency covered the important timespan when the two Sephardic communities, which had split in 1864, were reunited to form the Mikvé Israel – Emanuel Congregation in 1963.

Sarah Lopez Penha's experience in Barranquilla was entirely a consequence of her marriage to Jacob Senior, just like Hannah Sasso's life in St. Thomas came about as a consequence of her husband's appointment as cantor for the St. Thomas Hebrew Congregation. But unlike Hannah, Sarah did not have to work for a living. It is likely that during the five years before the demise of her husband, she spent most of her time taking care of her son, socializing with the other women of Barranquilla's elite, and attending charitable functions, receptions, and parties. As a widow, she was less likely to participate in some of these events in a city where social affairs were the raison d'être for women of her class. Sarah's life as a single mother must have become considerably less exciting than her married life had been, and some of Barranquilla's appeal must have worn off after her husband's death. Curaçao's newly developed residential area of Scharloo, where Sarah's sister Clara and her ever-expanding family were living, offered equal if not greater sophistication and comfort during the last decades of the nineteenth century. It is therefore not surprising that, eventually, Sarah Lopez Penha returned to Curaçao, whereas such a move was never considered by Hanna Sasso after her husband, Joshua Piza, passed away in St. Thomas.

Abraham Zacarías Lopez Penha

Abraham Zacarías Lopez Penha was the baby in the family. He was born on March 18, 1865 in Curaçao, three years after the death of his two brothers, Abraham Oriel and Aaron. A few weeks after he was born, his brother, Joseph, died from another epidemic disease that swept through Curaçao.[569] Grief must have permeated the household of Rachel and Haim Daniel Lopez Penha, and sadness must have been a pervasive sentiment during Abraham Zacarías's childhood. To make matters worse, his mother passed away when he was ten years old and a year later, in 1876, his father remarried.[570] Soon thereafter, he and his older spinster sister Esther were the only children of Haim Daniel and Rachel Maduro left living at home. His brothers David, Moses, and Elias had all migrated away from Curaçao, his sister Clara and her husband Isaac de Marchena had their own large household, and his sister Sarah, who had been living at home, married and moved to Barranquilla in 1877. That same year Abraham Zacarías's father and his new wife had a daughter called Rebecca.[571] It is likely that much attention was lavished on this new addition to the family, which, no doubt, represented a less than happy development for the young Abraham.

Abraham Zacarías was eager to emulate his older brothers and prove his mettle in foreign lands. In his twenty-first year, he moved to Barranquilla where his brother David had become a well-known figure. In 1886, when Abraham arrived, Barranquilla was an important center of commerce where astute businessmen often became rich in a few short years. Abraham Zacarías hoped to follow their example. However, although he tried, he was never as successful in business as his brother David had been. This was partially due to timing but also due to his particular set of talents. David had always been a businessman first and an author second, but Abraham Zacarías was definitely an author first and a businessman second. He wrote both poetry and prose and was generally considered a literary man. At the same time, he ran a bookstore and owned and published a number of literary magazines during his lifetime, including one called *El Siglo*.[572] His inability to succeed in business is made abundantly clear by the Colombian writer Carlos H. Palacio, who described Abraham Zacarías Lopez Penha as

> ...[having] the vastest knowledge, a literary culture so exotic in my native city [Barranquilla], which was primarily dedicated to industry and commerce, [so that he was] like "a carnation on the heights of the Chimborazo." [an inhospitable volcanic peak of the Andes] But Lopez Penha, aside from being highly educated, wanted to instruct my countrymen and he established a bookstore where one could find, at reasonable prices, famous works that were just published in France and Spain. I do not presume that by doing so he expect-

ed to conduct much useful business, because he did not.

We, his clients, were few in numbers, and we went to
the establishment not only to buy books, but to take
pleasure from the delightful and incisive conversation of
the owner. Lopez Penha, Jew, but [nevertheless] lacking
the business sense characteristic of his race ...[573]

Although his works are considered by some as early examples of the
Modernismo movement in Hispanic American literature, many were crit-
ical of his literary output. In 1907, Barranquilla's writer/philosopher,
Julio Enrique Blanco, wrote about him: "Reporter, journalist, novelist
and poet [...] he is all that in bits and pieces." And upon the publication
of Penha's second novel, *La Desposada de Una Sombra* – The Wife of a
Shadow – Blanco provided a left-handed compliment indicating that
this book was "better, or rather less silly or insipid, than the first one."
The well-known author from the Dominican Republic, Max Henriquez
Ureña, also a descendant of Curaçaoan Sephardic Jews, wrote extensive-
ly about the history of the *Modernismo* movement. In his analysis of this
literary movement, he calls Abraham Zacarías Lopez Penha "a poet of
little rank" and adds that Penha's poetic works were made up of some
verses which were good, very few which were very good, and others
which were bad and very bad.[574]

Some believe that much of the criticism of Penha's literary output had
an element of anti-Semitism or that those who disapproved of
Freemasonry were out to get him.[575] Yet others have tried to put the literary scene in Barranquilla in perspective.

In Barranquilla we believe that our easy triumphs in the
area of industry and progress, triumphs that we owe
mostly to the favor of God, which inspired the founders
of this city [to establish it] near an abundant[ly flowing]
river and a much travelled sea, will preserve and augur a
splendid and pleasant future. Here [in Barranquilla] we
look down with indifference, if not with disdain, at all
that is not of a commercial and industrial nature. In this

way an exaggerated mercantile environment has been
created, where intellects, who because of the law of
selection, were not born for such rough struggles, die and
languish like flowers on ice. [...] Nobody reads in
Barranquilla nor does anybody write [...] the few who
might be able to write do not do so because they are
certain that [their words] will not be read nor
understood. ... [576]

It is not surprising that in such a business-driven environment, surrounded by family and friends who were all successful businessmen,
Abraham Zacarías was viewed as an oddball. Nevertheless, he published
several books of fiction and poetry, helped immensely by his brother's
introductions and occasional financial assistance.[577]

It was probably difficult for the much younger man to live in the shadow of the popular and accomplished David Lopez Penha Jr., his beloved
eldest brother. Barranquilla's Jews and their descendants socialized in a
fairly small circle, and, although Abraham began to make a name for
himself as a poet, his artistic bent set him apart.

As was customary in those days, Abraham Zacarías Lopez Penha often
dedicated his poetry to important persons in politics and literature. Thus
he dedicated one of his poems to Ángel Pulido, a Spanish senator and
historian. At the end of the nineteenth century and in the early twentieth century, Pulido had become interested in the history of the unique
Hispanic culture of the descendants of the Spanish Jews banished in
1492, and Penha was clearly an admirer of Pulido's efforts. Another of
Abraham Zacarías's works is dedicated to Walt Whitman.[578]

Shortly after his brother David's untimely demise, Abraham published
a collection of poems under the title "Cromos" and dedicated the slim
volume *"a la memoria de mi muy querido hermano DAVID LÓPEZ-
PENHA YR." [sic]* – to the memory of my very dear brother David Lopez
Penha Jr. There is a picture of the author on the first page of this publication and under it is written "Abrahán Z. López Penha." The mis-
spellings of the Jr. in David's name and of his own first name, Abraham,
are odd, to say the least. The poems in this volume have nothing to do

with his brother and are almost all individually dedicated to Latin American men of the time, such as the concertist Julio Blasini, the Colombian writer Augusto N. Samper, the Curaçaoan poet David M. Chumaceiro, and the Salvadorian poet Rubén Darío.

Abraham Zacarías Lopez Penha's poetry not only appeared in literary magazines and in published collections, but also in the local newspaper. Barranquilla's weekly, *El Promotor*, ran regular ads for newly arrived books available at Penha's bookstore and occasionally also published his poetic creations. In the issue of February 13, 1892, for example, he published a poem entitled "Umbra" — Shadow — which romantically describes the fires of love, and which he dedicated to fellow poet Julio N. Vieco.[579] Later that year, another flowery poem of a romantic nature was published in *El Promotor* dedicated to Dr. Rafael Nuñez, President of Colombia.[580]

Penha's masculinity appears to have been questioned during his lifetime. Not only was he a poet living in the rough and tumble business world of Barranquilla, but his social skills left much to be desired. Stories abound about his often unusual public behavior. He would at times ignore people he knew quite well, pretending not to see them and bury his head in a book to avoid saying hello. Later in life he was also known to carry pieces of bricks in his pocket to throw at people who called him names when he walked the streets of Barranquilla.[581]

The modern-day Colombian historian, Dino Manco Bermúdez, attempts to dismiss suggestions that Abraham Zacarías Lopez Penha was a woman hater or that he may have had homosexual tendencies. Clearly there must have been rumors to this effect, which Manco Bermudez thought needed to be quelled.[582] In a conversation with Dr. Manco about this topic, he explained these rumors by saying: "Well, you know the adage here in Colombia – '*el soltero maduro, homosexual seguro*' – a mature single man is a sure sign of a homosexual." Yet, Manco Bermúdez believes that in the case of Abraham Zacarías Lopez Penha this assumption was incorrect. It is of interest to note that no such rumors existed about David Lopez Penha, Jr., who had also been a bachelor.

Be it as it may, Manco Bermúdez's theory that neither brother had married because of their obvious desire not to marry outside the faith and because of the limited number of Jewish women available to these men in Barranquilla may be too facile an explanation.[583] The fact is that two other brothers of David and Abraham Zacarías, both living in Santo Domingo, had married Catholic women. Therefore there was definitely a precedent for mixed marriages in this branch of the Lopez Penha family. Additionally, in the last decade of the nineteenth century when both David and Abraham Zacarías were of marriageable age, there were more mixed marriages among the Sephardim of Barranquilla than there were marriages within the Jewish faith. Hence it would not have been too shocking to the Jewish community of Barranquilla if these men had chosen to marry Catholic women. And finally, Curaçao had an abundance of Sephardic single women towards the end of the nineteenth century. In view of their many trips to this island, David and Abraham Zacarías actually had a larger pool of eligible Jewish women at their disposal than the small Jewish community of Barranquilla would imply.[584] Of course, Manco Bermudez may be right that the issue of marrying out may have been less appealing to these two Penha brothers than it had been to their siblings in the Dominican Republic and some of their peers living in Barranquilla. After all, their father, Haim Daniel Lopez Penha, had been a member of the *Beth Din* in Curaçao and a very active board member of the Mikvé Israel community. His children grew up in a home that attached great value to Jewish traditions, and it is possible that the two brothers in Barranquilla felt more strongly about the issue of intermarriage than the two who had migrated to Santo Domingo. In reality, we can only speculate about the reasons for David's and Abraham Zacarías's bachelorhood.

Like his brother David, Abraham Zacarías was proud of his Jewish ancestry. The front cover of one of his books states: "*El Libro de las Incoherencias lo perpetró A. Z. López Penha, judío español*" – The Book of Incoherences was perpetrated by A.Z. López Penha, Spanish Jew. This indicates that the author wanted to be sure that his readers knew that the romantic poems included in the volume came from the pen of a man who identified himself first and foremost as a Jew. [585]

In a short biography written by Alfredo de la Espriella, the author refers to Abraham Zacarías López Penha as a habitué of the social clubs who enjoyed playing cards and billiards, and loved serving one and all "spirited drinks." In spite of this view that portrays him as a somewhat charming "bon vivant," this biographer too indicates that there were others who found him harsh and insolent.[586] There is no doubt that Abraham Zacarías Lopez Penha was at best eccentric and quite often not an easy man to like.

Penha corresponded with authors, publishers, and politicians in many countries. Mordechay Arbell quotes from a letter written by Penha to Dr. Ángel Pulido in 1904, in which he provides a description of Jewish life in Barranquilla, apparently in response to questions posed by the historian.

> There are a few Sephardic families [here] from the colony of Curaçao, a Dutch island in the Antilles chain, north of Venezuela. I do not believe that there are any in other cities, with the exception of the young Republic of Panama, where there are quite a few Sephardim from Curaçao and St. Thomas, a Danish island in the Antilles. They are very favorably positioned. Their social standing has been and is quite distinguished. They have always held and continue to hold high positions in the banking industry and in commerce. The founder of the Compañía de Transportes, the most important river boat company that plies the waters of the river Magdalena (the principal artery of the entire republic), was my deceased brother, David Lopez Penha Junior, who used to head [that company's] board until his demise. The current administrative director is Mr. Jacob Cortissoz, a relative of mine and also a Sephardic Jew. There are two banks here and the chairman of the most important one, the Banco del Atlántico, is a Jew, Mr. Moisés de Sola; for a long time, the manager of the other bank, the [Banco] de Barranquilla, was David de Sola, who is currently the administrative manager of the Compañía del Acueducto de Barranquilla, one of the most important firms in the city.

As far as occupying positions in the government or serving in the militia, our status as foreigners, prevents us from doing so.

Referring to the language [meaning Ladino or Judeo-Spanish], we no longer speak it here for obvious reasons. Although our old predilection for Spain has cooled off – a result of [the passage of] time and of the freedom that is enjoyed in these countries – the majority [of the Sephardic Jews] still maintain a certain affection for it [Spain]. They enjoy absolute freedom.

We have no synagogue here nor intellectual centers. Jewish bookstores do not exist, since they are not necessary.[587]

It is striking to compare this man's writing to the eloquent, well-informed works produced by his brother David. But, although his non-fiction prose is uninspired, his dreamy poems often appealed to female audiences, both in Colombia and in his native Curaçao. The scrapbook of Leah Monsanto (1814-1902) of Curaçao contains various clippings of Penha's poetry, which she clearly must have valued and pasted in her album.[588] In Colombia he continues to be remembered by many as a pioneer of the *Modernismo* literary movement in America.[589]

The inheritance that Abraham Zacarías received from his brother's estate in the 1890s was not sufficient to ease his financial worries. He died destitute and abandoned in 1927 and is buried in the old Sephardic cemetery of the Cementerio Universal in his adoptive city of Barranquilla.[590] There is no doubt that in Barranquilla's commercial atmosphere of the late nineteenth and early twentieth century, Abraham Zacarías must have felt like a fish out of water. Yet, even though this city did not always value his artistic endeavors very highly during his lifetime, Penha never returned to live in Curaçao. Barranquilla had become his home.

As is often the case, time has been relatively kind to his memory. Today, when the name Lopez Penha is mentioned among modern-day Colombian historians, it is usually Abraham Zacarías's name and fame that is recalled first and not the many achievements by his financially successful and socially admired brother David. In this case, the legacy of the written word outweighed the recollection of commercial entrepreneurship.

SMITTEN BY HANDSOME BARRANQUILLEROS

On a raw and drizzly day in November of 2002, I spent several hours walking through the Jewish cemetery in Ouderkerk aan de Amstel, just outside of Amsterdam. The weather was Holland at its dreariest. Yet, in spite of the dark skies and the fact that I was walking among so many dead and forgotten Jewish ancestors of centuries gone by, I was very excited to be in this historic cemetery. Here in this wet and chilly spot, lay *"de zoon van het gloeiende Westen"* — the son of the blazing West [Indies].[591] This was the final resting place of David Lopez Penha Jr.

By the time of this visit, I had already uncovered many details about Penha's life, and I had also found a photograph of the handsome bachelor. I was smitten! I stood at his simple grave and thought about David at the prime of his life, addressing his friends at a party, calling a meeting to order at the Banco de Barranquilla, and consoling his sister Sarah when she was widowed. How sad that his life had ended so far from his beloved Curaçao and Barranquilla. Leaving a stone on the grave to indicate that he was still remembered after all these years, I walked out of that graveyard reluctantly. He had been so alive in the material that I had found! His speeches were so dramatic, his writing so logical, and his contributions to Barranquilla so all-encompassing that the David I had in my mind was the David shown in the photograph published in the volumes written by Isaac and Suzanne Emmanuel about the Jews of the Netherlands Antilles. Not this block of marble in this little Dutch town, but the young man with the bushy black beard and a head of thick slicked back hair that curled slightly over his right ear. That day in the cemetery of Ouderkerk aan de Amstel, it was almost as if a dear acquaintance had just died. I suddenly had to come to terms with his premature death – a death which had occurred more than one hundred year earlier.

It was then that I realized how immersed I had become in the lives of these long-gone Sephardim of the nineteenth century. And it would happen again in the ensuing years. When I learned about Jacob Cortissoz and his son Ernesto, I did not, at first, have access to their pictures. My admiration was limited to being in awe at how Jacob Cortissoz had pulled himself up by his bootstraps, and later, how Ernesto had been as enterprising and successful as his father. As their stories unfolded, I felt that I knew them. And when at some point, I finally came across their photographs, I studied their faces and knew that I would recognize them immediately should our paths ever cross.

In 2004 I had occasion to meet Ernesto Cortissoz's son, Ernesto Cortissoz Rodriguez, at his home in Barranquilla. He had been seven years old when his father died in the airplane accident and was well into his eighties when we met. Both he and his wife of sixty years were very alert and eager to share stories from years gone by. It was clear that this intelligent man possessed many of the same qualities as his brilliant father and grandfather. A chemical engineer, with a degree from Purdue University, he had returned to Barranquilla from his studies in the United States and had been one of the founders of the Universidad del Atlántico in that city. For a while he taught at the university and became Rector, a job that

Ernesto Cortissoz Alvares Correa
1884-1924

did not pay too well, causing him to take on a second job at a local beer conglomerate. Eventually he resigned from both jobs and went back to the United States for an advanced degree. This time he went with his wife, Doña Raquel Cabrera Forero, and studied at the University of Minnesota. His wife did not remember the Minnesota winters too fondly and called the three winters in the late 1940s, when she lived in the States, as the period of "forty below," referring to the many mornings when the radio announcer would indicate that the wind-chill temperature had dipped to these unpleasantly low levels.

In Minnesota, Ernesto Cortissoz Rodriguez began to research commercial uses for the wood from the tropical trees that grew in Colombia. Since it had already been determined that this wood was not suitable for the paper industry, he decided to investigate other possible applications, a study which he continued when he returned to Colombia. Here he eventually founded Láminas del Caribe in 1958, a factory that produced wood laminates.

While Don Ernesto was recounting his many business endeavors, my attention kept drifting to the large black and white photograph of his father, Ernesto Cortissoz, which hung prominently in his son's home. Unlike the current Ernesto, his namesake father had never aged and looked out from the picture frame with youthful assurance and energy. Another handsome Barranquillero with Curaçaoan Sephardic roots.

These were the beautiful people of Barranquilla at the turn of the century. In the souvenir books of the Club Barranquilla, Ernesto and Esther Cortissoz pose with other members of the Carnaval committee for the city's 1908 Carnaval celebrations, all wearing sashes over their handsome suits and dresses, ready to have a wonderful time. Even Abraham Zacarías Lopez Penha appears in one of the pictures wearing a fez in a crowd of men and women in costume dressed as *los turcos* – the Turks – prepared for the Carnaval events of 1912.

Their elders had been at the forefront of Barranquilla's growth, and, as the twentieth century began, the new generations continued to mold the city's development. Barranquilla was theirs. They were of Sephardic descent and had married into Catholic and Protestant families with Spanish, German, and English names, and now they were Barranquilleros. No longer foreigners, this was their home. They were Cortissoz Rodriguez, Alvares Correa Vengoechea, Cortissoz Buitrago, Salas Ponchet, a total blending of the immigrant population.

Today's descendants of Curaçao's Sephardim in Barranquilla are still very aware of their Jewish roots. They often attribute their commercial success to their Jewish ancestry. Frequently that reference merely seems to imply a genetic predisposition that allows Jews to succeed in business — a viewpoint about the Jewish people which is most often espoused by non-Jews. It is only after prompting that many of the non-Jewish descendants of the Sephardim agree that the network of contacts developed by the nineteenth century Sephardic Jews across the Caribbean and stretching to Europe and the United States may have had something to do with their ancestors' achievements as well.

Barranquilla in the twenty-first century has an active Jewish community, with a beautiful community center, a private Jewish day school, and several synagogues. The descendants of the original Sephardic immigrants may occasionally attend a graduation, bar mitzvah, or wedding of their Ashkenazi friends at one of these locations, but they are no longer part of the Jewish community of Barranquilla.

PART I I

Analysis and Conclusions

CHAPTER 6

GOING, GOING . . . GONE: A COMPARATIVE ANALYSIS

It was disconcerting to find out that only a handful of Jewish descendants of Curaçao's nineteenth century Sephardim still lived in the four loca-tions visited for this project. Even in present day Curaçao, there are fewer than 150 Jewish descendants left of the 1,500 Sephardic Jews who represented that island's flourishing Mikvé Israel community at the end of the eighteenth century. These numbers vividly and literally illustrate the term "decimate." They also hint at what might have been. Today, thousands of descendants of Curaçao's Sephardim populate the core islands of the Caribbean and the Caribbean periphery, but the vast majority is no longer Jewish. They and their more recent ancestors are the result of the large number of exogamous marriages which began to occur in the second half of the nineteenth century and which continued through the twentieth century.*

At first it seemed possible that the impetus for this complete religious assimilation might be that the Jewish men who had decided to leave Curaçao in the nineteenth century had been the more adventurous and rebellious members of the community. Or, perhaps, that the Jews who

---

* In view of the increased interest in the thousands of men and women who claim to descend from Jews who were forced to convert, it is important to emphasize that the non-Jewish descendants of Curaçao's Sephardim described in this book should not be included among these *bnei anousim* – children of forced converts.

219

Caribbean shores

were religiously less attached were the ones who emigrated. But careful examination of the ancestry and personal histories of these immigrants prior to migration did not yield sufficient data to confirm these hypotheses. It appeared that most of the men and women in all four locations came from families who had been active members of Curaçao's Jewish community in the years that preceeded their decision to migrate.

Close analysis of the immigrant stories and of the attitudes towards Jews that existed in the host societies did, however, reveal three key factors which affected the rate of assimilation in each locale. These factors are as follows:

1. The degree to which the host country was favorably inclined towards Jews.
2. The extent to which the migrants were able to create a fairly complete Jewish infrastructure in their new location.
3. The presence of a Hispanic culture.

First, when the host location was welcoming to the Jews, the likelihood of assimilation and integration into the host society was easier and more likely than if the host culture had anti-Semitic tendencies. Second, when the new migrants set up a Jewish infrastructure that could satisfy their religious needs and that additionally had similarities with the Mikvé Israel community they had left behind, they were less likely to assimilate. Such an infrastructure helped keep them together as a community, separate from the communities around them, and discouraged intermarriage. And finally, assimilation into a population descending from a Spanish culture was much more likely than assimilation with non-Jewish Danish, Dutch, English, or American populations. As is believed by many who studied the fate of the Sephardim after they left Spain: "When the Sephardim lived in Spain they were very Jewish – when they left Spain they became very Spanish."[592] Curaçao's Sephardim found that their social customs were more similar to those of the descendants of the Catholic Spanish colonizers of the Caribbean and the South American mainland than to those of the non-Hispanic colonizers of the region.

The intensity of these factors differed in each of the locations described in the preceeding chapters. By using the fairly simple two-variable matrix presented below, the speed of religious assimilation in various locations may be better understood. The horizontal axis shows the degree of welcome vis-à-vis the Sephardim and the vertical axis is indicative of the level of Jewish infrastructure in each location. The variable for the existence of a Hispanic culture in the host country can be superimposed on this model as an on/off switch, which would give an extra push towards assimilation if it were in the on position, that is, if the Jews migrated to a former colony of Spain.

	Jews are welcome in host location	Welcome extended to Jews is mixed	Jews are not welcome —anti-Semitism
High-functioning Jewish infrastructure	*Very slow assimilation*	*Little assimilation*	*Most Jews do not stay, and those who stay do not assimilate*
Some Jewish infrastructure	*Assimilation, but not first generation*	*Assimilation after several generations*	*Jews keep a low profile; little assimilation*
No Jewish infrastructure	*Complete and rapid assimilation*	*Assimilation after several generations*	*Few Jewish observances, but little assimilation*

The level of welcome extended by a host community is, of course, dependent on many variables such as the religious and racial history of the host country, the need for capital and entrepreneurial input, the level of unemployment, and so on. The brief macro-historical information provided for each of the four locations discussed in this work provides an outline of these variables that led to more or less welcoming environments.

Similarly, the likelihood of a Jewish infrastructure being put in place by migrating Jews is dependent on the degree of religiosity of the migrating population, the inclusion among the migrants of religiously learned lay leaders or rabbis and cantors, and the desire to marry within one's own group.

The level of welcome offered by the host countries and the degree of religious involvement by the newly arrived Sephardim and their descendants are discussed below in a summary fashion for each location in order to provide an overview of the comparative differences in the rate of religious assimilation among the Caribbean Sephardim of the nineteenth century.

ST. THOMAS, VIRGIN ISLANDS

In St. Thomas, the nineteenth century Curaçaoan Sephardim arrived to an existing community that already had put in place the necessities for Jewish communal life. Regular religious services, a synagogue building, a cemetery, and other ritual elements that facilitated religious observance had been established here since the late eighteenth century. With the mix of Ashkenazim and Sephardim, the Jewish community of St. Thomas was originally structured somewhat differently than the Mikvé Israel community of Curaçao. However, fairly soon after their arrival, the Curaçaoan Jews let their influence be felt. They made their imprint on the community by-laws of 1803, and St. Thomas's Beracha VeShalom began to resemble their old community in Curaçao.

The host environment that surrounded St. Thomas's Jews was extremely receptive to the migrants. While there were class distinctions defined primarily by the level of one's wealth and the color of one's skin, St. Thomas's society was pluralistic in nature, allowing people of many backgrounds and faiths to live together in relative harmony, each adhering to their own customs and religion. Additionally, the Danish government representatives on the island were quite tolerant of the Jewish residents, and so, in this welcoming environment and with a strong Jewish infrastructure in place, the Jewish Curaçaoan Diaspora in St. Thomas lived as proud Jews through the 1870s, not intermarrying, and, when necessary, going outside their small community to find suitable Jewish marriage partners. Clearly the position in the matrix for the Jewish community of St. Thomas in the nineteenth century was in the upper left-hand corner, the same location that would be assigned to the Curaçaoan Jewish community at this point in time.

	Jews are welcome in host location	Welcome extended to Jews is mixed	Jews are not welcome —anti-Semitism
High-functioning Jewish infrastructure	*Very slow assimilation* St. Thomas	*Little assimilation*	*Most Jews do not stay, and those who stay do not assimilate*
Some Jewish infrastructure	*Assimilation, but not first generation*	*Assimilation after several generations*	*Jews keep a low profile; little assimilation*
No Jewish infrastructure	*Complete and rapid assimilation*	*Assimilation after several generations*	*Few Jewish observances, but little assimilation*

The disappearance of the Jewish descendants of St. Thomas's early Sephardim of the nineteenth century was not originally caused by religious assimilation, but by the major economic setbacks the island experienced in the late 1860s and 1870s. As the economy spiraled downward, the descendants of the original migrants left for Curaçao, Panama, Costa Rica, and the United States where, more than a century later, many descendants of this second migratory wave still adhere to the Jewish religion.

CORO, VENEZUELA

In Coro, Venezuela, the Jews were met early on with strong anti-Semitism. In the 1830s this was enough for some of the Sephardic Jews to return to Curaçao, leaving behind whatever economic benefits they had expected from their earlier migration decisions. Those who stayed on and those who arrived later to live in Coro during the first period of Jewish settlement (1830-1855) tried valiantly to set up a Jewish infrastructure that would mirror that of their Curaçaoan community. In view of the anti-Jewish sentiments and the legal ambivalence regarding the right to construct a synagogue, the Coro Jews kept their observances quite private, holding religious services at the home of David Valencia and, later, in a room of the Senior residence with all the windows closed. For years they worshipped in this suffocating environmnent, and it was only in 1853 that they dared remedy this uncomfortable situation by asking for and receiving Mr. Senior's neighbor's permission to open some windows during services. Yet, within these constraints, they established regular Shabbat and holiday services, using the *Torah* owned by the Senior family as their precious centerpiece. They built their *cabana* during Sukkot, counted amongst their own several trained circumcisers as well as ritual slaughterers, and bought land for a Jewish cemetery as early as 1832. They even made an attempt to produce a religious text for the community, entitled *Principios elementales de instrucción religiosa y moral para la enseñanza de la juventud hebrea* – Elementary principals of religious and moral instruction for the teaching of Jewish youth. This 56-page booklet, translated into Spanish from French, was published in Caracas in 1845, and was found in some of the Jewish households of Coro.[593]

From their early settlement through the upheaval in 1855, when practically all of Coro's Jews left for Curaçao, Coro's location in the matrix model would be in the upper right-hand corner. As shown in the chart, the Sephardim who chose to stay in Coro before the 1860s were religiously active, despite the persisting anti-Semitic environment. Religious assimilation in Coro during this first period of settlement was minimal.

During the second settlement period, when the Jews returned to Coro in 1858-1859 after their claims with the Venezuelan government had been settled, the Sephardim were much less invested in the Jewish infrastructure. The cemetery was still in use, and, for some years, weekly services continued to be held at the home of one of the members of the Senior family. But the Jews now focused their attention on politics, large business enterprises, theatrical productions, literature, Freemasonry, and the community at large. Dietary laws were mostly ignored, and the community used traveling *mohels*, such as Moises Frois Ricardo, to circumcise their newborn sons.

During this period of Jewish settlement in Coro, its position in the matrix started to move down from the upper right-hand corner as the town's Jewish infrastructure became less complete. At the same time,

Coro's Catholics became somewhat more tolerant with occasional anti-Semitism primarily expressed in non-violent ways. The location of Coro's Jewish community in the matrix, therefore, moved diagonally downwards.

	Jews are welcome in host location	Welcome extended to Jews is mixed	Jews are not welcome —anti-Semitism
High-functioning Jewish infrastructure	*Very slow assimilation*	*Little assimilation*	*Most Jews do not stay, and those who stay do not assimilate* **Coro (pre-1860s)**
Some Jewish infrastructure	*Assimilation, but not first generation*	*Assimilation after several generations* **Coro (1860s–1900)**	*Jews keep a low profile; little assimilation*
No Jewish infrastructure	*Complete and rapid assimilation*	*Assimilation after several generations*	*Few Jewish observances, but little assimilation*

SANTO DOMINGO, DOMINICAN REPUBLIC

The placement in the matrix of Santo Domingo's Sephardic community is diagonally opposite to that of Coro during the first period of settlement. It is true that there were some anti-Semitic feelings among parts of the Dominican population, but the government and most of the elite class stood fully behind the Sephardic Jews of Curaçao who made their home in Santo Domingo in the nineteenth century. Expressions of anti-Semitism were isolated incidents, mostly recorded on paper and not affecting the day-to-day lives of the Jews. The Jews never suffered any loss of property or physical harm.

The Dominican Sephardim did not make any attempt at setting up a Jewish infrastructure for themselves. Religious services were held at various locations on a not-too-regular basis, and the Sephardim buried their dead in a separate area of the Catholic cemetery, never bothering to purchase land for their own cemetery. They relied on traveling circumcisers to circumcise their sons, and Jewish education was nonexistent.

This low level of Jewish infrastructure coupled with the welcoming environment in the Dominican Republic led to a rapid assimilatory process in Santo Domingo. The historian Enrique Ucko has described this integration as a fusion of the Jews and the Dominicans, which is exactly what would be indicated by the placement of Santo Domingo in the lower left quadrant of this matrix.[594]

	Jews are welcome in host location	Welcome extended to Jews is mixed	Jews are not welcome —anti-Semitism
High-functioning Jewish infrastructure	*Very slow assimilation*	*Little assimilation*	*Most Jews do not stay, and those who stay do not assimilate*
Some Jewish infrastructure	*Assimilation, but not first generation*	*Assimilation after several generations*	*Jews keep a low profile; little assimilation*
No Jewish infrastructure	*Complete and rapid assimilation* **Santo Domingo**	*Assimilation after several generations*	*Few Jewish observances, but little assimilation*

BARRANQUILLA, COLOMBIA

Barranquilla, Colombia, was a city accustomed to foreigners and as such was probably somewhat more open to Jews than other cities and towns in Colombia. Nevertheless, the country had gone straight from Spanish rule to independence without experiencing a prolonged period of exposure to more liberal ideas as occurred in the Dominican Republic during its Haitian occupation. The Roman Catholic Church was a powerful force in town, and the Jews tread carefully. Between the 1840s and the early 1870s there was only a minimal Jewish infrastructure in place for the Jews who called Barranquilla their home. It was not until 1874 that Barranquilla's Jews formally organized themselves as the Colombian Jewish community. Around that time they also purchased a cemetery plot and religious services became somewhat more regular and organized.

While there appears to have been no evidence of a strong, popularly supported anti-Semitic movement in Barranquilla after liberation from Spanish rule in the nineteenth century, there is no doubt that anti-Semitism existed among Barranquilleros and other Colombians. It was more prevalent than in the Dominican Republic and manifested itself primarily in the form of literary debates and sermons given by the Roman Catholic clergy. An example of these written expressions of disdain for the Jewish nation was the article written by José María Samper in 1875 which was rebutted so brilliantly by David Lopez Penha, Jr. There were also more unfortunate isolated violent incidents, when, for example, Moisés Lopez Penha was imprisoned for not kneeling during a Catholic procession that took place on the outskirts of the city in 1878, and was subsequently murdered in prison by hoodlums.[595] However, massive uprisings and violence against Jews as were experienced in Coro in the nineteenth century never happened in Barranquilla.

Barranquilla's placement in the model described above is at the bottom of the right-hand column at the start of the migratory process, when, in spite of the lack of a Jewish infrastructure, little religious assimilation took place due to underlying anti-Semitic sentiments among Catholics and their clergy. By the 1870s, when the Jewish community finally obtained some structure, the Jews had also become more accepted by the elite society of the city because of their commercial and financial successes. Thus Barranquilla's placement shifted to the center of the matrix after the official establishment of the Colombian Jewish Community of Barranquilla in the early 1870s. Before this time there had been few mixed marriages, but in the last quarter of the nineteenth century many more exogamous marriages occurred.

	Jews are welcome in host location	Welcome extended to Jews is mixed	Jews are not welcome —anti-Semitism
High-functioning Jewish infrastructure	*Very slow assimilation*	*Little assimilation*	*Most Jews do not stay, and those who stay do not assimilate*
Some Jewish infrastructure	*Assimilation, but not first generation*	*Assimilation after several generations* **Barranquilla (1870s–1900)**	*Jews keep a low profile; little assimilation*
No Jewish infrastructure	*Complete and rapid assimilation*	*Assimilation after several generations*	*Few Jewish observances, but little assimilation* **Barranquilla (pre-1870s)**

OVERVIEW

While not meant to take the place of an in depth analysis, the matrix used here is a simple vehicle for understanding the differences that were observed in the assimilatory processes in the four locations discussed in this book. By integrating the four matrices presented above into a single one as shown below, this comparative analysis can be summarized in a succinct manner. It offers a visual overview of the different ways in which the once-numerous Sephardim of the Caribbean were absorbed into the societies that became their new homes.

	Jews are welcome in host location	Welcome extended to Jews is mixed	Jews are not welcome —anti-Semitism
High-functioning Jewish infrastructure	*Very slow assimilation* **St. Thomas**	*Little assimilation*	*Most Jews do not stay, and those who stay do not assimilate* **Coro (pre-1860s)**
Some Jewish infrastructure	*Assimilation, but not first generation*	*Assimilation after several generations* **Barranquilla (1870s–1900) Coro (1860s–1900)**	*Jews keep a low profile; little assimilation*
No Jewish infrastructure	*Complete and rapid assimilation* **Santo Domingo**	*Assimilation after several generations*	*Few Jewish observances, but little assimilation* **Barranquilla (pre-1870s)**

Over time, attitudes towards Jews changed in some of the host countries. Similarly, the internal workings of the Jewish communities became more or less sophisticated. As a reflection of these trends, the placement in the matrix of the locations where the variables were changing had to be modified as well. Thus, even within the relatively short time span of the nineteenth century period selected for this study, this otherwise static model reflects a sense of motion and change.

By the early twentieth century, it is clear from the increasing number of exogamous marriages among the Jewish descendants of the Curaçaoan Sephardim of Coro and Barranquilla that the placement of the Jewish communities of these two locations had continued to move diagonally from the middle to the bottom left hand corner of the matrix, arriving at the same point of total assimilation to which the Jews of Santo Domingo had arrived at a much faster pace.

CHAPTER 7

THE IMPORTANCE OF POPULATION SIZE

There is no doubt that numbers play an important role in the ability of a minority group to set up a cultural or religious infrastructure that will allow it to maintain a self-identity among the general population. Small Jewish communities without an ordained rabbi to guide them must at the very least have a large enough critical mass to be viable. Such communities must also include some members with adequate levels of religious training and a willingness to educate and lead in order to ensure continuity. Communities that cannot achieve and maintain an adequate size with such built-in leadership are not likely to survive in the long term.

A study of the decline of small Jewish communities in the American South by Ira M. Sheskin reports that between 1960 and 1997 forty-four small Jewish communities, which had populations ranging between 100 and 499 in 1960, basically disappeared. At the same time, however, fifty-four of these communities still existed in 1997.[596] Sheskin identifies four reasons for the disappearance of some of these communities. They are as follows: outmigration in reaction to anti-Semitism, outmigration related to employment opportunities, intermarriage and assimilation, and general population decline of the locale. All of these factors were at play for the Caribbean Sephardim discussed in this book.

Lee Shai Weissbach also studied small American Jewish communities that had Jewish populations of at least 100 but less than 1000 in the 1870s. This study had similar findings. It found that economic conditions causing outmigration, accompanied by acculturation and religious assimilation, led to the disappearance or decline of a significant number of these communities. Of course there were communities such as Denver, Indianapolis, and Minneapolis, where the Jewish population went from triple digits in 1878 to low five digits in 1927. A town like Goshen, Indiana, on the other hand, had 125 Jews in 1878 and only 51 in 1927, causing the town's Shearith Israel congregation to disband in 1932.[597]

It appears from these studies that the hundred-person threshold is key to the development and maintenance of a working Jewish community. Communities of fewer than one hundred Jews appear to have been unable to sustain Jewish life without significant in-migration. Once the threshold size has been reached, however, size can become an interdependent variable, meaning that population growth or decline can encourage further population growth or decline, so that size influences size. Community growth generally fosters more growth by means of natural reproduction as well as by the resulting appeal of a particular location to additional immigrants. The Jewish community of Curaçao can be used as an example to illustrate this principle. In the first half of the eighteenth century, there was a sharp increase in the Sephardic migration from Europe to Curaçao. The flourishing Jewish community that resulted from this in-migration as well as from the large number of children born into the community brought about additional growth which continued until the economy of the small island could no longer support it, leading to the outmigration discussed in this book. Conversely, as the Jewish population of a place decreases, the smaller size leads to fewer options for endogamous marriages and a desire to leave for places of greater social and economic opportunity. Therefore, just as size can be an accelerator as Jewish communities grow, it can also cause further decline as the number of Jews decreases.

Through the first six or seven decades of the nineteenth century, the number of Jews in St. Thomas grew steadily, resulting in an active Jewish community which, at its height, counted 600 to 700 Jews. During the last two to three decades of the century, economic conditions reversed this trend by leading to outmigration which greatly reduced the number of Jews on the island. The small Jewish community that remained could not, in spite of its respectable Jewish infrastructure, sustain a Jewish life for the fewer than one hundred Jews who were left. Judah Cohen writes:

The St. Thomas congregation thus became a hollow center of sorts for Sephardic Jewish life in the northeast Caribbean. Just as Curaçao had served as the "parent" congregation to St. Thomas throughout much of the nineteenth century, so St. Thomas had become a place of origination for new congregations taking root in Panama and Costa Rica.[598]

The small number of descendants of Curaçao's Sephardim who still lived in St. Thomas in the mid- twentieth century either intermarried, left, or encouraged their offspring to leave, and eventually died out. As a consequence, today there is a complete absence of Sephardim on this island.

The Sephardim of Coro reached the threshold size fairly quickly after Venezuelan independence was achieved. Between 1830 and 1855, the Jews of Coro numbered almost 200 and had the necessary leadership to operate as a fairly well functioning Jewish community. After their hasty departure to Curaçao in 1855, however, fewer Jews returned to Coro in the late 1850s. The decreased community size and the presence of fewer knowledgeable Jews led to an increased number of intermarriages. These conditions eventually led to the demise of the Jews of Coro.

It is estimated that about one hundred Jews made their homes in Santo Domingo in the third quarter of the nineteenth century. Of the four Jewish communities discussed in this book, the community in Santo Domingo, even at its height, was the least viable. Political and economic instability during the early years after independence failed to attract a sufficient number of Jews. The threshold size of the Jewish population in Santo Domingo included few who were religiously learned which made it difficult to establish a Jewish infrastructure. Religious assimilation further reduced the group that was already marginal, resulting in an even smaller Jewish population, and, eventually, the extinction of Jewish Sephardim in the capital of the Dominican Republic.

In the early years of settlement in Barranquilla, the number of Jewish residents was too small to ensure the formal observance of Jewish life in a structured setting. It was not until more Jews arrived in that town that the Jewish community officially organized itself. It is estimated that close to 200 Jews lived in Barranquilla in the late 1860s and early 1870s when the Jewish community in which the Sephardim of Curaçao played a role was at its apex. It was only at this point in time that a formal Jewish community was created. This example shows once more that when the population reached a critical mass, it was also more likely that it would include Jewish leaders who could put in place the elements needed for a functioning Jewish community.

The Jewish population of the host communities to which the Curaçaoan Sephardim migrated varied according to the intensity of in and out-migration, religious assimilation, and natural growth. Based on the number of children in the families of the individuals discussed in this book, natural growth was never a problem among the Sephardim who migrated to these four locations.

		Children	
Sephardic Migrant	Location	Total	Surviving
Hannah Sasso Piza	St. Thomas	9	9
Benjamin Delvalle	St. Thomas	8	7
Jeudah Senior	Coro	3	2
Abraham Senior	Coro	4	4
Isaac Senior	Coro	7	6
Menases Capriles	Coro	13	13
Rafael de Marchena	Sto. Domingo	8	8
Benjamin de Marchena	Sto. Domingo	6	6
Moses Lopez Penha	Sto. Domingo	5	5
Elias Lopez Penha	Sto. Domingo	n/a	n/a
Jacob Alvares Correa	Barranquilla	9	9
Jacob Cortissoz	Barranquilla	14	12
David Lopez Penha Jr.	Barranquilla	0	0
Sara Lopez Penha Senior	Barranquilla	1	1
Abraham Zacarias Lopez Penha	Barranquilla	0	0
Average for 14 individuals		6.2	5.9

The average number of children in this group who lived to adulthood was 5.9, and if the two unmarried Lopez Penha brothers from Barranquilla are omitted, this average rises to 6.8 children. More children died before reaching adulthood in those days than is the case today. Mothers too succumbed to complications related to childbirth at a greater rate than is seen in the twenty-first century. Nevertheless, the immigrant Jews were pro-creating at a rate that, coupled with additional in-migration, allowed all four communities to arrive at a census count of between one hundred and five hundred Sephardic inhabitants during various periods of the nineteenth century – a size considered viable for the formation of a community. What happened to those communities once they had achieved such levels of viability differed by location.

In summary, in Coro and St. Thomas, outmigration* accelerated the demise of Sephardic life, reducing the community. This decline was further exacerbated by the intermarriages that resulted from the limited choices available to Jews of marriageable age in the smaller communities and additional outmigration. In Barranquilla and Santo Domingo, religious assimilation was the main reason for the reduction in size, which in turn led to additional exogamous marriages because of the scarcity of viable Jewish partners.

While the sizes of the Jewish communities discussed here were affected by religious assimilation, religious assimilation in turn was affected by size – by the number of eligible Jewish partners. It is therefore clear that size, although worthy of discussion, is an interdependent variable with regard to assimilation. It is therefore not included in the matrix presented earlier.

---

* Outmigration from Coro was primarily due to anti-Semitism, although in the latter part of the nineteenth century and the early twentieth century economic conditions also caused the Sephardim and their descendants to leave for more promising locations. Outmigration from St. Thomas was entirely due to the island's economic decline.

CHAPTER 8

FREEMASONRY AND THE CARIBBEAN SEPHARDIM

A fascinating and unexpected factor appears over and over again in the Sephardic immigrant stories presented in this book. All the men and most of their male descendants were members of the Freemasonry movement. This is not a trivial finding and requires further examination. If indeed Freemasonry was so important to the Curaçaoan Sephardim, what role did it play in their lives after they had moved away from the structured Mikvé Israel community that had been at the center of their existence on the Dutch island? Did Freemasonry to some extent replace the need for a spiritual center in those places where such a focus did not exist?

Freemasonry is not a religion. It is a fraternal order of men that encourages a life of high moral values and requires that its members believe in a Supreme Being. It has its own rites and procedures which are only known to its members, and the organization is totally non-denominational and tolerant of all religions. Although Freemasonry did not always welcome Jews in all the countries in which it existed, European Jews were members of Masonic lodges since the early eighteenth century.[599] In Curaçao the first Freemasonry lodge called L'Amitié was founded in 1757, followed in 1774 by a second lodge called Unión, and in 1785 by yet a third called De Vergenoeging.[600] Quite early in the history of Curaçaoan Freemasonry, the Sephardim had joined the fraternal order. The historian Emmanuel indicates that a document of 1774 refers to a Jewish lodge in Curaçao and that the Sephardim were the co-founders of both the Igualdad lodge in 1855 and the Acacia lodge in 1874.[601] The immigrants,

The Masonic Lodge, St. Thomas, U.S. Virgin Islands

therefore, had ancestors who had been both Jewish and Freemasons, and these men who left Curaçao for other Caribbean locales had themselves most likely been Freemasons in Curaçao as well, before they migrated to St. Thomas, Coro, Santo Domingo, and Barranquilla. It is therefore not surprising that upon arrival, they became involved in the Masonic movements in their host countries.

Even in St. Thomas, where the nineteenth century Jews had a well-functioning religious community, the Harmonic Lodge was an important element in the life of most of the Sephardim. On this island, where class distinctions were based primarily on levels of wealth, the Masonic lodge represented a place where the island's diverse population could get together in a spiritual and tolerant setting with friends, be they rich or poor, who clearly shared their common belief in the tenets of

Freemasonry. Many Sephardim who are buried in St. Thomas's Altona Jewish cemetery chose to have the Masonic square and compass symbol engraved on their tombstones, a sign of their strong feelings about this fraternal order.

In the other three locations discussed in this book, the local Masonic organizations had an even greater impact on the lives of the Sephardim.

In Coro, during the second period of Jewish settlement, and in Barranquilla, at the end of the nineteenth century, some of the cohesiveness that existed among the Jews in these two towns weakened as religious services began to take place less regularly. Concurrently, the Sephardim who had joined the local Masonic movements soon after they settled on the South American mainland began to focus more on the goings-on at their lodges. Towards the end of the century they were among the leaders of Freemasonry in Coro and Barranquilla.

As mentioned previously, David Curiel had been one of the founders of the first Masonic lodge of Coro in 1856, and Isaac Senior, his brothers, and his sons were all members of Coro's Unión Fraternal #44 and later the Fraternal #17 lodge. Also Manasés Capriles and his sons were Freemasons. Manasés, who achieved the high Masonic rank of 33rd degree, was the Grand Master of his lodge in Coro in 1886.

A large number of Jews belonged to Barranquilla's Masonic lodges as well. Among them were members of the Cortissoz and Alvares Correa families, who featured prominently among the leaders of the Masonic movement in Barranquilla at the end of the nineteenth century.

While anti-Semitism existed in these two locations, there was no trace of it at the Masonic gatherings. It was here, away from the sometimes less receptive atmosphere of those host cities, that Catholics and Jews socialized and, in the end, became comfortable enough with each other to become business partners and, eventually, in-laws.

In Santo Domingo, where the Jews never had a strong religious center, Sephardic Jews such as David Leon and Joshua Naar were among the co-founders of a Masonic lodge created in 1846, only a few years after the Dominican Republic became independent. They and other members of the Curaçaoan Jewish Diaspora, such as the De Marchenas, Penhas, and Henriquezes and their descendants, continued to be active members of

subsequent lodges in Santo Domingo. The easy mingling with other liberal members of Dominican society who were Freemasons complemented the warm reception given to the Jews in this country. To a great
extent these regular get-togethers at the local lodges, based on the spiritual and moral themes of Freemasonry, took the place of the practically
non-existant religious rituals and celebrations for the Sephardim of
Santo Domingo.[602]

The Freemasonry movement accelerated the socio-political integration of the Sephardic immigrants from Curaçao into the freethinking
societies of their host countries. While Freemasonry may have facilitated religious assimilation, it was by no means the cause of the gradual disappearance of Sephardic life in these locations. Yet it was a catalyst for a
leveling of the playing field. Particularly in the host countries that had
demonstrated some anti-Semitism towards the immigrant Jews,
Freemasonry's belief in universal brotherhood and tolerance paved the
way for an open-minded approach in many areas, including politics and
religion.

CHAPTER 9

GENDER AND CONTINUITY IN CURAÇAO*

This book has thus far focused on the lives of the migrating Curaçaoan Sephardim in their new places of residence. An important question remains: what was the impact of their departure on the community they left behind in Curaçao? A great deal of entrepreneurial talent left the island in the nineteenth century, and one wonders if Curaçao would have developed differently had these enterprising Jews stayed on the island. Perhaps the creative drive of many of the Sephardim who left could never have taken flight in such a small economic setting and with such limited resources as existed in Curaçao at the time. Nevertheless, it is fair to say that Curaçao's loss was the gain of many other communities, in the Caribbean and elsewhere, which benefited from the enterprising spirit of the newly arrived and their descendants.

A significant secondary effect of the departure of so many young men was the measurable disparity in the marriage rate of the Jewish women left behind on the island compared with that of their male counterparts. According to census data and less formal family histories, we know that during the initial phases of migration, few of the migrating Curaçaoan Jews were female. It is not surprising therefore that a gender imbalance among the Jewish population of Curaçao developed in the nineteenth

* Part of this chapter appeared in a Hadassah-Brandeis Institute working paper written by Josette Capriles Goldish, entitled "The Girls They Left Behind – Curaçao's Jewish Women in the Nineteenth Century," Waltham, MA 2002.

241

century. A summary of the population decline and the degree of this imbalance in the early years of outmigration is shown below.[603]

Curaçao's Jewish Population

	Women	Men	Girls	Boys	Total
1816	410	312	163	136	1021
1826	387	263	159	128	937
1835	380	270	100	114	864

These numbers show an overall decline from the 1500 Jews who lived in Curaçao in the late eighteenth century to 1021 in 1816, 937 in 1826, and 864 in 1835. In 1816, 57% of the adult population were women and 43% were men – the women outnumbered the men by a ratio of almost 4 to 3. Ten years later the percentage of women among the adult population had risen to 60%, meaning that for every three Jewish women there were two Jewish men in the community. In 1835 the percentage of women declined somewhat, but still stood at 58%. This gender disparity is believed to have existed throughout most of first half of the nineteenth century.

Curaçao's Jewish women in the nineteenth century were a sheltered group, although probably not more so than most elite white women in South America and the Caribbean. In social customs the Curaçaoan Jews were quite similar to the Spanish and creole elite societies of Latin America, and as such, the women had very specific roles that centered on the family. As the historian Marysa Navarro explains, "the mission of … elite married women [in Latin America] was to be faithful and obedient wives, appearing pious and virtuous, and to bear legitimate children, so that the lineage could be properly perpetuated."[604] While in other countries there are cases of more active involvement in community life by elite Latin American women of the nineteenth century,[605] this behavior was not evident among Curaçao's Jewish elite for much of the period of concern.

Nineteenth Century Curaçaoan Ladies of the Club Entre Nous

Bearing children kept the Curaçaoan Jewish women of that era quite busy indeed. The Sephardic families are believed to have averaged nine or ten children in those days, and girls were married off at such an early age that grandmothers who were thirty-five years old were not uncommon.[606] The men tended to be in their late twenties or older when they married. Although there were servants, and, until 1863 also house slaves, the large households consumed the married women's time. In their leisure time they may have embroidered, read, played music, or attended a special theater performance, but they rarely became involved in formal business ventures or politics.[607]

Many of Curaçao's Jewish women of the early nineteenth century could not read or write, precluding that activity in their spare time. A mark would often suffice to indicate their acquiescence to some contract or letter, as for example the circle drawn on the loan document between the elders of the Mikvé Israel community and Ribca Sasso, sister to the enterprising Hannah Sasso Piza. In numerous cases where their signatures appear on archival documents, they seem wobbly and very carefully traced, a sign of the writers' lack of familiarity with the written word. Illiteracy was extremely high on the island, though less so among the Sephardim than among the overall population. Schooling statistics show that a mere 260 children attended school in 1816 out of a total population of about 12,000, and, by the mid-nineteenth century, this number had barely reached 1,000, while the island's population had grown to 16,000.[608] More girls than boys are listed among the students, reflecting perhaps the larger number of girls in the general population as well, although it is possible that the boys were pulled out of the school system earlier in order to make a living.

While there are no known written narratives dealing specifically with Curaçao's Jewish women of the nineteenth century, it is plausible that their lives most closely resembled those of Latin American Catholic elite women during that period. The description below provides an image of such a society in Mexico.

> Organizing and attending family rituals represents a demanding occupation for Gómez women. A Gómez wife's desire to work for a living is not merely discouraged for traditional reasons: it is impractical, if the woman truly cares for the prestige of her nuclear family among the kinship network at large. In addition, she has to reckon with the social obligations to personal friends and business associates outside the family, as well as her in-laws' grandfamily and kinship network obligations.[609]

In Curaçao too there was little opportunity for married women to do anything beyond tending their homes and cultivating the kinship network. Most of their time outside the home was spent visiting other Sephardic families or participating in birthday or holiday celebrations.[610] Some of this socializing is thought to have been a significant component of their husbands' powerful business networks.[611] Secondary glory at best. Social roles, nevertheless, provided these married women an informal information-gathering and networking status in the business world. Sometimes, when Jewish merchants were away on business, powers of attorney were given to their wives to act in their stead during their absences. Usually, however, these women had to be assisted by a male member of the family, e.g. a father or brother.[612]

For the single women of this community, there were fewer responsibilities, and, often after the demise of parents, they led a life of economic and social poverty. It was not until the end of the nineteenth century that some of these single Jewish women together with some of their Christian friends organized the Club Entre Nous, which presented theatrical performances and raised funds for the creation of a park in downtown Willemstad. For the first time, the single women on the island felt empowered and able to contribute to the common good, and the activities of the club marked an important change in the self-perception of the Jewish women on the island.[613] For most of the nineteenth century, however, a single woman's life in Curaçao was not very desirable. Social conditions beyond their control, however, ensured a steady increase in the number of unmarried Sephardic women on the island as the century progressed.

As Jewish outmigration became part of everyday life in Curaçao and the number of eligible single Jewish marriage partners for Curaçao's Sephardic women declined, the disparity in the social acceptability of exogamous marriages for Jewish men versus Jewish women became apparent. As seen in the stories presented in this book, a large percentage of the migrating men and their descendants eventually married non-Jews in their new places of residence. A few did come back to Curaçao to find Jewish brides with whom they returned to the Dominican Republic, Venezuela, St. Thomas, or Colombia after the wedding ceremony. But among those living in the countries that were once colonies of Spain, such endogamous marriages with Curaçaoan Sephardic women became more the exception than the rule by the second half of the nineteenth century. While the option of marrying outside the Jewish faith existed for their off-island male counterparts, parental supervision and community pressure in Curaçao would not allow the Jewish women who were left behind to consider such possibilities. They had to find their partners among the island's dwindling pool of Sephardic Jews or remain single.

There were certain periods in the second half of the nineteenth century when the Jewish population of Curaçao saw sudden, temporary increases. These occurred for example in 1855, when more than 160 Jewish refugees from Coro, Venezuela arrived in Curaçao as a result of the anti-Semitic uprising in that town. But by the early 1860s, many of these Jews had returned to Venezuela. Another influx of Jews from St. Thomas showed up in Curaçao a few years later. This outmigration from St. Thomas took place after a hurricane devastated businesses on that island in 1867. Again, this increase in the Curaçaoan Jewish population was temporary and not as pronounced as the 1855 change in demographics. Many of the St. Thomas families left Curaçao after some time to join their friends and relatives in Panama in the last quarter of the nineteenth century.

These arrivals and departures of large groups of Jews in the second half of the nineteenth century make it difficult to analyze the imbalance in the Jewish male-female population on the island. It is therefore helpful to focus on the first half of the century, when the Curaçaoan Jewish gender imbalance was most uninterrupted, to determine the impact of this disparity. An analysis of fifteen years of the death registers of the Mikvé Israel Synagogue for the period 1885-1899 (see Appendix B) shows that 48 females and 16 males* who were born before 1826 passed away during this fifteen-year period. The cutoff date of 1826 was chosen to obtain

---

* For Jewish women reaching adulthood the average age at death during those years was 70.8 years, whereas the average age for the Jewish men was 58.4 years. Few men born before 1826 were still alive in 1885.

the cohort that became of marriageable age (by the community standards of those days) during the first half of the nineteenth century. This analysis found that 46% of the females died single and 31% of the males were bachelors at the time of their death. The higher incidence of single females ascertained on this macro level provides concrete evidence of the fate of the Jewish girls left behind in the Curaçaoan community while their brothers, cousins, and uncles who left for other shores widened their horizons and generally neglected to give the same priority to Jewish continuity as they did to their financial well-being.

This gender-based difference in marriage choices among the Sephardim in Curaçao and in the Caribbean Diaspora (where it existed to a lesser extent) was a very significant factor contributing to the decline of this Jewish subgroup in the Caribbean. It aggravated the effect of the many exogamous marriages by the Sephardic men and their descendants, since a disproportionate number of Sephardic women remained single and childless, hampering the growth of a community that had once been considered numerous.

CHAPTER 10

LA DONNA IMMOBILE: THE LIMITED OPTIONS FOR SEPHARDIC WOMEN

The question, of course, arises as to why it was primarily the single Jewish men who migrated to the Latin American locations. Why not young Jewish women as well? And why did not more young married couples leave Curaçao in search of economic betterment?

As mentioned previously, the Jewish woman's role in Curaçao was quite proscribed. As a young girl she was to behave herself in a lady-like way in her parents' home, and as a young adolescent she was expected to focus on being charming, well dressed, and sociable and appearing to be a good catch for a suitable young man with a promising future. There was no way that a Jewish woman from this community would be allowed to take off on her own and migrate to another country. Sometimes these prohibitions could be circumvented if the young woman in question had a married brother or sister living elsewhere whom she could visit for prolonged periods or move in with. But leaving her parents' home for any length of time on an unchaperoned trip was just not imaginable.

And how about the young married couples? In the nineteenth century, a Sephardic man usually did not ask a woman to marry him unless he was able to provide for her. Conversely therefore, the young married couples who lived in Curaçao were already fairly sure that the husband's income on the island had promise, otherwise, in general, they would not have entered into matrimony. There was therefore no urgent reason for

such a young couple to leave the island, unless the husband was particularly ambitious or unless a once comfortable level of income was threatened by changing circumstances.

An example of such a situation was the firing of Hazan Piza by the
Mikvé Israel community within a few years of his marriage to Hannah
Sasso. This led the couple and their young children to move to St.
Thomas, a move they could not have anticipated at the time of their
marriage. At that time, the cantor's steady income and leadership position would have been considered sufficient security for him to ask for her
hand.

Similarly, upon his return to Curaçao from Coro, David Senior had
married Sally Cohen Henriquez in 1856. Although David had his own
business in Curaçao at the time of his wedding, the young couple
returned to Coro for the second period of Jewish settlement in that town.
In this case David was able to compare his financial position in Curaçao
with the business he used to have when he lived in Coro. His accounting books make it very clear that he had done much better in Venezuela
than he was doing on the Dutch island where he had been born.
Therefore, in spite of the frightening experiences of 1855, David Senior
made the decision to go back to Coro with his young wife. Venezuela's
economic possibilities must have outweighed his safety considerations in
the anti-Semitic surroundings of Coro.

Unless the economics in Curaçao became really dire for a young married couple or unless the couple had previous connections with a
Caribbean location in what used to be the Spanish colonies, they were
hesitant to leave the comforts of the mother community on the Dutch
island for those locations. Such migratory decisions were left to their
younger, unmarried, and more adventurous brothers.

The truth is that while the Latin American countries were considered
promising and exciting, they were dangerous places to live. Politically
they were in flux, economically they no longer had the backing of a colonial power to finance growth and development; and, on top of these
unsettling issues, disease was often rampant in these areas of unfiltered
water, muddy streets, and overflowing rivers. How could a young husband ask a protected woman of Curaçao's Mikvé Israel community to go

to such places? It was not until these new locations were perceived to be more livable or until the situation for a family in Curaçao became really difficult financially that Jewish family units with unmarried children began to arrive in the Latin American locations discussed in this book. The single Jewish male immigrants who returned to Curaçao to find brides to bring back to Coro, Barranquilla or Santo Domingo, usually did so only after they had been able to establish themselves financially and were able to offer their wives a home environment in the host countries that was at least somewhat comparable to what they had been accustomed to in Curaçao.[614]

Migration to St. Thomas was different. Life in Charlotte Amalie in the first half of the nineteenth century was fairly similar to life in Willemstad – cargo being unloaded and ships being re-stocked in a busy harbor, store keepers hawking their wares, and the pleasure of living without worries about anti-Semitism and political unrest. St. Thomas, therefore, was perceived by many to be a safe haven with an often better economic potential than Curaçao. Although the Virgin Islands experienced more hurricanes than the Dutch islands off the coast of Venezuela, these occasional acts of God were not a major deterrent to migrating families.

As a consequence, the bulk of the Jews who settled in St. Thomas were not the young unmarried men who set out for Santo Domingo and Coro in search of their fortune. Indeed, when the first sizable influx of migrants joined the small number of Jewish families already living in St. Thomas in the 1790s, the newly arrived included mostly Jewish family units fleeing the political instability in French Saint Domingue and St. Eustatius.[615] The fact that these early migrants to St. Thomas included men, women, and children, set a precedent for subsequent immigrants to this Danish island. By 1846, 44% of the 330 individuals recorded in a partial census of Jews living in St. Thomas, were under 18 years of age, and, of those 18 years and older, 56% were women and 44% were men.[616] These data not only show that the St. Thomas Jewish community consisted of families, but they also indicate that the marriage choices for the Jewish men of St. Thomas were quite different from those faced by their brothers and male cousins in mid-nineteenth century Coro,

Barranquilla, and Santo Domingo, where there were few Jewish females to pick from. And even with a ratio of about five women for every four men on the Danish island, many of St. Thomas's Jews found their partners elsewhere, including in Curaçao, Europe, and the United States.

The question persists among those who are preoccupied with Jewish continuity as to why the young Sephardic men in the Latin American countries were not more concerned about this issue as well. Why did they choose to live in these places where, during the early years after their independence from Spain, few would think of bringing their wives and children? The most succinct answer to this question is this: economic opportunity. And in most cases this opportunity was actually realized.

Of course, the Latin American host locations were not totally devoid of Jewish women. There were some married Jewish couples among the very early immigrants of the 1830s and 1840s, such as Benjamin and Clara de Marchena in Santo Domingo, Jacob and Rachel Alvares Correa in Barranquilla, and Joseph and Deborah Curiel in Coro. Their daughters often married the single Jewish men who later joined these early settlers. Thus Julia Alvares Correa, whose parents had been among the Jewish pioneers of Barranquilla, married Jacob Cortissoz who arrived in that town a few decades later. Sarah Curiel, daughter of the early Coro settlers Joseph and Deborah Curiel, married the later arrival, Eliahu Haim Lopez da Fonseca.

Toward the second half of the nineteenth century, as these host locations became more developed, more Curaçaoan Jewish family units, as opposed to only their single sons, began to consider such moves. Among such couples were Joseph and Esther Cortissoz who left Curaçao with their children in the 1850s to settle in Venezuela. In the late 1840s Haim Daniel and Rachel Lopez Penha and their offspring temporarily lived in Santo Domingo. And similarly, Joseph and Bathsheba Capriles and their unmarried children moved to Venezuela in the late 1850s or early 1860s to join their many sons already living (and intermarried) in that country. But by the time these locations appeared acceptable enough to a larger number of Curaçao's Sephardic families, intermarriages had already become a frequent and socially accepted phenomenon in Santo Domingo, Barranquilla, and Coro, opening up marriage options for the children of those migrating Sephardic families that had not existed in Curaçao.

For many decades of the nineteenth century, the Jewish women born to the Curaçaoan Sephardim in the host locations behaved like their counterparts in Curaçao, marrying only Jews or remaining single. Much sooner than was the case in Curaçao and St. Thomas, however, their brothers began marrying Dominican, Venezuelan, and Colombian Catholics. These exogamous marriages tolerated in the Caribbean for the Sephardic male remained off-limits to the Sephardic female for at least another generation or two.

In Curaçao and St. Thomas, the Sephardic males of the nineteenth century often had premarital and extramarital affairs with non-Jewish women, but usually they did not marry these women, even when such unions resulted in children born out of wedlock. Community pressures in these two islands that had significant Jewish infrastructures prevented such marriages. Frequently, if the Jewish male in such an extramarital relationship was unattached, he would subsequently marry a Jewish woman to fit the expectations of his parents and others in the community. This was the case for St. Thomas's Samuel Piza, for example, who did not marry the Catholic woman he loved, but instead married the daughter of his half-brother while continuing the relationship with his true love on the side.

Not so among the Sephardim of Santo Domingo in the 1840s or of Coro and Barranquilla in the 1870s, where the men would often marry their Catholic partners. Thus, after Rafael de Marchena of Santo Domingo had fathered four children out of wedlock, he married their mother Justa Sanchez, and the couple had forty-two years of marital bliss without any apparent disruptions in the relationship with Rafael's Sephardic relatives.

True, there were not that many single Jewish women in these Latin American locations, but there were plenty in Curaçao, a place to which most of these men returned quite frequently. Nevertheless, once the first intermarriages began to take place in the host communities, few went back to the mother community specifically to find Jewish wives. And so, a large number of the first generation male Sephardim who migrated to the Dominican Republic and quite a few among the second and third generations of those who ended up in Venezuela and Colombia felt very much at home in their new settings and among new Catholic friends and did not perceive great pressures requiring them to marry within their faith. In Coro Josias Senior's brothers Seigismundo and Abraham married the two Molina sisters, and in Barranquilla, Ernesto and Rodolfo Cortissoz married the Catholic Rodriguez sisters.

It was not until a generation or two later, that some of the Sephardic women followed suit and began to marry out as well. Thus, for example, none of Manasés Capriles Ricardo's sisters entered into exogamous marriages. Three remained single and the other two married Sephardic Jews. On the other hand, eight of his ten brothers who moved to Venezuela entered into mixed marriages. Two generations later, only two of his forty-one known grandchildren married men with Sephardic names, while all the others, men and women, who married chose to marry out.

According to Jewish law, children of unions where the mother is Jewish are still considered Jewish by all branches of Judaism. But in the strong Catholic environment of the Latin American towns discussed in this book, the Jewish women who intermarried usually had to promise the Church and their in-laws that they would bring up their children in the Catholic faith. And quite often the women too would convert to Catholicism prior to or some time after the marriage. The Catholic offspring of the mixed marriage between the Sephardic Raquel Salas Cortissoz and Ignacio Segovia in Barranquilla were an example of children of a Jewish woman being brought up in the father's religion. Similarly, the conversion of the four daughters of Samuel Curiel and Hannah Rodriguez Pereira in Santo Domingo reflected the influence of the Church on females in mixed marriages as opposed to the leniency extended to the Jewish males who married Catholics.

Very infrequently did a Jewish man who chose to enter into a mixed marriage convert in order to marry a Catholic woman in these Spanish-speaking locations. None of the Sephardic men discussed in the first part of this book gave up their Jewish religion. Not Rafael de Marchena in Santo Domingo nor Seigismundo Senior in Coro nor the Cortissoz brothers in Barranquilla. Perhaps the Church found it imperative for a

Jewish mother to convert, because it was she who would most likely be in charge of the children's religious education. Therefore Church officials often insisted on the woman's conversion, so that she could properly guide her offspring. Since the man was expected to be less involved in his children's religious upbringing, it was not as important to press for the conversion of a Jewish man in a mixed marriage. Had the Jewish women, like the men, been able to resist such conversion, it still would have been difficult for them to raise the children of their mixed marriages in the Jewish faith. None of the Latin American locations had sufficient access to Jewish education for the children, while a Catholic education was readily available. Indeed, even throughout the twentieth century, parochial schools in Latin America had academic curricula that were far superior to those of public schools in the towns where public education existed. It was only natural for children of the elite families in Coro, Santo Domingo, and Barranquilla – Jewish and Catholic – to be sent to these schools.

And so the disparities between the lifestyles of Curaçaoan Sephardic men and women created situations where, in search of economic opportunities, the young men left the island, the young women on the Dutch island were left with fewer potential marriage partners of the Jewish faith, the migrating men were faced with limited marriage choices in Latin American locations, and the children of the resulting mixed marriages were almost always raised as non-Jews. The Jewish woman who was the key to continuity often did not marry, and, if she entered into a mixed marriage, she sometimes did not have the wherewithal to resist the Catholic influences in her surroundings. Religious assimilation occurred sooner in those host locations that had little or no Jewish infrastructure. It also occurred at a more rapid pace if, over time, the existing Jewish community lost some of the basic requirements for Jewish survival, such as religiously educated leaders, Jewish education for their children, ritual cirucumcisers, kosher butchers, and regularly scheduled Shabbat services. Furthermore, the increased acceptance of the Curaçaoan Sephardic Diaspora by the host population served to accelerate the lack of commitment that resulted from the internal shortcomings of these Jewish communities.

After the first few mixed marriages had taken place in Coro, Santo Domingo, and Barranquilla among the descendants of many who had been leaders of Curaçao's Jewish community and subsequently leaders of the communities in Coro and Barranquilla as well, the tone of acceptance was set. With no rabbinic authority to guide them, it became very difficult for Curaçao's Sephardim to survive as Jews once they moved away from the mother community.

CHAPTER 11

ENDURING TIES WITH CURAÇAO

And yet, and yet ... as the religious element disappeared among the Caribbean descendants of Curaçao's Sephardic Jews, the connection remained. The fact that 150 years after the migration of their Sephardic ancestors, their Catholic descendants still welcomed the Curaçaoan Sephardim who visited them in Coro, Santo Domingo, and Barranquilla as *primos* – cousins – was telling. Maybe this would not have seemed so unusual if the discovery of these family affinities had not coincided with so many revelations by American gentiles who, during the past decade, have suddenly found their Jewish roots. No such surprises occurred among the non-Jewish descendants of Curaçao's Sephardim still living in the Caribbean. When interviewed, these men and women were all well aware of their Jewish ancestry. For many, this ancestry went back four or five generations, and yet, they were able to talk about the connection with Curaçao's Jewish community as if it were only a generation or two ago that their forefathers had migrated to Santo Domingo or Coro.

What was it that made them think so fondly of the religion and place that had been part of the identity of great-great-grandparents they had never even met? Although it is difficult to give a definitive answer to this question, it would appear that this sense of connection had to do both with the oral history handed down by parents and grandparents as well as with the feeling that these ties with their Sephardic ancestors had positive connotations.

Many of the descendants of the Sephardic migrants discussed in this

Letter from S.E.L. Maduro & Sons of Curaçao to
Samuel Curiel & Co. of Santo Domingo

book had at one point or another benefited from the contacts their
ancestors had had with the Jews they had left behind in Curaçao. While
for some these contacts had been important in business, for almost all,
the historical ties with the Curaçaoan Jewish community was a cherished
part of their identity. They appeared to associate their Sephardic roots
with high morals, intelligence, creativity, and survival, and were grateful
and proud of these values that had been passed on to them by parents,
grandparents, and earlier ancestors. In a sense, therefore, the Sephardic
identity of the ancestor had been internalized by those who were no
longer Jewish because in their value system it was associated with all
these characteristics which they considered admirable.

For those who descend from the Jews of St. Thomas, the historical ties
with Curaçao are woven through the history of their ancestors' sojourn
on the Danish island. Many of the early leaders of St. Thomas's Jewish
community came from the Mikvé Israel community in Curaçao. These
included Reverend Abraham Jesurun Pinto, Hazan Joshua Piza, and
some years later, lay leaders Samuel Elias Levy Maduro, Benjamin
Delvalle and David Cardoze. In the nineteenth century, the Jews of St.
Thomas had also turned to Curaçao's Jewish community for advice on
religious issues and for assistance in times of religious disagreements. The
two separate visits by Rabbi Chumaceiro of the Mikvé Israel community
in 1857 and 1862 occurred at important times in the history of the St.
Thomas Jewish community. The first visit happened at a time when the
community had been without trained leadership for a while,[617] and
Chumaceiro's second visit came during a period of major disagreements
about St. Thomas's new Jewish preacher, Reverend Meyer H. Myers.[618]
On those occasions, Curaçao's Haham* gave several sermons that were
very well attended by the Jewish community, and he also served as an
intermediary in reuniting the disagreeing factions among the members of
the Hebrew Congregation of St. Thomas.

To descend from such learned ancestors was a positive attribute. That
these ancestors chose to turn to the mother community of Curaçao when

---

* A title which literally means "wise man" but which is often given to learned rabbis by
Sephardim.

circumstances required them to do so was a sign of their high regard for the leaders of that community. And, finally, to have participated in a second wave of migration by leaving St. Thomas when the economy of the Virgin Islands began to deteriorate, showed that they too, like their enterprising Curaçaoan ancestors, were a people who knew how to survive.

In the many family histories published by the Jewish descendants of St. Thomas's Sephardim now living in Panama, this Curaçaoan ancestry and the Mikvé Israel synagogue are given a place of honor. Alberto Osorio Osorio writes:

> This [synagogue] is our pride, our ancestor's roots, the sacred enclosure where our forefathers and founders of innumerable families learned about Judaism
>
> Curaçao's Mikvé Israel is a living monument to the inextinguishable faith that God revealed to Moses, our Teacher; [Moses] conferred [this faith] to the elders of Israel, and they [in turn passed it on] to the people. "We will listen and we will do" was the answer of the entire Congregation at the foot of [Mount] Horeb.
>
> In Curaçao, our parents listened to the Law, practiced it and took it [with them] in its entirety to remote latitudes.[619]

In a history of the Fidanque family, the family's roots are also carefully traced from Holland to Curaçao to St. Thomas and finally to Panama. In the introductory notes the author recalls:

> Curaçao became the most important Dutch settlement in the New World. The congregation Mikvé Israel reached a remarkable cultural and religious development, radiating its influence to other congregations in the Caribbean, and performing a very important role in various historical events ...[620]

These are the aspects of Curaçao's Sephardic community that have remained engrained in the memories of the Jewish descendants of those who left Curaçao for St. Thomas and a few generations later abandoned St. Thomas's shores for greater opportunities in Panama. Non-Jewish descendants of this nineteenth century St. Thomas community have also been documenting their ties to the original Sephardim from Curaçao. Over the course of the past six years, numerous e-mails have been exchanged with members of this group about their Curaçaoan Jewish ancestors.[621]

For most of these descendants of the Sephardic immigrants to St. Thomas, the historical memory of the Curaçaoan connection is mostly Jewish in nature. In Coro, however, the ties with Curaçao are much more multi-faceted. Ships had traveled back and forth between the Paraguaná peninsula and the Dutch island daily, carrying merchandise, letters, and passengers across the short distance that separated the Coriano Jews from their acquaintances and relatives. The Jews and their descendants in the two communities were not only related, they were business partners and friends. Those who remained Jewish in Coro also looked to Curaçao's Mikvé Israel for religious advice. And finally, all of them looked to the Dutch island as their haven on the many occasions when their Coriano neighbors exhibited xenophobic and anti-Semitic tendencies.

Through the end of the nineteenth century and the early twentieth century, the intensity of these contacts was maintained. Josias Senior's letters reveal all these aspects of the ties that persisted with his Curaçaoan counterparts. Most of the letters were business letters, but many also pertained to life cycle events. Among them is correspondence about a birthday party Senior was giving for his five-year old son in Coro, the announcement of a forthcoming wedding of Jacob Chumaceiro in Curaçao, condolences from Curaçao extended on the death of Alberto Henriquez and Efraim Curiel in Venezuela, and other communications in the same vein. In addition, often, during political upheavals or at times when the descendants of the Jewish immigrants to Venezuela had involved themselves in politics not to the liking of the ruling parties, they had the security that they could wait out such difficult times among their friends in Curaçao. Thus, in early 1900, Abraham Senior, Josias's brother, left for Curaçao to avoid some political difficulties, precipitating the unfriendly written exchanges with Father José Dávila González of Coro. This use of Curaçao as a political haven continued throughout the twentieth century, when, from time to time, Venezuelan descendants of many of the Sephardic families still living in that country sought refuge on the Dutch island for similar reasons. As a consequence, the face-to-face contacts were never disrupted for long.

The business connections that had led to financial success for many of Coro's Jews, coupled with the strong social bonds that were maintained, resulted in positive associations regarding the Jewish community on the nearby island among today's descendants of the Sephardic immigrants. They are proud of their friendships and family ties with the Henriquezes, Maduros, Seniors, and Caprileses in Curaçao and often search out their relatives many times removed when visiting the island. When asked why these Jewish ties are so important to them as Catholics, their replies are almost identical. They believe that their Sephardic ancestry guaranteed that they were brought up in homes where a moral life, liberal ideas, and education were valued above all.[622] Although no longer Jewish, they feel that they too have many of the qualities that made their Sephardic ancestors stand out as achievers and contributors to the well-being of the country they now consider home.

In Santo Domingo, situated much further away from Curaçao than Coro, personal and business contacts were maintained through many generations, although these interactions were less intense than those between Coro and Curaçao. Grandchildren of the original immigrants attended school on the Dutch island, Curaçaoan relatives traveled to the Dominican Republic to visit, and the Dominicans went back and forth to the island for prolonged stays during political unrest and also to visit friends. Some folks, like Samuel Curiel and his sons, had a business relationship and regular correspondence with S.E.L. Maduro & Sons and other companies in Curaçao. Even when, over time, such direct contact threatened to fade, something would happen to revive the ties among the following generations.

Thus, in 1936 and 1937, a flurry of correspondence with long-lost cousins many times removed ensued between Enrique de Marchena Dujarric of Santo Domingo and Benjamin Mendes Chumaceiro of

Curaçao. Enrique de Marchena Dujarric was a great grandson of Rafael de Marchena, and Benjamin Mendes Chumaceiro was Rafael's brother Benjamin de Marchena's grandson. Their correspondence was precipitated by the demise of a wealthy spinster, Lucy Jesurun, who had died intestate in Curaçao on November 4, 1936. Lucy's paternal grandmother had been a sister to Rafael and Benjamin de Marchena, and the descendants of her nieces and nephews in Curaçao, were searching the globe for potential heirs. The correspondence between Enrique and Benjamin suggests that the cousins did not know each other, and they address each other as *"estimado pariente"* – esteemed relative – in the multiple letters that went back and forth for several years regarding Lucy Jesurun's estate.[623] Long before the existence of the Internet, these relatives were persistent and found each other. The places of residence of these heirs to Lucy Jesurun's estate provide a snapshot of the reach of Curaçao's Jewish Diaspora in the 1930s. They included Curaçao, Aruba, the Dominican Republic, Cuba, Puerto Rico, Venezuela, New York, and New Jersey.[624] It is not known what the large number of far-flung relatives eventually inherited, but based on conversation with Enrique de Marchena y de Marchena in February of 2002, this exercise did not make any of them richer in discernable ways. It did, however, re-establish contact with long lost relatives.

Other serendipitous opportunities to reconnect have occurred over time. Julio Senior, grandson of the Curaçaoan immigrant by the same name, was the representative for Firestone in Santo Domingo in the mid twentieth century, and ended up conducting business with several members of the Jewish community on the Dutch island in that capacity. In the 1970s, Gloria Pinedo Stolk met her Curaçaoan mother's De Marchena cousins of Santo Domingo while she served as Venezuelan ambassador to the Dominican Republic from 1971 to 1973. And in 1999, the grandchildren of Rebeca and Moisés Salas Baiz reconnected with their Salas cousins in Curaçao during the family reunion which unexpectedly planted the seed for this book.

Interestingly, these exchanges between the descendants of the Sephardim from Santo Domingo and the Sephardim of Curaçao were not focused on religion. The relationships were usually social and famil-

ial, with occasional work-related contacts reviving the ties with
Curaçao's Jewish community. Yet, when the Dominicans who descend
from Curaçao's Sephardic immigrants are asked today about Curaçao or
their Curaçaoan connections, it is always their Jewish ancestry that they
emphasize, rather than, for example, the fact that their grandfather traded frequently with merchants in Curaçao or that their great grandfather
had a sister who had married into a very wealthy family on the island.
Instead, they mention the religious connection, even as they proudly
wear their crucifixes and consider themselves devout Catholics.

The image of the Sephardic Jew in Santo Domingo is that of an
upright, Caucasian, liberal-minded, and enterprising member of society,
whose descendants' names dot the landscape. Such names as Marchena,
Henriquez, Lopez Penha, and many others grace buildings, street signs,
and even the country's paper money. In this town it is almost a distinction to be a Catholic Jew.

After the first generation of immigrants, the exchanges between the
Sephardim of Barranquilla and those of Curaçao tended to be almost
entirely business related. More than fifty years after the De Solas had
migrated to Colombia, the Maduros in Curaçao maintained frequent
correspondence with them pertaining to import and export activities.
They also alerted each other regarding new commercial opportunities as
is evident, for example, in this letter received by Senior De Sola & Co.
of Barranquilla from S.E.L. Maduro & Sons in 1891.[625]

> Dear Friends,
> Without any letter of yours to refer to since our most
> recent of the 1st of last month, we are hereby writing
> you to introduce to you Mr. W. Rathjens, representative
> of a beer brewery in Hamburg, who would probably be
> able to do business with your respected firm, which to us
> would be a most pleasant event.
> Any [positive] indications that you may be able to
> give to [this gentleman whom] we recommend [to you]
> with regard to the realization of the purpose of his trip,
> would be highly appreciated.

Your affectionate friends and servants,
SEL Maduro & Sons

The Alvares Correa-Cortissoz families appear to have had less contact with the Jewish community in Curaçao during those same years. Nevertheless, when Ernesto Cortissoz decided to expand the SCADTA* flights beyond Colombia in the 1920s, Curaçao was among the first foreign destinations added. The harbor island in Curaçao where the Colombian planes used to land was nicknamed SCADTA Island until the mid twentieth century when the name fell into disuse.[626]

In the 1920s and 1930s, the Cortissoz co-owned a beer brewery in Barranquilla with the Osorio family. In 1932, the Santodomingo family of Barranquilla wanted to buy out the Osorios. The group of shareholders approached the Maduro's Bank of Curaçao to help finance this buy-out which left the Cortissoz with a minority share.[627] It appears that for certain business transactions these Jews and descendants of Jews in Barranquilla were still most comfortable with their counterparts in Curaçao, even though personal contacts had diminished over the years.

The Catholic descendants of Curaçao's Sephardim living in today's Barranquilla often mention their Sephardic heritage almost as a genetic trait that may account for their ancestors' success in business. In a city like Barranquilla which grew mostly because of the commercial prowess of its inhabitants, it should not be too surprising to find such feelings among those whose names are so closely associated with Barranquilla's entrepreneurial spirit of the nineteenth century.

It is clear that the enduring awareness of a valued relationship with the Sephardim of Curaçao among the descendants of the Sephardim who migrated to other Caribbean locations has much to do with proximity. The relatively small size of the region allowed for frequent interaction which established a mutual respect that was maintained for many generations. Whether the social ties or business ties were most important did not seem to matter too much. Where Judaism has remained a factor,

* SCADTA was the name of the commercial airline co-founded by Cortissoz in Barranquilla.

however, as among those who descend from the Sephardic Jews of St. Thomas who migrated to Panama, the bond among the two groups appears stronger. Yet, in most cases the fact that many of the descendants of the Sephardim of the Caribbean are no longer Jewish has not hampered the relationships. The numerous and large family reunions that have taken place in recent years among the Maduros, the Delvalles, the Capriles, and the Salas are testimony that these *primos* of various nationalities, races, and religions have enjoyed getting to know each other. The ancestral history that binds them and the pride they take in the roles played by their admired and enterprising Sephardic forebears is far stronger that any other elements that might separate them.

CHAPTER 12

HOW CAN WE SING THE SONG OF THE LORD ON ALIEN SOIL?

—Psalm 137:4

It has been almost seven years since I first started the research that led to this book. The road I have traveled has been entertaining and varied, and I have thoroughly enjoyed the trip. The most wonderful benefit of this research, of course, has been the new friends and connections I have made in the process. I have no siblings, and, as such, family means a lot to me, even when I have to go back five generations to find new cousins. And find them I did. I had no idea that some of the people I ended up writing about would actually be related to me. Of course I knew that I would discover a relationship with the De Marchenas who were mentioned in Julia Alvarez's novel and that most of the Caprileses I would find in Venezuela were also family. I never expected, however, to be related to David Lopez Penha Jr., appealing author, diplomat, and businessman, or to Grace Cardoze, the betrayed wife of one of Benjamin Delvalle's sons. And almost as an extra bonus, I was thrilled that when I met today's descendants of these Sephardim, we felt a natural affinity as if the centuries had not separated us.

One of the most fascinating connections I made during my research trips was with Adelaida Sourdis Nájera, Director of the Archivo General y Archivo Histórico de la Universidad de Jorge Tadeo Lozano in Bogotá,

Colombia. My very generous newly found cousin, Rodolfo Segovia Salas, had arranged for Adelaida to come to Barranquilla, where they had both grown up, to guide me through the archival sources in that city. As we got to know each other, Adelaida explained that her great-grandfather, Evaristo Sourdis, had been a Sephardic Jew of French descent, and that he had come to Barranquilla from St. Thomas where he had grown up in the mid nineteenth century. Upon his arrival in Colombia, Evaristo had married a Catholic woman from Cartagena, and his descendants were all Catholic. As Adelaida enumerated the names of members of the generations that came after Evaristo Sourdis, she mentioned that her grandfather, Evaristo's son, Arístides, had married a woman by the name of Raquel Henriquez Juliao who also had Sephardic ancestry. It did not take us long to discover that Raquel's grandmother, Sara Roiz Mendes, was a sister to Abigail Roiz Mendes. Sara Roiz Mendes was Adelaida's great-great-grandmother, and Abigail Roiz Mendes was not only my great-great-grandmother, but also the great-great grandmother of Rodolfo Segovia Salas who had made the necessary arrangements to facilitate my research efforts in Barranquilla. We were all *primos* – cousins.

My original intent for this project had been primarily to learn the answers to the questions I had when I started my research. Questions pertaining to particular individuals who had broken away from the community in which they grew up, finding new lives in new places. As I discovered the answers to those early questions, however, new mysteries appeared. The patterns that were revealed in the stories about the Sephardic immigrants led me to examine some overarching issues pertaining to the survival of small Jewish communities and even to the survival of Judaism as we know it today.

As I began to write the stories, it soon became clear that I was writing about the demise of a people. Whatever the Sephardim of Curaçao had represented in the late eighteenth century before outmigration was now pure history. This sub-group that had contributed so much to Caribbean development in the nineteenth century had essentially disappeared. It made me sad to realize this, even while I tried to remain objective and just relate the facts as I found them.

My Catholic friends who read preliminary drafts of this book accused

me of being harsh about Catholicism and anti-Semitism, and not understanding the mandates of the Church. My Jewish friends told me that I
did not seem to care enough when describing the vanishing Sephardim
of the Caribbean. Although I have tried to achieve a balanced view, it is
almost impossible for this work not to carry my voice. These are my people, and I care deeply about them and about my religious ancestry. Of
course, I have attempted to accurately document all the data presented
here in spite of my emotional reaction to what is truly the death of a culture. In the process I have gained a great deal of understanding about the
absorption of a minority group into a host community. Do I think that I
am one of the few who survived the fusion between Curaçao's Sephardim
and the large non-Jewish world that surrounded us? I suppose I have,
albeit by chance, because it could have gone either way. Had I stayed in
Curaçao, I might have married a non-Jew, many of whom were my dearest friends. The single Jewish male population on the island in the 1960s
when I was of marriageable age was quite small, and most of these men
had moved away and married American and Dutch women in the countries where they attended college. If I had married outside my religion my
children may or may not have been brought up Jewish, although, of
course, they would have been Jewish by birth.

But life took a different turn when I came to college in the United
States. To some extent I too intermarried. I came from one hundred percent Sephardic stock, barely observant of religious practices in the twentieth century "exotic" community where I grew up and moved to the
Boston area where I met and married an orthodox Ashkenazi Jew from
Cleveland, Ohio. I too integrated into my new host community, but for
me it was a life full of Judaism. Following a path I never dreamed of or
even knew existed, we raised our children in a day school, synagogue-
going, kosher home environment and centered our family life on the
extensive Jewish infrastructure of the eastern seaboard of the United
States. Yet, the stories contained in this book have caused me to wonder
how long we modern American Jews can avoid blending into the receptive world around us, even with the ever-so-rich Jewish infrastructure
that is in place in this country.

Not only do I worry about the fate of other small Jewish communities in the Caribbean and elsewhere, I have also become doubtful about our ability to survive as Jews in the long term. I believe that religious assimilation, which is already rampant, will continue to occur in the United States where Jews have been welcome for many generations. It happened here before, and it can happen again. Jewish descendants of the Sephardim who came to America's shores in the seventeenth century have all but disappeared. And the large number of Ashkenazi Jews who have become such an integral part of the American scene appear to be following the road of assimilation as well, albeit at a slower pace. Are we doomed to extinction?

In trying to answer the same question, Jonathan Sarna, in his impressive study of American Jewry, suggests that creative ways must be found to revitalize Jewish life in places where it appears to be in decline. An enhanced Jewish infrastructure that will capture the imagination and lifestyle of the Jewish population in such locations could result in a renaissance of sorts in these communities. The key creative elements would include, as Sarna puts it, "visionary leaders, committed followers, and generous philanthropists."[628] Where these three elements do not coincide, it would seem that, indeed, assimilation and intermarriage will lead to extinction. This is particularly the case for communities that are already diminished in size.

Assuming that such communities can muster the required leadership and funds imperative for them to focus on their own continuity, how exactly can they deal with the issue of size? The lessons of the four communities described in this work would suggest emphasis on the following issues: encouragement of in-migration of other Jews; incentives to remain in the community; discouragement of intermarriage and a welcoming approach to intermarried couples and their children once intermarriage does occur; encouragement of a Jewish upbringing and education for all children; and communal celebrations of holidays and important events.

There is no doubt that for a small community to execute such a strategic approach to ensure its survival, dedicated leadership and a great deal of capital will be required. It is not clear if financing for such marginal Jewish communities can be obtained. Nor is it clear that some of these small communities will be able to provide the necessary leadership from within, meaning that external professional assistance may be called for. In cases where such help is not forthcoming, these small Jewish communities too shall go the way of Coro, Barranquilla, and Santo Domingo. Or maybe they will be lucky and go through a revival cycle as occurred in twentieth century St. Thomas, where other Jews came and re-established communal life on the skeleton infrastructure that was left behind by the original founders.

In larger communities, Sarna's optimistic approach may enable Jewish life to remain a vibrant part of a nation's overall population for many centuries to come. There is no denying, however, that the world's Jewish population has been shrinking, and that even in Israel, intermarriage is on the rise.[629] Eventually, if this trend continues, the vicious circle of size and religious assimilation becomes undeniable and many once viable communities will, over time, disappear.

Appendixes

A. GENEALOGICAL CHARTS

(Courtesy of Sandra R. de Marchena)

A-1 Ancestors of Alfred John Moron

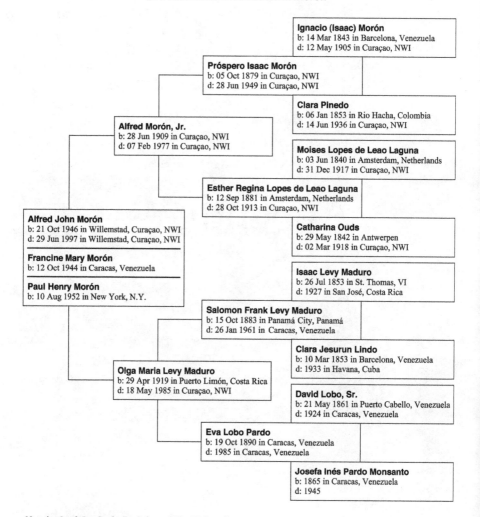

Ignacio (Isaac) Morón
b: 14 Mar 1843 in Barcelona, Venezuela
d: 12 May 1905 in Curaçao, NWI

Próspero Isaac Morón
b: 05 Oct 1879 in Curaçao, NWI
d: 28 Jun 1949 in Curaçao, NWI

Clara Pinedo
b: 06 Jan 1853 in Rio Hacha, Colombia
d: 14 Jun 1936 in Curaçao, NWI

Alfred Morón, Jr.
b: 28 Jun 1909 in Curaçao, NWI
d: 07 Feb 1977 in Curaçao, NWI

Moises Lopes de Leao Laguna
b: 03 Jun 1840 in Amsterdam, Netherlands
d: 31 Dec 1917 in Curaçao, NWI

Esther Regina Lopes de Leao Laguna
b: 12 Sep 1881 in Amsterdam, Netherlands
d: 28 Oct 1913 in Curaçao, NWI

Alfred John Morón
b: 21 Oct 1946 in Willemstad, Curaçao, NWI
d: 29 Jun 1997 in Willemstad, Curaçao, NWI

Catharina Ouds
b: 29 May 1842 in Antwerpen
d: 02 Mar 1918 in Curaçao, NWI

Francine Mary Morón
b: 12 Oct 1944 in Caracas, Venezuela

Isaac Levy Maduro
b: 26 Jul 1853 in St. Thomas, VI
d: 1927 in San José, Costa Rica

Paul Henry Morón
b: 10 Aug 1952 in New York, N.Y.

Salomon Frank Levy Maduro
b: 15 Oct 1883 in Panamá City, Panamá
d: 26 Jan 1961 in Caracas, Venezuela

Clara Jesurun Lindo
b: 10 Mar 1853 in Barcelona, Venezuela
d: 1933 in Havana, Cuba

Olga Maria Levy Maduro
b: 29 Apr 1919 in Puerto Limón, Costa Rica
d: 18 May 1985 in Curaçao, NWI

David Lobo, Sr.
b: 21 May 1861 in Puerto Cabello, Venezuela
d: 1924 in Caracas, Venezuela

Eva Lobo Pardo
b: 19 Oct 1890 in Caracas, Venezuela
d: 1985 in Caracas, Venezuela

Josefa Inés Pardo Monsanto
b: 1865 in Caracas, Venezuela
d: 1945

Note that Josefa Ines Pardo, Eva Lobo, and Olga Maduro all
married Sephardic men, but raised their children in their
mothers' Catholic religion.

A-2 Ancestors of Jeudah Senior

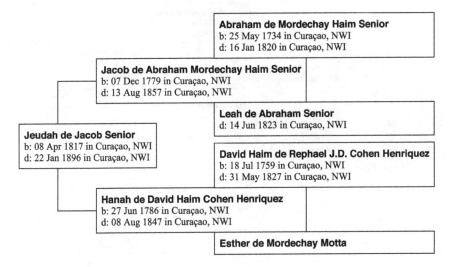

Abraham de Mordechay Haim Senior
b: 25 May 1734 in Curaçao, NWI
d: 16 Jan 1820 in Curaçao, NWI

Jacob de Abraham Mordechay Haim Senior
b: 07 Dec 1779 in Curaçao, NWI
d: 13 Aug 1857 in Curaçao, NWI

Leah de Abraham Senior
d: 14 Jun 1823 in Curaçao, NWI

Jeudah de Jacob Senior
b: 08 Apr 1817 in Curaçao, NWI
d: 22 Jan 1896 in Curaçao, NWI

David Haim de Rephael J.D. Cohen Henriquez
b: 18 Jul 1759 in Curaçao, NWI
d: 31 May 1827 in Curaçao, NWI

Hanah de David Haim Cohen Henriquez
b: 27 Jun 1786 in Curaçao, NWI
d: 08 Aug 1847 in Curaçao, NWI

Esther de Mordechay Motta

Note that Jeudah Senior's grandfather, Abraham de
Mordechay Haim Senior, was also the great-grandfather of
Isaac Senior whose ancestry is shown in A-3

A-3 Ancestors of Isaac de Abraham Mordechay Haim Senior

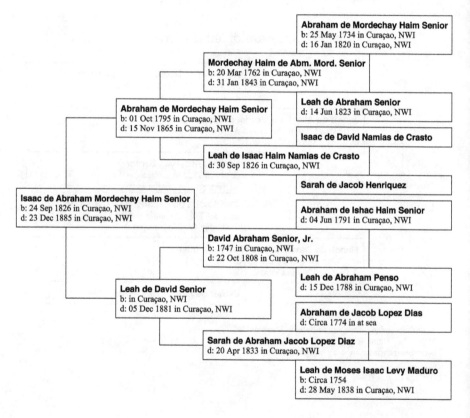

Abraham de Mordechay Haim Senior
b: 25 May 1734 in Curaçao, NWI
d: 16 Jan 1820 in Curaçao, NWI

Mordechay Haim de Abm. Mord. Senior
b: 20 Mar 1762 in Curaçao, NWI
d: 31 Jan 1843 in Curaçao, NWI

Leah de Abraham Senior
d: 14 Jun 1823 in Curaçao, NWI

Abraham de Mordechay Haim Senior
b: 01 Oct 1795 in Curaçao, NWI
d: 15 Nov 1865 in Curaçao, NWI

Isaac de David Namias de Crasto

Leah de Isaac Haim Namias de Crasto
d: 30 Sep 1826 in Curaçao, NWI

Sarah de Jacob Henriquez

Isaac de Abraham Mordechay Haim Senior
b: 24 Sep 1826 in Curaçao, NWI
d: 23 Dec 1885 in Curaçao, NWI

Abraham de Ishac Haim Senior
d: 04 Jun 1791 in Curaçao, NWI

David Abraham Senior, Jr.
b: 1747 in Curaçao, NWI
d: 22 Oct 1808 in Curaçao, NWI

Leah de Abraham Penso
d: 15 Dec 1788 in Curaçao, NWI

Leah de David Senior
b: in Curaçao, NWI
d: 05 Dec 1881 in Curaçao, NWI

Abraham de Jacob Lopez Dias
d: Circa 1774 in at sea

Sarah de Abraham Jacob Lopez Diaz
d: 20 Apr 1833 in Curaçao, NWI

Leah de Moses Isaac Levy Maduro
b: Circa 1754
d: 28 May 1838 in Curaçao, NWI

A-4 Ancestors of Abraham Raphael de Marchena

Abraham de Isaac Abraham de Marchena
b: 27 May 1770 in Curaçao, NWI
d: 29 Aug 1848 in Curaçao, NWI

Raphael de Abraham de Marchena
b: 29 Jan 1813 in Curaçao, NWI
d: 21 Oct 1879 in Santo Domingo

Esther de Jacob de Sola
d: 21 Nov 1814 in Curaçao, NWI

Abraham Raphael de Marchena
b: 16 Dec 1843 in Santo Domingo
d: 11 Feb 1917 in Paris (75) - Seine, France

Emilia de Marchena Sanchez
b: 1843 in Santo Domingo
d: 1927 in Ciudad Trujillo, Rep. Dominicana

Eugenio de Marchena Sanchez
b: 1845 in Curaçao or Santo Domingo
d: 1895

Julia de Marchena
b: 29 Aug 1846 in Santo Domingo
d: 1885 in Santo Domingo

(Francisca) Amelia de Marchena
b: 1850 in Ponce, Puerto Rico
d: 28 Feb 1941

Ofelia de Marchena
b: 1852
d: 1890 in Ciudad Trujillo, Rep. Dominicana

Dilia de Marchena
b: 1854
d: 1885

Rafael de Marchena
b: 1855
d: 1918

Alejo Sanchez
b: in Islas Canarias

Justa Sanchez
b: 1818 in Santo Domingo
d: 1905

Rosa Carreras

A-5 Ancestors of Eugenio Generoso de Marchena

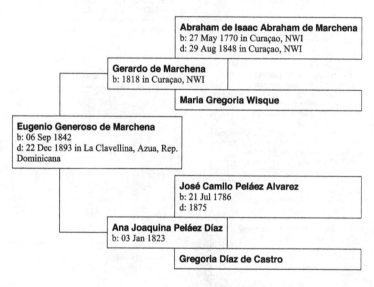

Abraham de Isaac Abraham de Marchena
b: 27 May 1770 in Curaçao, NWI
d: 29 Aug 1848 in Curaçao, NWI

Gerardo de Marchena
b: 1818 in Curaçao, NWI

Maria Gregoria Wisque

Eugenio Generoso de Marchena
b: 06 Sep 1842
d: 22 Dec 1893 in La Clavellina, Azua, Rep.
Dominicana

José Camilo Peláez Alvarez
b: 21 Jul 1786
d: 1875

Ana Joaquina Peláez Díaz
b: 03 Jan 1823

Gregoria Díaz de Castro

A-6 Ancestors of Jacob de Joseph Semah Cortissoz

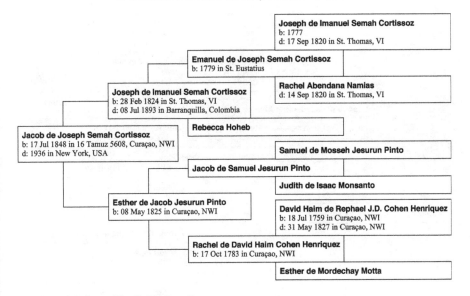

Note that Jacob Cortissoz and his wife, Julia Alvares Correa
(A-7), shared a common great-grandfather, Samuel de Mosseh
Jesurun Pinto.

A-7 Ancestors of Julia Alvares Correa

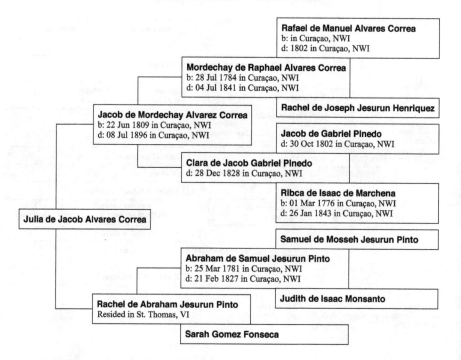

Note that Julia Alvares Correa and her husband, Jacob
Cortissoz (A-6), shared a common great-grandfather, Samuel de
Mosseh Jesurun Pinto.

B. ANALYSIS OF MARITAL STATUS AMONG CURAÇAO'S SEPHARDIM

Jewish Deaths in Curaçao 1885-1899
for Persons Born before 1826

Name	m/f	Born	Died	sgl/marr
Jeudith Jesurun	f	6/1/1797	3/15/1885	m
Esther Fidanque	f	9/15/1808	7/6/1885	m
Clara Senior	f	8/16/1800	10/19/1885	m
Rachel Alvarez Correa	f	6/3/1807	1/7/1888	m
Johebet Levy Maduro	f	2/17/1819	3/1/1888	m
Ribca Delvalle	f	9/5/1816	9/23/1888	m
Ribca Alvarez Correa	f	1/1/1812	2/23/1889	m
Clara Pinedo	f	11/29/1799	11/24/1889	m
Clara Levy Maduro	f	11/18/1820	4/23/1890	m
Batsebah Fidanque	f	7/26/1799	1/16/1891	m
Jeudith Jesurun Pinto	f	4/1/1811	3/21/1892	m
Jael Curiel	f	12/1/1813	4/6/1892	m
Abigail Penso	f	12/25/1812	12/28/1892	m
Rachel Valencia	f	8/6/1823	12/3/1893	m
Rebecca de Meza	f	2/8/1786	7/17/1894	m
Esther L. Maduro	f	12/27/1813	8/7/1894	m
Rachel Lopez Penha	f	3/2/1815	4/10/1895	m
Esther Pardo	f	4/13/1818	5/4/1895	m
Hannah Jesurun Henriquez	f	3/10/1814	11/19/1895	m

Sarah Henriquez	f	2/14/1815	7/30/1896	m
Clara Da Costa Gomez	f	10/20/1815	1/7/1897	m
Rachel Moreno Henriquez	f	7/14/1825	7/31/1897	m
Leah Senior	f	6/171811	7/16/1898	m
Rachel Senior de Polly	f	9/13/1825	8/23/1898	m
Sara Vda. de Samuel				
L. Maduro Jr.	f	8/30/1813	5/15/1899	m
Gracia Vda. Moisés				
Rois Mendez	f	9/25/1817	6/30/1899	m
Clara Osorio	f	11/21/1805	8/21/1885	s
Abigail Pardo	f	6/12/1807	8/21/1885	s
Clara Dovale	f	1/1/1814	5/20/1886	s
Rachel Jesurun	f	9/22/1808	2/16/1888	s
Grace de Sola	f	11/21/1824	4/14/1888	s
Jeudith Pereira	f	11/29/1810	5/22/1888	s
Leah Senior	f	3/24/1810	8/27/1888	s
Abigail Buenas Vivas	f	10/20/1811	10/16/1888	s
Esther Capriles	f	7/22/1814	11/15/1889	s
Clara Abinun de Lima	f	1/1/1810	3/16/1891	s
Jeudith de Castro	f	2/14/1806	2/15/1892	s
Ribca Pardo	f	8/30/1811	5/9/1892	s
Leah Abinun de Lima	f	6/11/1811	6/3/1892	s
Clara Pardo	f	3/19/1810	7/11/1893	s
Ribca Abinun de Lima	f	9/29/1810	11/23/1893	s
Rachel de Jeosuah de Sola	f	6/13/1820	8/2/1895	s
Silvania Capriles	f	11/30/1826	12/16/1896	s
Lea Henriquez Juliao	f	1/1/1814	3/25/1897	s
Jeudith Pardo	f	9/16/1819	4/13/1897	s
Sarah Hanah de Castro	f	3/11/1811	3/16/1898	s
Amathyste de Sola	f	6/6/1823	12/1/1898	s
Sarah Dovale	f	8/2/1821	11/7/1899	s
Gabriel Pinedo	m	3/30/1807	6/1/1885	m
Abraham Cardozo	m	1/1/1809	9/24/1885	m
Benjamin de Marchena	m	1/22/1811	11/28/1887	m
Moise Pereira	m	9/2/1822	2/25/1888	m

Mordechay Alvarez Correa	m	4/15/1816	2/8/1886	m
Benjamin Jesurun Jr.	m	6/4/1813	7/9/1889	m
Samuel de Casseres	m	11/19/1818	2/27/1891	m
Rafael Polly	m	10/21/1819	9/21/1894	m
David Abraham Jesurun	m	2/12/1812	4/22/1886	m
Jeudah Senior	m	4/8/1817	1/22/1896	m
Haim Daniel Lopez Penha	m	5/11/1820	2/2/1897	m
Jacob Haim Osorio	m	3/9/1810	7/2/1885	s
Mordechay Henriquez	m	5/3/1810	7/10/1886	s
Benjamin Leefmans	m	9/11/1823	7/7/1890	s
Abraham Isaac de Marchena	m	11/10/1825	5/26/1898	s
Samuel Levy Maduro Jr.	m	11/24/1811	12/15/1898	s

Total number of deaths: 64
Total number of women: 48
Total number of women who died single: 22 (46 % of deceased women)
Total number of men: 16
Total number of men who died single: 5 (31% of deceased men)

C. USE OF NAMES

Double Names

Many of the Sephardic names that appeared in Curaçao consisted of double names. It is believed that some of these double names originated by a person using both his father and mother's name in the sixteenth or seventeenth century, with the two names subsequently carried on by the descendants. This is the case, for example with the Levy Maduro family. At times the double names can also be indicative of pseudonyms used by the Sephardim as they attempted to escape persecution. In such cases one of the two names may be Jewish in nature, such as Cohen Henriquez.

Often, however, the double names are not of obvious Jewish ancestry, such as Lopez Henriquez, Lopez Penha, and Henriquez Juliao. The latter two reflect both the Spanish and Portuguese antecedents of the Caribbean Sephardim who carried these names. Over time, in Curaçao, some double names became most commonly used in abbreviated form, and occasionally this usage also appears in this text. To facilitate an understanding of these abbreviated forms, a partial listing is provided below.

Double name	Abbreviated as
Pereira Brandao	Brandao
Mendes Chumaceiro	Chumaceiro
Alvares Correa	Correa
Salom Delvalle	Delvalle
Lopez da Fonseca	Fonseca
Cohen Henriquez	Henriquez
Delvalle Henriquez	Delvalle
Lopez Henriquez	Henriquez

Moreno Henriquez	Moreno
Abinun de Lima	de Lima
Levy Maduro	Maduro
Henriquez Morón	Morón
Cohen Peixotto	Peixotto
Lopez Penha	Penha
Jesurun Pinto	Pinto
Israel Ricardo	Ricardo
Athias Robles	Robles
Semah Valencia	Valencia

Some Sephardic double names are almost always used in full and are generally not abbreviated. Among these are Gomes Casseres, Da Costa Gomez, Henriquez Juliao, and Namias de Crasto.

Names at Birth and Married Names

Curaçao has the dubious distinction of two influencing cultures: the Dutch culture, which represents the official norms on this tropical island, and the Latin American culture, which has strongly affected various aspects of life because of Curaçao's proximity to so many Spanish-speaking entities. Among the Sephardim the latter influence was dominant, and it became more so when the Curaçaoan Jews migrated to what were once Spanish colonies.

In this text the Latin way of naming is generally employed, meaning that the name consists of the given name, followed by the father's name, followed by the mother's name. Thus the son of Isaac Salas and Leah Baiz is referred to as Moisés Salas Baiz and the son of Abraham Senior and Rebecca Tavares is referred to as Jacob Senior Tavares. This is, of course, confusing, because a person not familiar with the names may think that Salas Baiz is one of the double names shown above, while this is not the case. At times people would shorten their names by merely adding the mother's initial, such as Moisés Salas B. or Hector Henriquez B.

Once a woman married, the name had the potential of becoming even longer, since the husband's name now had to be added. Thus Haydée Capriles Mendes Chumaceiro would become Haydée Capriles Mendes

Chumaceiro de Ricardo, when she married Louis Ricardo, although generally the mother's maiden name would be dropped at this point. In Curaçao such a person would be referred to in casual conversation as Haydée Ricardo. In Venezuela, where this lady lived for several years, she probably went by Haydée Capriles de Ricardo. In this text the usage of "de" preceeding the married name is often abandoned, i.e. Haydée Capriles Ricardo. Additionally, I frequently refer to a married woman by her maiden name, as is customary in Latin American countries. To complicate matters, the Dutch custom is the reverse in the case of married women, with the husband's name listed first, followed by the maiden name, e.g., Ilse Palm Chumaceiro as opposed to Ilse Chumaceiro Palm. This custom is not used in this text.

Finally, it is necessary to discuss those last names that start with "de," such as de Marchena, de Lima, de Jongh, and de Sola. In these cases, if the last name is the mother's name, the child will insert the word "y" after the father's name and before the mother's name. This is quite important, as I had occasion to find out. When enrolling at the Universidad Central de Venezuela in the sixties, I listed my name as Josette Capriles de Marchena, using the Spanish custom of listing the father's name followed by the mother's name. The administrative offices of the university assumed that Josette Capriles was married to a person called Marchena and assigned a married status to the student, listing her always under the letter "M." My enrollment forms should have read Josette Capriles y De Marchena, and it almost took an act of God to change the registration.

These last names starting with "de" also cause confusion when the person marries. Thus Elaine Jesurun, who married Hector de Marchena, said that she always felt that people thought she was stuttering when she gave her married name as Elaine Jesurun de De Marchena. She also decided to make it clearer that "De Marchena" was the actual name by capitalizing the "de." The author has used a capitalized "De" when these last names stand alone or appear as modifiers, for example, in "De Marchena believed ..." or "the De Marchena family."

As an aside, it is noted that the use of "de Marchena" as opposed to "Marchena" has very subtle meaning, since Marchena without the "de" is often an indication of illegitimacy. Yet among friends it is sometimes dropped for ease, e.g., Sandy Marchena.

NOTES

In general, those sources for which no page numbers are given either did not have page numbers or refer to the entire article, document, or book.

Introduction

1. Julia Alvarez, *In the Name of Salomé* (New York, NY: Penguin Group, 2001), p. 92.
2. Mordechai Arbell, *Comfortable Disappearance: Lessons from the Caribbean Jewish Experience* (Jerusalem, Israel: Institute of the World Jewish Congress, 1998).

Chapter 1 – Curaçao

3. Piet Huisman, *Sephardim – the Spirit That Has Withstood the Times* (The Netherlands: Huisman Editions, 1986), pp. 59–60.
4. Isaac S. Emmanuel and Suzanne A. Emmanuel, *History of the Jews of the Netherlands Antilles*, 2 vols. (Cincinnati: American Jewish Archives, 1970), p. 46.
5. Huisman, *Sephardim – the Spirit That Has Withstood the Times*, p. 66.
6. Emmanuel and Emmanuel, *History of the Jews of the Netherlands Antilles*, pp. 46–48.
7. Dr. Joh. Hartog, *Curaçao – Van Kolonie Tot Autonomie*, 2 vols. (Aruba: D. J. De Wit, 1961), p. 86.
8. Ibid., pp. 113–32.
9. Emmanuel and Emmanuel, *History of the Jews of the Netherlands Antilles*, p. 68.
10. Ibid., pp. 234–37.
11. Ibid.
12. Ibid., chapters XII and XIII.
13. Maritza Coomans-Eustatia et al, *Breekbare Banden – Feiten en Visies over Aruba, Bonaire en Curaçao Na de Vrede van Munster 1648-1998* (Bloemendaal, Netherlands: Stichting Libri Antilliani, 1998), p. 150.
14. H. Hoetink, *Het Patroon van de Oude Curaçaose Samenleving – Een Sociologische Studie* (Aruba, Netherlands Antilles: De Wit, N.V., 1958), pp. 37–40.
15. Emmanuel and Emmanuel, *History of the Jews of the Netherlands Antilles*, pp. 124–28.
16. Ibid., pp. 254–56.

17. Mikvé Israel – Emanuel, "Handwritten Documents Indicating Requests for Charitable Funds by the Indigent Members of the Mikvé Israel Community in the 18th and 19th Century" (Archives of Mikvé Israel – Emanuel Synagogue, Curaçao: various years).

18. Ibid.

19. Gary Elbow, "Scale and Regional Identity in the Caribbean," in *Nested Identities : Nationalism, Territory, and Scale*, ed. Guntram H. Herb and David H. Kaplan. (Lanham, MD: Rowman & Littlefield Publishers, 1999).

20. Frances P. Karner, *The Sephardics of Curaçao – a Study of Socio-Cultural Patterns in Flux*, Anjerpublikaties (Assen, Netherlands: Van Gorcum & Comp. N.V., 1969), p. 20.

21. xxi Casual conversations with Tanya Cohen Henriquez, 1964 – 1970.

22. Linda M. Rupert, *Roots of Our Future – a Commercial History of Curaçao* (Curaçao, Netherlands Antilles: Curaçao Chamber of Commerce and Industry, 1999), pp. 41-42.

23. Emmanuel and Emmanuel, *History of the Jews of the Netherlands Antilles*, p. 303.

24. Ibid., p. 305.

25. Ibid.

26. Ibid., p. 306.

27. Vida Lindo Guiterman, *Joshua Piza and His Descendants* (New York: 1928), p. 2.

28. Emmanuel and Emmanuel, *History of the Jews of the Netherlands Antilles*, pp. 305–06.

29. Ibid., pp. 307–09.

30. Ibid., p. 302.

31. Ibid., pp. 326–27.

32. Ibid., p. 326.

Chapter 2 – St. Thomas, Danish Virgin Islands

33. Johan Peter Nissen, *Reminiscences of a 46 Years' Residence in the Island of St. Thomas in the West Indies* (Nazareth, PA: Senseman & Co., 1838), p. 27.

34. John P. Knox, *A Historical Account of St. Thomas, W.I.* (New York: Charles Scribner, 1852), p. 162.

35. Judah M. Cohen, *Through the Sands of Time* (Lebanon, N.H.: University Press of New England, 2004), pp. 14–15.

36. Ibid., p. 25.

37. Isidor Paiewonsky, *Jewish Historical Development in the Virgin Islands, 1665–1959* (St. Thomas: 1959).

38. Cohen, *Through the Sands of Time*, p. 26.

39. Nissen, *Reminiscences of a 46 Years' Residence in the Island of St. Thomas in the West Indies*, p. 27.

40. Cohen, *Through the Sands of Time*, pp. 21–24.

41. Ibid., p. 32.

42. Emmanuel and Emmanuel, *History of the Jews of the Netherlands Antilles*, pp. 319–21.

43. Archival Collection of J.M.L. Maduro, "Register van Geboorenen en Overledenen van de Ned. Port. Israelitische Gemeente van het Eiland Curaçao 1722–1830" (Box 17, Centraal Bureau voor Genealogie, The Hague, Netherlands).

44. Isaac S. Emmanuel, *Precious Stones of the Jews of Curaçao* (New York: Bloch Publishing Company, 1957), pp. 366–67.

45. Sandra R. de Marchena, "Unpublished Genealogy of Curaçao's Sephardic Jews," (Miami, FL: 2007).

46. Emmanuel, *Precious Stones of the Jews of Curaçao*, pp. 366–67.

47. Emmanuel and Emmanuel, *History of the Jews of the Netherlands Antilles*, p. 306.

48. Mikvé Israel – Emanuel Archives, "Loan Document between Mikvé Israel Community and Ribca Sasso, January 18, 1822" (Curaçao). Note: 22 pesos and 4 reais was the fare needed to travel from Curaçao to St. Thomas (see also introduction reference 15). Although Ribca's promissory note does not mention this, we know that she did end up living on that island. Based on the date of this loan, she arrived there a few years before her sister Hannah Sasso.

49. Guiterman, *Joshua Piza and His Descendants*, p. 3.

50. De Marchena, "Unpublished Genealogy of Curaçao's Sephardic Jews."

51. Guiterman, *Joshua Piza and His Descendants*.

52. Emmanuel and Emmanuel, *History of the Jews of the Netherlands Antilles*, p. 326., Guiterman, *Joshua Piza and His Descendants*, p. 5.

53. St. Thomas Tidende, "Subscription List for Synagogue Building Fund," 30 March 1833.

54. Cohen, *Through the Sands of Time*, pp. 29–30.

55. Guiterman, *Joshua Piza and His Descendants*, p. 6.

56. Ibid., pp. 7–8.

57. Ibid., p. 8a.

58. The Occident, "Confirmation at St. Thomas," *The Occident and American Jewish Advocate* IV (1846).

59. Cohen, *Through the Sands of Time*, p. 83.

60. St. Thomas Tidende, "Announcement of School Led by Esther Jacobs," February 25, 1832.

61. St. Thomas Tidende, "Announcement of School Led by Isaac W. Williams," February 12, 1840.

62. St. Thomas Tidende, "Announcement of School Led by M.B. Simmonds," October 10, 1840.

63. St. Thomas Tidende, "Letter to the Editor by 'A Jewess'," May 24, 1856.

64. Cohen, *Through the Sands of Time*, p. 132.

65. Ibid., p. 144.

66. Emmanuel and Emmanuel, *History of the Jews of the Netherlands Antilles*, p. 981.

67. Paiewonsky, *Jewish Historical Development in the Virgin Islands, 1665–1959*.

68. Knox, *A Historical Account of St. Thomas, W.I.*, p.163.

69. Guiterman, *Joshua Piza and His Descendants*, pp. 42–43.

70. Ibid., pp. 48–52.

71. Ibid., p. 56.

72. American Jewish Archives, "Letter to Alliance Israélite Universelle Regarding Contributions from Panama, June 4, 1869, by Samuel Piza" (Alliance Israélite Universelle Microfilms, Roll # 772: Cincinnati, Ohio).

73. Vestindien Danmark Rentekammeret, "Virgin Islands Census Records, 1841–1911," in *Microfilm filmed for the Genealogical Society of Utah*, #GS0039453 (Salt Lake City, Utah: 1855).

74. Guiterman, *Joshua Piza and His Descendants*, pp. 92–93.

75. Ibid.

76. Ibid.

77. Cohen, *Through the Sands of Time*, pp. 120–21.

78. Ibid., pp. 121–23.

79. Guiterman, *Joshua Piza and His Descendants*, pp. 94–95.

80. American Jewish Archives, "Lists of St. Thomas Contributors to Alliance Israélite Universelle, March 10, 1876 and August 10, 1877, by D. Lindo" (Alliance Israélite Universelle Microfilms, Roll 772: Cincinnati, Ohio).

81. Guiterman, *Joshua Piza and His Descendants*, p. 96.

82. Jul. Margolinsky, *299 Epitaphs from the Jewish Cemetry (Sic) in St. Thomas, W.I. 1837–1916* (Copenhagen: 1957), p. 30.

83. Daniel Jacobs et al, *Code of Laws for the Government of the St. Thomas Hebrew Congregation Blessings and Peace and Acts of Piety* (New York, NY: Industrial School of the Hebrew Orphan Asylum, 1875).

84. De Marchena, "Unpublished Genealogy of Curaçao's Sephardic Jews."

85. Cohen, *Through the Sands of Time*, p. 143.

86. Ibid.

87. Paiewonsky, *Jewish Historical Development in the Virgin Islands, 1665–1959.*

88. Cohen, *Through the Sands of Time*, p. 167.

89. De Marchena, "Unpublished Genealogy of Curaçao's Sephardic Jews."

90. Ibid.

91. Emmanuel, *Precious Stones of the Jews of Curaçao*, p. 418. Another source indicates that Salomon Delvalle arrived in Curaçao in 1792, see René van Wijngaarden, *Engraved in the Palm of My Hands*, self-published limited edition ed. (Schoorls, Netherlands: Pirola, 2002), p. 98.

92. van Wijngaarden, *Engraved in the Palm of My Hands*, pp. 98–99.

93. Emmanuel and Emmanuel, *History of the Jews of the Netherlands Antilles*, p. 641.

94. Ibid., p. 473.

95. van Wijngaarden, *Engraved in the Palm of My Hands*, p. 98.

96. St. Thomas Tidende, "Description of Fire of December 31, 1831," *St. Thomas Tidende*, January 7, 1832.

97. St. Thomas Tidende, "Listing of Subscribers to Hurricane Relief Fund,"

October 18, 1871.

98. Dr. J.H Hertz, *The Pentateuch and Haftorahs – Hebrew Text, English Translation and Commentary*, Second ed. (London, England: Soncino Press, 1981), p. 855.

99. Emmanuel and Emmanuel, *History of the Jews of the Netherlands Antilles*, p. 801.

100. Ibid., p. 340.

101. Ibid.

102. Charles Gomes Casseres, "Genealogical Tree of the Family Gomes Casseres – Stretching over 5 Centuries (1470 to 1998)" (Curaçao: 1999), p. 11.

103. Informal reports run off the data available in De Marchena, "Unpublished Genealogy of Curaçao's Sephardic Jews."

104. Emmanuel and Emmanuel, *History of the Jews of the Netherlands Antilles*, p. 341.

105. van Wijngaarden, *Engraved in the Palm of My Hands*, p. 121.

106. Cohen, *Through the Sands of Time*, p. 29. and van Wijngaarden, *Engraved in the Palm of My Hands*, p. 122.

107. Judah M. Cohen, "Excel Spreadsheet of 1846 Census Data for St. Thomas" (based on Virgin Islands Census records, 1841–1911, 2003).

108. van Wijngaarden, *Engraved in the Palm of My Hands*, p. 122.

109. Vestindien Danmark Rentekammeret, "Virgin Islands Census Records, 1841–1911."

110. De Marchena, "Unpublished Genealogy of Curaçao's Sephardic Jews."

111. Conversation with David Knight, March 16, 2005.

112. St. Thomas Hebrew Congregation Archives, "Letter from the Board to Vice Governor of St. Thomas, April 1, 1867" (Box 42: Charlotte Amalie, St. Thomas).

113. St. Thomas Hebrew Congregation Archives, "Letter to Governor Regarding Synagogue by-Laws Revisions, April 12, 1872," signed by Benjamin Delvalle (Box 42: Charlotte Amalie, St. Thomas).

114. Jacobs et al, *Code of Laws for the Government of the St. Thomas Hebrew Congregation Blessings and Peace and Acts of Piety*.

115. De Marchena, "Unpublished Genealogy of Curaçao's Sephardic Jews."

116. Announcements in various issues of the *Tidende*.

117. Edith deJongh Woods, April 10, 2005.

118. John D. Woods, "A Short History of the Harmonic Lodge 356 E.C.," in *Harmonic Lodge No. 356 E.C. – 175th Anniversary – October 19, 1993* (Charlotte Amalie, St. Thomas: 1993).

119. Ibid.

120. Ibid.

121. deJongh Woods, April 10, 2005

122. Woods, "A Short History of the Harmonic Lodge 356 E.C."

123. College Park National Archives, MD, "List of Inventory of B. Delvalle's Furniture, Records of the Government of the Virgin Islands" (Record # 55: 1876).

124. Sita Levy Likuski, e-mail, March 26, 2003.

125. St. Thomas Times, "Advertisement for the Alliance - New Delvalle

Venture," February 17, 1875.

126. St. Thomas Tidende, "Advertisement for Sale of Household Furniture by Isaac B. Delvalle," November 11, 1876.

127. René van Wijngaarden, May 1, 2005.

128. Dr. Joh. Hartog, *Het Verhaal der Maduro's en Foto-Album van Curaçao 1837–1962 Uitgegeven Ter Gelegenheid van het Honderd Vijfentwintigjarig Bestaan van S.E.L. Maduro & Sons N.V.* (Aruba: D.J. de Wit, 1962), p. 74.

129. American Jewish Archives, "Letter to Central Committee of Alliance Israélite Universelle Regarding Contributions from St. Thomas, May 11, 1864, by N.M. Nathan" (Alliance Israélite Universelle Microfilms, Roll # 772: Cincinnati, Ohio).

130. American Jewish Archives, "Letter to the Central Committee of the Alliance Israélite Universelle, February 4, 1895, by Jb. B. Delvall," (Alliance Israélite Universelle Microfilms, Roll # 772: Cincinnati, Ohio).

131. Emmanuel and Emmanuel, *History of the Jews of the Netherlands Antilles*, p. 403.

132. Emmanuel, *Precious Stones of the Jews of Curaçao*, p. 418.

133. Casual conversations in 1999 and 2000 by the author with Jossy Capriles and Ruth (Doe) Delvalle of Curaçao.

134. De Marchena, "Unpublished Genealogy of Curaçao's Sephardic Jews."

135. Ibid.

136. Cohen, *Through the Sands of Time*, p. 147.

137. *The St. Thomas Times Almanac* (Charlotte Amalie, St. Thomas: St. Thomas Times, 1877).

138. Det Kongelige Bibliotek, "Letter from Grace Cardoze Delvalle to David Simonsen, Dated Nov 28, 1907" (Oriental and Judaica Collections, The David Simonsen Archives, Copenhagen, Denmark).

139. De Marchena, "Unpublished Genealogy of Curaçao's Sephardic Jews."

140. Ibid.

141. St. Thomas Tidende, "Obituary for Judith De Castro Delvalle," June 24, 1871.

142. Margolinsky, *299 Epitaphs from the Jewish Cemetry (Sic) in St. Thomas, W.I. 1837–1916*, p. 34.

143. De Marchena, "Unpublished Genealogy of Curaçao's Sephardic Jews."

144. Margolinsky, *299 Epitaphs from the Jewish Cemetry (Sic) in St. Thomas, W.I. 1837–1916*, p. 34.

145. Benjamin Delvalle, "Last Will and Testament of Benjamin Delvalle and His Wife Judith Delvalle, Born De Castro, May 3, 1864," in *National Archives, College Park, MD, Record #55* (St. Thomas).

146. Frederik C.Gjessing and William P. Maclean, *Historic Buildings of St. Thomas and St. John* (London: Macmillan Education Ltd., 1987).

147. Edith deJongh Woods, "Wimmelkafts Gade No. 10 – the Masonic Hall," *The Daily News*, June 22, 2000, p. 25.

148. Cohen, *Through the Sands of Time*, p. 193.

149. Ibid., pp. 195–200.

150. De Marchena, "Unpublished Genealogy of Curaçao's Sephardic Jews."

151. Nadhji Arjona, *La Familia Fidanque: Cien Años en Panamá – the Fidanque Family: Centennial Anniversary in Panama 1885–1985* (Panama: Impresora Panamá, S.A., 1986), p. 30.

152. De Marchena, "Unpublished Genealogy of Curaçao's Sephardic Jews."

153. Cohen, *Through the Sands of Time*, p. 192.

154. De Marchena, "Unpublished Genealogy of Curaçao's Sephardic Jews."

155. Cheryl Pinto, handwritten correspondence, May 12, 2003.

156. Rabbi Stanley T. Relkin, "A Farewell to Rabbi Sasso," in *Private papers of Marguín Valencia Salas*, (Curaçao, after 1966).

157. Private Papers of Marguín Valencia Salas, "Invitation to Solemn Thanksgiving Service in St. Thomas" (Curaçao: St. Thomas, V.I., 1964).

158. Cohen, *Through the Sands of Time*, p. 215.

159. Ibid.

160. Ibid., p. 192.

Chapter 3 – Coro, Venezuela

161. Maria Victoria Uribe, "Los Ocho Pasos de la Muerte del Alma: La Inquisición en Cartagena de Indias," *Boletín Cultural y Bibliográfico* XXIV, no. 14 (1987).

162. Hartog, *Curaçao – Van Kolonie Tot Autonomie*, p. 275. and Archival Collection of J.M.L. Maduro, "Letter from B. Bernagie to the States General of the Netherlands, Accompanied by Letters About the Imprisonment of Phillip Henriquez" (Box 24: 1700).

163. Maduro, "Letter from B. Bernagie to the States General of the Netherlands, Accompanied by Letters About the Imprisonment of Phillip Henriquez."

164. Mordechai Arbell, *Spanish and Portuguese Jews in the Caribbean and the Guianas*, ed. Dennis C. Landis and Ann P. Barry (Providence: The John Carter Brown Library, 1999), pp. 262–65.

165. Ramón Aizpurua, *Curazao y la Costa de Caracas – Introducción al Estudio de Contrabando en la Provincia de Venezuela en Tiempos de la Compañía Guipuzcoana 1730–1780* (Caracas, Venezuela: 1993), pp. 25–29.

166. Ibid., p. 29.

167. Guillermo Morón, *A History of Venezuela*, trans. John Street (New York, NY: Roy Publishers, Inc., 1963), pp. 74–75.

168. Aizpurua, *Curazao y la Costa de Caracas – Introducción al Estudio de Contrabando en La Provincia de Venezuela en Tiempos de la Compañía Guipuzcoana 1730–1780*, pp. 239–53.

169. Frank Safford and Mark Palacios, *Colombia – Fragmented Land, Divided Society* (New York: Oxford University Press, 2002), pp. 96–97.

170. Ibid., p. 92.

171. John V. Lombardi, *Venezuela – the Search for Order, the Dream of Progress*

(New York-Oxford: Oxford University Press, 1982), pp. 139–51.

172. Safford, *Colombia – Fragmented Land, Divided Society*, pp. 96–97.

173. Lombardi, *Venezuela – the Search for Order, the Dream of Progress*, pp. 139–51.

174. Isidoro Aizenberg, *La Comunidad Judía de Coro 1824–1900* (Caracas, Venezuela: Biblioteca de Autores y Temas Falconianos, 1983), p. 29.

175. Ibid., p. 30.

176. De Marchena, "Unpublished Genealogy of Curaçao's Sephardic Jews."

177. Carlos Gonzales-Batista, *Documentos para la Historia de las Antillas Neerlandesas* (Coro, Estado Falcón, Venezuela: Universidad Nacional Experimental 'Francisco de Miranda', 1997), p. 177.

178. Aizenberg, *La Comunidad Judía de Coro 1824–1900*, p. 37.

179. Archivo Histórico de la Asamblea Nacional, "1825 Census of Coro" (Gaceta de Venezuela. Trimestre 1, Nº 11. Valencia, Venezuela, page 6, March 20, 1831).

180. Aizenberg, *La Comunidad Judía de Coro 1824–1900*, p. 39.

181. José Rafael Fortique, *Los Motines Anti-Judíos de Coro* (Maracaibo, Venezuela: Ed. Puente, 1973), p. 68.

182. Aizenberg, *La Comunidad Judía de Coro 1824–1900*, p. 38.

183. Maarten Jan Bakkum, *La Comunidad Judeo-Curazoleña de Coro y el Pogrom de 1855*, ed. Centro de Investigaciones Históricas del Estado Falcón Instituto de Cultura del Estado Falcón (Caracas, Venezuela: Editorial Ex Libris, 2001), p. 14.

184. Aizenberg, *La Comunidad Judía de Coro 1824–1900*, pp. 36–39.

185. Ibid., p. 40.

186. Ibid., pp. 39–47.

187. Bakkum, *La Comunidad Judeo-Curazoleña de Coro y el Pogrom de 1855*, p. 28.

188. Gonzales-Batista, *Documentos para la Historia de las Antillas Neerlandesas*, p. 201.

189. Emmanuel and Emmanuel, *History of the Jews of the Netherlands Antilles*, p. 995.

190. De Marchena, "Unpublished Genealogy of Curaçao's Sephardic Jews."

191. Isaac S. Emmanuel, *The Jews of Coro, Venezuela* (Cincinnati, OH: American Jewish Archives, 1973), p. 29.

192. The Jewish Chronicle, "News from Coro, Venezuela," November 12, 1847.

193. Aizenberg, *La Comunidad Judía de Coro 1824–1900*, p. 101.

194. Ibid.

195. The Jewish Chronicle, "News from Coro, Venezuela,"

196. Gonzales–Batista, *Documentos para la Historia de las Antillas Neerlandesas*, p. 210.

197. Ibid., p. 244.

198. Ibid., p. 245.

199. Ibid., pp. 178–79.

200. Ibid., p. 170.

201. Ibid., p. 189.

202. Ibid., p. 183.

203. Ibid., p. 208.

204. UNEFM – Archivo Histórico de Falcón, "Certifications of Shipments Made by Henriquez, Maduro y Senior" (AHC-UNEFM, Sección Instrumentos Públicos, LXVI (1851–1854), F151v, 152, 152v, 226, 226v, Coro, Venezuela: 1852).

205. Aizenberg, *La Comunidad Judía de Coro 1824–1900*, p. 53.

206. Emmanuel, *The Jews of Coro, Venezuela*, p. 10.

207. Aizenberg, *La Comunidad Judía de Coro 1824–1900*, p. 64.

208. Bakkum, *La Comunidad Judeo-Curazoleña de Coro y el Pogrom de 1855*, pp. 59–62.

209. Aizenberg, *La Comunidad Judía de Coro 1824–1900*, pp. 63–64.

210. Ibid., p. 74.

211. UNEFM – Archivo Histórico de Falcón, "Letter from Jeudah Senior to I.A. Senior & Hijo, Asking Them to Collect Some Debts in Coro for Him," (Fondo Senior, Coro, Venezuela, Box V, July 10, 1895).

212. UNEFM – Archivo Histórico de Falcón, "Purchase of Goats on Behalf of Jeudah Senior" (AHC-UNEFM, SIP LXVIII (1858–1862), F 183–183v, Coro, Venezuela: 1859).

213. UNEFM – Archivo Histórico de Falcón, "Sale of a Dutch Schooner Owned by Jeudah Senior" (AHC-UNEFM, SIP LXVIII (1858–1862), F 195–195v, Coro, Venezuela: 1859).

214. UNEFM – Archivo Histórico de Falcón, "Protest Filed against Federal Forces on Behalf of Jeudah Senior" (AHC-UNEFM, SIP LXVIII (1858–1862), F 358–358v, Coro, Venezuela: 1861).

215. Emmanuel, *The Jews of Coro, Venezuela*, p. 27.

216. Mikvé Israel – Emanuel Archives, "Death Registers by Year for Mikvé Israel Community" (Willemstad, Curaçao: various).

217. Hartog, *Het Verhaal der Maduro's en Foto-Album van Curaçao 1837–1962 Uitgegeven Ter Gelegenheid van het Honderd Vijfentwintigjarig Bestaan van S.E.L. Maduro & Sons N.V.*, pp. 39–48.

218. Emmanuel and Emmanuel, *History of the Jews of the Netherlands Antilles*, p. 360.

219. Ibid., p. 730.

220. Ibid., p. 736.

221. Pauline Pruneti Winkel, *Scharloo – a Nineteenth Century Quarter of Willemstad, Curaçao: Historical Architecture and Its Background* (Edizioni Poligrafico Fiorentino, 1987), p. 57.

222. Emmanuel and Emmanuel, *History of the Jews of the Netherlands Antilles*, p. 365.

223. Pruneti Winkel, *Scharloo – a Nineteenth Century Quarter of Willemstad, Curaçao: Historical Architecture and Its Background*, p. 57.

224. Emmanuel and Emmanuel, *History of the Jews of the Netherlands Antilles*, p. 996.

225. Archival Collection of J.M.L. Maduro, "Scrapbook of Leah Monsanto of Curaçao" (Not yet catalogued in 2003 in collection at Centraal Bureau voor-, The Hague, Netherlands).

226. De Marchena, "Unpublished Genealogy of Curaçao's Sephardic Jews."

227. Charles Gomes Casseres, *Bewoond Scharloo* (Curaçao: Amigoe, N.V., 2000), p. 108.

228. Julio Senior, June 7, 2006.

229. De Marchena, "Unpublished Genealogy of Curaçao's Sephardic Jews."

230. Emmanuel, *The Jews of Coro, Venezuela*, p. 12.

231. Bakkum, *La Comunidad Judeo-Curazoleña de Coro y el Pogrom de 1855*, p. 101.

232. Blanca de Lima, *Coro: Fin de Diáspora – Isaac A. Senior e Hijo: Redes Comerciales y Circuito Exportador (1884–1930)*, Colección Monografías (Caracas. Venezuela: Comisión de Estudios de Postgrado, Facultad de Humanidades y Educación – Universidad Central de Venezuela, 2002), p. 22.

233. De Marchena, "Unpublished Genealogy of Curaçao's Sephardic Jews."

234. UNEFM – Archivo Histórico de Falcón, "Accounting Entries by David A. Senior in His 'Livro de Comercio'," (Fondo Senior, Coro, Venezuela, not catalogued: 1851–1858).

235. De Marchena, "Unpublished Genealogy of Curaçao's Sephardic Jews."

236. Emmanuel, *The Jews of Coro, Venezuela*, pp. 33–34.

237. Emmanuel, *Precious Stones of the Jews of Curaçao*, p. 496.

238. A. Senior in His 'Livro de Comercio'."

239. de Lima, *Coro: Fin de Diáspora – Isaac A. Senior e Hijo: Redes Comerciales y Circuito Exportador (1884–1930)*, p. 21.

240. Ibid., pp. 28.

241. Ibid., pp. 28–29 and pp. 221–25.

242. Ibid., pp. 61–63.

243. Ibid., p. 186.

244. De Marchena, "Unpublished Genealogy of Curaçao's Sephardic Jews."

245. UNEFM – Archivo Histórico de Falcón, "Letter from Josias Senior in Curaçao to His Brothers and Sister in Coro" (Fondo Senior, Coro, Venezuela, Box V, October 21, 1895).

246. Ibid.

247. Emmanuel, *The Jews of Coro, Venezuela*, pp. 35.

248. Ibid., pp. 50.

249. de Lima, *Coro: Fin de Diáspora – Isaac A. Senior e Hijo: Redes Comerciales y Circuito Exportador (1884–1930)*, p. 222.

250. Ibid., p. 40.

251. De Marchena, "Unpublished Genealogy of Curaçao's Sephardic Jews."

252. Helen Salas, November, 2002.

253. Emmanuel, *The Jews of Coro, Venezuela*, pp. 35.

254. Ibid., pp. 51–52.

255. de Lima, *Coro: Fin de Diáspora – Isaac A. Senior e Hijo: Redes Comerciales y Circuito Exportador (1884–1930)*, p. 223.

256. De Marchena, "Unpublished Genealogy of Curaçao's Sephardic Jews."

257. UNEFM – Archivo Histórico de Falcón, "Letter from David A. Senior in

Curaçao to Josias Senior in Coro" (Fondo Senior, Box 32, p. 243, Coro, Venezuela: 1899).

258. Aizenberg, *La Comunidad Judía de Coro 1824–1900*, pp. 107–09.

259. de Lima, *Coro: Fin de Diáspora – Isaac A. Senior e Hijo: Redes Comerciales y Circuito Exportador (1884–1930)*, p. 46.

260. UNEFM – Archivo Histórico de Falcón, "Letter from Julius L. Penha to I.A. Senior & Hijo" (Fondo Senior, box 32, page 8, Coro, Venezuela: 1899).

261. UNEFM – Archivo Histórico de Falcón, "Letter from Moses S.L. Maduro of Curaçao to Josias Senior of Coro" (Fondo Senior, box 10, Coro, Venezuela, October 26, 1896).

262. UNEFM – Archivo Histórico de Falcón, "Letter from C. G. Pinedo of Maracaibo to I.A. Senior & Hijo" (Fondo Senior, Box V, Coro, Venezuela, March 19, 1897).

263. UNEFM – Archivo Histórico de Falcón, "Letter from José Puri of Havana, Cuba to I.A. Senior & Hijo" (Fondo Senior, Box V, Coro, Venezuela, March 19, 1897).

264. UNEFM – Archivo Histórico de Falcón, "Letter from Edwin Senior in Curaçao to Josias Senior in Coro" Fondo Senior, Box 32, Coro, Venezuela, July 1, 1899).

265. Ibid.

266. UNEFM – Archivo Histórico de Falcón, "Letter from J.D. Capriles to Josias L. Senior" (Fondo Senior, Box 26, p. 563, Coro, Venezuela: 1898).

267. Aizenberg, *La Comunidad Judía de Coro 1824–1900*, p. 117.

268. Ibid., p. 124.

269. de Lima, *Coro: Fin de Diáspora – Isaac A. Senior e Hijo: Redes Comerciales y Circuito Exportador (1884–1930)*, p. 19. – This was a sign that not all of Coro's Jews had stayed away from Coro between 1855 and 1858.

270. Ibid., pp. 19–20.

271. Aizenberg, *La Comunidad Judía de Coro 1824–1900*, p. 130.

272. Ibid., p. 128.

273. de Lima, *Coro: Fin de Diáspora – Isaac A. Senior e Hijo: Redes Comerciales y Circuito Exportador (1884–1930)*, p. 45.

274. Private Archives of César Maduro Ferrer, Coro, Venezuela, "Letter Signed by Josias L. Senior et. al. Directed to José Dávila González, February 18, 1900," (uncatalogued papers: Coro, Venezuela).

275. Private Archives of César Maduro Ferrer, Coro, Venezuela, "Letter Signed by R. Piña Castro et. al., February 20, 1900" (uncatalogued papers: Coro, Venezuela).

276. Private Archives of César Maduro Ferrer, Coro, Venezuela, "Public Letter by Father José Dávila González, February 24, 1900" (uncatalogued papers: Coro, Venezuela).

277. Dr. G. E. van Zanen, *David Ricardo Capriles, Student Geneesheer Schrijver, Curaçao 1837–1902*, Anjerpublikaties (Assen, Netherlands: Van Gorcum & Comp. N.V., 1969), p. 66.

278. de Lima, *Coro: Fin de Diáspora – Isaac A. Senior e Hijo: Redes Comerciales y*

Circuito Exportador (1884–1930), p. 42.

279. American Jewish Archives, "Letter to the Alliance Israélite Universelle Regarding Contributions from Venezuela, July 17,1874, by E. De Sola," (Alliance Israélite Universelle Microfilms, Roll # 772: Cincinnati, Ohio).

280. De Marchena, "Unpublished Genealogy of Curaçao's Sephardic Jews."

281. American Jewish Archives, "Letter to the Alliance Israélite Universelle Regarding Contributions from Venezuela, July 29, 1881, by E. De Sola," (Alliance Israélite Universelle Microfilms, Roll # 772: Cincinnati, Ohio).

282. American Jewish Archives, "Letter to the Alliance Israélite Universelle Regarding Contributions from Venezuela, March 16, 1886, by E. De Sola," (Alliance Israélite Universelle Microfilms, Roll # 772: Cincinnati, Ohio).

283. Emmanuel, *The Jews of Coro, Venezuela*, p. 14.

284. Thelma Henriquez, June 24, 2004

285. Maduro, "Scrapbook of Leah Monsanto of Curaçao."

286. Casual conversation with Helen Salas, November 2002.

287. Edna Molina Senior de Suarez, June 24, 2004.

288. van Zanen, *David Ricardo Capriles, Student Geneesheer Schrijver, Curaçao 1837–1902*, p. 66.

289. Ibid., pp. 65–67.

290. José Luis Alvarez Ortiz, "Unpublished Genealogy and Notes of the Capriles Family" (Caracas, Venezuela: 2000).

291. Ibid.

292. Ricardo de Sola, *Los Sefarditas – Lazos de Unión entre Curazao y Venezuela* (Caracas, Venezuela: self published, 1991), p. 46.

293. Emmanuel and Emmanuel, *History of the Jews of the Netherlands Antilles*, p. 297.

294. Ibid., p. 298.

295. Ibid., pp. 800–01.

296. John de Pool, *Del Curaçao Que Se Va* (Panama: 1935), p. 283.

297. de Sola, *Los Sefarditas – Lazos de Unión entre Curazao y Venezuela*, p. 48.

298. Emmanuel and Emmanuel, *History of the Jews of the Netherlands Antilles*, p. 298.

299. Emmanuel, *Precious Stones of the Jews of Curaçao*, p. 298.

300. Josette Capriles Goldish, "Analysis of the Journal of Circumcisions of Moises Frois Ricardo," *American Jewish History* 91, no. 2.

301. Abraham Levy-Benshimol, *Los Sefardíes, Vínculo Entre Curazao y Venezuela* (Caracas, Venezuela: Museo Sefardí de Caracas, 2002), p. 73.

302. Emmanuel and Emmanuel, *History of the Jews of the Netherlands Antilles*, p. 857.

303. Moises Frois Ricardo, "Record of Birth and Circumcision Beginning from the 26th January 1840 Corresponding to the 21st Sebat 5600, Kingston, Jamaica," in *Private Archives of Ricardo de Sola* (Caracas, Venezuela: 1840–1878).

304. De Marchena, "Unpublished Genealogy of Curaçao's Sephardic Jews." and Alvarez Ortiz, "Unpublished Genealogy and Notes of the Capriles Family."

305. Blanca de Lima, "El Legado de una Comunidad: Los Sefarditas de Coro," *Maguén*, July/September 2001, p. 29.

306. Blanca de Lima, *The Coro and La Vela Railroad and Improvement Company 1897–1938* (Coro, Venezuela: Centro de Investigaciones Históricas "Pedro Manuel Arcaya" UNEFM, 1995), p. 49.

307. Ibid., p. 45.

308. Ibid., p. 51.

309. Ibid., p. 50.

310. de Lima, "El Legado de una Comunidad: Los Sefarditas de Coro," p. 16.

311. Ibid., pp. 13 – 18.

312. Ibid., p. 18.

313. de Lima, *The Coro and La Vela Railroad and Improvement Company 1897–1938*, p. 50.

314. De Marchena, "Unpublished Genealogy of Curaçao's Sephardic Jews."

315. de Lima, *The Coro and La Vela Railroad and Improvement Company 1897–1938*, pp. 69–77.

316. Ibid., pp. 77–80.

317. Ibid., p. 87.

318. S.E.L. Maduro and Sons, "Copiador de Cartas – Files by Year" (Willemstad, Curaçao: various years).

319. Ibid., March 26, 1901.

320. De Marchena, "Unpublished Genealogy of Curaçao's Sephardic Jews."

321. Ibid.

322. Aizenberg, *La Comunidad Judía De Coro 1824–1900*, pp. 141– 42.

323. Ibid., pp. 143–44.

324. Private Archives of Ricardo de Sola, "Freemasonry Certificate of David Ricardo Issued in Coro, Venezuela" Caracas, Venezuela: 1886).

325. Alvarez Ortiz, "Unpublished Genealogy and Notes of the Capriles Family."

326. Ibid.

327. De Marchena, "Unpublished Genealogy of Curaçao's Sephardic Jews."

328. Deborah Capriles de Petit, June 24, 2004.

329. Aizenberg, *La Comunidad Judía de Coro 1824–1900*, pp. 121–24.

330. Ibid., pp. 124–25.

331. Archival Collection of J.M.L. Maduro, "Individuals of Curaçaoan Origin Who Have Held Distinguished Posts in Venezuela, as Listed by J.M.L. Maduro" (Box 3, Centraal Bureau voor Genealogie, The Hague, Netherlands).

332. Alvarez Ortiz, "Unpublished Genealogy and Notes of the Capriles Family."

Chapter 4 – Santo Domingo, Dominican Republic

333. Frank Moya Pons, *The Dominican Republic: A National History* (New Rochelle: Hispaniola Books, 1995), pp. 62–63.

334. María Rosario Sevilla Soler, *Santo Domingo Tierra de Frontera (1750–1800)*

(Sevilla: Escuela de Estudios Hispano Americanos, 1980), pp. 409–58.

335. Carlos Esteban Deive, *Heterodoxia e Inquisición en Santo Domingo 1492–1822* (Santo Domingo: Taller, 1983), p. 155.

336. Ibid., pp 157–58.

337. H. Hoetink, *The Dominican People, 1850–1900 : Notes for a Historical Sociology*, trans. Stephen K. Ault (Baltimore: John Hopkins University Press, 1982), p. 21.

338. Moya Pons, *The Dominican Republic: A National History*, p. 116.

339. Martin D. Clausner, *Rural Santo Domingo: Settled, Unsettled, and Resettled* (Philadelphia: Temple University Press, 1973), pp. 81–82.

340. Deive, *Heterodoxia e Inquisición en Santo Domingo 1492–1822*, p. 340. and Moya Pons, *The Dominican Republic: A National History*, pp. 122–41.

341. Mordechai Arbell, "Referred to by Enrique de Marchena in His Manuscript."

342. Emmanuel and Emmanuel, *History of the Jews of the Netherlands Antilles*, pp. 940–42.

343. Enrique Ucko, *La Fusión de los Sefardíes con los Dominicanos* (Ciudad Trujillo, Republica Dominicana: Imprenta La Opinión, 1944), p. 26.

344. Moya Pons, *The Dominican Republic: A National History*, pp. 174–83.

345. De Marchena, "Unpublished Genealogy of Curaçao's Sephardic Jews."

346. Ucko, *La Fusión de los Sefardíes con Los Dominicanos*, p. 24.

347. Enrique de Marchena y de Marchena, "Unpublished Manuscript of the History of the De Marchenas in the Dominican Republic" (Santo Domingo: 2001).

348. Emmanuel and Emmanuel, *History of the Jews of the Netherlands Antilles*, p. 47.

349. Ibid., pp. 260–61.

350. Ibid., p. 267.

351. Mikvé Israel – Emanuel Archives, "Letter from Abraham de Marchena Refusing Payment, November 11, 1819" (Willemstad, Curaçao).

352. Emmanuel and Emmanuel, *History of the Jews of the Netherlands Antilles*, p. 955.

353. Ibid., p. 916.

354. De Marchena, "Unpublished Genealogy of Curaçao's Sephardic Jews."

355. Sevilla Soler, *Santo Domingo Tierra de Frontera (1750–1800)*, pp. 50–56.

356. De Marchena y de Marchena, "Unpublished Manuscript of the History of the De Marchenas in the Dominican Republic."

357. Archivo General de la Nación, "Marriage Registrations 1848–1852, November 9, 1848" (Santo Domingo, D.R.).

358. Ibid.

359. Ibid.

360. Cándida Amelia Cohen de Marchena, "Unpublished Memoirs of Cándida Amelia Cohen De Marchena" (Santo Domingo, Dominican Republic: 1967).

361. De Marchena y de Marchena, "Unpublished Manuscript of the History of the De Marchenas in the Dominican Republic."

362. De Marchena, "Unpublished Genealogy of Curaçao's Sephardic Jews."

363. Inés Roux de Bézieux, November 8, 2001.

364. Michel Hadengue, January 3, 2002.

365. Ucko, La Fusión de los Sefardíes con los Dominicanos, pp. 19–20.

366. De Marchena y de Marchena, "Unpublished Manuscript of the History of the De Marchenas in the Dominican Republic."

367. Capriles Goldish, "Analysis of the Journal of Circumcisions of Moises Frois Ricardo."

368. Emmanuel and Emmanuel, History of the Jews of the Netherlands Antilles, p. 369.

369. De Marchena y de Marchena, "Unpublished Manuscript of the History of the De Marchenas in the Dominican Republic."

370. Cohen de Marchena, "Unpublished Memoirs of Cándida Amelia Cohen De Marchena."

371. Ibid.

372. Kai Schoenhals, Dominican Republic, ed. Kai Schoenhals, vol. III, World Bibliographical Series (Oxford, England: Clio Press Ltd., 1990), p. xix.

373. Enrique de Marchena – Dujarric, "Presencia Hebrea en la República Dominicana," in Presencia Judía en Santo Domingo, ed. Alfonso Lockward (Santo Domingo: Taller, 1994), p. 98.

374. De Marchena y de Marchena, "Unpublished Manuscript of the History of the De Marchenas in the Dominican Republic."

375. Ibid.

376. Ibid.

377. Eva Abraham-van der Mark, "Marriage and Concubinage among the Sephardic Merchant Elite of Curaçao," in Women & Change in the Caribbean, ed. Janet Momsen (Bloomington, IN: Indiana University Press, 1993), p. 43.

378. Carlos Larrazabal Blanco, Familias Dominicanas, multi vols. (Santo Domingo, D.R.), Vol. V, p. 47.

379. Hoetink, The Dominican People, 1850–1900: Notes for a Historical Sociology, p. 24.

380. Moya Pons, The Dominican Republic: A National History, pp. 272–73.

381. "Letter to Braulia de Marchena Signed by the President of the Dominican Republic Ulyssis Heureaux, June 10, 1893" (Private Collection of Enrique de Marchena y de Marchena: Santo Domingo, D.R.).

382. Hoetink, The Dominican People, 1850–1900: Notes for a Historical Sociology, p. 90.

383. De Marchena – Dujarric, "Presencia Hebrea en la República Dominicana," p. 108.

384. J. Agustín Concepción, Proyección Curazoleña en Santo Domingo (Santo Domingo: Editora Nivar, 1985), p. 47.

385. Ibid., p. 19.

386. Ibid., p. 20.

387. Cohen de Marchena, "Unpublished Memoirs of Cándida Amelia Cohen De

Marchena."

388. Emmanuel, *Precious Stones of the Jews of Curaçao*, p. 81.

389. Enrique de Marchena y de Marchena, August 17, 2001.

390. De Marchena, "Unpublished Genealogy of Curaçao's Sephardic Jews."

391. Aizenberg, *La Comunidad Judía de Coro 1824–1900*, p. 39.

392. De Marchena, "Unpublished Genealogy of Curaçao's Sephardic Jews."

393. Emmanuel and Emmanuel, *History of the Jews of the Netherlands Antilles*, p. 47.

394. Ibid., p. 304.

395. Ibid., p. 311.

396. Emmanuel and Emmanuel, *History of the Jews of the Netherlands Antilles*, pp. 306–07.

397. Ibid., pp. 805–13.

398. The Occident, "(News Items from) Puerto Cabello, Venezuela," *The Occident and American Jewish Advocate* XI (1853): p. 79.

399. Ibid.: p. 534.

400. The Occident, "(News Items from) Puerto Cabello, Venezuela," *The Occident and American Jewish Advocate* XIII (1855): p. 202.

401. Emmanuel and Emmanuel, *History of the Jews of the Netherlands Antilles*, p. 1080.

402. De Curaçaosche Courant, "Notification to the Public," September 19, 1863.

403. Emmanuel and Emmanuel, *History of the Jews of the Netherlands Antilles*, p. 393.

404. Ibid., p. 394.

405. Ibid., p. 880.

406. De Marchena, "Unpublished Genealogy of Curaçao's Sephardic Jews."

407. Juan Hormazabal Salas, November 15, 2001.

408. S.E.L. Maduro and Sons, "Letter to Samuel Curiel & Co. of Santo Domingo, March 15, 1901," in *Archives of S.E.L. Maduro & Sons* (Curaçao).

409. Ibid.

410. Henry Zvi Ucko, "The Ancient Jewish Cemetery in Ciudad Trujillo, Dominican Republic," in *Henry Zvi Ucko Papers, Southern Historical Collection, Manuscripts Department, Wilson Library, University of North Carolina* (Chapel Hill, NC: after 1957).

411. Private Papers of Juan Hormazabal Salas, "Listing of Founding Members of Club Unión, 1892" (Santo Domingo, Dominican Republic: Sociedad Dominicana de Bibliófilos, 1892).

412. De Marchena, "Unpublished Genealogy of Curaçao's Sephardic Jews."

413. Josette Capriles Goldish, *The Girls They Left Behind – Curaçao's Jewish Women in the Nineteenth Century*, Working Paper No. 11, Hadassah International Research Institute on Jewish Women at Brandeis University (Waltham, MA: 2002).

414. editor Home Journal of the Young Men's Hebrew Association of Curaçao, "Arrivals," November 15, 1889.

415. De Marchena, "Unpublished Genealogy of Curaçao's Sephardic Jews."

416. Ibid.

417. Hormazabal Salas.

418. Adelaida Sourdis Nájera, *El Registro Oculto – Los Sefardíes del Caribe en la Formación de la Nación Colombiana 1813–1886* (Bogotá: Academia Colombiana de Historia, 2001), p. 42.

419. Ibid., pp. 125–29.

420. Ibid., p. 131.

421. De Marchena, "Unpublished Genealogy of Curaçao's Sephardic Jews."

422. Emmanuel and Emmanuel, *History of the Jews of the Netherlands Antilles*, p. 441.

423. Private papers of Dr. Manuel Galán-Salas, "Collection of Newspaper Clippings Pertaining to Salas and Curiel Families" (Santo Domingo, Dominican Republic).

424. De Marchena, "Unpublished Genealogy of Curaçao's Sephardic Jews."

425. Sourdis Nájera, *El Registro Oculto – Los Sefardíes del Caribe en la Formación de la Nación Colombiana 1813–1886* , p. 142.

426. Hormazabal Salas.

427. Olga Salas de Galán, "An Essay on Religion," (Santo Domingo, Dominican Republic: unknown date).

428. De Marchena, "Unpublished Genealogy of Curaçao's Sephardic Jews."

429. Emmanuel, *Precious Stones of the Jews of Curaçao*, p. 454.

430. Emmanuel and Emmanuel, *History of the Jews of the Netherlands Antilles*, p. 969.

431. De Marchena, "Unpublished Genealogy of Curaçao's Sephardic Jews."

432. The Jewish Chronicle, "News Items – St. Domingo," June 19, 1846, p. 153.

433. Ricardo, "Record of Birth and Circumcision Beginning from the 26th January 1840 Corresponding to the 21st Sebat 5600, Kingston, Jamaica."

434. Abraham Mendes Chumaceiro, "Bij de Dood van David Lopez Penha Jr. – Een Brief aan Zijn Grijzen Vader," in *A.M. Chumaceiro A*z. *– Onpartijdig Pionier Op Curaçao*, ed. Henny E. Coomans and Maritza Coomans-Eustatia (Bloemendaal, Netherlands: Stichting Libri Antilliani, 1893), p. 506.

435. De Marchena, "Unpublished Genealogy of Curaçao's Sephardic Jews."

436. Emmanuel and Emmanuel, *History of the Jews of the Netherlands Antilles*, p. 359.

437. De Marchena, "Unpublished Genealogy of Curaçao's Sephardic Jews."

438. Emmanuel and Emmanuel, *History of the Jews of the Netherlands Antilles*, p. 805.

439. Ibid., p. 357.

440. Elias López Penha, "Reivindicación," (Santo Domingo, D.R.: 1883), p. 5.

441. Ibid., p. 3.

442. Ibid., pp. 5–6.

443. De Marchena, "Unpublished Genealogy of Curaçao's Sephardic Jews."

444. Marianela Lopez Penha, Conversation, February 7, 2002.

445. The New York Times, "Educator Challenges Bevin," June 16, 1946, p. 4.

Chapter 5 – Barranquilla, Colombia

446. Capt. Charles Stuart Cochrane, *Journal of a Residence and Travels in Colombia During the Years 1823 and 1824*, 2 vols. (Reprinted by AMS Press, Inc., New York, NY, 1971, 1825), p. 476.

447. Eduardo Posada Carbó, *Una Invitación a la Historia de Barranquilla*, ed. Martha Cárdenas, Historia Contemporánea y Realidad Nacional No. 17 (Bogotá, Colombia: Fondo Editorial CEREC, 1987), p. 17.

448. Cochrane, *Journal of a Residence and Travels in Colombia During the Years 1823 and 1824*, pp. 76–77.

449. Safford, *Colombia – Fragmented Land, Divided Society*, p. 180.

450. Manuel Rodríguez Becerra and Jorge Restrepo Restrepo, *Los Empresarios Extranjeros de Barranquilla 1820–1900* (Bogotá, Colombia: Facultad de Administración de la Universidad de los Andes, 1987), pp. 9–10.

451. Adelaida Sourdis Nájera, "Los Judíos Sefardíes en Barranquilla – El Caso de Jacob y Ernesto Cortissoz," (Cartagena, Colombia: Universidad Jorge Tadeo Lozano, Sección del Caribe, May 1999), pp. 5–6. and Dino Manco Bermúdez and José Watnik Barón, *Nuestras Gentes – Primera Generación* (Barranquilla, Colombia: Escala Impresores Ltda., 2000), p. 48.

452. Rodolfo Segovia Salas, June 20, 2004.

453. Sergio Paolo Solano, "Comercio, Transporte y Sociedad en Barranquilla en la Primera Mitad del Siglo XIX," *Boletín Cultural y Bibliográfico*, 1989, p. 2.

454. Sourdis Nájera, "Los Judíos Sefardíes en Barranquilla – El Caso de Jacob y Ernesto Cortissoz," p. 70.

455. Emmanuel, *Precious Stones of the Jews of Curaçao*, pp. 231–32.

456. Emmanuel and Emmanuel, *History of the Jews of the Netherlands Antilles*, pp. 317–18.

457. *El Promotor*, "Announcement of the Death of Rachel Jesurun Pinto de Alvares Correa," December 12, 1891.

458. De Marchena, "Unpublished Genealogy of Curaçao's Sephardic Jews."

459. Cohen, *Through the Sands of Time*, p. 32.

460. Emmanuel and Emmanuel, *History of the Jews of the Netherlands Antilles*, p. 824.

461. Eduardo Posada Carbó, *The Colombian Caribbean, a Regional History* (Clarendon Press, 1996), p. 190.

462. Emmanuel and Emmanuel, *History of the Jews of the Netherlands Antilles*, p. 824.

463. Sourdis Nájera, *El Registro Oculto – Los Sefardíes del Caribe en la Formación de la Nación Colombiana 1813–1886*, pp. 3–4.

464. Ibid., pp. 156–57.

465. De Marchena, "Unpublished Genealogy of Curaçao's Sephardic Jews."

466. Karner, *The Sephardics of Curaçao – a Study of Socio-Cultural Patterns in Flux*, p. 12.

467. Mikvé Israel – Emanuel Archives, "Letter to Synagogue Board with Request for Financial Assistance, Written by Jacob Jesurun Pinto, February 16, 1837," (Curaçao).

468. Sourdis Nájera, *El Registro Oculto – Los Sefardíes del Caribe en la Formación de la*

Nación Colombiana 1813–1886, p. 133.

469. Ricardo, "Record of Birth and Circumcision Beginning from the 26th January 1840 Corresponding to the 21st Sebat 5600, Kingston, Jamaica."

470. Eudacia Cortissoz, "Letter to Moises Frois Ricardo, July 19, 1867," in *Private Archives of Ricardo de Sola* (Caracas, Venezuela). and Ricardo, "Record of Birth and Circumcision Beginning from the 26th January 1840 Corresponding to the 21st Sebat 5600, Kingston, Jamaica."

471. Sourdis Nájera, "Los Judíos Sefardíes en Barranquilla – El Caso de Jacob y Ernesto Cortissoz," p. 6.

472. *El Promotor*, "Listing of Shareholders of the Banco de Barranquilla," *El Promotor*, February 22, 1873.

473. Posada Carbó, *Una Invitación a la Historia de Barranquilla*, p. 21.

474. *El Promotor*, "Open Letter to the President of Colombia," May 31, 1873.

475. *El Promotor*, "Response Regarding Excessive Freight and Tardiness of The 'Ferrocaril De Bolívar' by Aquileo Parra for the Executive Branch of Colombia," June 14, 1873. This formal notification furthermore tried to placate the management of the 'Ferrocaril de Bólivar' with a basic lesson in the laws of supply and demand by informing the company that the decrease in freight fees would be more than offset by the increase in the volume of transported goods.

476. *El Promotor*, "Listing of Founding Shareholders of the 'Compañía de Omnibus'," March 29, 1873

477. Sourdis Nájera, "Los Judíos Sefardíes en Barranquilla – El Caso de Jacob y Ernesto Cortissoz," pp. 9–11.

478. Sourdis Nájera, *El Registro Oculto – Los Sefardíes del Caribe en la Formación de la Nación Colombiana 1813–1886*, pp. 139–42.

479. *El Promotor*, "'Acueducto de Barranquilla' – Summary of Shareholders Meeting of July 14, 1879," July 19, 1879.

480. *El Promotor*, "Announcement of First Test of Water Processed by the 'Acueducto De Barranquilla'," Feb 28, 1880.

481. *El Promotor*, "Editorial About Inauguration of the 'Acueducto De Barranquilla'," March 27, 1880.

482. *El Promotor*, "'Acueducto De Barranquilla' – Summary of Shareholders Meeting of July 11, 1892," July 16, 1892.

483. Sourdis Nájera, "Los Judíos Sefardíes en Barranquilla – El Caso de Jacob y Ernesto Cortissoz," p. 15.

484. Sourdis Nájera, *El Registro Oculto – Los Sefardíes del Caribe en la Formación de la Nación Colombiana 1813–1886*, pp. 145–46.

485. *El Promotor*, "Announcement of Formation of 'Compañía Teatro Barranquilla'," July 7, 1888.

486. Julio Hoenigsberg, *100 Años de Historia Masónica de la Respetable Logia El Siglo XIX No. 24–1* (Barranquilla, Colombia: 1964), p. 21.

487. Ibid., pp. 27–28.

488. Ibid., insert at p. 30.

489. *El Promotor*, "Letter to the Editor of *El Promotor*," June 14, 1873.

490. Ibid.

491. Manco Bermúdez, *Nuestras Gentes – Primera Generación*, pp. 138–39.

492. Ibid., p. 146.

493. Ibid., p. 153.

494. Manco Bermúdez, *Nuestras Gentes – Primera Generación*, p. 145.

495. Miguel García-Bustamente, *Ernesto Cortissoz – Conquistador de Utopías* (Colombia: Lerner Ltda., 1994), pp. 30–31.

496. American Jewish Archives, "Letter to the Alliance Israélite Universelle Regarding Contributions from Barranquilla, Colombia, March 13, 1874, by J.I. Senior," (Alliance Israélite Universelle Microfilms, Roll # 772: Cincinnati, Ohio).

497. American Jewish Archives, "Letter to the Alliance Israélite Universelle Regarding Contributions from Barranquilla, Colombia, May 22, 1884, by D. H. Senior," (Alliance Israélite Universelle Microfilms, Roll # 772: Cincinnati, Ohio).

498. American Jewish Archives, "Letter to Alliance Israélite Universelle Regarding Contributions from Colombia, July 13, 1870, by Jacob Alvares Correa," (Alliance Israélite Universelle Microfilms, Roll # 772: Cincinnati, Ohio).

499. Sourdis Nájera, *El Registro Oculto – Los Sefardíes del Caribe en la Formación de la Nación Colombiana 1813–1886*, p. 74.

500. Sourdis Nájera, "Los Judíos Sefardíes en Barranquilla – El Caso de Jacob y Ernesto Cortissoz," p. 9.

501. Ibid.

502. Archival Collection of J.M.L. Maduro, "J.M.L. Maduro Genealogical Notes for Cortissoz Family Prepared by J.M.L. Maduro" (Box 19, Centraal Bureau voor Genealogie, The Hague, Netherlands).

503. García-Bustamente, *Ernesto Cortissoz – Conquistador de Utopías*, pp. 13–14.

504. Hoenigsberg, *100 Años de Historia Masónica de la Respetable Logia El Siglo XIX No. 24–1*, p. 62.

505. Andres Vilora-Terán et al, *Barranquilla – Estudio Sociológico Documental para una Monografía Histórica de la Ciudad* (Barranquilla, Colombia: Editorial Efemérides, 1995), p. 439.

506. As quoted in García-Bustamente, *Ernesto Cortissoz – Conquistador de Utopías*, p. 54.

507. Sourdis Nájera, "Los Judíos Sefardíes en Barranquilla – El Caso de Jacob y Ernesto Cortissoz," p. 17.

508. García-Bustamente, *Ernesto Cortissoz – Conquistador de Utopías*, p. 69.

509. Ibid., pp. 90–93. This airline later became the country's largest airline, Avianca, which is still in operation in the twenty-first century.

510. Advertising pamphlet obtained from Michèle Veldhahn of Curaçao.

511. Sourdis Nájera, *El Registro Oculto – Los Sefardíes del Caribe en la Formación de la Nación Colombiana 1813–1886*, pp. 150–52.

512. Judith Segovia de Falquez, November 15, 2004.

513. García-Bustamente, *Ernesto Cortissoz – Conquistador de Utopías*, p. 30. and Ernesto Cortissoz Rodriguez, November 17, 2004.

514. Rodolfo Segovia Salas, October 11, 2005.

515. Dino Manco Bermúdez and José Watnik Barón, *Vidas Destacadas* (Barranquilla, Colombia: Man Comunicaciones, 2001), pp. 190–91.

516. Mendes Chumaceiro, "Bij de Dood van David Lopez Penha Jr. – Een Brief aan Zijn Grijzen Vader," p. 505.

517. Ibid., p. 504.

518. Ibid., p. 505.

519. De Marchena, "Unpublished Genealogy of Curaçao's Sephardic Jews."

520. Mendes Chumaceiro, "Bij de Dood van David Lopez Penha Jr. – Een Brief aan Zijn Grijzen Vader," p. 505.

521. Dr. David R. Capriles, *Nota Biográfica del Modesto Joven Dd. Lopez Penha, Jr.* (Curaçao: A. Bethencourt & Hijos, 1882), p. 7.

522. De Marchena, "Unpublished Genealogy of Curaçao's Sephardic Jews."

523. Capriles, *Nota Biográfica del Modesto Joven Dd. Lopez Penha, Jr.*, p. 4.

524. Ibid., p. 14.

525. David Lopez Penha Jr., "Discurso de D. Lopez Penha Jr. en el 63o Aniversario del Acta de Independencia Firmada en Cartagena en 1811, Speech of November 11, 1874," (Barranquilla, Colombia), p. 5.

526. David Lopez Penha Jr., *Los Israelitas y sus Detractores – Carta al Señor Doctor José María Samper.* (Barranquilla, Colombia: Imprenta Americana, May 1875), p. 4.

527. Ibid., pp. 12–14.

528. Ibid., p. 19.

529. *El Promotor*, "Description of Shareholders Meeting of 'Banco de Barranquilla' Held on Feb 28, 1873," March 8, 1873 and Diario de Bolívar, "1873 Incorporation Papers, Constitution and Shareholders of 'Banco de Barranquilla'," *Diario de Bolívar*, Jan 17 through 19, 1883, no. 3015, page 60.

530. *El Promotor*, "Announcement of 'Cia. Colombiana de Transporte' Advertising Their Ships and Destinations," August 16, 1890.

531. David Lopez Penha Jr., "Balance De 31 De Marzo De 1893," in *Private Accounts of David Lopez Penha, Jr.* (Curacao: Private Collection of Joyce Senior de Waard, 1893).

532. *El Promotor*, "Listing of Donors for the Creation of the 'Cementerio Universal'," Aug 23, 1873.

533. *El Promotor*, "Announcement of Bazaar to Benefit New Hospital Building," Oct 25, 1873.

534. *El Promotor*, "Listing of Contributions to the 'Iglesia De Nuestra Señora del Rosario'," June 25, 1892.

535. *El Promotor*, "Description of Show Put on by Girl Students at The 'Colegio de Niñas'," Jan 3, 1880.

536. American Jewish Archives, "Letter to Alliance Israélite Universelle Regarding Contributions from Colombia, July 13, 1870, by Jacob Alvares Correa."

537. Th. Ch. L. Wijnmalen, "Les Possessions Néerlandaises dans les Antilles" (Amsterdam, Netherlands: 1888), p. 43. and Hartog, *Curaçao – Van Kolonie Tot Autonomie*, pp. 744–45.

538. *El Promotor*, "Announcement of Arrival and Departure of Dutch Warship," Jan 23, 1888.

539. Manco Bermúdez, *Vidas Destacadas*, p. 186.

540. Casual phone conversation with Rodolfo Segovia Salas, October 11, 2005.

541. *El Promotor*, "Welcoming Back David Lopez Penha Jr.," Nov. 17, 1888.

542. *El Promotor*, "Description of Visit to Barranquilla by Ferdinand de Lesseps," January 3, 1880.

543. *El Promotor*, "Announcement of Trip by David Lopez Penha Jr. to Visit Count De Lesseps in Panama," Feb 13, 1886.

544. *El Promotor*, "Description of Celebration of Princess Wilhelmina's Birthday," Sept 5, 1891.

545. *El Promotor*, "Description of Celebration of 400th Anniversary of Discovery of America," October 15, 1892.

546. Moises Lopez Penha and David Lopez Penha, "Generations of the Lopez Penha Family," (1878).

547. Manco Bermúdez, *Vidas Destacadas*, p. 190.

548. Ibid., pp. 190–91.

549. Francisco Parias Vargas, "David Lopez Penha, Jr.," *El Anotador*, November 5, 1893.

550. Manco Bermúdez, *Vidas Destacadas*, p. 190.

551. De Marchena, "Unpublished Genealogy of Curaçao's Sephardic Jews."

552. Emmanuel and Emmanuel, *History of the Jews of the Netherlands Antilles*, p. 996.

553. "Legal Document Issued by Curaçao's Burgelijke Stand," in *Private Collection of Joyce Senior de Waard* (Curaçao: 1877).

554. "Legal Documents Pertaining to Dispute of Estate of Jacob Isaac Senior in Barranquilla, Colombia," in *Private Collection of Joyce Senior de Waard* (Curaçao: 1884).

555. "Legal Document Issued by Curaçao's Burgelijke Stand."

556. Ibid.

557. Archives-AJHS, "Birthregister for the Jewish Community of Curaçao," (New York: on microfilm at the American Jewish Historical Society, various years).

558. "Legal Documents Pertaining to Dispute of Estate of Jacob Isaac Senior in Barranquilla, Colombia."

559. Archives-AJHS, "Birthregister for the Jewish Community of Curaçao."

560. Alvarez Ortiz, "Unpublished Genealogy and Notes of the Capriles Family."

561. van Zanen, *David Ricardo Capriles, Student Geneesheer Schrijver, Curaçao 1837–1902*, pp. 65–68.

562. "Legal Documents Pertaining to Dispute of Estate of Jacob Isaac Senior in Barranquilla, Colombia."

563. Ibid.

564. Charles H. Emerson, "Barranquilla en 1898," in *Barranquilla y Sabanilla durante el Siglo XIX (1852–1898)*, ed. José Ramón Llanos and Iveth Florez (Ediciones Clio Caribe, 1898), pp. 128–33.

565. *El Promotor*, "Welcoming Back David Lopez Penha Jr. "

566. *El Promotor*, "Notice from Sarah Lopez Penha Senior Indicating That Jacob Cortissoz Will Be in Charge of the Liquidation of Her Husband's Estate," April 20, 1889.

567. Emmanuel, *Precious Stones of the Jews of Curaçao*, p. 525.

568. Joyce Senior de Waard, December 2, 2004.

569. De Marchena, "Unpublished Genealogy of Curaçao's Sephardic Jews."

570. Ibid.

571. Ibid.

572. Manco Bermúdez, *Vidas Destacadas*, p. 144.

573. As quoted in Ibid., p. 151.

574. Ramón Illán Bacca, "El Modernismo en Barranquilla," *Boletín Cultural y Bibliográfico* XXX, no. Número 33.

575. Manco Bermúdez, *Vidas Destacadas*, pp. 148–49.

576. Illán Bacca, "El Modernismo en Barranquilla," quoting an editorial in the local newspaper Rigoletto.

577. Manco Bermúdez, *Vidas Destacadas*, p. 151.

578. Ibid., p. 162.

579. Abraham Zacarías Lopez Penha, "Umbria," *El Promotor*, Feb 13, 1892.

580. Abraham Zacarías Lopez Penha, "Nupcial," *El Promotor*, Nov 12, 1892.

581. Illán Bacca, "El Modernismo en Barranquilla,"

582. Manco Bermúdez, *Vidas Destacadas*, pp. 160–61.

583. Ibid., p. 159.

584. Capriles Goldish, *The Girls They Left Behind – Curaçao's Jewish Women in the Nineteenth Century.*

585. Manco Bermúdez, *Vidas Destacadas*, pp. 171–72.

586. Alfredo de la Espriella, "Abraham Zacarías López-Penha," in *Historia General de Barranquilla – Personajes* (Barranquilla, Colombia: Academia de la Historia de Barranquilla, 1995).

587. As quoted by Mordechai Arbell, "El Asentamiento de Judíos Caribeños en Paises Liberados de España: Colombia y la República Dominicana" (paper presented at the Congreso Judío Latinoamericano, 2001).

588. Maduro, "Scrapbook of Leah Monsanto of Curaçao."

589. Manco Bermúdez, *Vidas Destacadas*, p. 182.

590. Ibid., p. 171.

591. Mendes Chumaceiro, "Bij de Dood van David Lopez Penha Jr. – Een Brief aan Zijn Grijzen Vader," p. 503.

Chapter 6 – Going, Going . . . Gone: A Comparative Analysis

592. Mordechai Arbell, *Lecture Given at the Center for Jewish History, November 12, 2002* (New York, NY).

593. Aizenberg, *La Comunidad Judía de Coro 1824–1900*, p. 105.

594. Ucko, *La Fusión de los Sefardíes con los Dominicanos*

595. Archival Collection of J.M.L. Maduro, "Notes Pertaining to Curaçaoan Jews Living Elsewhere, Written by J.S. Da Silva-Rossa" (Box 8, Centraal Bureau voor Genealogie, The Hague, Netherlands).

Chapter 7 – The Importance of Population Size

596. Ira M. Sheskin, "The Dixie Diaspora: The 'Loss' of the Small Southern Jewish Community," *Southeastern Geographer* Vol. XXXX, no. 1.
597. Lee Shai Weissbach, "Decline in an Age of Expansion: Disappearing Jewish Communities in the Era of Mass Migration," *American Jewish Archives Journal* 49 (1997).
598. Cohen, *Through the Sands of Time*, pp. 145–46.

Chapter 8 – Freemasonry and the Caribbean Sephardim

599. Paul M. Bessel, "Freemasonry & Judaism," http://www.bessel.org. (1995).
600. Hartog, *Curaçao – Van Kolonie Tot Autonomie*, pp. 395–96.
601. Ibid., p. 478.
602. H.H. Lopez Penha, *La Masonería en Santo Domingo, Primer Tomo* (Ciudad Trujillo, Dominican Republic: Editora Stella, 1956), pp. 45–47.

Chapter 9 – Gender and Continuity in Curaçao

603. Emmanuel and Emmanuel, *History of the Jews of the Netherlands Antilles*, p. 302 and p. 47.
604. Marysa Navarro, "Women in Pre-Columbian and Colonial Latin America and the Caribbean," in *Women in Latin America and the Caribbean*, ed. Marysa Navarro and Virginia Sanchez Korrol (Bloomington, IN: Indiana University Press, 1999), p. 49.
605. Silvia Marina Arrom, *The Women of Mexico City, 1790–1857* (Stanford, CA: Stanford University Press, 1985), p. 176. and María de la Luz Parcero, *Condiciones de la Mujer en México durante el Siglo XIX* (México, D.F.: Instituto Nacional de Antropología e Historia, 1992), pp. 22–23.
606. Emmanuel and Emmanuel, *History of the Jews of the Netherlands Antilles*, p. 261.
607. Rupert, *Roots of Our Future – a Commercial History of Curaçao*, p. 55.
608. Hartog, *Curaçao – Van Kolonie Tot Autonomie*, pp. 866–68.
609. Larissa Adler Lomnitz and Marisol Perez-Lizaur, *A Mexican Elite Family, 1820–1980: Kinship, Class, and Culture* (Princeton, NJ: Princeton University Press, 1987), p. 190.
610. Karner, *The Sephardics of Curaçao – a Study of Socio-Cultural Patterns in Flux*, p. 20.
611. Rupert, *Roots of Our Future – a Commercial History of Curaçao*, p. 56.
612. Nolda C. Romer-Kenepa, "Curaçaose Vrouwen in de Slavenmaatschappij (Eind 18de Eeuw en Eerste Helft 19de Eeuw)," in *Mundu Yama Sinta Mira – Womanhood in Curaçao*, ed. Richenel Ansano, et al (Curaçao: Fundashon Publikashon

Curaçao, 1992), pp. 28–29.

613. Capriles Goldish, *The Girls They Left Behind – Curaçao's Jewish Women in the Nineteenth Century*.

Chapter 10 – La Donna Immobile: The Limited Options for Sephardic Women

614. A later example of this was the author's grandfather, Moisés de Marchena (1888–1950), who migrated to Cuba in the early twentieth century after he became engaged to Sarah Salas of Curaçao. Family lore has it that the two were engaged for seven or eight years, unable to marry since Moisés did not have the wherewithal to support a wife. A letter written by Moises's mother Clara de Marchena to Sarah in 1913 implies that this may indeed have been the case. Moisés spent most of 1918 in Cuba trying to get settled and accumulating some wealth so that he could finally marry his fiancée of many years and move his new bride to the beautiful Vedado section of Havana. The couple were finally wed on August 3, 1918 in Curaçao and moved to Cuba immediately thereafter. Two of their three children were born in Havana, but the sudden decline in the sugar market exhausted Moisés's finances and Moisés, Sarah, and their children returned to Curaçao around 1924 and continued to live there for the remainder of their lives.

615. Cohen, *Through the Sands of Time*, pp. 14–15.

616. Cohen, "Excel Spreadsheet of 1846 Census Data for St. Thomas."

Chapter 11 – Enduring Ties with Curaçao

617. Cohen, *Through the Sands of Time*, pp. 94–95.

618. Ibid., pp. 97–100.

619. Alberto Osorio Osorio, *Los Osorios Sefardíes – Rutas y Legados* (Panama: 1991), p. 118.

620. Arjona, *La Familia Fidanque: Cien Años en Panamá – the Fidanque Family: Centennial Anniversary in Panama 1885–1985*, p. 12.

621. A recent example is extensive correspondence in April of 2006 between the author and Ana María Piza of Costa Rica about her Sephardic ancestry.

622. Capriles de Petit, Henriquez, Molina Senior de Suarez.

623. "Letter to Benjamin Mendes Chumaceiro Detailing Descendants of Rafael de Marchena for the Purpose of an Inheritance, Signed by Enrique de Marchena Dujarric, March 24, 1937," in *Private Collection of Enrique de Marchena y de Marchena* (Santo Domingo, D.R.). and "Letter to David C. Leon and Enrique de Marchena of Santo Domingo and Attachment Pertaining to Illegitimate Children, Signed by Benjamin Mendes Chumaceiro, April 19, 1937," in *Private Collection of Enrique de Marchena y de Marchena* (Santo Domingo, D.R.).

624. Notary Public, "Official Document Submitted to the Court in Curaçao Pertaining to the Distribution of the Estate of Lucy Jesurun" (1937).

625. S.E.L. Maduro and Sons, "Letter to Senior De Sola & Co. Of Barranquilla, Colombia, May 13, 1891," in *Archives of S.E.L. Maduro & Sons* (Curaçao).
626. Michèle van Veldhoven, e-mail December 17, 2005.
627. Cortissoz Rodriguez, November 17, 2004.

Chapter 12 – How Can We Sing the Song of the Lord on Alien Soil?

628. Jonathan D. Sarna, *American Judaism – a History* (New Haven, CT: Yale University, 2004), p. 374.
629. Sergio Dellapergola, "Global Perspectives on Jewish out-Marriage," presented at *International Roundtable on Intermarriage, December 18, 2003* (Brandeis University, Waltham, MA), Table 1.

BIBLIOGRAPHY

Abraham-van der Mark, Eva. "Marriage and Concubinage among the Sephardic Merchant Elite of Curaçao." In *Women & Change in the Caribbean*, edited by Janet Momsen. Bloomington, IN: Indiana University Press, 1993.

Aizenberg, Isidoro. *La Comunidad Judía de Coro 1824-1900*. Caracas, Venezuela: Biblioteca de Autores y Temas Falconianos, 1983.

Aizpurua, Ramón. *Curazao y la Costa de Caracas – Introducción al Estudio de Contrabando en la Provincia de Venezuela en Tiempos de la Compañía Guipuzcoana 1730-1780*. Caracas, Venezuela, 1993.

Alvarez, Julia. *In the Name of Salomé*. New York, NY: Penguin Group, 2001.

Alvarez Ortiz, José Luis. "Unpublished Genealogy and Notes of the Capriles Family." Caracas, Venezuela, 2000.

American Jewish Archives. "Letter to Alliance Israélite Universelle Regarding Contributions from Colombia, July 13, 1870, by Jacob Alvares Correa." Alliance Israélite Universelle Microfilms, Roll # 772: Cincinnati, Ohio.

———. "Letter to the Alliance Israélite Universelle Regarding Contributions from Barranquilla, Colombia, March 13, 1874, by J.I. Senior." Alliance Israélite Universelle Microfilms, Roll # 772: Cincinnati, Ohio.

———. "Letter to the Alliance Israélite Universelle Regarding Contributions from Barranquilla, Colombia, May 22, 1884, by D. H. Senior." Alliance Israélite Universelle Microfilms, Roll # 772: Cincinnati, Ohio.

———. "Letter to Alliance Israélite Universelle Regarding Contributions from Panama, June 4, 1869, by Samuel Piza." Alliance Israélite Universelle Microfilms, Roll # 772: Cincinnati, Ohio.

———. "Letter to Central Committee of Alliance Israélite Universelle Regarding Contributions from St. Thomas, May 11, 1864, by N.M. Nathan." Alliance Israélite Universelle Microfilms, Roll # 772: Cincinnati, Ohio.

———. "Letter to the Alliance Israélite Universelle Regarding Contributions from Venezuela, July 17, 1874, by E. De Sola." Alliance Israélite Universelle Microfilms, Roll # 772: Cincinnati, Ohio.

———. "Letter to the Alliance Israélite Universelle Regarding Contributions from Venezuela, July 29, 1881, by E. De Sola." Alliance Israélite Universelle Microfilms, Roll # 772: Cincinnati, Ohio.

———. "Letter to the Alliance Israélite Universelle Regarding Contributions from Venezuela, March 16, 1886, by E. De Sola." Alliance Israélite Universelle Microfilms, Roll # 772: Cincinnati, Ohio.

———. "Letter to the Central Committee of the Alliance Israélite Universelle, February 4, 1895, by Jb. B. Delvalle." Alliance Israélite Universelle Microfilms,

Roll # 772: Cincinnati, Ohio.

———. "Lists of St. Thomas Contributors to Alliance Israélite Universelle, March 10, 1876, and August 10, 1877, by D. Lindo." Alliance Israélite Universelle Microfilms, Roll 772: Cincinnati, Ohio.

Arbell, Mordechai. Comfortable Disappearance: Lessons from the Caribbean Jewish Experience. Jerusalem, Israel: Institute of the World Jewish Congress, 1998.

———. "El Asentamiento de Judíos Caribeños en Paises Liberados de España: Colombia y la República Dominicana." Paper presented at the Congreso Judío Latinoamericano 2001.

———. Lecture Given at the Center for Jewish History, November 12, 2002. New York, NY.

———. "Referred to by Enrique de Marchena in His Manuscript." Santo Domingo, Dominican Republic.

———. Spanish and Portuguese Jews in the Caribbean and the Guianas. Edited by Dennis C. Landis and Ann P. Barry. Providence: The John Carter Brown Library, 1999.

Archives, St. Thomas Hebrew Congregation. "Letter from the Board to Vice Governor of St. Thomas, April 1, 1867." Box 42: Charlotte Amalie, St. Thomas.

———. "Letter to Governor Regarding Synagogue By-Laws Revisions, April 12, 1872." Signed by Benjamin Delvalle. Box 42: Charlotte Amalie, St. Thomas.

Archives-AJHS. "Birthregister for the Jewish Community of Curaçao." New York: on microfilm at the American Jewish Historical Society, various years.

Archivo General de la Nación. "Marriage Registrations 1848-1852, November 9, 1848." Santo Domingo, Dominican Republic.

Archivo Histórico de la Asamblea Nacional. "1825 Census of Coro." Gaceta de Venezuela. Trimestre 1, Nº 11. Valencia, Venezuela, page 6, March 20, 1831.

Arjona, Nadhji. La Familia Fidanque: Cien Años en Panama - the Fidanque Family: Centennial Anniversary in Panama 1885-1985. Panama: Impresora Panamá, S.A., 1986.

Arrom, Silvia Marina. The Women of Mexico City, 1790-1857. Stanford, CA: Stanford University Press, 1985.

Bakkum, Maarten Jan. La Comunidad Judeo-Curazoleña de Coro y el Pogrom de 1855. Centro de Investigaciones Históricas del Estado Falcón Instituto de Cultura del Estado Falcón. Caracas, Venezuela: Editorial Ex Libris, 2001.

Bessel, Paul M. "Freemasonry & Judaism." http://www.bessel.org, 1995.

Capriles, Dr. David R. Nota Biográfica del Modesto Joven Dd. Lopez Penha, Jr. Curaçao: A. Bethencourt & Hijos, 1882.

Capriles de Petit, Deborah. June 24, 2004.

Capriles Goldish, Josette. "Analysis of the Journal of Circumcisions of Moises Frois Ricardo." American Jewish History 91, no. 2.

———. The Girls They Left Behind - Curaçao's Jewish Women in the Nineteenth Century, Working Paper No. 11, Hadassah International Research Institute on Jewish Women at Brandeis University. Waltham, MA, 2002.

Clausner, Martin D. Rural Santo Domingo: Settled, Unsettled, and Resettled.

Philadelphia: Temple University Press, 1973.

Cochrane, Capt. Charles Stuart. *Journal of a Residence and Travels in Colombia During the Years 1823 and 1824.* 2 vols: Reprinted by AMS Press, Inc., New York, NY, 1971, 1825.

Cohen, Judah M. "Excel Spreadsheet of 1846 Census Data for St. Thomas." Based on Virgin Islands Census records, 1841–1911, 2003.

———. *Through the Sands of Time.* Lebanon, N.H.: University Press of New England, 2004.

Cohen de Marchena, Cándida Amelia. "Unpublished Memoirs of Cándida Amelia Cohen de Marchena." Santo Domingo, Dominican Republic, 1967.

Concepción, J. Agustín. *Proyección Curazoleña en Santo Domingo.* Santo Domingo: Editora Nivar, 1985.

Coomans-Eustatia et al, Maritza *Breekbare Banden – Feiten en Visies over Aruba, Bonaire en Curaçao Na de Vrede van Munster 1648–1998.* Bloemendaal, Netherlands: Stichting Libri Antilliani, 1998.

Cortissoz, Eudacia. "Letter to Moises Frois Ricardo, July 19, 1867." In *Private Archives of Ricardo de Sola.* Caracas, Venezuela.

Cortissoz Rodriguez, Ernesto. November 17, 2004.

De Curaçaosche Courant. "Notification to the Public." September 19, 1863.

de la Espriella, Alfredo. "Abraham Zacarías López-Penha." In *Historia General de Barranquilla – Personajes.* Barranquilla, Colombia: Academia de la Historia de Barranquilla, 1995.

de la Luz Parcero, María. *Condiciones de la Mujer en México Durante el Siglo XIX.* México, D.F.: Instituto Nacional de Antropología e Historia, 1992.

de Lima, Blanca. *Coro: Fin de Diáspora – Isaac A. Senior e Hijo: Redes Comerciales y Circuito Exportador (1884-1930),* Colección Monografías. Caracas. Venezuela: Comisión de Estudios de Postgrado, Facultad de Humanidades y Educación - Universidad Central de Venezuela, 2002.

———. "El Legado de una Comunidad: Los Sefarditas de Coro." *Maguén,* July/September 2001.

———. *The Coro and La Vela Railroad and Improvement Company 1897–1938.* Coro, Venezuela: Centro de Investigaciones Históricas "Pedro Manuel Arcaya" UNEFM, 1995.

De Marchena – Dujarric, Enrique. "Presencia Hebrea en la República Dominicana." In *Presencia Judía en Santo Domingo,* edited by Alfonso Lockward. Santo Domingo: Taller, 1994.

De Marchena, Sandra R. "Unpublished Genealogy of Curaçao's Sephardic Jews." Miami, FL, 2007.

De Marchena y de Marchena, Enrique. August 17, 2001.

———. "Unpublished Manuscript of the History of the De Marchenas in the Dominican Republic." Santo Domingo, 2001.

de Pool, John. *Del Curaçao Que Se Va.* Panama, 1935.

de Sola, Ricardo. *Los Sefarditas – Lazos de Unión Entre Curazao y Venezuela.* Caracas, Venezuela: self published, 1991.

de Waard, Joyce Senior. December 2, 2004.

Deive, Carlos Esteban. *Heterodoxia e Inquisición en Santo Domingo 1492–1822*. Santo Domingo: Taller, 1983.

deJongh Woods, Edith. April 10, 2005.

———. "Wimmelkafts Gade No. 10 – the Masonic Hall." *The Daily News*, June 22, 2000.

Dellapergola, Sergio. "Global Perspectives on Jewish out-Marriage." presented at *International Roundtable on Intermarriage, December 18, 2003*. Brandeis University, Waltham, MA.

Delvalle, Benjamin. "Last Will and Testament of Benjamin Delvalle and His Wife Judith Delvalle, Born De Castro, May 3, 1864." In *National Archives, College Park, MD, Record #55*. St. Thomas.

Det Kongelige Bibliotek. "Letter from Grace Cardoze Delvalle to David Simonsen, Dated November 28, 1907." Oriental and Judaica Collections, The David Simonsen Archives, Copenhagen, Denmark.

Diario de Bolívar. "1873 Incorporation Papers, Constitution, and Shareholders of Banco De Barranquilla." *Diario de Bolívar*, January 17 through 19, 1883.

El Promotor. "'Acueducto de Barranquilla' - Summary of Shareholders Meeting of July 14, 1879." July 19, 1879.

———. "'Acueducto de Barranquilla' – Summary of Shareholders Meeting of July 11, 1892." July 16, 1892.

———. "Announcement of Arrival and Departure of Dutch Warship." Jan 23, 1888.

———. "Announcement of Bazaar to Benefit New Hospital Building." Oct 25, 1873.

———. "Announcement of 'Cia. Colombiana de Transporte' Advertising Their Ships and Destinations." August 16, 1890.

———. "Announcement of First Test of Water Processed by the 'Acueducto De Barranquilla'." Feb 28, 1880.

———. "Announcement of Formation Of 'Compañía Teatro Barranquilla'." July 7, 1888.

———. "Announcement of the Death of Rachel Jesurun Pinto de Alvares Correa." December 12, 1891.

———. "Announcement of Trip by David Lopez Penha Jr. to Visit Count De Lesseps in Panama." Feb 13, 1886.

———. "Description of Celebration of 400th Anniversary of Discovery of America." October 15, 1892.

———. "Description of Celebration of Princess Wilhelmina's Birthday." Sept 5, 1891.

———. "Description of Shareholders Meeting of 'Banco de Barranquilla' Held on Feb 28, 1873." March 8, 1873.

———. "Description of Show Put on by Girl Students at the 'Colegio de Niñas'." Jan 3, 1880.

———. "Description of Visit to Barranquilla by Ferdinand de Lesseps." January 3,

1880.

———. "Editorial About Inauguration of the 'Acueducto De Barranquilla'." March 27, 1880.

———. "Letter to the Editor of *El Promotor*." June 14, 1873.

———. "Listing of Contributions to the 'Iglesia de Nuestra Señora del Rosario'." June 25, 1892.

———. "Listing of Donors for the Creation of the 'Cementerio Universal'." Aug 23, 1873.

———. "Listing of Founding Shareholders of the 'Compañía de Omnibus'." March 29, 1873.

———. "Listing of Shareholders of the 'Banco de Barranquilla'." February 22, 1873.

———. "Notice from Sarah Lopez Penha Senior Indicating That Jacob Cortissoz Will Be in Charge of the Liquidation of Her Husband's Estate." April 20, 1889.

———. "Open Letter to the President of Colombia." May 31, 1873.

———. "Response Regarding Excessive Freight and Tardiness of the 'Ferrocaril de Bolívar' By Aquileo Parra for the Executive Branch of Colombia." June 14, 1873.

———. "Welcoming Back David Lopez Penha Jr." Nov. 17, 1888.

Elbow, Gary. "Scale and Regional Identity in the Caribbean." In *Nested Identities: Nationalism, Territory, and Scale*, edited by Guntram H. Herb and David H. Kaplan. Lanham, MD: Rowman & Littlefield Publishers, 1999.

Emerson, Charles H. "Barranquilla en 1898." In *Barranquilla y Sabanilla Durante el Siglo XIX (1852-1898)*, edited by José Ramón Llanos and Iveth Florez. Barranquilla: Ediciones Clio Caribe, 1995.

Emmanuel, Isaac S. *Precious Stones of the Jews of Curaçao*. New York: Bloch Publishing Company, 1957.

———. *The Jews of Coro, Venezuela*. Cincinnati, OH: American Jewish Archives, 1973.

Emmanuel, Isaac S., and Suzanne A. Emmanuel. *History of the Jews of the Netherlands Antilles*. 2 vols. Cincinnati: American Jewish Archives, 1970.

Fortique, José Rafael. *Los Motines Anti-Judíos de Coro*. Maracaibo, Venezuela: Ed. Puente, 1973.

García-Bustamente, Miguel. *Ernesto Cortissoz - Conquistador de Utopías*. Colombia: Lerner Ltda., 1994.

Gjessing, Frederik C., and William P. Maclean. *Historic Buildings of St. Thomas and St. John*. London: Macmillan Education Ltd., 1987.

Gomes Casseres, Charles. *Bewoond Scharloo*. Curaçao: Amigoe, N.V., 2000.

———. "Genealogical Tree of the Family Gomes Casseres – Stretching over 5 Centuries (1470 to 1998)." Curaçao, 1999.

Gonzales-Batista, Carlos. *Documentos para la Historia de las Antillas Neerlandesas*. Coro, Estado Falcón, Venezuela: Universidad Nacional Experimental Francisco de Miranda, 1997.

Guiterman, Vida Lindo. *Joshua Piza and His Descendants*. New York, 1928.

Hadengue, Michel. January 3, 2002.

Hartog, Dr. Joh. *Curaçao - Van Kolonie Tot Autonomie*. 2 vols. Aruba: D. J. De Wit, 1961.

————. *Het Verhaal der Maduro's en Foto-Album van Curaçao 1837–1962 Uitgegeven Ter Gelegenheid van het Honderd Vijfentwintigjarig Bestaan van S.E.L. Maduro & Sons N.V.* Aruba: D.J. de Wit, 1962.

Henriquez, Thelma. June 24, 2004.

Hertz, Dr. J.H. *The Pentateuch and Haftorahs – Hebrew Text, English Translation, and Commentary.* Second ed. London, England: Soncino Press, 1981.

Hoenigsberg, Julio. *100 Años de Historia Masónica de la Respetable Logia El Siglo XIX No. 24–1.* Barranquilla, Colombia, 1964.

Hoetink, H. *Het Patroon van de Oude Curaçaose Samenleving – Een Sociologische Studie.* Aruba, Netherlands Antilles: De Wit, N.V., 1958.

————. *The Dominican People, 1850-1900: Notes for a Historical Sociology.* Translated by Stephen K. Ault. Baltimore: John Hopkins University Press, 1982.

Home Journal of the Young Men's Hebrew Association of Curaçao, editor. "Arrivals." November 15, 1889.

Hormazabal Salas, Juan. November 15, 2001.

Huisman, Piet. *Sephardim – the Spirit That Has Withstood the Times.* The Netherlands: Huisman Editions, 1986.

Illán Bacca, Ramón. "El Modernismo en Barranquilla." *Boletín Cultural y Bibliográfico* XXX, no. Número 33.

Jacobs et al, Daniel *Code of Laws for the Government of the St. Thomas Hebrew Congregation Blessings and Peace and Acts of Piety.* New York, NY: Industrial School of the Hebrew Orphan Asylum, 1875.

Karner, Frances P. *The Sephardics of Curaçao – a Study of Socio-Cultural Patterns in Flux,* Anjerpublikaties. Assen, Netherlands: Van Gorcum & Comp. N.V., 1969.

Knight, David. March 16, 2005.

Knox, John P. *A Historical Account of St. Thomas, W.I.* New York: Charles Scribner, 1852.

Larrazabal Blanco, Carlos. *Familias Dominicanas.* multi vols. Santo Domingo, Dominican Republic.

"Legal Document Issued by Curaçao's Burgelijke Stand." In *Private Collection of Joyce Senior de Waard.* Curaçao, 1877.

"Legal Documents Pertaining to Dispute of Estate of Jacob Isaac Senior in Barranquilla, Colombia." In *Private Collection of Joyce Senior de Waard.* Curaçao, 1884.

"Letter to Benjamin Mendes Chumaceiro Detailing Descendants of Rafael de Marchena for the Purpose of an Inheritance, Signed by Enrique de Marchena Dujarric, March 24, 1937." In *Private Collection of Enrique de Marchena y de Marchena.* Santo Domingo, Dominican Republic.

"Letter to Braulia de Marchena, Signed by the President of the Dominican Republic Ulyssis Heureaux, June 10, 1893." In Private Collection of Enrique de Marchena y de Marchena. Santo Domingo, Dominican Republic.

"Letter to David C. Leon and Enrique de Marchena of Santo Domingo and Attachment Pertaining to Illegitimate Children, Signed by Benjamin Mendes Chumaceiro, April 19, 1937." In *Private Collection of Enrique de Marchena y de Marchena.* Santo Domingo, Dominican Republic.

Levy-Benshimol, Abraham. *Los Sefardíes, Vínculo Entre Curazao y Venezuela*. Caracas, Venezuela: Museo Sefardí de Caracas, 2002.

Likuski, Sita Levy. e-mail, March 26, 2003.

Lombardi, John V. *Venezuela - the Search for Order, the Dream of Progress*. New York – Oxford: Oxford University Press, 1982.

Lomnitz, Larissa Adler, and Marisol Perez-Lizaur. *A Mexican Elite Family, 1820–1980: Kinship, Class, and Culture*. Princeton, NJ: Princeton University Press, 1987.

Lopez Penha, Abraham Zacarías. "Nupcial." *El Promotor*, Nov 12, 1892.

———. "Umbria." *El Promotor*, Feb 13, 1892.

Lopez Penha, Elias. "Reivindicación." Santo Domingo, Dominican Republic, 1883.

Lopez Penha, H.H. *La Masonería en Santo Domingo, Primer Tomo*. Ciudad Trujillo, Dominican Republic: Editora Stella, 1956.

Lopez Penha Jr., David. "Balance de 31 De Marzo De 1893." In *Private Accounts of David Lopez Penha, Jr*. Curacao: Private Collection of Joyce Senior de Waard, 1893.

———. "Discurso de D. Lopez Penha Jr. en el 63o Aniversario del Acta de Independencia Firmada en Cartagena en 1811, Speech of November 11, 1874." Barranquilla, Colombia.

———. *Los Israelitas y Sus Detractores – Carta al Señor Doctor José María Samper*. Barranquilla, Colombia: Imprenta Americana, May 1875.

Lopez Penha, Marianela. Conversation, February 7, 2002.

Lopez Penha, Moises, and David Lopez Penha. "Generations of the Lopez Penha Family." 1878.

Maduro, Archival Collection of J.M.L. "Individuals of Curaçaoan Origin Who Have Held Distinguished Posts in Venezuela, as Listed by J.M.L. Maduro." Box 3, Centraal Bureau voor Genealogie, The Hague, Netherlands.

———. "J.M.L. Maduro Genealogical Notes for Cortissoz Family Prepared by J.M.L. Maduro." Box 19, Centraal Bureau voor Genealogie, The Hague, Netherlands.

———. "Letter from B. Bernagie to the States General of the Netherlands, Accompanied by Letters About the Imprisonment of Phillip Henriquez." Box 24, 1700.

———. "Notes Pertaining to Curaçaoan Jews Living Elsewhere, Written by J.S. Da Silva-Rossa." Box 8, Centraal Bureau voor Genealogie, The Hague, Netherlands.

———. "Register van Geboorenen en Overledenen van de Ned. Port. Israelitische Gemeente van het Eiland Curaçao 1722–1830." Box 17, Centraal Bureau voor Genealogie, The Hague, Netherlands.

———. "Scrapbook of Leah Monsanto of Curaçao." Not yet catalogued in 2003 in collection at Centraal Bureau voor Genealogie, The Hague, Netherlands.

Manco Bermúdez, Dino, and José Watnik Barón. *Nuestras Gentes – Primera Generación*. Barranquilla, Colombia: Escala Impresores Ltda., 2000.

Manco Bermúdez, Dino, and José Watnik Barón. *Vidas Destacadas*. Barranquilla, Colombia: Man Comunicaciones, 2001.

Margolinsky, Jul. *299 Epitaphs from the Jewish Cemetry (Sic) in St. Thomas, W.I. 1837–1916*. Copenhagen, 1957.

Mendes Chumaceiro, Abraham. "Bij de Dood van David Lopez Penha Jr. - Een Brief aan Zijn Grijzen Vader." In A.M. *Chumaceiro Az. - Onpartijdig Pionier Op Curaçao*, edited by Henny E. Coomans and Maritza Coomans-Eustatia. Bloemendaal, Netherlands: Stichting Libri Antilliani, 1893.

Mikve Israel - Emanuel. "Handwritten Documents Indicating Requests for Charitable Funds by the Indigent Members of the Mikve Israel Community in the 18th and 19th Century." Archives of Mikve Israel - Emanuel Synagogue, Curaçao, various years.

Mikve Israel - Emanuel Archives. "Death Registers by Year for Mikve Israel Community." Willemstad, Curaçao, various years.

———. "Letter from Abraham De Marchena Refusing Payment, November 11, 1819." Willemstad, Curaçao.

———. "Letter to Synagogue Board with Request for Financial Assistance, Written by Jacob Jesurun Pinto, February 16, 1837." Curaçao.

———. "Loan Document between Mikve Israel Community and Ribca Sasso, January 18, 1822." Curaçao.

Molina Senior de Suarez, Edna. June 24, 2004.

Morón, Guillermo. *A History of Venezuela*. Translated by John Street. New York, NY: Roy Publishers, Inc., 1963.

Moya Pons, Frank. *The Dominican Republic: A National History*. New Rochelle: Hispaniola Books, 1995.

National Archives, College Park, MD. "List of Inventory of B. Delvalle's Furniture, Records of the Government of the Virgin Islands." Record # 55, 1876.

Navarro, Marysa. "Women in Pre-Columbian and Colonial Latin America and the Caribbean." In *Women in Latin America and the Caribbean*, edited by Marysa Navarro and Virginia Sanchez Korrol. Bloomington, IN: Indiana University Press, 1999.

Nissen, Johan Peter. *Reminiscences of a 46 Years' Residence in the Island of St. Thomas in the West Indies*. Nazareth, PA: Senseman & Co., 1838.

Notary Public. "Official Document Submitted to the Court in Curaçao Pertaining to the Distribution of the Estate of Lucy Jesurun." 1937.

Osorio Osorio, Alberto. *Los Osorios Sefardíes - Rutas y Legados*. Panama, 1991.

Paiewonsky, Isidor. *Jewish Historical Development in the Virgin Islands, 1665–1959*. St. Thomas, 1959.

Paolo Solano, Sergio. "Comercio, Transporte y Sociedad en Barranquilla en la Primera Mitad del Siglo XIX." *Boletín Cultural y Bibliográfico*, 1989.

Parias Vargas, Francisco. "David Lopez Penha, Jr." *El Anotador*, November 5, 1893.

Pinto, Cheryl. handwritten correspondence, May 12, 2003.

Posada Carbó, Eduardo. *The Colombian Caribbean, a Regional History*: Clarendon Press, 1996.

———. *Una Invitación a la Historia de Barranquilla*. Edited by Martha Cárdenas, Historia Contemporánea y Realidad Nacional No. 17. Bogotá, Colombia: Fondo Editorial CEREC, 1987.

Private Archives of César Maduro Ferrer, Coro, Venezuela. "Letter Signed by Josias

L. Senior et al Directed to José Dávila González, February 18, 1900." uncatalogued papers: Coro, Venezuela.

———. "Letter Signed by R. Piña Castro et al, February 20, 1900." uncatalogued papers: Coro, Venezuela.

———. "Public Letter by Father José Dávila González, February 24, 1900." uncatalogued papers: Coro, Venezuela.

Private Archives of Ricardo de Sola. "Freemasonry Certificate of David Ricardo Issued in Coro, Venezuela." Caracas, Venezuela, 1886.

Private Papers of Dr. Manuel Galán-Salas. "Collection of Newspaper Clippings Pertaining to Salas and Curiel Families." Santo Domingo, Dominican Republic.

Private Papers of Juan Hormazabal Salas. "Listing of Founding Members of Club Unión, 1892." Santo Domingo, Dominican Republic: Sociedad Dominicana de Bibliófilos, 1892.

———. "Marriage Document – Ketubah – of Moises Salas Baiz and Rebecca Curiel." Santo Domingo, Dominican Republic, 1894.

Private Papers of Marguín Valencia Salas. "Invitation to Solemn Thanksgiving Service in St. Thomas." Curaçao: St. Thomas, V.I., 1964.

Pruneti Winkel, Pauline. Scharloo – a Nineteenth Century Quarter of Willemstad, Curaçao: Historical Architecture and Its Background: Edizioni Poligrafico Fiorentino, 1987.

Relkin, Rabbi Stanley T. "A Farewell to Rabbi Sasso." In Private papers of Marguín Valencia Salas. Curaçao, after 1966.

Ricardo, Moises Frois. "Record of Birth and Circumcision Beginning from the 26th January 1840 Corresponding to the 21st Sebat 5600, Kingston, Jamaica." In Private Archives of Ricardo de Sola. Caracas, Venezuela, 1840-1878.

Rodríguez Becerra, Manuel, and Jorge Restrepo Restrepo. Los Empresarios Extranjeros de Barranquilla 1820–1900. Bogotá, Colombia: Facultad de Administración de la Universidad de los Andes, 1987.

Romer-Kenepa, Nolda C. "Curaçaose Vrouwen in de Slavenmaatschappij (Eind 18de Eeuw en Eerste Helft 19de Eeuw)." In Mundu Yama Sinta Mira – Womanhood in Curaçao, edited by Richenel Ansano, et al. Curaçao: Fundashon Publikashon Curaçao, 1992.

Roux de Bézieux, Inés. November 8, 2001.

Rupert, Linda M. Roots of Our Future – a Commercial History of Curaçao. Curaçao, Netherlands Antilles: Curaçao Chamber of Commerce and Industry, 1999.

S.E.L. Maduro and Sons. "Copiador de Cartas – Files by Year." Willemstad, Curaçao, various years.

———. "Letter to Samuel Curiel & Co. of Santo Domingo, March 15, 1901." In Archives of S.E.L. Maduro & Sons. Curaçao.

———. "Letter to Senior De Sola & Co. of Barranquilla, Colombia, May 13, 1891." In Archives of S.E.L. Maduro & Sons. Curaçao.

Safford, Frank, and Mark Palacios. Colombia – Fragmented Land, Divided Society. New York: Oxford University Press, 2002.

Salas de Galán, Olga. "An Essay on Religion." Santo Domingo, Dominican

Republic, unknown date.

Salas, Helen. November 2002.

Sarna, Jonathan D. *American Judaism – a History*. New Haven, CT: Yale University, 2004.

Schoenhals, Kai. *Dominican Republic*. Edited by Kai Schoenhals. Vol. III, World Bibliographical Series. Oxford, England: Clio Press Ltd., 1990.

Segovia de Falquez, Judith. November 15, 2004.

Segovia Salas, Rodolfo. June 20, 2004.

———. October 11, 2005.

Senior, Julio. June 7, 2006.

Sevilla Soler, María Rosario. *Santo Domingo Tierra de Frontera (1750-1800)*. Sevilla: Escuela de Estudios Hispano Americanos, 1980.

Sheskin, Ira M. "The Dixie Diaspora: The 'Loss' of the Small Southern Jewish Community." *Southeastern Geographer* Vol. XXXX, no. 1.

Sourdis Nájera, Adelaida. *El Registro Oculto–Los Sefardíes del Caribe en la Formación de la Nación Colombiana 1813-1886*. Bogotá: Academia Colombiana de Historia, 2001.

———. "Los Judíos Sefardíes en Barranquilla–El Caso de Jacob y Ernesto Cortissoz." Cartagena, Colombia: Universidad Jorge Tadeo Lozano, Sección del Caribe, May 1999.

———. "Sefardíes y Ashkenazis en Barranquilla en la Segunda Mitad del Siglo XIX–Negocios y Compañías Comerciales." In *Paper presented at XII Congreso Colombiano de Historia*, 27. Popayán, Colombia, 2003.

St. *Thomas Tidende*. "Advertisement for Sale of Household Furniture by Isaac B. Delvalle." November 11, 1876.

———. "Announcement of School Led by Esther Jacobs." February 25, 1832.

———. "Announcement of School Led by Isaac W. Williams." February 12, 1840.

———. "Announcement of School Led by M.B. Simmonds." October 10, 1840.

———. "Description of Fire of December 31, 1831." St. *Thomas Tidende*, January 7, 1832.

———. "Letter to the Editor By 'A Jewess'." May 24, 1856.

———. "Listing of Subscribers to Hurricane Relief Fund." October 18, 1871.

———. "Obituary for Judith de Castro Delvalle." June 24, 1871.

———. "Subscription List for Synagogue Building Fund." March 30, 1833.

St. *Thomas Times*. "Advertisement for the Alliance–New Delvalle Venture." February 17, 1875.

The Jewish Chronicle. "News from Coro, Venezuela." November 12, 1847.

———. "News Items–St. Domingo." June 19, 1846.

The New York Times. "Educator Challenges Bevin." June 16, 1946.

The Occident. "Confirmation at St. Thomas." *The Occident and American Jewish Advocate* IV (1846).

———. "(News Items from) Puerto Cabello, Venezuela." *The Occident and American Jewish Advocate* XIII (1855).

———. "(News Items from) Puerto Cabello, Venezuela." *The Occident and American*

Jewish Advocate XI (1853).

The St. Thomas Times Almanac. Charlotte Amalie, St. Thomas: St. Thomas Times, 1877.

Ucko, Enrique. *La Fusión de los Sefardíes con los Dominicanos.* Ciudad Trujillo, Republica Dominicana: Imprenta La Opinión, 1944.

Ucko, Henry Zvi. "The Ancient Jewish Cemetery in Ciudad Trujillo, Dominican Republic." In *Henry Zvi Ucko Papers, Southern Historical Collection, Manuscripts Department, Wilson Library, University of North Carolina.* Chapel Hill, NC, after 1957.

UNEFM–Archivo Histórico de Falcón. "Accounting Entries by David A. Senior in His 'Livro de Comercio'." Fondo Senior, Coro, Venezuela, not catalogued, 1851-1858.

———. "Certifications of Shipments Made by Henriquez, Maduro y Senior." AHC-UNEFM, Sección Instrumentos Públicos, LXVI (1851-1854), F151v, 152, 152v, 226, 226v, Coro, Venezuela, 1852.

———. "Letter from C. G. Pinedo of Maracaibo to I.A. Senior & Hijo." Fondo Senior, Box V, Coro, Venezuela, March 19, 1897.

———. "Letter from David A. Senior in Curaçao to Josias Senior in Coro." Fondo Senior, Box 32, p. 243, Coro, Venezuela, 1899.

———. "Letter from Edwin Senior in Curaçao to Josias Senior in Coro." Fondo Senior, Box 32, Coro, Venezuela, July 1, 1899.

———. "Letter from J.D. Capriles to Josias L. Senior." Fondo Senior, Box 26, p. 563, Coro, Venezuela, 1898.

———. "Letter from Jeudah Senior to I.A. Senior & Hijo, Asking Them to Collect Some Debts in Coro for Him." Fondo Senior, Coro, Venezuela, Box V, July 10, 1895.

———. "Letter from José Puri of Havana, Cuba to I.A. Senior & Hijo." Fondo Senior, Box V, Coro, Venezuela, March 19, 1897.

———. "Letter from Josias Senior in Curaçao to His Brothers and Sister in Coro." Fondo Senior, Coro, Venezuela, Box V, October 21, 1895.

———. "Letter from Julius L. Penha to I.A. Senior & Hijo." Fondo Senior, box 32, page 8, Coro, Venezuela, 1899.

———. "Letter from Moses S.L. Maduro of Curaçao to Josias Senior of Coro." Fondo Senior, box 10, Coro, Venezuela, October 26, 1896.

———. "Protest Filed against Federal Forces on Behalf of Jeudah Senior." AHC-UNEFM, SIP LXVIII (1858-1862), F 358-358v, Coro, Venezuela, 1861.

———. "Purchase of Goats on Behalf of Jeudah Senior." AHC-UNEFM, SIP LXVII (1858-1862), F 183-183v, Coro, Venezuela, 1859.

———. "Sale of a Dutch Schooner Owned by Jeudah Senior." AHC-UNEFM, SIP LXVIII (1858-1862), F 195-195v, Coro, Venezuela, 1859.

Uribe, Maria Victoria. "Los Ocho Pasos de la Muerte del Alma: La Inquisición en Cartagena de Indias." *Boletín Cultural y Bibliográfico* XXIV, no. 14 (1987).

van Veldhoven, Michèle. e-mail December 17, 2005.

van Wijngaarden, René. May 1, 2005.

————. *Engraved in the Palm of My Hands.* self-published limited edition ed. Schoorls, Netherlands: Pirola, 2002.

van Zanen, Dr. G. E. *David Ricardo Capriles, Student Geneesheer Schrijver, Curaçao 1837-1902,* Anjerpublikaties. Assen, Netherlands: Van Gorcum & Comp. N.V., 1969.

Vestindien Danmark Rentekammeret. "Virgin Islands Census Records, 1841-1911." In *Microfilm filmed for the Genealogical Society of Utah,* #GS0039453. Salt Lake City, Utah, 1855.

Vilora-Terán et al, Andres. *Barranquilla–Estudio Sociológico Documental para una Monografía Histórica de la Ciudad.* Barranquilla, Colombia: Editorial Efemérides, 1995.

Weissbach, Lee Shai. "Decline in an Age of Expansion: Disappearing Jewish Communities in the Era of Mass Migration." *American Jewish Archives Journal* 49 (1997).

Wijnmalen, Th. Ch. L. "Les Possessions Néerlandaises dans les Antilles." Amsterdam, Netherlands, 1888.

Woods, John D. "A Short History of the Harmonic Lodge 356 E.C." In *Harmonic Lodge No. 356 E.C.–175th Anniversary - October 19, 1993.* Charlotte Amalie, St. Thomas, 1993.

INDEX

PHOTO CREDITS

All photographic editing by Suzanne Goldish

ABOUT THE AUTHOR

Josette Capriles Goldish was born in Curaçao, Netherlands Antilles, and is a descendant of Sephardim who have lived on the island since 1659. Josette has had a varied professional background, working as a computer programmer in the 1960s, as an energy and environmental researcher in the 1970s, as a financial analyst and CFO in the 1980s, as a business and financial consultant in the 1990s, and, most recently, as a researcher of Caribbean Jewry.

She holds a bachelor's degree in economics from M.I.T. and a graduate degree from the Sloan School of Management at M.I.T. She is currently a research associate at the Hadassah-Brandeis Institute in Waltham, Massachusetts, and resides in the Boston area.

CPSIA information can be obtained
at www.ICGtesting.com
Printed in the USA
JSHW030924271222
35404JS00001B/21

9 781558 764941